Twentieth ~~Century~~

PITTSBURGH

VOLUME 2

The Post-Steel Era

ROY LUBOVE

University of Pittsburgh Press

Pittsburgh and London

Published by the University of Pittsburgh Press, Pittsburgh, Pa., 15260
Copyright © 1996, University of Pittsburgh Press
All rights reserved
Manufactured in the United States of America
Printed on acid-free paper

Designed by Jane Tenenbaum

Library of Congress Cataloging-in-Publication Data
Lubove, Roy.
    Twentieth-century Pittsburgh : government, business,
and environmental change.

    Vol. 2: The post-steel era.
    Includes bibliographical references and indexes.
    1. City planning—Pennsylvania—Pittsburgh.
2. Pittsburgh (Pa.)—Politics and government.   3. Urban
renewal—Pennsylvania—Pittsburgh.   4. Pittsburgh (Pa.)—
Politics and government.   5. Pittsburgh (Pa.)—Social
conditions.   6. Title.
HT168.P48L6   1994   307.1′216′0974886   94-26215
ISBN 0-8229-5551-2 (v. 1)
ISBN 0-8229-3892-8 (v. 2 : cl : acid-free paper)
ISBN 0-8229-5566-0 (v. 2 : pb : acid-free paper)

A CIP catalogue record for this book is available from the British Library.
Eurospan, London

Twentieth-Century Pittsburgh

VOLUME 2

CONTENTS

PREFACE

Pittsburgh is exceptional among American cities in having been reborn twice since 1945. Renaissance I reconstructed the central business district, launched large-scale renewal projects throughout the city, created Point State Park, generated significant infrastructure improvements, launched ACTION-Housing and, not least, moved forward in air pollution abatement and flood control. Renaissance II, usually associated by Pittsburghers with the onset of the Caliguiri mayoralty (1977), gave birth to a flock of new office buildings in the Golden Triangle, as well as a new level of commitment to neighborhood revitalization (already launched during the Flaherty administration). In contrast to the Mellon-Lawrence era, it witnessed a much greater emphasis upon cultural development, expressed in ambitious plans for a downtown cultural district, and support for major cultural enterprises like the Carnegie Science Center and Warhol Museum. Lately, it has dawned upon Pittsburghers that their rivers might be used for something other than industrial waste discharge.

The spearhead of Renaissance II, as earlier, was a public-private partnership (but with the addition of a significant nonprofit sector and a transformed Urban Redevelopment Authority). The effectiveness of this partnership led to its elevation to a virtually uncontested norm of governance in Pittsburgh (with the exception of the Peter Flaherty administration, 1970–1977).[1] Although elite-based, the public-private partnership has been flexible enough to adapt its agenda to changing social conditions. Thus the public, corporate, and foundation sectors have been significantly involved in assisting and funding neighborhood organizations, creating a system of subsidized empowerment. In essence, Pittsburgh governance and public policy formulation has been rooted in a public-private partnership ideology that discouraged confrontational strategies of change in favor of consensus building.

Renaissance II is usually conceived as synonymous with a new generation of downtown office buildings. It would be useful, however, to define it more broadly as an effort to reconstruct Pittsburgh's economy, its system of neighborhood citizen organizations, and its cultural image.[2] One of the most dramatic contrasts between Renaissance I and Renaissance II in this broadly conceived reconstruction process was the prominent role played by nonprofit organizations in Renaissance II. The research universities (University of Pittsburgh and Carnegie Mellon University) and the medical centers emerged as economic development agencies and sources of expanding employment. The working-class neighborhoods of Pittsburgh participated in the reconstruction process through their own community development corporations. Nonprofit organizations emerged in the 1980s to nurture advanced technology and entrepreneurship. A highly significant force influencing social as well as cultural development were the private foundations. In funding and defining the civic agenda of Renaissance II, private foundations supplemented (and to a degree supplanted) the contribution of corporations and government. More flexible and less accountable than government or corporations to external pressure, foundations comprised a powerful element in the civic coalition.

Amenities or quality of life considerations have become part of the competitive universe in which communities must struggle. In the 1980s, industrial communities in particular had to confront basic issues defining their identity, their function, and their hopes for survival. Historians and others have focused mainly on economic issues and industrial relations. But quality of life concerns have also emerged as part of the economic development process—as another way to enhance a community's competitive advantage. Pittsburgh's strategic geographic location and easy access to the vital raw materials needed for iron and steel production had determined its economic character and industrial preeminence in the past. Renaissance II had to address new ways of maintaining a competitive advantage in the post-steel era. Corporations once integral to the history of Pittsburgh have departed, been absorbed, gone bankrupt. Those that remained were less rooted in the local community, more oriented to the international economy, more preoccupied with survival (and, in the 1980s, resisting takeovers). The question, then, became: what comes after a century of steelmaking for Pittsburgh? How could it reestablish a competitive edge in a more fluid economic universe? The civic coalition recognized that Pittsburgh had to exploit the features of its environment and culture that were distinctive and would attract the kind of population and economic development it desired. In effect, quality of life considerations had to be coordinated with economic development to a greater degree than was the case in the previous century of steelmaking. Organizations like the Pittsburgh History & Landmarks Foundation, Pittsburgh Cultural Trust, Carnegie Museum, and Historical Society of Western Pennsylvania were conspicuous in this process, becoming cultural entrepreneurs and developers. (ACTION-Housing, on the other hand, demonstrated the potential for nonprofit entrepreneurship in the realm of social service.)

In summary, Pittsburgh's civic culture was rooted in a partnership strategy that favored consensus and added the foundations and the new breed of entrepreneurial, development-oriented nonprofits to the coalition of Renaissance II. These nonprofits representing education and research, health and medicine, advanced technology and entrepreneurship, neighborhood development and cultural metamorphosis, testified to the controlling objective of the Renaissance II era—to modernize the Pittsburgh area economy, to transform it into a diversified professional, service, research, information processing, and advanced technology economy graced by an improved quality of life.

Renaissance II was an extraordinary episode in American urban history. It marked a widespread commitment on the part of a city's public and private leaders to abandon its industrial past and create a new economic and cultural identity. Few—outside the unemployed workers and residents of the devastated steel-based communities of the region—objected. To the contrary, many Pittsburghers (not just members of the elite) acquiesced in relegating the area's steel-centered, heavy industry legacy to the care of historians and preservationists. What evolved in its place was a strategy of modernization encompassing economic diversification (with an emphasis on professional services), nurture of the advanced technology and research sectors, a reduced but streamlined, more efficient, and more competitive manufacturing component, and a new awareness of the direct economic benefits of cultural vitality and heightened quality of life and their role in enhancing the community's image as a place to live and do business.[3] Involved in every aspect of this transformation was the Urban Redevelopment Authority under the chair-manship of John Robins (1977–1993). Thus G. Evan Stoddard, former director of the URA's Economic Development Department, defined the agency's strategy as "consistent with the modernization-diversification-quality of life" agenda.[4]

ACKNOWLEDGMENTS

Many faculty at the University of Pittsburgh, and many in the community contributed enormously to the writing of this book. The former include Morton Coleman, Director, Institute of Politics, and Professor of Social Work; and James Cunningham, Professor of Social Work; Edward Muller, Professor of History; and Robin Jones, Director, Urban Studies Program. They were all participants in events I examine and endured incessant requests for discussions, documents, and manuscript review. I do not blame them if they are relieved the book is finished.

The same is true of those in the community who likewise helped shape the events I describe. The following put up with multiple interviews, manuscript checks, or both: Jo DeBolt, Executive Director, Mon Valley Initiative; Michael Eversmeyer, Preservation Planner, Department of City Planning; Robert Gangewere, Editor, *Carnegie Magazine*; Sandra Phillips, Executive Director, Pittsburgh Partnership for Neighborhood Development; Richard Swartz, Director of Development, Bloomfield-Garfield Corporation; Arthur Ziegler, President, Pittsburgh History & Landmarks Foundation; Jonathan Zimmer, Executive Director, ACTION-Housing, Inc.

Others at the University of Pittsburgh, in government, and nonprofit agencies also deserve great credit for their willingness to review the manuscript or discuss the operations of their organizations. I would like to thank Roger Ahlbrandt, Dean, School of Business Administration, Portland State University; Henry Beukema, Executive Director, McCune Foundation; Caroline Boyce, Executive Director, Preservation Pennsylvania (former Executive Director, Oakland Planning and Development Corp.); David Brewton, Executive Director, Breachmenders, Inc.; Carol Brown, President, Pittsburgh Cultural Trust; Mark Bunnell, former City Planning Department; Raymond Christman, President, Technology Development and Education Corporation; Cathy Cairns, former Executive

Director, Aliquippa Alliance for Unity and Development; August Carlino, Executive Director, Steel Industry Heritage Corporation; Tom Croft, Executive Director, Steel Valley Authority; James DeAngelis, Graduate School of Public and International Affairs, University of Pittsburgh; John DeSantis, Chairman, Historic Review Commission; Lu Donnelly, Historic and Preservation Consultant; Jane Downing, former Director, Department of City Planning; David Epperson, Dean, School of Social Work, University of Pittsburgh; Bob Erickson, Project Director, Steel Valley Authority; Rebecca Flora, Executive Director, South Side Local Development Company; Robert Fogelson, Professor of History and Urban Planning, Massachusetts Institute of Technology; Randolph Harris, Community Organizer, Steel Industry Heritage Corporation; Joan Ivey, former Chairman, Historic Review Commission; William Keyes, Historical Society of Western Pennsylvania; Walter Kidney, Architectural Historian, Pittsburgh History & Landmarks Foundation; Karen LaFrance, Executive Director, East Liberty Development Inc.; Charles McCollester, Associate Director, Pennsylvania Center for Labor Relations, Indiana University of Pennsylvania; Arden Melzer, Professor of Social Work, University of Pittsburgh; Curt Miner, former Folklore Coordinator, Johnstown Area Heritage Association; Nancy Noszka, Executive Director, Lawrenceville Development Corporation; Wesley Posvar, former Chancellor, University of Pittsburgh; Raymond Reaves, Director, Allegheny County Planning Department; Larry Ridenour, Planning Project Manager, Allegheny County Department of Planning; John Robin, former Chairman, Urban Redevelopment Authority; Meyer Schwartz, former Professor of Social Work, University of Pittsburgh; Edward Sites, Professor of Social Work, University of Pittsburgh; Tracy Soska, Director, Continuing Education, School of Social Work, University of Pittsburgh, former Director, Westinghouse Valley Human Services Center; John Stephen, Executive Director, Friends of the Riverfront; G. Evan Stoddard, former Director, Economic Development Department, Urban Redevelopment Authority; Rev. William Thomas, former Chairman, Mon Valley Initiative; Michael Weber, Provost and Academic Vice President, Duquesne University; Michael Weir, Pennsylvania Economy League; Richard Wells, Professor Emeritus, School of Social Work, University of Pittsburgh.

Assistance in the accumulation of photograph materials was provided by the staff of the Carnegie Library; Randolph Harris, Community Organizer, Steel Industry Heritage Corporation; Norma Madden, Urban Redevelopment Authority.

This book was originally sponsored by the River Communities Project, School of Social Work, University of Pittsburgh, James Cunningham, Director, and David Epperson, Dean, with partial financial support provided by the PPG Industries Foundation.

Twentieth-Century Pittsburgh

VOLUME 2

I

Elegy for a Bygone World

The message of the 1963 *Economic Study of the Pittsburgh Region* was that Pittsburgh's economy had remained in the nineteenth century despite changing technological and market conditions.[1] The six-county, 4,500-square-mile region under study (Allegheny, Armstrong, Beaver, Butler, Washington, and Westmoreland Counties) suffered, accordingly, from slow population growth, a lag in employment opportunities compared to other metropolitan areas, above-average unemployment, underrepresentation of small firms, an excess of population in nonproductive age groups, a higher than average proportion of blue-collar workers. By 1900, the Pittsburgh region's economic mix possessed two distinctive features: an overspecialization in coal, iron, and steel, heavy electrical machinery, and glass, clay, and stone products, as well as a concentration of the labor force in the large plants required for those activities. The metals industries alone employed about 125,000 workers in 1960, representing two-fifths of manufacturing employment and one-seventh of total employment. The average manufacturing plant employed 109 persons, compared to the national average of 52.

Overspecialization in heavy industry and the concomitant concentration of workers in large plants were associated with two other characteristics of the regional economy. The coal industry, though attenuated, still employed a larger percentage of the work force in the primary or extractive sector than was true for any other metropolitan area. At the same time, the region ranked lowest in tertiary employment (trade and services); large-scale heavy industry did not provide an environment that spawned a great number of small suppliers and businesses.

Although social scientists perceived that the Pittsburgh economy had reached a mature plateau and that diversification was necessary to prevent economic arteriosclerosis, a casual look at the region in the early 1960s might suggest otherwise. Arriving here in 1963, after nearly a decade in the more sylvan ambience of New England and upstate New York, I encountered a city that seemed more like a scene out of Dickens's Coketown—one that would not have been altogether alien to Andrew Carnegie or Henry Clay Frick had they returned to earth.

Pittsburgh thirty years ago was a rich feast for a historian. Legendary figures like Carnegie and Frick, Jones and Laughlin, Schwab, Westinghouse, Mellon, or Heinz seemed more real in Pittsburgh—where they had lived and brought the second industrial revolution to America. The steel mills, still exploding with a primeval energy, testified to their presence, as did the many philanthropies associated with their names. To experience the noise and heat of the mills and visit the mill communities precipitated an awareness of the typical working-class experience—the long journey from southern and eastern Europe in the late nineteenth century, the harsh life of a Pittsburgh steel worker and, ultimately, attainment of middle-class affluence after World War II.[2]

Whatever the statistics concerning the erosion of population, commercial activities, and employment opportunities in the mill towns, the physical presence of heavy industry—steel above all—was inescapable. Driving to or from downtown along the Parkway East, one passed the steel complex of Jones & Laughlin, its great blast furnaces breathing fire like a metallic dragon. On the opposite side of the Monongahela River was J&L's South Side Works, substantially expanded in the 1950s with the assistance of the Urban Redevelopment Authority.

Leaving Pittsburgh, heading up the Mon Valley, one reached Homestead in a few minutes, site of the immense plant of the United States Steel Corporation (a name redolent with history, not yet the blank USX). Most famous of the Mon Valley mill towns because of the bloody strike of 1892, Homestead was a familiar place to many Pittsburghers with young children. One traversed Eighth Avenue, Homestead's bustling main thoroughfare, en route to Kennywood—the venerable, still pop-

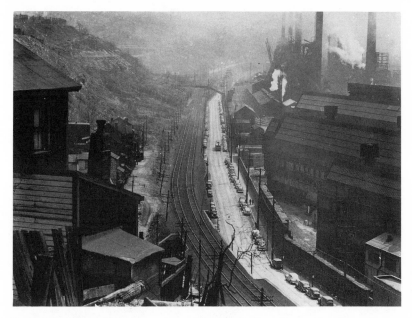

Jones & Laughlin mills before construction of the Parkway East, 1948. *Photo: Carnegie Library of Pittsburgh*

ular amusement park (recently supplemented by a nearby water park, Sandcastle).

Heading upriver again, one soon encountered the formidable Carrie Furnaces of U.S. Steel in Rankin. Preservationists hope to include them—still partly standing, but silent—with a section of Homestead in a steel heritage park. The Edgar Thomson Works of U.S. Steel in Braddock came next. This plant, with its forest of tall chimneys puffing smoke like demented tobacco addicts, was the base of Andrew Carnegie's steel empire, and Braddock was the site of his first library. The plant remains in operation with a much reduced work force.[3] The Duquesne Works of U.S. Steel followed. Nestled in a bend of the Monongahela, it was the site of the (now demolished) Dorothy Six blast furnaces. Continuing upriver, heading out of the deep bend, one reached McKeesport, home of U.S. Steel's National Works. In better days, McKeesport's downtown was a thriving shopping center for the surrounding mill towns. The Irvin Works of U.S. Steel in West Mifflin, still intact, loomed up across the river from McKeesport.

At Clairton, USX has kept a coke plant in operation—a source of frequent complaints from environmentalists over its pollution record.

J&L mills, Oakland, with the J&L South Side works across the Monongahela River.
Photo: Carnegie Library of Pittsburgh

Viewed from across the river in the 1960s, the Clairton Works had the aura of a lunar landscape. Standing in the midst of a desolate post-atomic-bomb terrain, one was enveloped in a cloud of metallic-tasting fog. All the mill towns have experienced hard times, but Clairton had descended altogether into a municipal purgatory by the early 1990s; "The bankrupt city is without its own police department and reliant on the Pennsylvania State Police. This protection amounts to no more than a two-officer patrol at any given time and is proving woefully inadequate at controlling drug traffic and other crime at two county Housing Authority projects, according to residents."[4]

Heading upriver from Clairton, one passed the Allegheny County line into Washington County, where the Donora Works of U.S. Steel still functioned in 1963. Renowned among environmentalists for a lethal air inversion in 1948, Donora was an unlikely site for what was arguably the finest continental restaurant in the region—the Redwood Inn. Donora was reachable from Pittsburgh via Route 837, which carried one through or past all the mill towns mentioned. The Donora Works, in 1966, were the first of the U.S. Steel Mon Valley steel mills to be closed and demolished; a full decade later, a visitor would encounter a scene of stark desolation in the business district. Past Donora in Westmoreland County were the Monessen and Allenport Works of Wheeling-Pittsburgh Steel.

Adjoining Allegheny County to the northwest was Beaver County. Driving out of Pittsburgh along Route 65, which parallels the Ohio River, one might visit Old Economy Village in Ambridge. This notable preservation project commemorated the utopian pastoral community established by the Rappites in the 1820s. The Rappites were pietists who lived by a code of biblical literalism and primitive Christian simplicity. Yet there was beauty in their lives and villages; it was expressed in the simple vernacular of their architecture and handicrafts and the care devoted to their horticulture. Across the river, in unintended but outlandish contrast to everything for which Economy stood, stretched the six-mile-long, 779-acre Aliquippa Works of Jones & Laughlin. And to the west of Aliquippa in Beaver County was the Midland Works of Crucible Steel. These two plants, established around 1909–1911, marked the final phase of large-scale steel production facilities in the region.

It was not only the shutdown of steel plants that decimated the heavy industrial sector. A short distance from Pittsburgh along the Parkway East was the Turtle Creek Valley. Here, in East Pittsburgh and Wilmerding, respectively, were the vast Westinghouse Electric and Westinghouse Air Brake Corporation plants. Once employing thousands, the "great Westinghouse works [had become] a mere repair shop for used generator machinery" by the mid-1980s.[5]

The severe recession of the early 1980s precipitated the decision by U.S. Steel and other steel companies to close down their plants in the Pittsburgh area. Attrition turned into swift decapitation of an entire industry built over the course of a century. Between 1982 and 1987, U.S. Steel abandoned its blast furnace complexes at Rankin (1982) and Duquesne (1984), and its mills at Duquesne (1984), Clairton, except for a coke plant (1984), Homestead (1986), and McKeesport (1987). The Donora Works, as mentioned earlier, had been closed in 1966. Jones & Laughlin (LTV Steel) closed its South Side and Hazelwood plants in 1985, while keeping the Hazelwood coke plant in operation. At about the same time, J&L shut down its Aliquippa Works in Beaver County. Wheeling-Pittsburgh closed its Monessen Works in Westmoreland County in 1986.[6]

A combination of competitive pressures, market changes, low-cost imports, overcapacity, rigidity and miscalculations by management, labor, and government, as well as productivity problems in the older plants of Pittsburgh—and the Northeast generally—explain the industrial Götterdämmerung. According to John P. Hoerr, in his magisterial study of labor relations in the Mon Valley:

> Perhaps the key mistake of the entire period, the one that would start an unraveling process that has not ended, came in the 1950s. The domestic industry expanded its capacity from 100 million to 149 million tons during that decade . . . [and] they expanded in the wrong way, building large, new, open hearth shops. The more efficient basic oxygen furnace (BOF) had already been invented in Germany. . . . The domestic industry stuck with open hearths because they provided greater volumes of steel to feed large rolling mills.

Subsequently, the companies found themselves on a treadmill; they raised prices to maintain profit margins as unit costs escalated, further reducing their competitive status in an increasingly international market. Decades of adversarial labor relations based on unilateral company control of the production process ensured that even the threat of extinction prevented a cooperative response: "The union's short term goal was to push to the limit for economic benefits, regardless of whether they would be generated solely by the growth of the steel business, or whether the consumer of steel would have to chip in by paying higher prices."[7]

The shutdown of the steel industry in the Pittsburgh region involved more than jobs.[8] Swept away was an intergenerational way of life that provided a sense of continuity, security, family cohesion, and communality. The mill towns had been created for the single purpose of producing steel, but around that function the workers had created an encompassing social system. Its loss defined the real cost of deindustrialization. Hoerr, a McKeesport native, vividly portrays the allure of a life in steelmaking:

> For young men in the mill towns of those days, there was a very tangible sense of having to make an implicit bargain with life from the outset. There were two choices. If you took a job in the mill, you could stay in McKeesport among family and friends, earn decent pay, and gain a sort of lifetime security (except for layoffs and strikes) in an industry that would last forever. You traded advancement for security and expected life to stick to its bargain.[9]

Young men graduated from high school and entered the mill "just like their fathers, brothers, uncles and grandfathers before them." The work was hard and sometimes dangerous, but it provided a "sense of identity and self-respect." In Homestead, the steel works were known to locals as the "thirteenth grade" and "Riverside Academy." Bill Gorol, Jr., went to work there in 1977, like his father in 1944, his grandfather in 1913, and his great-grandfather in the 1890s.[10] Beyond work and family, there were many other institutions that built and sustained a sense of identity in the mill town world: neighborhood, ethnic club or fraternity, church, union, athletic association, tavern. The mill communities were not at all bereft of cultural life, but it was working-class rather than boutique culture.

Anyone whose encounter with the Pittsburgh area mill towns during the postwar decades was limited to the industrial section suffered from a misconception of their ecology. They were built according to a pattern, like the New England mill towns of the mid-nineteenth century. The steel plants, like the textile mills, usurped the flatland along the river. Railroads, rather than canals, serviced the steel works. Past the main avenue that paralleled the mill, one ascended the slopes and moved farther from the forbidding industrial sector. Attractive neighborhoods of

USS Publicity photo ca. 1950. *Photo: United States Steel Corporation*

well-tended homes, gardens, and churches materialized. They expressed pride and a sense of permanence.

Many remember the Mon Valley mill towns as lively, friendly places to be in the expansive years of World War II and its aftermath: "The narrow brick streets of the mill towns were filled with streetcars, automobiles, workers going to and from the plant, and shoppers carrying big brown paper bags." Braddock in the 1940s laid claim to five movie theaters, dozens of car dealerships, "retail shops galore." An old-time resident of Rankin, a half-mile chunk of earth overlooking the river between Swissvale and Braddock, reminisced about life there in the 1930s: "Oh, it was nice. Everybody was friendly. Everybody had their own little clubs to go to. We had a lot of stores. It was an awfully nice community."[11] But the mill town, like the steelworker, was vulnerable— both depended upon a single industry for prosperity and survival. In Homestead, for example, U.S. Steel provided jobs for the handicapped, cleaned the streets with company equipment, and burned the city's garbage in its open-hearth facilities. But when the godfather packed up and left, there was no one to take his place. Braddock, the "Little Pittsburgh" of the Mon Valley's Indian Summer, turned derelict—a stroll down Braddock Avenue by the early 1990s was like "taking a trip down death row" in view of the pervasive crack scene. The population had peaked at 22,000 in the 1950s, descending to about 5,300 by the mid-1980s. The plant had once employed 6,000 at fourteen open-hearth furnaces and five blast furnaces; employment had dropped to a mere 650 jobs by the 1980s. Carnegie's handsome library, his first such gift, was closed in 1974—but was not torn down and has since undergone restoration. The Braddock scene had a postapocalypse ambience: "Plywood covers the smashed windows of vacant buildings. . . . Weeds grow in empty lots. The handful of stores still open wear iron grates as defensive shields. Pockets of idled men mill about on shabby street corners."[12]

The decisive shutdown of the steel industry throughout the Pittsburgh region in the 1980s devastated a once stable and prosperous working-class way of life. Simply put, the drift of the mill towns toward smaller, poorer, older populations dramatically quickened (many steelworkers had already moved out to the suburbs after World War II). The progress made by the growing number of black steelworkers in the post-1960s era abruptly ended. The tax base of the mill towns eroded at

USS Works, Homestead, 1970s. *Photo: Author*

exactly the time when vastly increased health and welfare services were most needed. Steel industry contraction and economic diversification in the Pittsburgh region may have been necessary and desirable. But the cost of the transition was unevenly distributed; it fell disproportionately upon one generation of workers and their communities. It was a wrenching industrial revolution in reverse.[13]

If an unemployed steelworker neither left the region nor retired on a pension, his skills and the security he had known proved to be liabilities in seeking employment. Proficiency in steelmaking was not readily transferable to an economy expanding toward services and advanced technology. The ease with which he had found work within the steel industry, probably with the aid of family or friends, resulted in a lack of experience and confidence when forced to look for another job: "Man, I've worked since I was sixteen. I had one job after another. Before you quit one job, you had another one lined up. You never went months without work. This is all new to me, trying to find a job. I've tried like hell, there's nothing out there." It was difficult to accept what was never supposed to happen. A longtime Homestead steelworker explained, "Everybody felt the mill would always be there. On that basis they went out and bought cars, houses, and all. . . . We have no experience in this. . . . For seventeen years, I went down to the shop each day and they tell you what you are doing that day. Now where am I going?"

Over generations, the expectation had been that one was set for life in a familiar round of work, family, friends, community. "It was easy," a former steelworker observed; "you went to work, had a few beers afterward, and then went home. You had a lot of money for the wife and kids. You had nice vacations. You bought anything you wanted."[14]

. The relationship between steelworkers and steel companies was both contentious and paternalistic. The companies fiercely defended managerial prerogatives and made every effort to discourage initiative on the part of workers or unions. Rules, regulations, and an elaborate hierarchical bureaucracy typified U.S. Steel labor policy. Throughout its history, U.S. Steel "regarded hourly workers as an undifferentiated horde, incapable of doing anything more than following orders and collecting the paycheck." In response, Hoerr writes, the workers and union "had no concern for competitiveness and rejected the idea that [they] bore any responsibility for seeing that the plant operated efficiently."[15]

When the steel industry crumbled, mill towns as well as workers had difficulty adjusting. The steel communities, which had existed only to produce steel and had depended on the companies for their economic sustenance, suddenly had to cope with an unwanted freedom and need to make decisions about the future. Steelworkers, similarly, had to cope with the loss of security, sense of worth, and identity—all of which were wrapped up in the jobs that would never return. A railroader in the Homestead plant, a third-generation employee, perceived the challenge confronting the former steelworkers and their communities: "Blue collar is traditional. Things are planned out for you. Someone is taking care of you, rather than you taking care of yourself. Now it is more survival of the fittest. You need the tools to achieve your goals."[16]

A major effort to analyze the human consequences of deindustrialization was the River Communities Project (RCP) of the School of Social Work at the University of Pittsburgh. Directed by James Cunningham, who had guided ACTION-Housing's neighborhood urban extension experiment in the 1960s, the RCP produced two surveys of Aliquippa, another of East Pittsburgh and Turtle Creek, and a volume of essays dealing with "survival and resilience" in the Mon Valley.[17] These studies were supplemented by more specialized research concerning the impact of deindustrialization upon the elderly, women, children, the unemployed, and blacks.[18] Another study examined a community-university effort to promote youth enterprise in Aliquippa, Monessen, and the East Liberty district of Pittsburgh.[19]

Not surprisingly, the research confirmed that massive economic dislocation and unemployment were generating widespread social problems in a context of fragmented and impoverished governments: "Disinvestment turns vital centers of production into shrinking retirement communities" that are increasingly "sustaining themselves with social security and pension checks."[20] Critical issues included loss of health insurance for many families, public education systems that had been geared to supplying recruits for the mills rather than for college, river- and rail-based transportation systems representative of the paleotechnic era that provided poor access to interstate highways or the airport, outmigration of the younger, better-educated population, racial tensions, and crime.

Cunningham found that survival techniques for Aliquippa residents included belt tightening, sharing, appealing to support networks, and the ministrations of churches, unions, and social agencies. A consistent theme of the River Communities Project is the vital role of family as a buffer against deprivation. The norm in these mill towns was "intergenerational reciprocity." Family was the supreme refuge. Elderly parents supporting adult children carried much of the burden.[21] Family cohesion characteristic of mill town life, together with government and industry pension programs, helped to mitigate the impact of massive deindustrialization in the Pittsburgh region.

The social work origins of the River Communities Project are expressed in its emphasis upon the plight of individuals and families, their efforts to cope with conditions that undermined their capacity for self-support, the threat to their self-respect resulting from unaccustomed dependency, and the role of community and social agencies. People were often slow to accept assistance from social agencies for fear of compromising their self-respect. Social service professionals interviewed for the Turtle Creek study "felt they could provide more assistance if community residents would let them." Pride kept residents of Duquesne "from accepting services and goods not earned directly by their own labor."[22] Resistance to entitlements or welfare was widespread: "People of the distressed communities still cling proudly to their spirit of self-reliance. They would rather go without or borrow from a relative than apply to a social agency."[23] Such repudiation of assistance from strangers was indeed a vestige of a bygone world.

Cunningham believed that the conflict between need and pride might be reconciled through community organization efforts, transforming dispirited or powerless individuals into a unified force for renewal and re-construction. The community organization theme was prominent at the outset of the project—the Aliquippa report released in 1984. Noting the dismal condition of municipal government—political squabbling within Aliquippa's city council, alienation of a black population that lacked representation, layoff of police officers and other municipal work-ers, deterioration of the B.F. Jones Memorial Library, declining revenues, and increasing debt—Cunningham stressed the need for community cohesion in order to "restore some vitality and sweetness to life in Ali-quippa." Since it was beyond the capacity of government to act, lead-ership would have to come from a "broad community task force."[24] This response to the deindustrialization crisis had to compensate, also, for the absence of regional organization. Allegheny County was fragmented into 130 fiercely independent local jurisdictions. Individual communities had no choice but to adopt a self-help strategy.[25]

Aliquippa illustrated, in microcosm, the variety of self-help expedi-ents in the Ohio and Mon Valleys. As always, "churches and family networks" were among the primary sources of assistance and survival. Under Anglican auspices, a "Community of Celebration" was organized, "committed to being a sign of the celebration of Jesus Christ in the whole of life and to being a friend of the poor and the oppressed." Also church inspired was "People Helping People," a nonprofit corporation formed by the Greater Aliquippa Ministerial Association in 1983. The Aliquippa Salvation Army Corps Community Center was another of the religious agencies that "help Aliquippa survive."[26]

Supplementing family, ethnic associations, fraternal organizations, and churches were the efforts of more formal social agencies and agencies for employment retraining. Between 1984 and 1986, for example, no fewer than four training centers opened in Aliquippa. They included the Beaver Valley Job Training Partnership, established through the federal Job Training Partnership Act of 1983. But the many programs in the region in the 1980s had limited success. They did not necessarily lead to jobs, or they led to jobs incommensurate with the age, experience, and needs of the unemployed worker.[27]

Worker-initiated, and reminiscent of the 1930s, were the unem-ployed workers' committees that operated outside the union structure. Following the mass layoffs of 1981, a coalition of these groups in 1982 established the Mon Valley Unemployed Steelworkers Committee (later Mon Valley Unemployed Committee). The Beaver County Unemployed Committee was created in 1985 by former LTV workers in Aliquippa; the following year witnessed the organization of the Mid-Mon Valley Unemployed Committee. In the winter of 1986 these groups formed a federation known as the Unemployed Council of Southwestern Pennsylvania. These worker-controlled committees were significant as an effort to combine assistance and self-respect. They devoted considerable attention to seeking trade readjustment allowances and help for the unemployed. A highly charged issue in the period was mortgage foreclosure; the worker committees acted to prevent sheriff's sales of homes and played a key role in formulating the Pennsylvania Homeowners Emergency Mortgage Assistance Program (1983). The committees were also active in organizing food banks.[28]

The River Communities Project's 1984 report on Aliquippa had urged the creation of a "broad community task force" to assume leadership in revitalization. Although this report and the other community surveys contained a multitude of proposals for economic and social development, none received greater emphasis than the need for community organization. In Aliquippa, for example, Cunningham saw fragmentation, factionalism, "local government frustrated and making little progress," an absence of "unified planning and action." Any comeback depended, ultimately, "on the ability of local people to move beyond fragmentation."[29]

There is an intriguing resemblance between these perceptions and those of the celebrated Pittsburgh Survey of 1907–1908, which emphasized the disparity in power and organization between the economic-corporate and social sectors in the region. But the survey, a quintessential example of middle-class reform perspectives in the early twentieth century, saw redemption through expansion of the regulatory powers of government; it was a vision of rule by technocratic benevolence. Very different was Cunningham's latter-day social work concept of redemption by community-based process. Aliquippa would only degenerate if it awaited salvation through external forces—government or corporate. It had to take control of its own destiny, "unite to plan and act, make demands on outside institutions, and start to make a few things better."[30] Evolving out of the first Aliquippa report, and from proposals made by

Cunningham and Cathy Cairns at a May 1984 "Comeback Conference" at the University of Pittsburgh, was the Aliquippa Alliance for Unity and Development (AAUD), organized in the summer of that year.

The beneficiary of funding from the Heinz Endowments, the AAUD developed a complex three-track program. The first of these, according to Cathy Cairns, executive director from 1984 to 1993, was the creation of a social service and health network which, by 1990, was serving nearly 2,000 residents of southern Beaver County. The second track, education and youth employment, encompassed "basic literacy and math skills, computer education, and apprenticeship training programs, linked to real jobs." An adult program, established in 1989, provided "customized" job training. The third AAUD track featured economic development programs. Its accomplishments included designation of the area as a state enterprise zone and establishment of two business incubators (inexperienced and low-income entrepreneurs were assisted by the social service and education divisions). Other initiatives in the economic sphere included studies of the economic prospects of the community, tax reform (encouraging LTV use or sale of its mill property), federal funding of infrastructure improvements to improve access to the mill site and to downtown, and the county's purchase of some 120 acres of the mill. The Aliquippa Alliance, by 1993, "owned or controlled over 10 percent of the city's useable commercial square footage, located mostly in the downtown."[31]

The AAUD was not an isolated phenomenon (although its original intention to dissolve in three to five years was unique and improbable). It was paralleled in the 1980s by the creation of a Community Development Corporation (CDC) network in Pittsburgh neighborhoods and the Mon Valley Initiative (a federation of Mon Valley CDCs). What these organizations represented, in a context of community and neighborhood demoralization and dissolution, was a quest for strategies for reconstruction. More specifically, they sought a mixture of economic development, community revitalization, social service, and citizen empowerment strategies that might improve the quality of life. They were also de facto substitutes for the governments and corporations upon whom the communities had previously depended for services and livelihood.

An underlying theme of the RCP was that deindustrialization was irreversible. However, an alliance of labor and church dissenters emerged in the 1980s who contested the valedictions for steel production in the Mon Valley. They were sustained by the belief that deindustrialization was not the product of irreversible global and domestic impersonal forces, but of a calculated policy of disinvestment by banks and corporations. If so, it could be reversed. A labor historian, David L. Rosenberg, stated the argument for deindustrialization by design. According to Rosenberg, two processes, "deindustrialization and the planning of Pittsburgh, have been closely connected and the Allegheny Conference on Community Development (ACCD) has played and continues to play a crucial role in both." A narrowly based elite organization, the ACCD aspired to attain "balance and diversity in the regional economy" at the expense of the traditional industrial sector. Critical to Rosenberg's argument was his examination of the conference's Executive Committee which, from 1968 to 1990, revealed (to Rosenberg's satisfaction) a pattern of Mellon domination. "The possibility of global overcapacity and competition from foreign imports could not have been entirely unanticipated by conference planners, when, in their role as bank directors, they must have participated in the banks' investment policies."[32] Expanded world capacity, he concludes, generated a flood of exports that competed with regional production.

This line of analysis, favored by church and labor groups spawned in the early 1980s, raises several significant economic issues. Was it economically viable to modernize the aged industrial plants in the Pittsburgh region in competition with newer plants closer to markets farther west? Would not modernization itself have entailed substantial labor reductions? Was it not imperative for the Pittsburgh region to diversify an economy long burdened by excessive reliance on metals fabrication? Although the United States needed to retain a significant manufacturing sector (as critics of deindustrialization argued), did it have to be in Pittsburgh?[33] Or how much manufacturing, and what kind, was appropriate for Pittsburgh's post-steel economy?

There is another issue raised by Rosenberg's, and similar, critiques. One gets the impression that the disinvestment policy was devised by a narrow corporate and financial elite that could anticipate a decline of union power as a fringe benefit. In reality, the policy was favored (or at least not resisted) by a wide range of community interests who recognized the possibility of significant economic and environmental transformation. Those with a new vision of economic reconstruction, who saw the historic industrial sector as an economic liability, gave a chilly reception to the idea of reindustrialization.

The tactics of the closely aligned Denominational Ministry Strategy (DMS), and Network to Save the Mon-Ohio Valley, were disastrous. They generated a backlash that deflected attention from their critique of the investment policies of Pittsburgh banks and corporations. The DMS was formed in 1979 by Lutheran and Episcopal clergy. The Network, an alliance of DMS and labor dissidents, followed in 1982. They focused their protests against disinvestment on Mellon Bank. But the appointment of Charles Honeywell as strategist resulted in a kind of self-destructive radical theater. Formerly employed by the Shadyside Action Coalition, a neighborhood group, Honeywell had been influenced by the late Saul Alinsky, the radical community organizer based in Chicago. From Alinsky he learned that change could be precipitated by consciousness-raising confrontation. In Pittsburgh, consciousness raising included dumping sacks of pennies in Mellon bank lobbies and depositing fish in safety deposit boxes. A tactic that precipitated vehement condemnation was the invasion of a Christmas pageant dinner at the Shadyside Presbyterian Church. On December 16, 1984, four masked men tossed balloons inflated with dye and skunk water at the celebrants, a group that presumably included representatives of the Pittsburgh corporate elite.

By early 1983, the Protestant church hierarchies had repudiated the DMS. As the DMS became increasingly obsessed with battling and discrediting the Lutheran leadership, which had defrocked two of the pastors, it forgot about corporations, banks, mill town deterioration, and reinvestment. A group of the dissidents occupied Trinity Lutheran Church in Clairton for a week and had to be evicted by the sheriff.[34]

A more sober effort to promote reindustrialization was embodied in the Tri-State Conference on Steel, and the Steel Valley Authority (SVA). Organized in 1979, Tri-State not only protested against wholesale deindustrialization, but attempted to create an institutionalized basis for worker and community involvement in the investment process. According to Staughton Lynd, workers in Youngstown, Ohio, and the Pittsburgh region, beginning in 1977, began exploring the concept that

> private decisions with catastrophic social consequences are really public decisions, that some kind of community property right arises from the long-

standing relation between a company and a community, and that the power of eminent domain . . . should be used to acquire industrial facilities when corporations no longer wish to operate them.[35]

Initially, Tri-State attempted to persuade individual borough councils to acquire manufacturing plants. When Crucible Steel in Midland abandoned production in 1982, for example, Tri-State urged the locality to acquire the property through eminent domain and to issue bonds to finance the purchase of the plant. The following year, Tri-State joined protests against Mellon Bank policies concerning the Mesta Machine Company's bankruptcy proceedings in West Homestead. Worker groups demanded that Mellon release company assets to pay back wages and benefits. A Save Mesta Committee created by Tri-State and others proposed that the municipality acquire the plant. Although the borough council did approve the creation of a nine-member authority, the scheme was vetoed by the mayor. Here, as elsewhere, municipal authorities feared potential legal liabilities or financial burdens.

Tri-State's efforts to save the Dorothy Six blast furnace and oxygen process furnace in Duquesne (shut down in 1984) also failed. A feasibility study issued by Lazard Freres in January 1986 declared that market conditions and financing prospects were too poor, the costs of furnace improvements and a continuous caster too high. Also futile were efforts to prevent the loss of the American Standard Corporation plants in Swissvale (Union Switch & Signal) and Wilmerding (Westinghouse Air Brake). A Save the Brake and Switch Coalition, including the Tri-State Conference, lost a court action to prevent the Radice Corporation (which had acquired Union Switch & Signal in October 1985) from dismantling the property.[36]

The determination to thwart deindustrialization was reaffirmed by the creation of the Steel Valley Authority in 1985. It was incorporated with nine members (including Pittsburgh) in January 1986. But local concerns over liabilities, costs, and municipal independence constricted its ability to function effectively. Even more important was the continued lack of private investment capital for acquisition and development.[37]

Nothing more dramatically symbolized the industrial era in Pittsburgh than the coke facilities and blast furnaces of J&L near the downtown center, and the 110-acre plant spreading along the South Side flatland. LTV closed the latter facility in 1985, giving the newly created

SVA an opportunity to demonstrate that worker and community initiative could revitalize the steel industry. The object was to restart the two electric furnaces that had been installed in the 1970s (when 5,000 workers toiled at the plant) and produce rough slabs for sale. But six years and $600,000 later, LTV, South Side residents, and City Council members had lost patience with the inability of SVA to utilize the property.

LTV had already cleared forty-five acres of the site by the spring of 1991, when two development forces converged. Gustine Company, a local realtor, expressed interest in the entire site for a mixed-use project involving housing, retailing, small businesses, and warehouses. Simultaneously, the South Side Planning Forum issued a report (funded by LTV and prepared by the South Side Local Development Company) urging a similar mixed-purpose project. Any prospect for housing would be lost, however, if the idled electric furnaces were restarted.

Early in July 1991, two Pittsburgh councilmen urged demolition of the entire plant in order to exploit "a magnificent opportunity for a mixed-use development project."[38] At the same time, the Gustine Company announced its intention to create a $50 million residential and commercial complex on the 110-acre site, including a marina and riverfront parks. Pittsburgh newspapers were eager to write an obituary for

Demolition of LTV South Side works, 1984. *Photo: Author*

steel production within the city's limits. According to the *Pittsburgh Press*, "It is time to begin an orderly planning process for reusing this prime parcel. Sounding the death knell for the electric furnaces is the painful first step." The *Pittsburgh Post-Gazette* contended that the SVA had "left a legacy of false hopes" and it was "time to move on. Bring on riverfront development in the South Side."[39] The Gustine project never materialized and, by 1994, the site had become a leading candidate for a riverboat gambling complex—provided such "gaming" is approved by the state legislature in 1995.

Efforts to halt the erosion of the industrial sector in the Pittsburgh region failed through a convergence of market forces and a strong consensus within the civic coalition that the local economy had to be diversified and modernized. Robert Erikson, project director for SVA, complained that LTV wanted $35 million for a site it hoped to purchase for $10 million. But $120 million of investment capital would not flow to what seemed a lost cause at the time—an unfavorable market for steel slabs, the high cost of scrap steel needed for production, and the expense of installing a continuous caster. Although conceding that the prospects for restarting the electric furnaces on the South Side were negligible, Erikson defended the aspiration to preserve manufacturing jobs: "We're moving closer toward earning money in less productive ways. We're becoming a tourist destination. . . . Now rich foreign tourists are coming here and we're making the beds."[40]

The deindustrialization of the Pittsburgh region produced a social tragedy—thousands of unemployed workers and an intergenerational way of life destroyed. Whole communities of stable, independent, hard-working families dissolved in the 1980s. Although worker and community groups made little progress in preserving the steel-based industrial sector or reviving the mill towns, they did raise fundamental issues of economic policy. This was true, especially of the Tri-State Conference and the SVA.

Tri-State/SVA have argued consistently that a balanced, vigorous regional economy requires an extensive manufacturing sector. "A retail-service economy cannot exist in a vacuum; it ultimately depends upon those sectors, such as basic manufacturing, that export to the larger markets. . . . Sophisticated medical care, chic restaurants, specialized legal services and higher education are all part of the *consumer* economy, not the *productive* economy." Advanced technology, with its limited job potential, "should be *applied* to our metalmaking and metalworking industries, not seen as a *replacement* for them."[41]

Tri-State/SVA never accepted the argument of the steel industry that steel production had become unprofitable and that it was therefore necessary to abandon steel in favor of more diversifed investment. The labor groups insisted that steelmaking was profitable enough, but not as profitable as alternative avenues of investment. The problem was that U.S. Steel and other steel corporations failed to modernize and remain competitive, preferring to channel their funds into other "more lucrative businesses." The industry strategy was to run plants into the ground and shift profits into nonsteel investments such as petrochemicals and natural gas (while American banks were financing the modernization of foreign steel companies). According to a Tri-State Conference report,

> While foreign steel firms modernized and prepared their industries to challenge American dominance, U.S. Steel was apparently content to just rake in the profits. Later, rather than face the technological challenge posed by Japanese super mills . . . with their basic oxygen furnaces and continuous casters, U.S. Steel disinvested from its steel business into oil, chemicals, plastics and real estate.[42]

Along with the role of manufacturing in a regional economy, Tri-State/SVA also raised fundamental and enduring issues of industrial relations—what a company owes to its labor force and to the community. Thus Charles McCollester condemned as irrational and irresponsible the casual abandonment of the skilled Pittsburgh regional labor force. It did not make economic sense to toss away such a valuable resource.[43] Similarly, Tri-State objected that "an entire generation of skilled industrial workers is being cut out of the nation's economic life and left idle. . . . A century-old culture based upon the making, shaping and fitting of metal is being needlessly and thoughtlessly obliterated." It was not all right to "hurt people economically—in ways that damage their children, their families, their communities—as long as you do it in the name of your property rights." A new principle was needed: that economics and technology "should be subordinated to the preservation and nurturing of community."[44] In essence, the concept of property rights had to be extended to include a voice for workers and communities. Banks and corporations should not have unilateral power to impoverish an entire region. Surveying the mill town scene in late 1993, a reporter concluded that "the industrial towns that line southwestern Pennsylvania's rivers have become the region's Third World, increasingly disadvantaged and increasingly unable to take care of themselves."[45]

2

Economic Development Strategy in the Post-Steel Era

The Federal Reserve Bank of Cleveland compared the economic mix of four cities—Cincinnati, Cleveland, Pittsburgh, and Columbus—from the mid-1960s to the mid-1980s. It found that Pittsburgh had experienced the most "dramatic transformation" over the period; the city's manufacturing base dropped from 37 percent of total employed to 16 percent. Pittsburgh had evolved from the most industrialized to the least industrialized of the four cities. It lost half its manufacturing jobs but doubled the service component. Pittsburgh thus exemplified a determination "to break with the apparent security of the past" rather than entrust the community's future to "familiar but declining industries."[1]

This transformation of Pittsburgh was not the product of a regional plan, and no single agency exerted an influence akin to the Allegheny Conference in Renaissance I. Nonetheless, an informal consensus evolved in response to the evaporation of the region's century-old heavy industry constellation. Just as Renaissance I was precipitated by a crisis situation in the aftermath of World War II, the opportunity for modernization in the 1980s was made possible by economic shocks that loosened the stranglehold of heavy industry. The Federal Reserve reported,

> The [traditional] industries' demand for labor drove up wages and employed the best and the brightest. . . . Their desire to build new plants tied up financial resources. Their large scale of operation cornered resources and

markets. . . . [As] these dominant industries matured, institutions and coalitions formed to preserve the industries.[2]

A realization that modernization of the economy was now possible and imperative governed the emerging consensus. The key to successful modernization would be diversification. A modernized, diversified economy, in turn, would be characterized by (1) a vigorous service, professional, and small-business sector, (2) advanced technology, research, and information processing, (3) a smaller but more efficient and technologically sophisticated manufacturing sector, and (4) attention to quality of life concerns. (One might add to the modernization aspirations the upgrading of an aging and incomplete infrastructure). As in Renaissance I, public-private partnerships would be prominent, but nonprofit organizations would play a more significant role in the partnerships, as would state government in the context of diminished federal aid.

According to University of Pittsburgh economist David B. Houston, who holds an alternative "Marxist interpretation" of Pittsburgh's economic evolution, the 1980s witnessed the triumph of finance over production capitalism. Mellon interests, he argues, had long been dominant in the region, and it was in the "nonproductive realms of accumulation that they saw both their past and their future." Pittsburgh, under the Mellon aegis, had shifted "from a center producing surplus value to one managing and circulating surplus value." The workers had nothing to say about this process, which transformed them into part of an internationalized proletariat competing with the "urbanized peasants of the third world." Renaissance I had simply been an effort to "remake . . . Pittsburgh in a form more suitable for its new nonproductive functions."[3]

One of the hazards of Marxist economics and historiography is reductionism: dogma becomes reality and substitutes for an effort to deal with the complexity and contradiction of the world as it is. Finance capitalism, in Pittsburgh and elsewhere, was only one element in the transformation of the international economy; the wrenching adjustments demanded of a community like Pittsburgh, whose dinosaur economy was neither competitive nor a source of growth long before 1945, were not exclusively the product of Mellon Bank policies.[4]

The recession era of 1979–1983 and its aftermath, which devastated the Pittsburgh region, also generated prescriptions that were not Marxist but depended upon a high degree of federal initiative and spending. Thus

Morton Coleman and James Cunningham, faculty members in the University of Pittsburgh School of Social Work, proclaimed the need for a "new national economic policy," involving the creation of an industrial competitiveness bank to provide capital to declining regions; TVA-like projects; a reborn Reconstruction Finance Corporation; national industrial planning; major expansion of the Jobs Partnership Training Act; government procurement contracts that would promote job retention; and a kind of public works program geared toward improving the infrastructure.[5]

The context for this kind of advocacy was a long era of federal expansionism, from New Deal and World War II programs, to urban renewal, civil rights, and antipoverty initiatives, including Medicare and Medicaid. Indeed, many of the projects from Pittsburgh's Renaissance I (1945–1970) had depended upon federal renewal, antipoverty, and revenue-sharing funds. But political circumstances had changed by the 1980s, including a resurgence of conservatism, increased awareness of the liabilities associated with federal mandates and regulations, and the exponential growth of federal deficits. By the 1980s and 1990s, many Americans desired to reduce federal interference. In the words of Stephen Goldsmith, mayor of Indianapolis,

> While local governments are trying to devolve authority, decentralize decision making, privatize service delivery and deregulate their markets, Congress is ordering the federal government to stop us. . . . Through its actions Washington demonstrates the disturbing attitude that it understands the problems of America's cities better than those of us who live in them. By making laws that increasingly restrict local options, paralyze local leadership and prevent local problem solving, Congress has nullified the federal government's role as partner to the cities and transformed it into one of urban America's chief problems.[6]

In retrospect, the massive federal spending for urban renewal and social programs in the 1960s and 1970s may have created a fool's paradise, a state of mind that encouraged evasion of hard-core issues relating to municipal tax resources, spending priorities, an area's economic mix, or its competitive market status. If city authorities could balance the budget by means of external transfer payments, one did not have to worry about creating a viable municipal economy. And, not surprisingly, city officials favored programs for which funding was available; this did not necessarily coincide with what the community most needed. The Pittsburgh Regional Planning Association's *Economic Study of the Pittsburgh Region* in 1963 clearly portrayed the economic obsolescence and the imperative of modernizing and diversifying the Pittsburgh economy, but it hardly caused a ripple while the community was awash in federal dollars (and guidelines). The shutdown of the Pittsburgh area's heavy industry complex after 1979, combined with constricted federal funding, finally forced a serious reappraisal of the region's economic prospects. Limited federal funding, compared to the Renaissance I era, thus had its advantages: local leaders now had to confront the region's competitive advantages and liabilities and devise a long-term strategy for a more diversified and balanced economy.

Roger Ahlbrandt, a leading advocate and publicist for advanced technology, also briefly yearned for grand planning in response to the economic breakdown of the early 1980s in the Pittsburgh area. He complained in 1984 that "a grand vision charting the future of our region is lacking" and that what was needed was "a commitment at the highest levels . . . to form a broad-based coalition to form an overall structure or framework to guide the numerous activities already underway." Subsequently, Ahlbrandt abandoned expectations of centralized economic and community planning in favor of an emphasis on the Pittsburgh partnership tradition as the basis for regional reconstruction. The partnership mechanism, he recognized, now encompassed an expanded range of participants, compared to Renaissance I—"the private sector, universities, civic agencies, and nonprofit corporations." The state of Pennsylvania, as suggested before, had also become a significant participant. Unconstrained by political boundaries, private and nonprofit organizations and coalitions could, to a degree, overcome the fragmentation produced by 130 local jurisdictions in Allegheny County alone. Finally, Ahlbrandt acknowledged that grand visions and plans might not be necessary, after all, because the many initiatives embodied in the network of public, private, nonprofit agencies and partnerships amounted to "many of the elements of what would have gone into a comprehensive plan."[7]

One of the earliest and most important assessments of the region's future prospects came from the Allegheny Conference. It organized an Economic Development Committee in 1981 that established nine task forces to examine the issues deemed most vital to the region: advanced technology, manufacturing, services, corporate headquarters, international trade, infrastructure, human resources, business climate, and quality of life. Embedded in the dry, lifeless prose of its report, published in 1984, was a vision of a modernized twenty-first-century economy rooted in diversification. Raymond Christman, director of the Economic Development Committee, affirmed that diversification was a high priority. The committee's chairman, Konrad Weis, agreed that the overarching objective was to create a "business climate where diversity can flourish." "We must diversify," according to the *Pittsburgh Press.* "This time we must build new industries, new jobs, new outlooks, new styles of life, and clear away the atmosphere of decline and decay. This time we must reinvent Pittsburgh."[8] A decade later, Timothy Parks, president of the Pittsburgh High Technology Council, reflected, "We knew that development through diversity would be best for Pittsburgh's economy. If the steel experience taught us anything, it was to avoid the vulnerability that comes from dependence on a single industry."[9]

If diversification was the key to the redemption of Pittsburgh, then nurturing an already substantial service sector was vital. The objective was to translate existing market forces into a more self-conscious strategy of economic development—to push the region in a direction it was already heading toward.

> Pittsburgh is a regional center for health services, with 38 hospitals and over 85,000 employees. It is an educational center with three major universities and numerous colleges and related institutions. The region has become a leading regional financial center. And it has one of the highest concentrations of engineers, technicians, and scientists in the country.

Health, educational, and business support services had increased by 115,000 jobs between 1960 and 1983, representing a rise from 15 percent to 27 percent of the labor force. Most of the nonmanufacturing employment in southwestern Pennsylvania, 85 percent, was concentrated in the four-county Pittsburgh SMSA that included Allegheny, Beaver, Washington, and Westmoreland Counties.[10]

Another response to the economic upheaval was the appointment by the Allegheny County Commissioners of a Mon Valley Commission in May 1986 to devise a revitalization strategy. The study area encompassed 140 square miles, thirty-eight governments, forty-nine public authorities, and a population of more than 270,000. The main corridor, Route 837, presented a scene of "dilapidated mills, shopping districts and houses." The image and the reality coincided—the valley was "frequently seen as an undesirable place in which to shop, live, locate a business or invest." Like the Allegheny Conference, the Mon Valley Commission in its February 1987 report emphasized diversification as the key to modernization and revitalization. "Although the retention of some steelmaking plants— especially smaller steel or steel product makers—is a commission goal, the consensus is that diversification will be a key to future employment." The "consensus" included a recognition that an expanded service sector would be the engine of diversification. "Service," according to the commission, "is the key word, as the Greater Pittsburgh area's growth assets change from coal and steel to universities, research and development expertise, and its value as a center for corporate headquarters."[11]

As to the status of manufacturing, the Pittsburgh region in the decade after 1974 experienced a loss of 100,000 manufacturing jobs (two out of five). Of the 75,000 manufacturing jobs lost since 1980, 40,000 were in primary metals. By 1987, manufacturing accounted for only 14 percent of employment in the Pittsburgh metropolitan area, a drop from 25 percent in 1979.[12] Nonetheless, manufacturing would play a role in the regional strategy for modernization and diversification. But as defined by the ACCD, the "future orientation of Pittsburgh's manufacturing will likely be toward light manufacturing that relies on customized production and precision type processes."[13] The demise of the specialized, large-plant, heavy-industry economy made possible a new entrepreneurship based on smaller, more competitive, technologically sophisticated firms. To encourage this evolution, the Mon Valley Commission recommended the creation of a business technical assistance center, while the Allegheny Conference favored a small-business research and development program at the local universities. Already in existence was the Southwestern Pennsylvania Economic Development District (SPEDD), organized in 1965 as a nine-county agency eligible for funding from the federal Appalachian Regional Commission. Its small-business loan program was expanded in the 1980s to include the creation of small-business incubators.[14] But despite pro forma expressions of interest in manufacturing as part of a diversification strategy, it ranked low in the hierarchy of economic concerns in the early 1980s.[15]

The future of the Mon Valley would depend partly on the ultimate disposition of the steel plant sites. It would also depend on improved transportation facilities. The mill towns had been self-contained communities that relied upon rail and water transportation. A modern highway system had never been created, not to mention convenient access to the Pittsburgh airport. This circumstance not only inhibited the establishment of businesses requiring accessible air and highway connections; it also created burdens for those in the area seeking employment or educational opportunities. A Mon Valley Expressway, linking Pittsburgh with West Virginia, has long been considered vital to the economic prospects of the valley. Strongly supported by the Mon Valley Progress Council, a mid-Mon consortium of community leaders, it had been authorized by the state legislature in 1985 within the framework of a toll road expansion program. According to the chairman of the Washington County commissioners, the expressway was essential because " 'there are a lot of people along that 78-mile stretch that are hurting. The expressway is the only thing that will bring them out of the economic doldrums.' " Despite such claims, the idea has prospered slowly as a result of funding and routing difficulties, as well as doubts that it will provide a stimulus to economic growth.[16]

Pittsburgh's hegemony during the industrial era had been rooted in several competitive advantages: access to raw materials for steel production, superior river and rail transportation, proximity to markets, and the superior coking coal of the Connellsville region. But now the issue arose of defining Pittsburgh's competitive advantage in the post-steel era. Why should business firms remain in or move to the Pittsburgh area? Why should entrepreneurs, professionals, technicians, and others favor Pittsburgh over other communities? To compensate for the loss of the decisive competitive advantages of the steel era, it was necessary to exploit every circumstance that might increase the area's appeal as a place to do business, work, and live. Thus the modernization process involved a more self-conscious concern with quality of life issues than had Renaissance I.

The economic development strategy of the Allegheny Conference emphasized the need for amenities to strengthen Pittsburgh's competitive appeal. "A region's quality of life and basic livability are particularly important for service-based businesses of all kinds. Enhancing Pittsburgh's image in this regard can be particularly helpful to firms as they compete to retain or attract engineering and other technical talent."

Equally important, developing and promoting the cultural, recreational, and environmental advantages of the region were essential to overcoming one of the greatest obstacles to economic development—the longstanding negative image of Pittsburgh as a smoky inferno populated by philistines and drones. In fact, these negative perceptions were regarded by the Allegheny Conference as a serious obstacle to economic development. "Time and again, Pittsburgh's negative image was mentioned as a barrier to recruiting talent, attracting businesses, and giving the Pittsburgh market area the economic stature it deserves."[17]

Clearly, creating a new image was vital to the success of the modernization process, and this required the development of Pittsburgh as a postindustrial center of culture as well as medical, educational, and other quality of life assets. Indeed, culture and amenities were translated into a force promoting economic development. The performing and visual arts, recreation, and historic preservation nurtured tourism, provided jobs, increased the tax base, and "averted social costs" caused by the absence of "lively streets and vital neighborhoods." The Mon Valley Commission suggested that "recreation and leisure activities could become one of the Valley's major industries, given the natural beauty of the land and its proximity to the rivers."[18]

Since knowledge rather than locational factors increasingly governed modern economic life, enhancing the quality of life would brighten the prospects for establishing Pittsburgh as a mecca for advanced technology—a key element in the regional modernization strategy. The entrepreneurs, scientists, technicians, and university personnel needed to develop advanced technology would understandably favor communities that offered not just jobs but a superior way of life.

Advanced or high-technology firms were defined by the Allegheny Conference as those with "high levels of research and development expenditures, a large number of employees with scientific or technical backgrounds, or both." The implications of high technology for employment and economic development were far-reaching. The conference reported: "Advanced technology development can provide opportunities for the start up of new service-related as well as new manufacturing businesses. And it can have application and provide economic benefit to traditional manufacturing activity, not just to new ventures."[19] As in the services sector, market forces had created a significant advanced technology sector in the Pittsburgh area. What was necessary by the early 1980s, as the heavy-industry complex slid into history, was to consciously nurture high technology as part of a broader modernization strategy. Thus Pittsburgh already claimed two major research universities and more than 415 advanced technology companies employing nearly 34,000 in the early 1980s; these included 180 companies employing more than 25,000 in electronics production. All this constituted a critical mass that could spin off new companies and establish Pittsburgh as a national advanced technology center. It would be necessary for the financial, corporate, and university communities to provide the venture capital, technical assistance, and research to "support and encourage the entrepreneur," who represented the "foundation for the desired business creation and growth."[20]

Three older nonprofit organizations played a significant role in helping to define and implement the advanced technology–based modernization strategy. These included, besides the Allegheny Conference, the Regional Industrial Development Corporation (RIDC), and Penn's Southwest Association (both of which had been established by the Allegheny Conference). Penn's Southwest was created in 1972 to help market the region and attract new companies.[21] Its director, Jay Aldridge, took the initiative in 1981 in efforts to expand the advanced technology sector in the regional economy.[22] Besides consulting university faculty such as Angel Jordan, provost of CMU, he approached several high-technology entrepreneurs and executives. The consensus was to nurture the burgeoning high-technology enterprise already in Pittsburgh rather than attempt to import it.[23] Also prominent in efforts to link the advanced technology, academic, and business worlds were Roger Ahlbrandt and CMU's Raj Reddy and Dwight Sangrey.[24] As a result of these efforts in the early 1980s, a comprehensive infrastructure (both for-profit and nonprofit) was created in Pittsburgh to promote advanced technology entrepreneurship, research, funding, and technical assistance.[25]

One of the first of the new organizations designed to nurture advanced technology was the Pittsburgh High Technology Council, established in 1983.[26] Its mission was promotion, education, and advocacy. According to its first (and only) executive director, Timothy Parks, the council would help "build an identity for this new, emerging sector of the Western Pennsylvania Economy."[27] A second component in the support system was the Enterprise Corporation, a nonprofit also created in 1983. The "dream" of CMU faculty member Jack Thorne, the Enterprise Corporation provided a "practical textbook on building businesses in Pittsburgh." Supported initially with grants from the Richard King Mellon Foundation and Western Pennsylvania Advanced Technology Center, it provided early funding for small companies as well as management advice and workshops. Also providing management assistance was the CEO Network, sponsored by the Allegheny Conference, which matched executives in established firms with those in emerging advanced technology companies.[28]

The Allegheny Conference and Enterprise Corporation helped establish the Pittsburgh Seed Fund, and a CEO Venture Fund was initiated by the Pittsburgh High Technology Council. These venture capital funds were important components of the advanced technology infrastructure created in the 1980s. From a handful of firms at the beginning of the decade who were not necessarily investing in the Pittsburgh area, the number tripled by the end of the decade.[29]

A later (1991) addition to the advanced technology advocacy network was the Technology Development and Education Corporation. An independent, nonprofit spinoff of the Pittsburgh High Technology Council, it was created to help manufacturers remain competitive through technology, assist biomedical researchers with commercial application of their work, and unify the regional economic development network. A significant responsibility was oversight of the Southwestern Pennsylvania Industrial Resource Center (SPIRC), one of eight created in 1988 to provide small manufacturers with technical and managerial assistance. A state Department of Commerce program, the SPIRC dispatched engineers to give small manufacturers a state-subsidized operations review in the hopes of improving their efficiency and competitiveness.[30]

The corporation's president, Ray Christman, had been Pennsylvania's secretary of commerce from 1987 to 1991. Previously, he had served as director of economic development for the Allegheny Conference and as executive director of the Pittsburgh Urban Redevelopment Authority. Along with Jay Aldridge of Penn's Southwest, Christman's initiatives while secretary of commerce were instrumental in persuading the Sony Corporation to select the former Volkswagen plant in New Stanton, Westmoreland County, thirty-five miles east of Pittsburgh, as the site for

TV picture tube production. This announcement in April 1990 was succeeded by a Sony decision ten months later to devote another plant to the assembly of TV sets. The combined investment was projected at $370 million. Both state and local officials anticipated not only new production jobs, but also supplier opportunities for local small businesses and manufacturers.[31]

The Sony decision to establish a major production facility in Westmoreland County dramatized the increased importance of state government in regional economic development in Pittsburgh (and nationally). Although Sony manufactured TV tubes in San Diego, the company decided to establish a production facility closer to its largest markets. Christman and Aldridge first met Sony officials in the spring of 1989, when "Aldridge and his staff at Penn's Southwest did their usual outstanding job of marketing the area to Sony." After the site had been selected, the Department of Commerce participated in the crucial negotiations over the $38 million state assistance package, (which would include low-interest loans and grants for conversion of the former auto plant, infrastructure, and employee training). Sony held options on an additional 400 acres, and Westmoreland County planned to develop 200 more acres into industrial parks. According to Christman, "Our plan from the beginning, unlike with the Volkswagen project, has been to fully develop the land around this plant and make it one of the prime pieces of industrial property in the state."[32]

The president of Sony Engineering and Manufacturing of America reported, " 'We finally decided on Pittsburgh because of proximity and people—and maybe Ray Christman.' "[33] Governor Robert P. Casey had also been involved in the successful negotiations.[34] Apart from the potential for job creation and economic development, the Sony project was significant for what it revealed about the state's economic policy. In essence, it was a policy highly congruent with the advanced technology emphasis of the Pittsburgh region—the Sony TV tubes would be made by robots and automated machinery. State officials expected that the Sony plants would draw electronic and advanced technology manufacturing to Western Pennsylvania. According to Timothy Parks of the Pittsburgh High Technology Council, Sony was " 'really a benchmark in the development of the Pittsburgh high-tech community.' " Christman declared that the Sony project "seemed to symbolize our transformation to

a new economy based on high technology and advanced manufacturing";
it revealed the "growing nexus between manufacturing and high technology in the region."[35]

Also exemplifying a modernization strategy that linked manufacturing and advanced technology and that incorporated state government
into the regional partnership network was the creation of a coalition to
establish a maglev (magnetic levitation) industry in Western Pennsylvania. Consisting of regional companies, universities, labor representatives,
and government officials, the maglev coalition was strongly supported
by the administration of Governor Robert Casey. Casey recommended
a $2 million state grant to enable the coalition to compete for a $725
million federal contract for a prototype project extending nineteen miles
from downtown to Greater Pittsburgh International Airport. " 'What
we're looking at here,' " Casey proposed, " 'is a substantial state investment in a new technology that can mean tens of thousands of good
paying jobs in southwestern Pennsylvania.' "[36] As of 1994, however, the
maglev proposal consisted of little more than aspirations, studies, and
reports.

A major state contribution to reclamation of the moribund Mon
Valley was the funding of several mill site redevelopment projects sponsored by the Regional Industrial Development Corporation (RIDC).
Also involved in advanced technology projects in the city of Pittsburgh,
the RIDC emerged as one of the key nonprofit instruments of the economic revitalization strategy in the 1980s. According to Frank Brooks
Robinson, its president since 1981, the agency's mission was to stimulate
economic growth and create jobs; more specifically, it was to redirect the
economy from smokestack to high tech and "to strengthen and diversify
the regional economy." Manufacturing would be part of a diversified
economy. Robinson disagreed with those who argued that the region
should ignore manufacturing in favor of high tech; to the contrary, high
tech could induce "certain kinds of manufacturing" to migrate to Pittsburgh.[37]

Following a charter revision in 1962 permitting the RIDC to function as a development agency, it established three suburban industrial
parks. The first was the O'Hara Industrial Park, 600 acres, begun in
1964 on the site of the old county workhouse. This was followed by
Thorn Hill Industrial Park, begun in 1971; straddling Marshall in Al-

legheny County and Cranberry in Butler County, it totaled 925 acres. Park West, 580 acres, begun in 1979, was located in Findlay and North Fayette Townships near the Pittsburgh International Airport. The three parks, by early 1991, housed more than 200 companies and 15,000 employees.[38]

A state legislative committee held hearings in the fall of 1991 on the operations of the RIDC. Its chairman, state representative Tom Murphy of Pittsburgh's North Side—now Pittsburgh's mayor—complained that the RIDC was using public funds to develop suburban industrial parks that were drawing businesses from distressed areas in Pittsburgh and the Mon Valley, or from one part of Allegheny County to another. The relocation of three Pittsburgh companies in the fall of 1990 to RIDC Park West near the airport (and the decision of Conrail to establish a service center there) epitomized the problem. Murphy claimed, in essence, that the RIDC was not implementing the goal of the Pennsylvania Industrial Development Authority Act "to help businesses relocate and create jobs in distressed areas."[39] In addition, it sold land at below market value, competing unfairly with private enterprise in suburban areas where the free market was working satisfactorily. Private developers echoed this complaint, adding that they were not even permitted to operate in the industrial parks.

In response to these charges, Robinson argued that the RIDC's industrial parks had generated development in the northern and western suburbs of Allegheny County. At Park West near the airport, for example, few developers were anxious to operate there before the RIDC arrived because of the topography, lack of utilities, and infrastructure. O'Hara had been created at the request of a county commissioner who desired to see the old county workhouse transformed into a site for light industry and research. In essence, RIDC had been a "risk-taker investing in the development of properties long before private development interests paid any attention." It was only after these projects became successful, Robinson charged, that "private developers object[ed] about the unfair advantages enjoyed by RIDC." Murphy had also complained that the RIDC Park West was located in Allegheny County's most booming real estate market—the airport corridor west of Pittsburgh. Yet firms paid one-third the market rate for their land, $80,000 rather than $240,000 an acre.

Robinson, however, objected to speculative development in RIDC projects; increased land prices, resulting from private speculative involvement, would presumably conflict with the RIDC's mission to help firms grow.[40] Robinson also contested Murphy's charge that the RIDC parks drew businesses from "distressed areas, putting them in places that by any measure are very healthy indeed." Robinson explained that companies could not be forced to locate where they did not want to go, and that the RIDC did not "try to convince companies to relocate from one county or region in our service area to another."[41] Furthermore, corporations (especially foreign ones) were highly conscious of their surroundings. This made spacious industrial parks appealing and increased the difficulty of encouraging firms to remain or relocate in urban centers lacking large enough tracts for contemporary commercial or industrial development.[42]

Clarke Thomas, formerly local affairs editor for the *Pittsburgh Post-Gazette*, wrote in 1991: " 'Jobs!' That's the answer you'll get from government officials up and down the line when you ask them to name the greatest pressure on them nowadays."[43] Thomas adds that this meant economic development—new businesses or government projects—and not old-fashioned patronage or make-work. Perhaps the pressure to create jobs explains the motivation of critics of the RIDC in the state legislature.[44] As job advocates, they criticized the RIDC's alleged lack of involvement in the city of Pittsburgh and Mon Valley.[45]

Yet RIDC operated three University Technology Development Centers in the Oakland section of Pittsburgh, managed the Software Engineering Institute, and participated in the development of the URA's Pittsburgh Technology Center. In addition, it had taken charge of three projects in the Mon Valley and East Pittsburgh–Turtle Creek area that would help shape the future of that region. These projects, the creation of industrial parks on former mill sites, were financed in part by the state of Pennsylvania, which operated several grant and loan programs for industrial site redevelopment.[46] The goal, besides the creation of jobs, was economic stimulation and diversification in the mill towns—the projected industrial parks would accommodate a variety of small businesses and manufacturing.

Allegheny County had acquired from USX in 1988 the 135-acre National Tube Works in McKeesport and the 240-acre Duquesne Works.

Both mills were transferred in 1990 to the RIDC, which had also purchased the 92-acre Westinghouse Plant in East Pittsburgh at the end of 1988. The three sites were rechristened the Industrial Center of McKeesport, City Center of Duquesne, and Keystone Commons, respectively.[47] Robinson believed that Keystone Commons exemplified the diversification upon which the future of the Mon Valley depended: "traditional types of industry—machine shops, pipe and generator facilities—would be followed by offices, high-tech companies, and research and development laboratories."[48]

But the demolition and redevelopment of defunct steel plants presented unique problems—a learning experience even for an experienced builder of industrial parks like the RIDC. Robinson reflected, " 'We weren't naive when we got into this, but I must say the scope and cost has been a real eye-opener in dealing with everything from old buildings and transformers to asbestos and what I call 'rainbow water.' "[49] Former industrial sites throughout the Pittsburgh region often posed formidable pollution cleanup problems and expenses. At Duquesne and McKeesport, according to Joseph Hohman, former Allegheny County director of development, cleanup costs could run as high as $14 million (of which 70 percent was asbestos-related). Piecemeal demolition and sale of scrap or equipment would help pay for the toxic substance removal, but liability insurance costs ran as high as $500,000 annually. The combination of toxic substance problems, ongoing demolition, and inadequate infrastructure obstructed the recruitment of tenants. Keystone Commons, which required less demolition and toxic clean-up, progressed faster.[50]

Widespread complaints had emerged by the mid-1990s about the failure of the state legislature and Department of Environmental Resources to reduce the burdens and uncertainties of brownfield reclamation arising from toxic waste liability. The situation encouraged greenfield development with its destruction of open space and agricultural land: "Potential investors cannot and will not pay for unreasonable cleanup when other, less costly alternatives are available."[51]

A private developer, the Park Corporation, had purchased the 310-acre Homestead Works in 1988 along with the 130-acre Carrie Furnace complex across the Monongahela River in Rankin. This property was also scheduled to become, after formidable challenges of demolition, grading, hazardous substance removal, road and utility installation, another industrial park; there was, however, virtually no development on the site by the end of 1994.[52]

Both Hohman and Robinson cautioned that it might be a long time before the market could absorb the space in these industrial parks. A broader issue was whether the industrial parks, along with business incubators and community development corporations, would revive the former mill towns. The overwhelming emphasis upon jobs (and the remaining legacy of the era of coke and steel in Braddock, West Mifflin, and Clairton) has discouraged alternative visions of community development. A minister and member of the board of the Tri-State Conference on Steel asserted that job creation came before "community beautification." There was, in fact, a moral issue involved in "remaking the Mon Valley towns into bedroom communities. Condos on the riverbanks, marinas, museums, etc., are ideas that target people who do not currently live in the valley. They do not address the needs of the people devastated by the job holocaust."[53]

As late as 1988, many in the Mon Valley refused to abandon the conviction that steel production would return. Proposals made by an American Institute of Architects design team at an international conference in Pittsburgh, March 1988, aroused considerable resentment because the designers assumed that there was no prospect for revitalization of the steel industry. They presented a vision of steel mill property in Homestead converted into a glass-enclosed international garden festival (with restaurants and theater) as well as a factory outlet–flea market and auto racetrack in McKeesport. Bob Anderson, a spokesman for the Rainbow Kitchen in Homestead, responded that it was " 'sad for America that this is the idea—to build flower festivals for the unemployed.' " There seemed to be no common ground between those who viewed the issue as jobs immediately, preferably industrial ones, and those who believed that the mill towns had to abandon that industrial heritage and pursue a fresh vision. The chairman of the design team was apparently surprised by the stubborn refusal of Mon Valley residents to admit that steel production was finished in the idled plants: "There is so much handwringing and concern that the team doesn't understand the economic hardships of the mills closing—but the team does understand

USS Works, Homestead, late 1980s. *Photo: Author*

that. The question is, where do we go from here?" Dreams of a resurrection of heavy industry persisted into the 1990s, when you would "hear people who still bristle at the memory of the talk of major floral gardens and similar projects . . . espoused by architects and planners."[54] The issue was much clearer in Pittsburgh—the creation of a postindustrial universe.

3

University, City, and Strategy 21

Allegheny County released a document in the fall of 1991 entitled *Our Future, 2001, Our Choice.* It was a report to county residents based on extensive citizen participation. In the realm of economic development, the authors of the report anticipated that "our universities can help to create new businesses by spinning off academic research into concepts and products that will succeed in the marketplace."[1] Their economic role by the 1980s, however, extended beyond academic, scientific, or biomedical research, and the nurture of advanced technology. The University of Pittsburgh emerged as the largest employer in the city of Pittsburgh by the 1990s. University-based educational and medical services dramatically expanded the service sector and helped maintain both the employment and tax base of Pittsburgh (although the substantial concentration of nonprofit educational and cultural institutions in the city also reduced the tax base). Not least, the universities engaged in major capital development projects in the 1980s and 1990s. These also provided employment and helped Pittsburgh survive the loss of its manufacturing base.[2]

In the fall of 1992, the University of Pittsburgh began planning a massive building and facility upgrading program. This was part of a $2 billion Pennsylvania initiative—Operation Jump Start—launched in 1991 to stimulate the state economy. It allocated nearly $470 million to institutions of higher education. The University of Pittsburgh's share,

$69.1 million, was supplemented by $70.6 million in university funds.[3] Unrelated to this, the University Medical Center began construction of a $35 million research center atop the Presbyterian Hospital parking garage, and a $55 million office tower.[4]

Pittsburgh is not unique in witnessing the emergence of the research university as an economic catalyst. In the South, according to the *New York Times*, the University of Alabama at Birmingham, had become the "state's hotbed of ideas and progress," its largest employer, and manager of its major hospital. The University of North Carolina at Charlotte created the new town of University City, "which has attracted numerous corporations and improved the region's economy."[5] But the evolution of research universities into economic development agencies is part of a broader phenomenon in Pittsburgh and elsewhere—the emergence of the nonprofit sector as an economic revitalization instrument, providing continuity, employment, and growth in the midst of national and international economic reconstruction. The diversified service base created by the nonprofit sector provides a buffer against the disruptions produced by corporate mergers, takeovers, bankruptcies, or reduced civic involvement.

In providing educational, medical, social welfare, or cultural services, the nonprofit organization has become a kind of expansive entrepreneur involved in capital development as well as a broadening range of services. The rise of nonprofit entrepreneurship and community leadership is rooted in the demand for such services in contemporary life combined with government funding in the name of economic development. The contrast between the city of Pittsburgh and the regional mill towns in the post-steel era dramatizes the vital role of the nonprofit sector in community revitalization. The loss of the steel industry in the Mon Valley and elsewhere in the region had been so devastating because these communities lacked the many educational, medical, social service, and cultural nonprofit groups that eased the transition for Pittsburgh. This greatly magnified role of development-oriented nonprofits differentiates Renaissance I and II. According to Alberta Sbragia, a University of Pittsburgh political scientist, city officials have "moved beyond an exclusive focus on supporting and bargaining with the private sector. . . . Pittsburgh has already recognized that certain nonprofit organizations are economic engines, and thus should receive public-sector attention."[6]

The expanded role of the state of Pennsylvania in economic development also distinguished Renaissance I from Renaissance II and the post-steel era. Two state programs, in particular, helped propel the research universities—the University of Pittsburgh and Carnegie-Mellon University—into the era of advanced technology research and economic growth. The first of these programs was established during the administration of Governor Richard Thornburgh. Elected in 1978, Thornburgh appointed a Commission on Choices for Pennsylvanians in 1979 that recommended that the state devise policies to promote the service and advanced technology component of the economy.[7] This led to the Ben Franklin Partnership, established in 1982. It linked institutions of higher education to the private sector through the creation of four advanced technology centers in 1983. These included the Western Pennsylvania Advanced Technology Center (later renamed the Ben Franklin Technology Center of Western Pennsylvania), sponsored and managed by the University of Pittsburgh and Carnegie Mellon.

The center acted as a conduit to link academic research with business. Most of its funding was awarded to research and development projects undertaken by universities and companies, supplemented by entrepreneurship support and training programs. Another program, Manufacturing 2000, was administered by the Ben Franklin Technology Center and provided grants to manufacturers for improving production processes rather than developing new products.[8] Statewide, the Ben Franklin Partnership distributed $25 million in 1991, of which nearly $6 million was allocated to the Western Pennsylvania center; total state funding from 1983 to 1990 was $181 million. Matching private sector funds totaled nearly $460 million, and educational institutions contributed $114 million.

The programs funded in Western Pennsylvania in the early 1990s illustrate the kind of advanced technology research and development favored by the Ben Franklin Partnership: new computer applications, biotechnology, advanced materials, robotic and intelligence systems, environmental technologies.[9] The Western Pennsylvania technology center claimed to have created 3,711 jobs in its first decade and to have played a role in launching 208 new companies and developing 89 new products or processes.[10]

Advanced technology research in the Pittsburgh region was also supported by the federal government (much of it related to defense objectives). The spectacular expansion of the University of Pittsburgh's health and medical center was financed by federal dollars as well. In effect, the state and federal governments, and the regional civic coalition, entered into a partnership with the research universities. The latter provided each level of government with research considered vital for defense, medical progress, or economic development, while the universities expanded and magnified their role in the community. They piped state and federal funds into the Pittsburgh region, provided employment, nurtured the advanced technology economy, sponsored construction projects, established Pittsburgh as an international center of medical research and treatment (University of Pittsburgh) and computer science and robotics (Carnegie-Mellon). It is necessary to examine this broader context of university and community before turning to Strategy 21, the second of the Pennsylvania programs that linked the research universities with advanced technology and economic development.

When Richard Cyert became president of Carnegie Mellon University in 1972, the university received $13 million in research funds. By 1990, the total had climbed to $123 million (including $89 million in federal funding of which $50. 7 came from the Department of Defense). Highly regarded by business leaders, Cyert also won corporate support for university programs.[11] During the Cyert administration, CMU (along with Pitt) would exemplify the emergence of the entrepreneurial nonprofit entity in the realm of higher education. Responding to a perceived market for advanced technology and applied research, both universities aggressively pursued contract research opportunities from public and private sources. Their explosive entrepreneurship and its economic implications for Pittsburgh, as suggested earlier, helped the city make the transition from a manufacturing to a diversified service economy.

CMU's leap to international prominence in advanced technology research was foreshadowed by merger with the Mellon Institute. Located in the Oakland district between the two universities, housed in a neoclassical structure dominated by rows of colossal Ionic columns, Mellon Institute was established in 1910 as an industrial research department at the University of Pittsburgh; it became a privately endowed, independent institution in 1913. Specializing in applied chemistry, physics, and biology, the institute was experiencing financial difficulties by the 1960s and merged with Carnegie Mellon in 1967. As CMU directed its research emphasis to advanced technology, the institute shifted its focus to such fields as process engineering, advanced materials, and computerized rail systems.[12]

Corporate funding enabled CMU to establish a Robotics Institute in 1978, a key component in its advanced technology empire (along with its Computer Science Department). Besides artificial intelligence research, the institute studied the potentialities of robots to assist the handicapped and contribute to toxic cleanup and space exploration. A Magnetics Technology Center followed in 1982.[13] A major coup took place in 1984 when the Department of Defense awarded the university, through competitive bidding, a five-year, $103 million contract to establish a Software Engineering Institute (SEI). Its purpose was to develop computer software applicable to weapons development. The SEI had a powerful impact in several respects: it dramatized and reinforced the aspiration of many to transform Pittsburgh into a center of advanced technology research in the post-steel era; it helped define the role of the research universities in the process; and it suggested the possibility of creating a new image for the Pittsburgh region.

Governor Thornburgh acclaimed the SEI as " 'an important breakthrough for the region, changing its image away from the smokestacks. . . . I think it has the potential to be historic.' " Similarly, James Colker, president of the Pittsburgh High Technology Council, believed it would force outsiders to discard any vision of Pittsburgh as a declining smokestack town.[14] This revolt against the smokestack image, spearheaded by the research universities, was reinforced in January 1990 when CMU announced its selection as the site for the Eleventh Sematech Center of Excellence. Created in 1987, Sematech was a consortium of semiconductor manufacturers who began funding the research centers in 1989 in the hopes of developing and marketing a superior semiconductor design.[15]

The status of CMU (and of Pittsburgh) as an international center of robotics research and technology was enhanced in the spring of 1994 when CMU and NASA announced the creation of the NASA Robotics Engineering Consortium. Its objective was the application of robotic space technology to the more mundane requirements of agriculture, transportation, construction, or underseas exploration. Linking advanced technology research and entrepreneurship to neighborhood development, the Urban Redevelopment Authority of Pittsburgh (URA) acquired a six-acre site in Lawrenceville (at Forty-first Street along the Allegheny River) to serve as national headquarters for the NASA Robotics Engineering Consortium.[16]

The collaboration between CMU and Pitt in several advanced technology projects in the mid-1980s contributed to the image of a revitalized Pittsburgh where the research universities symbolized the new strategy for economic development. These partnerships included joint management of the Ben Franklin Technology Center and the Enterprise Corporation; the successful bid (with Westinghouse) for National Science Foundation funding for creation of a Supercomputing Center in 1986; participation in Strategy 21 and its funding of the Pittsburgh Technology Center; and a Biotechnology Clinical and Research Center created in 1983 (comprising the Nuclear Magnetic Resonance Research and Development Institute, and Pittsburgh Cancer Center).[17]

The *Pittsburgh Press* reported in 1990, "The mills have rusted . . . and Pitt has become an economic linchpin of the region." When Wesley Posvar became chancellor in 1967, the university's budget was $90 million and total employment stood at 5,000; by 1990, the budget had reached $630 million ($1.1 billion, including the medical and health center), and it employed 12,000 persons (9,000 in Pittsburgh). Like Cyert, Posvar represented a new breed of university administrator—one who viewed higher education as a form of entrepreneurship, a provider of services to government, business, and the local community. Indeed, Posvar explicitly envisioned a partnership between the university and the business world; such an alliance would be " 'the key to improving American economic competitiveness, social inequities, and unstable foreign relations.' "[18]

The University of Pittsburgh, in conformity with this vision, vastly expanded its applied research activities in the almost quarter-century Posvar administration. These included the advanced technology partnerships with CMU—Ben Franklin, Pittsburgh Technology Center, Supercomputer. But the most dramatic example of the conception of the university as a center of applied research and partner to business was the creation of the University of Pittsburgh Applied Research Center (U-Parc). U-Parc originated in Chevron's acquisition in 1985 of Gulf Oil, whose headquarters had long been in Pittsburgh (but closed down after the takeover). Posvar persuaded Chevron to donate to Pitt the Gulf research center located in Harmar Township ten miles to the northeast. Chevron agreed—the transfer took place in March 1986—and added $3 million to the gift. Consisting of fifty-four buildings on eighty-five acres, U-Parc accommodated 130 companies and 1,200 workers by the early 1990s. A university advertisement offered tenants "offices, wet and dry labs, instrumentation and computer systems, conference and training facilities and a 100-seat auditorium," not to mention proximity to major universities and a "secluded setting near shopping centers, restaurants, and hotels."[19]

In the fall of 1991, Posvar's successor, J. Dennis O'Connor, announced a significant new initiative in applied research and advanced technology. The U.S. Air Force had awarded the university a $5 million, two-year grant to create a center for developing advanced materials. The research would encompass high performance materials (alloys, polymers, protective coatings); electro-optical systems (eye protection against lasers, computer switching devices); catalysts (alternative fuels, hazardous waste detoxification); biotechnology (memory-enhancing drugs to treat Alzheimer's disease, sensors to monitor therapy). O'Connor described the new center as a " 'powerful resource for industry,' " and its codirector, engineering professor Fred Pettit, anticipated that the center would work closely with companies (especially smaller firms) to market new materials and processes.

A second center was established at Pitt in the fall of 1991. The National Aeronautics and Space Administration awarded the university a $5 million, five-year grant for a regional center to serve as mid-Atlantic headquarters for NASA's Regional Technology Transfer Center network. Its purpose was to transfer NASA technology into the private sector.[20]

More comprehensible, and closer to the life of the average citizen of Pittsburgh, was the university's medical and health center. In common with other U.S. cities—for example, Waterbury, Connecticut—medical offices, facilities, and hospitals have replaced factories in Pittsburgh; like higher education, provision of health care has spurred the economic rejuvenation of communities. The largest private employers in Waterbury, following the demise of its brass industry, were two hospitals. In 1991, some 10,000 workers in Danbury, 12.6 percent of the labor force, made their living in the health field.[21]

In Pittsburgh, by 1991, health services claimed 11 percent of the work force, and were "critical in transforming Pittsburgh's economy from steel to services. . . ."[22] Like higher education, hospitals and medical services not only provided a source of employment, but helped sustain a wide range of other services and suppliers. Although the expansion needs of hospitals have created conflicts with neighborhood residents, they have become indispensable economic anchors as employers and development engines. An example is Pittsburgh's North Side, where Allegheny General Hospital employs 5,000 persons (20 percent of whom are residents of the district). The hospital also works with community groups to advise on expansion plans, and it offers employment, educational, mortgage, and health programs.[23]

The $300 million Partnership for Medical Renaissance, launched in 1987, exemplified the link between higher education, health care, and Pittsburgh's economic development. This partnership included Presbyterian University Hospital, Eye and Ear Hospital, and the Medical and Health Care Division of the university—later renamed the University of Pittsburgh Medical Center. The center included Presbyterian University Hospital, Montefiore University Hospital, the Pittsburgh Cancer Institute, Western Psychiatric Institute, Pitt's health science schools, and a number of other services. It should be noted, also, that Presbyterian University and nearby Children's Hospital are the renowned organ transplant institutions within the Oakland medical complex.

The combination of expanded facilities, new construction, and property purchases had, by 1992, more than doubled the size of the university medical center—from 1.5 million to 3.7 million square feet—and affected every aspect of medical care: educational, clinical, and research activities. Major new construction projects included a Biomedical Science Tower for basic and clinical research; a D wing for radiation oncology and cardiology; a "2-3 Infill Building" to house the Magnetic Resonance Imaging Center, a digestive disorders center, and a new cardiothoracic intensive care unit; and a medical research facility supplementing the Biomedical Science Tower.[24]

A second nucleus of Pitt's health-related applied research is the Center for Biotechnology and Bioengineering, established in 1987. Its director, Jerome Schultz, is dedicated to bridging the gap between laboratory and product development (technology transfer) and establishing ties with

" 'larger firms interested in the kind of research our faculty do.' " This implied encouragement of faculty entrepreneurship.

> Each would-be entrepreneur must find funding to develop a prototype for consideration by venture capitalists. To secure this, funding, Schultz is working with the Ben Franklin Partnership and Pittsburgh Biomedical Development Corp. , which provide bridge funding between a University research project . . . and a development project.[25]

Besides exemplifying Pitt's resolve that the university "should be a leader in economic growth and development," the center hopes to serve as a model of interdisciplinary research and education, bringing together scientists, engineers, and clinicians.[26]

Shrinking government and corporate funding has encouraged university-sponsored efforts at technology transfer and commercialization. The results have been mixed, at best. Besides lack of experience, there are conflict of interest problems—is the university a center of scientific research or scientific entrepreneurship? More broadly, how far can institutions dedicated to education and research pursue economic development objectives? How much capital can universities afford to risk?[27] Pitt's and CMU's experience in marketing the Pittsburgh Technology Center (to be discussed) suggests that the institutions were not overendowed with commercial knowhow.[28]

The Strategy 21 program of 1985 helped to finance the Biotechnology Center's facility on the site of the former Jones & Laughlin (LTV) steel plant between Second Avenue and the Monongahela River, not far from downtown Pittsburgh. Strategy 21 originated in the efforts of state representative Tom Murphy (D–North Side) to persuade Pittsburgh and Allegheny County officials in late 1984 and early 1985 to coordinate public and private requests for capital funding. Strengthening his case was the introduction of a bill in January 1985 providing up to $200 million for a Philadelphia Convention Center. Murphy suggested to Tom Foerster, chairman of the Allegheny County commissioners, that he devise a way to set priorities. In February, Foerster requested Robert Pease, executive director of the Allegheny Conference, to serve as convener and coordinator of a committee to prepare a comprehensive capital funding request.[29] This led to a coalition that included representatives of the city and county governments, the corporate sector, the Pennsylvania Economy League, Pitt, and CMU. An initial meeting in March resulted in funding requests totaling an exorbitant $650 million; Murphy suggested it would be expedient to limit the total to the $200 million requested for the Philadelphia Convention Center project. The final report was released in June.[30]

The public-private partnership that devised Strategy 21 reflected an "incremental, bargaining, coalition-building, short-run, information-limited, opportunity-based method of regional policy"; it expressed the preferences of the corporate and university sector in contrast to "those who would be outside of a technology-driven economy."[31] But however opportunistic or noninclusive, Strategy 21 was significant in revealing a fairly coherent strategy of economic development driven by the imperative of diversification. According to its 1985 proposal document,

> The economy of 21st century Pittsburgh must be positioned to take maximum advantage of emerging economic trends toward advanced technology and international marketing and communications systems. A diversified economic base must be created that includes light as well as heavy manufacturing, that capitalizes on the region's natural resources, and that promotes a new mix of large and small businesses marked by a renewed spirit of entrepreneurship and university-linked research and development.[32]

Among the most important of the funding requests, reflecting the global orientation of the post-steel regional economic strategy, was the creation of a new airport, and an accompanying seven-mile Southern Expressway linking the Parkway West to the Beaver Valley Expressway and the new terminal. These projects, according to the Pittsburgh-Allegheny Partnership which devised Strategy 21, would not only improve the region's appeal as a corporate headquarters and enhance its international competitiveness; they would also stimulate development in the adjoining western suburbs—Findlay, Moon, and Robinson Townships. Groundbreaking for the new Midfield Terminal at the Pittsburgh International Airport took place in July 1987, and the terminal opened in October 1992, along with the Southern Expressway.

Occupying 12,000 acres, the $700 million terminal and airport, the first to be constructed in a major city since Dallas–Fort Worth in the mid-1970s, is closely tied to the fortunes of USAir.[33] Using Pittsburgh as a hub, USAir occupies fifty of the seventy-five gates and pays many of the bills. The new terminal was to be both a symbol and generator of a Pittsburgh region "balanced on high-technology industries, corporate offices and service industries"; it was "to mean as much to further development and diversification as it does to area aviation." The determination to launch a "first-class" international airport testified to local leaders' commitment to "building a new diversified economy and reaching for global markets." It was Pittsburgh's "key to competing in the world economy of the twenty-first century."[34]

The predicted economic impact of the new terminal included $9.5 billion in expenditures in the 1990s, the creation of 17,600 new jobs in Allegheny County, and as many as 40,000–50,000 in a six-county region over the same period.[35] But the crystal ball was cloudy. The environs of the airport had experienced some residential and commercial investment by 1992, despite the recession of the early nineties. Projects included "Whispering Woods," a $35 million project encompassing 229 one-family homes; "Woodfield," $8 million, 35 one-family homes; "Cherrington Corporate Center," $45 million, six office buildings, two hotels, conference facilities, and golf course. In addition, British Airways had invested more than $13 million in terminal retail facilities.[36]

A staff member of the University of Pittsburgh Center for Social and Urban Research contended, " 'If we are smart in how we promote this facility, it will become this region's key infrastructure for the long term. Just look down the Parkway West today at all the corporation headquarters near the airport.' "[37] Yet the airport's economic stimulus had not lived up to expectations by the mid-1990s.

> What emerges beyond the vision of a modern airport with vast economic potential is a region which government officials battle over political turf, the economy is threatened by the instability of a major employer [USAir], taxes are inordinately high and some existing buildings and land are haunted by environmental neglect.[38]

Although Midfield Terminal and other proposals included in Strategy 21 reflected a fairly coherent development strategy, the political, corporate, university, and technocratic partnership that formulated Strategy 21 had difficulty defining a vision for the Mon Valley. Indeed, its most decisive assessment was negative: "Dependence on a single economic base—the metals industry—has jeopardized the economic survival of this region." The less than electrifying recommendations included a Metals Retention/Reuse Study and small-scale projects, mostly infrastructure improvements, for various communities from Homestead to Glassport and Pitcairn (located to the east somewhat distant from the Monongahela River).[39]

The potential long-term impact of the new airport upon the economy and demography of the city of Pittsburgh was not clear. According to a CMU analysis, the competitive advantages of the Midfield Terminal area (amenities, infrastructure, flexible use of varied topography, ample parking) threatened the "city's ability to compete for jobs, business, and investment." Jack Wagner, former president of the Pittsburgh City Council, agreed that the airport would become the economic growth center of the region. However, both the city and the Mon Valley lacked good road connections to the airport: "Without immediate improvements, we will lose businesses, residents, conventions, visitors, jobs for our residents and all of the economic returns associated with the new airport."[40]

The Strategy 21 projects that directly benefited Pittsburgh might, on the other hand, serve as a countervailing force—attracting investment, visitors, and population. These were large-scale operations including the Pittsburgh Technology Center and a group of Allegheny River projects: the Carnegie Science Center, enhancements of the North Shore, Herr's Island (Washington's Landing), and the Strip District. Taken together, they exemplified an economic development strategy designed to liberate Pittsburgh from any lingering blue-collar, heavy industry image. Twenty-first-century Pittsburgh would be economically diversified, strong in advanced technology and professional services, and, not least, would be a community where quality of life considerations were incorporated into development policy.

The Pittsburgh Technology Center, conceived before Strategy 21, was wrapped into the 1985 package of capital funding proposals for the state legislature.[41] Its evolution makes clear the continued prominence of the Urban Redevelopment Authority in shaping the Pittsburgh environment as well as the emergence of a broadened civic coalition in the post-steel era. The URA had purchased the forty-nine-acre site for the center from the Park Corporation in 1983 for $3.5 million. In cooperation with the RIDC, development coordinator, the URA prepared a plan for a research park, cleared the site, and enlisted the participation of the two universities, described by the *Pittsburgh Press* as "new power brokers" in regional economic development (along with neighborhood organizations, high-tech entrepreneurs, and multinational corporations).[42] The state of Penn-

Washington's Landing, Herr's Island, a major URA project. *Photo: Pittsburgh Urban Redevelopment Authority*

sylvania belonged in the list of power brokers; it had, by 1988, contributed to the Technology Center $16.7 million for development, $14 million for the University of Pittsburgh building, and $17 million for CMU.

The URA viewed the project as nothing less than the embodiment of "Pittsburgh's evolution from a town founded on heavy industry to a city on the cutting edge of innovative research and technology." It would "secure Pittsburgh's place as a leader in the technology sector while symbolizing the dynamic transformation of the City's economy." This new economy would be diversified and "strongly tied to research, new product development and advanced technology."[43] CMU President Richard Cyert anticipated the creation of a "beautiful place that becomes a statement of the new Pittsburgh." He wished the city to be "recognized as the software capital of the world." Similarly, Pitt's President Wesley Posvar described the Technology Center as a harbinger of Pittsburgh's status as "biotech valley," "an incubator for an exciting new industry that will . . . infuse new economic vitality into the area." And the center exemplified the conviction of Governor Robert Casey that "new technology has got to be the leader in establishing economic development in this state."[44] Accompanying these visions were optimistic predictions of the job and tax benefits that the center would provide. According to Mayor Caliguiri, it was the "most important economic development project undertaken in Pittsburgh in the past forty years."[45]

Whatever the aspirations, several circumstances combined to slow the pace of development and, for a time, the Pittsburgh Technology Center was something of an embarrassment to the URA. Apart from a sign announcing the project and the URA's site preparation, the land was barren until early 1991. At best, it could not have progressed speedily because of the large number of participants—URA, local and state governments, two universities. The recession of the early 1990s resulted in additional delays and the scaling down of the universities' plans for private-sector funding and tenants.[46] Private-sector participation was also thwarted when toxic waste testing uncovered cyanide on the site, arousing the concern of the state Department of Environmental Resources (DER). Located ten to fifteen feet underground, below the concrete slabs upon which the J&L plant had been built, the cyanide was not the legacy of steel production, but of an earlier Pittsburgh Gas Works, a coal gasification company. Addressing this problem dominated URA efforts in 1989 and led to a relocation of the projected CMU structure. Following DER toxic clearance in the summer of 1990, Pitt began construction of its Center for Biotechnology and Bioengineering in early 1991, which opened early in 1993. Between this structure and the CMU research facility are 1,000 feet of unmarketable land polluted by cyanide.[47]

The Technology Center acquired its first private tenant when Union Switch & Signal announced plans in March 1993 to build a research and engineering center. A manufacturer of computerized control equipment for rail transit, the company proposed to erect a 170,000-square-foot facility and provide 450 jobs initially, with the number rising to 700. A strong inducement for Union Switch & Signal's decision to choose the site was access to the research expertise of the two universities. Another was the availability of low-interest state loans, the URA's construction of a 649-space parking facility, and its transfer of four acres to the RIDC, which would construct the building.[48]

The URA's landscaping plans for the Technology Center reflected the quality of life concerns that formed part of the economic development strategy (including riverfront reclamation). "The project's master plan calls for the creation of a campus-like setting combining a riverwalk, tree-covered walkways, and a greensward consisting of a variety of grasses and wildflowers."[49] The same concept—aesthetic improvements in combination with commercial development—influenced the renewal plans for Washington's Landing (formerly Herr's Island) on the Allegheny River. A two-mile long island about two miles upriver from the Golden Triangle, it had once accommodated various industries, including meat processing and crunching animal remains for bone meal. By the 1960s it had deteriorated into a blighted wasteland. As with the Pittsburgh Technology Center, a redevelopment plan conceived in the 1970s was recycled into a Strategy 21 proposal.

The plan recommended transforming the island into a commercial, residential, and recreational magnet with corporate conference facilities, light manufacturing "aimed at attracting advanced technology activities," waterfront housing, retail shops, a marina, and a public park. The URA envisioned Washington's Landing as Pittsburgh's "waterfront jewel."[50] Groundbreaking for the first structure, an office building, took place in the fall of 1987. Further development was thwarted the next year when toxic wastes were discovered in one section. Encapsulation began in 1989, resulting in the discovery of additional contamination and the need for still more remediation. Here was a "cautionary tale" for other cities with faced with reclamation of industrial sites: "As legitimate concerns about industrial waste have mounted, they have inspired new regulations that have expanded the budgets and prolonged the timetables of redevelopment."[51] Encapsulation was completed in 1990 and the island's reclamation proceeded. By 1992, the Three Rivers Rowing Association had established its rowing center, the Sports Technology Group began construction of a tennis equipment manufacturing facility, a marina opened with 75 wet and 150 dry slips, and the DER announced a decision to establish its regional headquarters on the Island. The URA, meanwhile, continued to develop the plans for a park, tennis courts, and river trails.[52]

A North Shore (Allegheny River) renewal program—like Washington's Landing and the Pittsburgh Technology Center—had also been conceived earlier and was spooned into the Strategy 21 proposal of 1985.[53] A Three Rivers Stadium project also exemplified post-steel Pittsburgh in which enhancing the quality of life would be part of the new diversity. By the late 1970s, the URA had selected for renewal a ninety-one-acre tract along the North Side bank of the Allegheny, extending from Three Rivers Stadium on the west to the Sixteenth Street Bridge on the east. The plan called for high-rise condos, townhouses, a marina, and extending the shoreline Roberto Clemente Memorial Park.[54] Responding to the suggestions of developers that the plan should require a unifying and aesthetic element, the URA (in cooperation with the city, Allegheny Conference, and the private sector) created Allegheny Landing, a sculpture park fronting on the river between the Sixth and Seventh Street Bridges. The URA then selected (1981) a developer for a three-and-a-half-acre site above the park, resulting in two office buildings completed in 1983. At this point, the city eyed the Three Rivers Stadium section of the North Shore as a potential multiuse development with shopping plazas, a hotel, a children's amusement and education complex, an outdoor festival site, a marina, offices, and a science and technology center.[55]

According to Strategy 21, the stadium development project, combined with Washington's Landing and the proposal for a mixed-use riverfront parcel in the Strip District (the wholesale-retail food market and restaurant district paralleling the Allegheny River along Penn Avenue and Smallman Street above Eleventh Street) would transform the riverfront, promote tourism, and enhance the quality of life in Pittsburgh. However, the Stadium redevelopment plan led only to the creation of the Carnegie Museum's Science Center, described in Strategy 21 as a symbol of Pittsburgh's emerging leadership in advanced technology. Construction of the museum began in the fall of 1989, and it opened in 1991. Yet, as of 1994, the Stadium and Science Center area remains mostly a sea of parking lots, warehouses, and expressways.

4

A Second Renaissance

A survey by the Pittsburgh Finance Department of employment trends in the 1982–1992 decade documented the city's transition from a manufacturing to a diversified service center. Manufacturing employment, 21,447 in 1982, had dropped to 10,385 in 1992 (from 10.19 percent to 4.15 percent of total employment). Hospital employment, 28,185 in 1982, increased to 37,311 a decade later (9.83 percent to 11.72 percent); health care increased from 4,315 to 8,426 jobs over the decade (2.05 percent to 3.37 percent). Higher education grew from 21,650 jobs to 32,560 (7.55 percent to 10.23 percent). Employment in the restaurant sector leaped dramatically—from 4,470 in 1991 to 10,571 in 1992. High-technology jobs, 2,800 in 1981, rose to 5,523 in 1992 (2.2 percent). Corporate administrative office employment dropped sharply from 13,534 in 1982 to 6,010 in 1992 (2.4 percent), but jobs in finance increased from 14,802 to 18,535 (7.41 percent of the total).[1]

Despite its shrinking population, Pittsburgh experienced significant growth and vitality in the cultural sector in the 1980s—music, art, theater, ballet, opera. The Golden Triangle, over the decade, experienced the creation of a Cultural District as well as a massive new wave of high-rise office construction. North Shore redevelopment added the Carnegie Science Center in 1991 to Allegheny Landing and Roberto Clemente Memorial Park, and the Andy Warhol Museum opened in 1994.[2] South Side revitalization included the commercially successful Station Square (launched in the 1970s), East Carson Street shops and restaurants, and the city's Riverside Park. The rejuvenation of the Strip District, the historic wholesale-retail produce market section, included the establishment of the Society for Contemporary Crafts,[3] the Historical Society of Western Pennsylvania's Regional History Center (scheduled to open in 1996), and a complex of restaurants and night spots.

Thanks to these developments, Pittsburgh by the late 1980s was proclaimed to be "America's most promising postindustrial experiment." Renowned for its medical and health facilities, computer programming and robotics, Pittsburgh had become the yardstick for other cities stricken by industrial decline. The city had experienced a "revitalization beyond compare," a dramatic restructuring into a "robust, diversified economy" in which heavy industry had become marginal but culture and education flourished. Arguably the "safest, most affordable city in the nation," it retained a small-town charm and neighborhoods with a strong sense of identity. Pittsburgh, in essence, had transformed itself from a production-oriented community to one that offered an agreeable way of life. Indeed, Pittsburgh's quality of life, "once ridiculed . . . has become a catalyst in its comeback."[4] Even Duisburg, an industrial community in Germany's Ruhr Valley seeking models for economic revitalization, turned to Pittsburgh for clues. Duisburg's city manager had visited Pittsburgh and declared he had seen a successful example of economic transition.[5] Most outside commentators did not dwell on the continuing economic plight of the former mill towns, the growth of low-paid service-sector employment, the struggle of working-class neighborhoods to remain viable, or the declining population of Pittsburgh.

Visitors were also impressed by the "spirit of cooperation" in Pittsburgh, encompassing business, government, and nonprofit organizations. However, this cooperative ethic so characteristic of Renaissance I had evaporated in the administration of Mayor Peter Flaherty (1970–1977). Succeeding David L. Lawrence (1946–1959) and Joseph M. Barr (1959–1969), Flaherty had distanced himself from the Democratic party machine and run as an independent. He also distanced himself from the Allegheny Conference and corporate community. Flaherty was less concerned with corporate-driven development than with fiscal discipline, lean municipal government, neighborhood improvement, and reducing the tax burden of the ordinary citizen.[6] His balanced budgets and reductions in taxes and the municipal payroll were an anomaly in the twilight years of the Great Society. The retrenchment policy now appears significant, in retrospect, as an early effort to adapt municipal government in Pittsburgh to demographic realities. Pittsburgh's population, 676,806 in 1950, fell to 604,332 in 1960 and to 520,117 when Flaherty become mayor in 1970. Yet the city's taxes, payroll, and number of employees had continued to grow. A test case of Flaherty's resolve to reduce and reorganize the labor force was his elimination of Teamster drivers as water meter installers, resulting in an unsuccessful strike. By the end of Flaherty's administration, the city work force had dropped from 7,000 to 5,252.[7]

To some extent, Flaherty translated personal idiosyncracy into public policy; a near obsession with independence and autonomy precluded the cooperative relations with the corporate elite his predecessors had enjoyed. But Pittsburgh, and the challenge of governance, had also significantly changed by 1970. Lawrence and Mellon were gone, along with the kind of authority they could command; the mayor of Pittsburgh, Flaherty observed, now had " 'to confer with all groups of people, people in the neighborhoods, businessmen and merchants. . . . When Dave Lawrence was mayor he only saw whom he wanted to see.' "[8] Events of the 1960s and 1970s—the civil rights movement, community action and neighborhood organization, growing disillusionment with large-scale urban renewal and its social dislocations, the beginnings of historic preservation, with its emphasis on conservation rather than demolition of older structures—complicated the decision-making process and reduced the relative power of the business-centered civic coalition. John P. Robin, Mayor Lawrence's executive secretary, also saw that the "spirit of the times" had changed by 1980. "Today . . . the delays in the courts . . . are quite murderous. It's amazing we get anything done." No longer could the Allegheny Conference decree that "so-and-so will be done."[9]

The frosty relationship between Flaherty and the corporate sector was epitomized in the remarks of Edward J. Magee, former executive director of the Allegheny Conference; he complained to historian Stefan Lorant that "a few months after Mayor Flaherty took office in 1970 everything was over; all programs came to a standstill."[10] Worst of all, Flaherty vehemently opposed Skybus, a mass transit system endorsed not only by a segment of the corporate community but by the Democratic majority of the county commissioners and the Pittsburgh Democratic party organization. Skybus would have involved the construction of an elevated, operator-free people mover to the South Hills. Its corporate and political advocates viewed Skybus as the basis, in turn, for a mass-transit manufacturing industry in the Pittsburgh area. Apart from Flaherty's alienation from the corporate and political elite, he resisted Skybus because the two proposed stations in Pittsburgh would not benefit the city much and because he perceived a conflict between the technology and public safety: operatorless cars, a possible power failure while traveling in cars forty feet or more in the air, vandalism. Flaherty blocked any progress on Skybus through a series of legal obstacles.[11] Ultimately, a Port Authority Special Task Force created in 1974, chaired by John Robin, endorsed a consultant's recommendation for a light rail system to the South Hills. This was constructed (at a cost of $542 million) in the 1980s along with a four-station subway loop in the Golden Triangle. Another transportation project delayed by Flaherty was the East Street Valley Expressway cutting through the city's North Side to the suburban North Hills. Revived and constructed during the Caliguiri administration, it accelerated a real estate boom in the North Hills.[12]

The mayor and the Allegheny Conference also quarreled over the location and other details of a convention center for Pittsburgh, but a threat by the state in 1974 to withdraw funding for the project encouraged cooperation.[13] By September, the conference and the Mayor's Convention Advisory Committee agreed on the location of the convention center and its operation by the Public Auditorium Authority. Built along the Allegheny River between Penn Avenue, Fort Duquesne Boulevard, and Tenth and Eleventh Streets, the David L. Lawrence Convention Center was not only too small and architecturally undistinguished; it failed to exploit the proximity of the river. In all, it has stood since 1981 as an object lesson in poor urban design—with its faults attributable more to the state than the city. Its size limitations have ever since been a special source of aggravation for the city's economic development promoters, who bemoan all the business going to Philadelphia, Cleveland, and elsewhere.[14] In short, it exemplifies the penalties for civic design that is neither beautiful nor efficient.

Flaherty was the only mayor since the inception of Renaissance I in 1945 who lacked a strong commitment to Golden Triangle development.

This indifference represented another source of conflict with the corporate sector. In keeping with his independent and populist agenda, Flaherty shifted funds from downtown to city neighborhoods. His successor, Richard Caliguiri (1977–1988), also embraced neighborhood revitalization as a pivotal goal of Renaissance II after Flaherty resigned in April 1977 to join the Carter administration as deputy attorney general. But Caliguiri restored the central business district as a vital concern of municipal government. It had to function as the service, entertainment, and cultural anchor for a new postindustrial city.[15] Renaissance II signified more than a catalogue of office buildings and transportation projects, or neighborhood improvements. Caliguiri recognized (later into his administration, if not at the beginning) that Pittsburgh confronted a crisis at least equal to that following World War II. Its century-old economic base was shattered by the 1980s, and the city required a fundamental reconstruction of its economy and quality of life.

An interview in 1987 with Stefan Lorant, a year before Caliguiri's premature death of amyloidosis, clearly reveals the mayor's broader perspective, one fully compatible with the economic development strategy of the Allegheny Conference and Strategy 21. Caliguiri proclaimed the conference's *Strategy for Growth* of 1984 to be a "blueprint for Pittsburgh's future." He envisioned Pittsburgh resurrected as a modernized, diversified metropolis poised for the twenty-first century:

> We turned into a service and retailing center, a center for heath care, a city of transplants, a city of High Technology, a city of Robotics, of computer programming. We became a world major research center. . . . We are spending over a billion dollars on R&D. These efforts will reinvigorate our economic picture, breathe new life in the old industries.[16]

The eruption of new downtown office towers generated by the restored public-private partnership (and favorable market conditions), the rapid transit projects, the cultural initiatives of the 1980s supported by the Caliguiri administration all provided tax revenues and employment. More important, they provided the office space, infrastructure, and quality of life improvements that Caliguiri hoped would facilitate Pittsburgh's transition from a paleotechnic nineteenth-century economy of coal and steel to a post-steel economy rooted in advanced technology, information processing, professional services, and cultural vitality.

Two key organizational initiatives supported the ambitious development program of the Caliguiri era. In 1977 he created the Mayor's Development Council. Consisting of city department heads and chaired by the mayor's executive secretary, David Matter, it met weekly to coordinate all development activities. Five years later, in 1982, the departments of Housing and Economic Development were merged into the Urban Redevelopment Authority (URA). These changes made possible a more centralized, coordinated development process. In addition, the Pittsburgh Home Rule Charter of 1975 had strengthened the powers of the mayor's office.[17] Finally, the achievements of the Caliguiri administration owed much to the executive abilities of David Matter. He guided the entire development process, and like John Robin in the Lawrence administration, linked city government to the corporate and business sector.[18]

But Caliguiri's determination to redirect the Pittsburgh economy, his restoration of the public-private partnership, and administrative reorganizations do not fully explain the torrent of private investment in the central business district. At the time Caliguiri assumed office in 1977, a shortage of prime office space in the Golden Triangle was becoming acute; by 1980, the occupancy level was nearly 100 percent.[19] Although a few major office buildings had appeared between the late sixties and mid-seventies (U.S. Steel, Pittsburgh National, One and Two Oliver Plaza, Westinghouse), nothing was added after 1975.[20] Then, in the decade of Renaissance II, the public-private coalition produced 6.6 million square feet of new office space, along with hotel and cultural facilities.[21] Major structures included One Oxford Centre (forty-six stories) with its upscale shopping mall; Philip Johnson's PPG Place for Pittsburgh Plate Glass, a cluster of six Gothic glass cathedrals adjacent to Market Square; One Mellon Bank Center (fifty-four stories) located off Grant Street and Fifth Avenue, across from H. H. Richardson's renowned Romanesque county courthouse and jail; the twenty-seven-story Federated Investors Tower and the 615-room Vista International Hotel (twenty-eight stories), which together comprised Liberty Center, across from the Convention Center; Two Chatham Center, in the vicinity of the Civic Arena, and the controversial Lower Hill redevelopment of Renaissance I; Riverfront Center (twenty stories) at Fort Pitt Boulevard and Stanwix Street; CNG Tower (built by Consolidated Natural Gas), topped by a distinctive arched pediment and located on Liberty Avenue close to Heinz Hall and Plaza; and Fifth Avenue Place, at Fifth and Liberty Avenues, punctuated at the top by a tall pencil-like mast. One of Pittsburgh's most unique interior spaces—the Jenkins Arcade Building—was demolished for Fifth Avenue Place. CNG Tower replaced the Moose Building, a noteworthy Beaux-Arts structure.[22]

Pittsburgh's cultural scene had been enriched in the 1970s by the conversion of the old Penn Theater into Heinz Hall, opened in 1971

PPG Building, headquarters for PPG Industries, part of Renaissance II and the revitalization of the downtown business district, 1980s. *Photo: Courtesy of PPG Industries, Inc.*

(adjoined in 1979 by Heinz Hall Plaza, an outdoor space and dining area). The magnificently refurbished Heinz Hall became the home of the Pittsburgh Symphony and other performing arts groups. In the fall of 1974 the exhibition area of the Carnegie Museum of Art in the Oakland section increased dramatically with the opening of the Scaife Gallery. The emergence of quality of life concerns as part of the economic development strategy of the 1980s was then reflected in a surge of cultural and historic preservation projects during the Renaissance II years. As in the case of Heinz Hall, another old movie palace, the Stanley Theater, was converted into the Benedum Center for the Performing Arts; with its remarkably deep stage, it serves as the base for the Pittsburgh Opera and Pittsburgh Ballet Theater. The creation of this second cultural anchor in downtown Pittsburgh was supervised by the Pittsburgh Cultural Trust. Established in 1984 and strongly supported by the Heinz Foundation, the Trust was created to develop a cultural district and contribute to downtown economic revitalization. (This will be discussed more fully in chapter 9.)

One Oxford Centre. *Photo: Author*

Consolidated Natural Gas Tower. *Photo: Courtesy Lincoln Property Company*

Historic preservation flourished during the Caliguiri administration (though not necessarily because of the mayor's efforts). With URA assistance, the old Pennsylvania Railroad Station was recycled into an apartment and condominium complex dubbed the "Pennsylvanian." On a larger scale, the Pittsburgh History & Landmarks Foundation enhanced the city's tax base through its Station Square project—restaurants, shops, offices, and a hotel housed in the former terminal and other buildings that served the Pittsburgh & Lake Erie Railroad. The city created a Historic Review Commission in 1979 to enforce the newly enacted preservation ordinance.

According to John P. Robin, "Pittsburgh in the eighties is overcoming the constraints of its urban geography. . . . For the first time in the city's history there is an opportunity to treat central Pittsburgh—the heartland of the urban region—as an integrated whole."[23] By the early 1990s, the enlarged downtown included the North Shore and South Side and had moved eastward to encompass the Strip District and its riverfront (where the Historical Society of Western Pennsylvania announced plans to establish a Regional History Center in the recycled Chautauqua Lake Ice Company building on Smallman Street close to the Convention Center).

Pittsburgh's 300-acre Strip District is bounded, roughly, by the Allegheny River, Liberty Avenue, the Convention Center, and Fortieth Street. Food merchants began to concentrate there in the early twentieth century. The Lower Strip, along Penn Avenue and Smallman Street, following construction of a Produce Terminal, had become the city's wholesale food center by the 1920s.

The Strip's character as a lively, low-rise, mixed-use, historic precinct anchored in the wholesale food trade was threatened three times in the last quarter century. The Penn-Central Railroad planned to redevelop the Strip up to Twenty-first Street, forcing a relocation of the food industry. This scheme was thwarted by the Penn-Central's bankruptcy; otherwise, the area might have been homogenized by a conventional 1960s renewal project. Then, in 1980, it was eyed by the City Planning Commission as a blighted area ripe for redevelopment. The railroad produce terminal was acquired by the city from Conrail for $1.1 million, but Caliguiri favored renovating the five-block-long facility and keeping the wholesale food market in Pittsburgh. The next threat to the character of the Strip came from the Jack Buncher Company. Buncher, one of the city's major land and real estate tycoons, had acquired much of the Penn Central property in the Strip. In collaboration with the Rouse Company, he proposed a festival market in 1986. This scheme failed because of the city's reluctance to provide the massive subsidies requested by the developers against a limited equity, the diminishing success of festival markets nationally, and, not least, the existence of a highly successful restaurant-retail-entertainment complex in Station Square.[24]

The Strip survived and prospered as an example of renewal by preservation and adaptation. It evolved, during Renaissance II, into Pittsburgh's colorful international retail food bazaar. A stroll along Penn Avenue from Sixteenth to Twenty-eighth Streets is a food aficionado's encounter with paradise: Italian, Greek, Middle Eastern, and oriental specialties, fresh flowers, fruits, and vegetables, fish, cheese, baked goods, meals "at the working person's prices." A cultural dimension was added to the Strip in the 1980s when the Society for Contemporary Crafts abandoned the Allegheny River town of Verona in favor of Smallman Street. Like the Pittsburgh Center for the Arts in Shadyside, the society mounts exhibits that satisfy high professional standards. The cultural significance of the Strip will be greatly enhanced upon completion of the Regional History Center.

The opening of the Metropol night club at Smallman and Sixteenth Streets in 1988 foreshadowed the emergence of the Strip as a mecca for the nightlife crowd. The decisive event was the opening of Phase I of a complex called "The Strip—Down by the Riverside" in 1991–1992. The developer, WETCO, opened a night spot, Donzi's, on a 420-foot floating boardwalk along the Allegheny in the summer of 1991 (along with a grill area and pool). This was followed by Crewser's Restaurant and the Riverwatch, a banquet room above Crewser's. Buster's Crab opened in 1992. These facilities would not win any design awards for their shedlike character and unpaved, rutted parking lots off Smallman Street. But the Allegheny River scene from the boardwalk precipitates visions of more (and better designed) riverfront development for recreational, cultural, and entertainment uses.[25]

The future of the Strip will depend, in part, on how well the night spot, wholesale produce, retail, and cultural uses can coexist. Land prices have increased significantly in the Lower Strip, tripling in five years to $12 per square foot.[26] Commercial success and market forces could accomplish what abortive schemes for large-scale renewal failed to do—sterilize and homogenize a colorful urban precinct. The pressure on land prices might be alleviated if the various commercial and amusement activities were to extend beyond Twenty-fourth Street—presently an unpopulated and barren region of warehouses and light manufacturing. The long-term interests of the Strip (and the other sections of the greater downtown) might also be served by an increase in the residential population that, in 1990, numbered a negligible 275 persons.[27]

The decision of the Caliguiri administration to save and restore the produce terminal was critical to preserving the Strip's character as a unique, mixed-use precinct of Pittsburgh close to downtown and the Allegheny River. More broadly, the Caliguiri administration had resurrected the public-private partnership that, in turn, made possible a vast increase in Golden Triangle office space. It also presided over the initiation or completion of major transportation projects—the four-station downtown subway linked to light-rail-vehicle transit to the South Hills, the unbottling of the East Valley Expressway, the express busway connecting the East End and adjoining suburbs to downtown.[28] Most important, perhaps, Richard Caliguiri believed that Pittsburgh had to redefine its economy and competitive advantages; thus he endorsed the post-steel economic development strategy advocated by the Allegheny Conference and expressed in Strategy 21. This included the quality of life improvements needed to compete effectively for an educated, professional middle class required by a post-steel economy.

Caliguiri's successor as mayor, Sophie Masloff (1988–1993), was a product of the old-line Democratic party machine with its strong ties to organized labor. In two respects the Masloff administration espoused key elements of postwar municipal policy: the public-private partnership and efforts to maintain the vitality of downtown. Partnerships, she declared, were a "big component of making . . . things happen in Pittsburgh"; indeed, cooperation with business and community leaders was "the only way to make things happen in this city."[29] A key objective of the partnership, in turn, was to ensure that the downtown would remain the core of the Pittsburgh region, its "symbolic and functional heart" and a dominant location for jobs, economic development, culture, entertainment, and shopping.[30] But her administration was largely oblivious to the economic and community development benefits of historic preservation and its role in protecting the city's cultural heritage.

If measured by the expansion of office space and jobs[31] or by cultural activity, the nearly half-century determination to preserve the vitality of Pittsburgh's downtown was reasonably successful. As a retail shopping entrepot, however, it would never be confused with Chicago's Magnificent Mile. The picture is mixed. The city acknowledges both the neglect of retail activity and its importance to downtown vitality:

> The City is now focusing on a major role of the downtown which has not been previously addressed in public policy: the shopping core. . . . The importance of a lively urban retail district goes well beyond providing good places to shop. The retail environment is a fabric which holds together a commercial core. Colorful and active storefronts along city streets create a lively and safe public environment which attracts occasional shoppers as well as developers and businesses.[32]

Although three department stores remain in the Golden Triangle (Saks, Kaufmann's, and Lazarus—formerly Horne's),[33] two of the main downtown arteries—Fifth and Forbes Avenues—can serve future archaeologists as a guide to fast food and discount store culture. A "Fifth and Forbes" revitalization proposal by the mayor's office in 1990 (which included sidewalk widening, new lampposts, colorful banners) never materialized. It is doubtful whether these cosmetic improvements could have overcome the more fundamental problems of downtown retailing— suburban competition and the parking and traffic congestion invariably cited in any survey of shoppers.[34] It is also doubtful that the partiality toward food courts in latter-day office towers such as PPG and Fifth Avenue Place can increase the allure of the downtown.

What compensates for these limitations and gives the central business district a distinct personality are its impressive setting between rivers and a large concentration of late nineteenth- and early twentieth-century neoclassical and Beaux-Arts architecture. Neither of these assets was appreciated during Renaissance I. The rivers, cut off from pedestrian traffic by parkways, had no impact as a design element, and the creation of a new Pittsburgh justified, it seemed, the elimination of any vestige of the old. Yet it is the pool of surviving historic structures that distinguishes downtown Pittsburgh from much of urban America. These architecturally significant buildings provide visual spectacle and involvement, and they compensate for the conspicuous absence of public art and sculpture.

A commitment to the downtown's vitality, within a new economic framework, was clearly enunciated by the Pittsburgh City Planning Department.

> the changing structure of the economy is leading to a shift in employment from the riverfront industrial districts to the commercial centers of the Central Business District and Oakland; . . . riverfront industrial tracts will be the focus of increasing development interest. These tracts will be redeveloped for the new commercial, light industrial, residential, and recreational uses that take best advantage of what are now considered to be high amenity locations.
>
> With a solid research infrastructure . . . Pittsburgh is a legitimate center for high tech development. Specialization in software, robotics, biomedical research, chemicals, and business services affords a wide range of growth industries to diversify the economy as well as the labor force.[35]

The Planning Department would help implement the development strategy emerging in the 1980s identified with the Allegheny Conference, Strategy 21, the research universities, city and county government, the cultural nonprofit organizations, the advanced technology community, and, not least, the Urban Redevelopment Authority.

Although the Planning Department was closely involved in the development process, the key public operating agency, as in Renaissance I, was the URA.[36] It had, however, undergone a significant metamorphosis. As early as the 1960s, the agency began its evolution from a large-scale redevelopment and real estate " 'clear 'em out and tear 'em down' " program to one that encompassed housing and neighborhood economic assistance as well as large-scale projects.[37] After the 1960s, furthermore, the projects would minimize neighborhood disruption or residential displacement (as was true of the Pittsburgh Technology Center, Strip District, North Shore and Stadium, Washington's Landing, or the downtown office and hotel construction of Renaissance II). The housing and economic assistance programs of the URA were largely directed toward neighborhood revitalization. By the 1980s the URA would proclaim that "the public/private partnership that the URA helped forge in Pittsburgh 40 years ago has evolved into what today might more accurately be called a 'public/private/neighborhood' partnership."[38]

The transformation of the redevelopment process in Pittsburgh resulted, in part, from the social experiments and upheavals of the 1960s:

Pittsburgh Technology Center: University of Pittsburgh Biotechnology Building, on the site of the J&L mills. *Photo: Author*

ACTION-Housing's Neighborhood Urban Extension, a neighborhood-centered historic preservation consciousness beginning with the creation of the Pittsburgh History & Landmarks Foundation in 1964, the community action component of the federal antipoverty program, the social planning advocacy in the City Planning Department, and civil rights agitation. These movements nourished a reaction against urban renewal that ignored the historic and social fabric of neighborhoods and communities, or provided no voice for ordinary citizens. Especially important was the lesson of the Hill District—the large-scale displacement of residential population for the Civic Arena (intended as a first component of an abortive cultural center in the Lower Hill) and then the April 1968 riots. "That form of citizen involvement," observed the URA, "was an emphatic statement of residents' determination to have a key voice in deciding their own future. It also confirmed that conventional renewal could not work in the Hill District."[39] Significantly, Pete Flaherty, elected mayor the following year, shifted the city's renewal emphasis to the neighborhoods. G. Evan Stoddard, former director the URA's Economic Development Department, maintains that Flaherty's neighborhood orientation played an important role in redefining the URA's function.[40]

Equally important in redefining the role of the URA were changes in how federal housing and renewal funds were allocated. "Between 1963

Three Rivers Stadium: a bowl detached from the river in a wasteland of parking areas. *Photo: Author*

and 1967," according to the URA, "major emphasis was given to continuous efforts to adapt Pittsburgh's urban renewal plans to housing assistance programs emerging from Washington." These included the 1965 funding provision for rehabilitation grants and low-interest loans, leading initially to housing improvement efforts in East Liberty, Homewood North, and Garfield. Thus, as early as the mid-1960s, urban renewal in Pittsburgh was "moving toward 'save our neighborhoods' types of activity."[41] Funding for neighborhood improvement was greatly increased with the inauguration of the federal Community Development Block Grant system in 1974. Reinforcing the URA's role in economic assistance, housing, and neighborhood improvement was its absorption of the city's departments of Housing and Economic Development in 1982.

Presiding over both eras in the life of the Pittsburgh URA was John P. Robin. Born in the Hill District in 1912, Robin attended the University of Pittsburgh. The Depression forced him to drop out in his senior year before graduating, thwarting his dream of a career in biology.[42] He then worked as a reporter for the *Pittsburgh Post-Gazette* (1934–1936). In 1936, he became secretary to Mayor Cornelius D. Scully. By the time he entered the army in 1943, Robin had gained extensive administrative and legislative experience and, most important, won the confidence of David L. Lawrence. Robin encouraged Lawrence to run for mayor in 1945 and became his executive secretary when Lawrence assumed office in 1946. Lawrence appointed Robin executive director of the Urban Redevelopment Authority in 1948, where he served until 1954. In the Renaissance I era, Robin was to Lawrence what Wallace Richards was to Richard King Mellon: adviser, spokesman, and link between government and the corporate world.[43]

Robin left for Harrisburg in 1955 to become secretary of commerce. He returned to Pittsburgh the same year as president of the newly created Regional Industrial Development Corporation (RIDC). In 1957 he joined the Old Philadelphia Corporation as executive vice-president. This enabled him to operate again in his natural habitat—the world of urban affairs. He managed the nationally significant Society Hill and Independence Mall redevelopments (through which he first experienced the creative possibilities of historic preservation as an urban redevelopment strategy).[44]

Robin joined the Ford Foundation in 1963, specializing in Far Eastern and African urban affairs. His ten years with the Ford Foundation included service as consultant to the Calcutta Metropolitan Planning Organization and preparation of an international urban survey. Allegheny Conference President Henry Hillman and University of Pittsburgh Chancellor Wesley Posvar were instrumental in getting Robin back to Pittsburgh in 1973 as a program adviser to the conference and named University Professor of Public Affairs. Caliguiri, upon becoming mayor in 1977, appointed him chairman of the URA.[45]

Robin would always define Renaissance I as an era when a cohesive alliance of civic, business, and technical professionals "saved Pittsburgh from becoming a large-scale Gary or . . . Newark, a city that has lost its real reason for being and has become a very drab, gradually declining mill town. . . . What many of us did from 1945 to the present day . . . was to save Pittsburgh from that." With a certain nostalgia, if not regret, he also interpreted that earlier time as an era when the techniques of obstructionism had not yet been perfected: "The idea was new and ideas of public protest and the difficulties you can cause a government were not as well known as they now are." The election of Flaherty not only shattered the civic-business coalition, but also ostensibly "deprogrammed" the URA—the coalition's key instrument of environmental intervention. Its new chairman was Bruce Campbell, the mayor's executive secretary, and a "stern Gladstonian apostle of retrenchment." The

URA lost staff to the City Planning Department, meetings were scheduled for Friday afternoons, and the agency published no annual reports or other documents between 1969 and 1979. (Even worse, the City Planning Department published no annual reports between 1962 and 1988.)[46]

But the evisceration was more apparent than real. The URA's responsibilities increased during the period as redevelopment concepts were extended to cover the entire community as opposed to merely removing blight in designated areas. New legislation and funding encouraged loans, tax abatements, and subsidies for neighborhood conservation and rehabilitation:

> The movement has been from the particular to the holistic, from a simple declared public purpose in the elimination of blight to a series of public interventions . . . and from programs operative only in limited and legally defined areas to a looser and looser definition—now so broad in some instances, such as low interest home repair loans, to include the whole City.[47]

Robin thus recognized that the agency to which he returned as chairman in 1977, at the outset of Renaissance II, was greatly transformed from the one he left in 1954; and he promised that "there will be something for everybody in a new prospectus of redevelopment in Pittsburgh."[48] The Caliguiri administration's decision to transfer to the URA functions formerly carried out by the departments of Housing and Economic Development was another phase in the agency's evolution into the city's most comprehensive instrument of economic revitalization.

The Pennsylvania Economy League examined the economics of downtown development during Renaissance II, including the role of the URA. It calculated that a public investment of little more than $10 million for nine Renaissance II projects (mostly in tax abatements totaling $7.38 million) would ultimately return $26 million annually in city and county property taxes, and school district taxes. The nine projects were One Oxford Centre, One Mellon Bank Center, Two Chatham Center, Riverfront Center, Liberty Center, PPG Place, Penn Station, CNG Tower, Fifth Avenue Place. Moreover, the city's $10 million investment generated more than $922 million in private investment. Adding the Benedum Center to the total increased the private investment to nearly $950 million.[49]

At least half the projects would not have materialized without government assistance in the form of land assembly, tax abatements, low-interest loans to developers, business relocation assistance, or street improvements. The most important of these mechanisms was land acquisition, and the URA was the primary vehicle for this, as well as for low-interest loans and grants. URA land assembly made possible Liberty Center, One Mellon Bank Center, Penn Station (the "Pennsylvanian"), and Two Chatham Center. Although the land for PPG Place went directly from owners to developers, the URA helped the company to relocate displaced businesses, assisted PPG with design and site plans, and planned the reconstruction of the full twenty-six-acre Market Square redevelopment site.[50]

As a development agency, the URA was unique. No other municipal institution combined so many functions: initiator, catalyst, coordinator, planner, funding agent, provider of technical assistance, and (not least) land assembly. It participated significantly not only in the Golden Triangle projects of Renaissance II, but also the large-scale developments previously discussed: the Pittsburgh Technology Center, Washington's Landing, the Stadium–North Shore, the Strip District, and Station Square. In some cases, like Liberty Center, it initiated the development process. The URA acquired the site, which adjoins the Convention Center, in 1979 and offered it for development the next year. It selected the Grant-Liberty Development Group's proposal for an office tower and hotel on the two-and-a-half-acre site (but the sale did not occur until 1984). The URA also provided the developers with two large loans toward site acquisition and construction. Similarly, the URA's initiative in saving Pennsylvania Station and the Strip's produce terminal in 1980 provided object lessons in historic landmark recycling and ensured the survival of the wholesale produce business in the Strip District. An additional URA responsibility during Renaissance II was preparation of all city applications for federal Urban Development Action Grants (UDAG). These provided leverage for private investment. Two such grants, totaling $5.8 million in the early 1980s, generated $29 million in private investment in the early, vulnerable period of Pittsburgh History & Landmarks Foundation's Station Square. Similarly, a URA-generated UDAG for $17 million in 1986 was a vital component in financing the CNG Tower and converting the Stanley Theater into the Benedum Center for the Performing Arts.[51]

G. Evan Stoddard, former director of the URA's Economic Development Department, has defined the challenge confronting an older industrial center like Pittsburgh.

> The change in the city's economic functions—from a supplier of manufactured goods to a business and professional service center—has resulted in tremendous dislocations of companies and workers, a need to find new uses for old buildings, and unexpected growth in the city's office and institutional center. A large decline in the city's population accompanied these changes, the result both of suburban choices and of people's leaving the city to follow work, which in turn undermined the city's shopping districts.[52]

The centrifugal forces remain powerful, and the central city still suffers from many competitive disadvantages—land assembly limitations, congestion, old building stock, a legacy of environmental pollution, and a smaller, older, less affluent population. Simultaneously, the city's tax base dwindles while it must maintain the infrastructure and public services created for a much larger population. These circumstances help explain the creation in Pittsburgh of a comprehensive, multipurpose development agency with the resources to promote the post-steel economic development strategy and cope with the liabilities of a former heavy-industry metropolis. Even so, Stoddard is not sure that Pittsburgh can "continue to meet the expectations and needs of the region and of its own populace" without a system of regional cost sharing.[53]

This regionalism is a viewpoint also expressed lately by the Allegheny Conference on Community Development. A few years ago the Conference was frequently criticized for lacking any regional perspective. A favorite parlor game in Pittsburgh by the mid-1980's's was speculation over whether the Conference remained a significant force in the life of the community. Roger S. Ahlbrandt, Jr., for example, argued that its corporate participants "could not chart unfamiliar territory. They were stymied by regional problems extending far beyond the Downtown corporate headquarters base." And, as an early advocate for an advanced technology strategy for the region, Ahlbrandt complained that the "high-technology community, despite its visibility and importance to the region, is not a participating member of the power structure. The corporate leadership at the Allegheny Conference, Penn's Southwest and RIDC is still primarily in the hands of the older, traditional companies." The Conference, according to Ahlbrandt, should address itself to such regional issues as unemployment, mill town fiscal distress, and the area's image of poor management-labor relations."[54]

For some, the Conference's "reputation as the trailblazer of the public-private partnership is more history than present fact." Critics even complained that it had "degenerated into a report-writing luncheon club that abdicated . . . its responsibility to help the city weather its worst crisis since the depression." It was neither willing nor able to commit itself "to a comprehensively articulated strategy for revitalizing the manufacturing base of this region."[55] Much of this criticism seemed rooted in a sense of frustration and nostalgia. No one seemed to be in charge while a whole region suffered an economic disaster; and the frustration partly discharged itself upon the organization that had once before mobilized the public and private sectors to save Pittsburgh from an enveloping obsolescence. But the Conference's role in Renaissance I was based on a set of special circumstances that could not be replicated. The authority of Mellon and Lawrence was unique. The problems confronting Pittsburgh at the close of World War II could be alleviated through engineering, construction, and money. The economic and social conditions of the 1980s were less amenable to solution. Finally, Pittsburgh was a major corporate headquarters in the 1950s, the corporate world was stable, and many local executives were longtime residents of the community with time to devote to civic concerns.[56]

Ahlbrandt and Coleman, in a report published early in 1987 based on interviews with twenty-one executives, examined the corporate leadership's conception of civic responsibility and public policy.[57] A nostalgia seemed to operate at this level, too, as some looked back to a golden age: "When R. K. Mellon was alive, and he and Dave Lawrence were working together, there was a lot of initiative coming out of the Conference. With the passing of that kind of power and the Conference having to just sort of weigh all of the interests of a group . . . it was much more difficult . . . to exercise very strong initiatives." In contrast to Renaissance I, when "the companies brought their heavy-hitters together and they got it done," the Conference now had to proceed by consensus: "If the chairman doesn't sense that almost everyone sitting around that table is in favor of something, it isn't going to fly."[58]

Corporation leaders also voiced concern over the increased demands on their time that compromised their ability to exercise civic leadership.

Some heads of global corporations were "not in town very often, and they were not as close to what is happening in Pittsburgh as they are to what's happening in Hong Kong." Douglas Danforth, Westinghouse CEO and chairman of the Allegheny Conference, put it succinctly: "With corporate raiders roaming the land and foreign competitors snatching market share, CEOs are so busy running their companies they simply have less time to spend on civic affairs than their predecessors."[59] It was unfortunate for the Conference that chairmen in the 1980s such as James Lee of Gulf Oil and Howard Love of National Intergroup were "distracted" by company problems (a takeover of Gulf and an unsuccessful attempt at diversification in the case of National Intergroup).[60]

The most consistent attitude expressed by the executives was their endorsement of an economic development strategy rooted in modernization and diversification—advanced technology and research; education, medical, financial, legal, and other professional services; improved infrastructure. If the mill towns could not participate in this modernization process, they faced a bleak future. It was not clear whether there would be sufficient demand for businesses to locate in the various industrial parks and incubators in progress—Duquesne, McKeesport, East Pittsburgh, Homestead. Under any circumstances, they agreed that improved infrastructure was imperative: "If the old mills sit there and nothing is done about the highway system, the communities will die." Executives also expressed concern that the image of adversarial labor relations might undermine regional economic development and that local politicians suffered from a labor bias. "The problem, I think, is that the politicians used their chips carrying union messages rather than getting a good infrastructure for the Valley."[61] It was doubtful whether politicians could make economic development decisions independent of this bias.

By the mid-1980s, the obsession with the fate of the Mon Valley and Ohio River communities devastated by the shutdown of the steel industry led to an misconception of the Conference's role. This was reinforced by the tendency to look back at Renaissance I as a golden age of civic redemption (the present always suffers by comparison with some past ideal, irrespective of changed circumstances).[62] The problem that confronted the Allegheny Conference was less lack of accomplishment than lack of focus. Beginning in the late 1960s, it had kept expanding its agenda until its identity and purpose had become blurred.

There were two constants in the history of the Conference. From the time it was organized in the 1940s, the Allegheny Conference was committed to the public-private partnership as the instrument of effective change in Pittsburgh. This concept would subsequently permeate the local civic culture and influence the creation of economic development coalitions in other communities. A study of urban development and local business leaders in 1977 found that the redevelopment of Pittsburgh's Golden Triangle "became a model for other cities. Philadelphia, Baltimore, Wilmington, Syracuse, St. Louis, Cleveland, and Detroit, among others, have launched their own versions of the Pittsburgh Renaissance and have adopted the Allegheny Conference as a model for the formation of a public-private partnership."[63] Cleveland Tomorrow, organized in 1982, was very similar in program and organization to the Conference; it consisted of the chief executive officers of local corporations who operated by consensus and, as was always the case with the Conference, could not send substitutes to meetings.[64] Thus the Allegheny Conference was the original prototype for what later would be termed the "corporatist decision-making structure" (the accommodation of politics and economics in a single coalition), or the "new convergence" of local government, business elites, and professional staffs working on behalf of economic growth.[65]

A second source of continuity in the history of the Conference has been a commitment to downtown renewal and improvement. This largely shaped the Conference's agenda and identity during Renaissance I. Park Martin, its first executive director, described the challenge confronting the newly established public-private partnership:

> But the town was run down, its atmosphere was dirty and almost repellent to many people. . . . The waterfronts were not improved to any great extent. There had been no new office buildings built for twenty-five years. The tax base was falling. The assessed valuations in the Triangle were declining quite materially and the future did not appear bright."[66]

John J. Grove, appointed assistant director of the Allegheny Conference in 1952, declared that the "really exciting aspect of the Pittsburgh Renaissance was the rejuvenation and revitalization of the downtown area, and this *was done with purpose and intent, it wasn't an accident by any means.*" Former Mayor Joseph Barr, in a 1972 interview, agreed with the priorities of the Conference. It was right, he argued, "in doing the project downtown before the others because that got a lot of tax money in and you never could have moved the neighborhoods unless you did downtown first."[67] Embodied in the Conference's dedication to the Golden Triangle was an implicit urban theory (along with the element of self-interest)—that a city depended upon the concentrated resources of a flourishing downtown for its economic and cultural progress.

Despite the expanded and diffused agenda that the Conference would develop after 1968, it never abandoned the downtown custodianship. Although the Conference in the 1970s had cooperated with the Flaherty administration in pushing forward the Convention Center, the relationship had soured over Flaherty's indifference to downtown development and the fight over skybus. With the ascension of Caliguiri, the "traditional pattern of cooperation" was restored.[68] Symbolic of the restoration, and of the Conference's role as catalyst, was its initiative in the Grant Street reconstruction program. It had solicited foundation funding for consultants and, in a 1978 report, proposed the transformation of this major downtown artery into a "stately 'Grand Boulevard' that could serve as a model for other downtown street improvements."[69] Conference staff and city officials reviewed the plans, and the Conference volunteered to try to raise $750,000 in private contributions for landscaping in addition to city expenditures.

The Grant Street project signified a new direction in the Conference's downtown strategy. It had been identified in Renaissance I with large-scale improvements—smoke and flood control, Gateway Center, Point Park, parkways, the abortive Lower Hill cultural acropolis. During Renaissance II, however, it turned to the "streetscapes and public spaces that do so much to determine the flavor of a city" and to cultural development. Thus in the early 1980s it collaborated with the URA in planning for Market Square redevelopment as well as the North Shore's Allegheny Landing riverfront park; and it sponsored a report proposing improvements for Mellon Square Park—the Smithfield Street oasis of cascading waterfalls, sculpture, and plantings that was a legacy of Renaissance I (for which it helped raise funds). Such quality of life improvements were considered necessary to the creation of a modernized, competitive post-steel economy.[70]

When Robert Pease became executive director of the Allegheny Conference staff in 1968, however, the most pressing issue was not economic development or quality of life, but civil and social turbulence. Originally from Nebraska, Pease received an engineering degree from CMU in 1949 under the GI Bill. Hired by the university, he worked on construction plans and then joined the URA in 1953. His responsibilities there included the Lower Hill and Children's Hospital projects. He then served as the URA's executive director (1958–1968). He believes that the suffering he witnessed in North Africa during the war precipitated a sensitivity to human and social issues, and he guided the Allegheny Conference toward a new social agenda that addressed itself to the black community, education, health, and, by the mid-1980s, community organization in the Mon Valley. The crabby relations with the Flaherty administration also encouraged a move toward a social program.[71]

In 1968 the Conference created Employment, Economic Development and Education Committees. In conjunction with the Pittsburgh branch of the National Alliance of Businessmen, the Employment Committee pursued job opportunities for the "disadvantaged, chronically unemployed." In later years, the Conference helped reorganize the Private Industry Council of Pittsburgh–Allegheny County, and cooperated with it in the development of training and employment programs (such as SWEEP, which helped disadvantaged high school students acquire job skills, or JOBSTART, which sought to educate and train dropouts age eighteen to twenty-two).

The Economic Development Committee initiated a Minority Entrepreneur Loan Program. Working in cooperation with Pittsburgh's major banks, the program between 1968 and 1973 provided nearly $14 million in loans or loan guarantees to 588 minority applicants seeking an opportunity to become entrepreneurs. During the same period, the Conference supplied staff assistance to more than 200 organizations involved in human services or social action.[72] Both the minority entrepreneurship and human services activities were funded though a Conference Special Fund established in 1968 with contributions from corporations, foundations, and individuals.

The Conference Education Committee financed a pilot program in repair skills for the unemployed at Goodwill Industries and worked with the Board of Education to develop programs that would link the schools and business community as well as improve teacher performance. A major commitment to education occurred in 1978 when the Conference established an Education Fund. It initially supported a Mini-Grant Program that encouraged teachers to undertake curriculum improvements; a Partnerships-in-Education Program designed to link local businesses with schools; and an educator-in-residence plan to bring distinguished educators to the city. A Grants-to-Principals Program was added to encourage schoolwide innovation. In 1981 the Conference funded a review of school arts programs and prepared a community art resources directory in the hope of developing a coordinated and comprehensive arts curriculum. In 1985, the Conference organized an urban math collaborative funded by the Ford Foundation; this involved a collaborative effort among the Pittsburgh school district, businesses, and universities to improve the skills of math teachers.[73] The Conference also helped launch a McKeesport Education Fund that in 1987 evolved into the Mon Valley Education Consortium. Some of the Conference's educational initiatives aroused national interest. The Ford Foundation requested it to prepare a handbook to assist localities to develop teacher grant programs, and the Conference's Education Fund led to a national organization based in Pittsburgh known as the Public Education Fund.

The Conference agenda broadened in 1980 when it added health care. In cooperation with foundations, corporations, and the University of Pittsburgh's School of Public Health, it launched a Health Policy Institute to conduct research on the cost and quality of health care in Western Pennsylvania. Early studies included hospital utilization and the implications for health care of the region's aging population. The research was oriented to administrators and others who could improve the delivery of health services. In addition, the Conference participated in organizing the Pittsburgh Business Group on Health in 1981—an association of health service purchasers seeking ways to maintain quality and control costs. Also oriented to cost containment was the Pittsburgh Program for Affordable Health Care. Organized under Conference leadership, it brought together labor, business, health care, and community representatives to explore ways to reduce in-patient hospitals stays, provide the aged with community-based services in lieu of institutionalization, and encourage hospitals to eliminate excess capacity.

Around 1980, the Conference defined a new area of social concern: "community revitalization—the preservation and renewal of urban residential areas and neighborhood business districts."[74] It became the conduit for matching funds from the New York–based Local Initiatives Support Corporation (LISC) to support neighborhood development organizations. LISC-Pittsburgh funding, for example, enabled the Manchester Citizens' Corporation to rehabilitate more than seventy-five housing units. In 1985, the Conference dedicated half the funds to community organization in the Mon Valley, and in 1987 it organized the Mon Valley Development Team to help create community development corporations throughout the area. The rapid growth of these organizations led in 1988 to the establishment of the Mon Valley Initiative—a coalition (initially) of thirteen citizen-controlled development corporations.

As suggested earlier, the problem confronting the Conference by 1990 was not lack of accomplishment, but lack of focus. Conference President Vincent A. Sarni (chairman and CEO of PPG Industries), surveying the organization's prospects that year, declared that its strength had "been in its ability to convene local leadership to agree on a civic agenda, and then to build the will to implement solutions." But the increasing "diversity and fragmentation of interests" in the Pittsburgh area presented a challenge: "With so many new civic organizations, is there still an agenda for the Conference?"[75] What could the Conference contribute beyond what was offered by local government planning and development agencies, influential foundations like the those of the Heinz family or the Pittsburgh Foundation, the nonprofit advanced technology advocacy groups, or the Pittsburgh Cultural Trust? A new agenda was, in fact, defined between 1990 and 1992; it signified the most dramatic Conference reorientation since 1968 when director Pease expanded the emphasis on economics and downtown to include a diverse social program. Thus, the retirement of Robert Pease in 1990 had more than symbolic significance. Richard Stafford, his successor as executive director in 1991, would pursue a new regional planning policy that the Conference hoped would also maximize Western Pennsylvania's political resources.[76]

The Conference did not entirely lack a regional perspective prior to the 1980s; it was incorporated into its economic development and transportation goals. The Regional Industrial Development Corporation (1955) and Penn's Southwest (1972) encompassed nine counties and expressed an early commitment to diversification of the regional economy. Improving the transportation infrastructure was always essential to the Conference's economic development objectives. By 1973 it was already advocating a regional transportation policy; the Pittsburgh region "must have a 'catch up' game plan if it is to get a transportation system appropriate to the current year, let alone to the year 2000." In fact, the Conference defined transportation as "the region's most conspicuous public failure; the time lag in developing a transportation system that is within our technological capacity."[77] These aspirations help explain the infatuation with skybus and the bitterness engendered by the obstruction posed by the Flaherty administration.

The regional perspective embodied in the Conference's advocacy of transportation improvements intensified in the 1980s.[78] The economic development strategy of 1984 placed great emphasis upon the need to upgrade the entire regional infrastructure:

> The vitality of any region depends on its transportation systems, and Pittsburgh's roads, bridges, railroads, waterways, and airports, as well as its water and sewer facilities, need substantial improvement if they are to support a vigorous economy.[79]

To define priorities and funding possibilities in this area, the Conference created a Transportation Improvements Steering Committee in 1985.

The Allegheny Conference's evolving (but still undefined) regional agenda progressed in 1985–1987 when it midwifed the organization of Mon Valley community development corporations. More important, however, in expressing the emergent regional outlook was the Conference's participation in creating the Southwestern Pennsylvania Growth Alliance in 1989. This was a consortium of nine counties and nineteen representatives (two from each county and the mayor of Pittsburgh). Paralleling the Southwestern Regional Planning Commission (1962 successor to the Pittsburgh Regional Planning Association), the alliance was an advocacy organization designed to "serve as the consensual voice of the region in Harrisburg and Washington." Reporting to the Conference in 1991, Vincent Sarni advanced the regional blueprint further with proposals for a "regional human development corporation" and a strategy of functional cooperation to transcend the "fragmented and outdated local government systems now in place." Specifically, Sarni suggested adoption of the Pennsylvania Economy League's proposal for a "regional assets district" to support and develop recreational and cultural facilities.[80]

The Allegheny Conference and the Pennsylvania Economy League (Western Division) partially merged in the spring of 1992 in order to strengthen the organizational basis for regional advocacy. They maintained separate governing boards, but shared a single executive director (Stafford) as well as office facilities. The Economy League had been a key research and policy analyst for the Conference since its inception, and brought into the alliance a network of regional offices and county boards.[81] Along with the Economy League affiliation, the Conference participated in the formation of an Allegheny Policy Council on Youth and Workforce Development. This brought under one umbrella the Conference Education Fund and several other agencies. The intention to pursue the creation of a regional asset district was reaffirmed, and the Conference emphasized the need for regional alliances in order to achieve economic development and transportation goals (such as an airport-downtown transit corridor). Although the Conference joined with Pittsburgh and Allegheny County in submitting a fourth edition of Strategy 21, it anticipated a subsequent partnership with the Southwestern Pennsylvania Growth Alliance in preparing a regional Strategy 21.[82]

The Allegheny Conference in 1984 defined the economic development strategy that would characterize Pittsburgh in the post-steel era. Then, in the early 1990s, it redefined itself and actively advocated a regional consciousness in Western Pennsylvania—essential, according to Stafford, to enhancing the region's quality of life and its competitive position in a global economy. Prospective business investors and others, he suggested, possessed a de facto regional outlook; they considered the assets or liabilities of the region more than just a single community. But the Pittsburgh region, historically, has been notoriously fragmented. A multiplicity of political jurisdictions jealously guard their prerogatives. Within this framework, the city of Pittsburgh has been kept in a financial straightjacket by the state legislature. Although the city has experienced a drastic loss of population since the 1950s, and its tax base has been eroded by the departure of many corporations as well as taxpayers, the suburban- and rural-dominated state legislature guards against the city's attempts to tax nonresidents.

The regional asset district proposal represents, in part, an effort to break this impasse by providing a financing mechanism for recreational and cultural resources throughout the area—not just those in the city.[83] The funding of Pittsburgh's cultural facilities, meanwhile, became a critical issue as the mayor's office declared war in 1991 on the North Side Aviary, and subsequently, on Phipps Conservatory in Schenley Park, the Highland Park Zoo, and the Schenley Park golf course. From the administration's viewpoint, these are regional amenities and should not be so heavily subsidized by a revenue-starved city. By 1993, all these institutions had reorganized under nonprofit management (except for the zoo, which was scheduled for privatization).[84]

The first test of a regional asset district proposal in the state House of Representatives (November 1992) confirmed the absence of a regional consciousness sufficient to overcome the suburbs' aversion to being taxed by the city. The defeated measure would have authorized a 1 percent sales tax in the southwestern counties on top of the state's 6 percent tax; in Allegheny County, funds would have been divided between the city, county, and a regional assets district board. With the strong support of mayor-elect Murphy and the entire political and civic establishment of Pittsburgh, a Regional Assets District was approved by the state legislature in December 1993 that authorized a 1 percent sales tax for Allegheny County. Anticipated revenues of $106 million are to be divided equally among cultural institutions and city and county governments (who will have to reduce taxes by an equal amount).[85]

5

Pittsburgh Neighborhoods: A System of Subsidized Empowerment

Renaissance I was not neighborhood-oriented. It was dominated by smoke and flood control, highway improvement, downtown revitalization, industrial and institutional expansion. Large-scale neighborhood-based renewal projects such as Allegheny Center and Chateau Street (North Side), East Liberty Pedestrian Mall and Traffic Circle (East End), and the Civic Arena–Chatham Center in the Lower Hill (near downtown) suffered from the architectural and design flaws characteristic of the period nationally. The East Liberty project probably did not cause the decline of the business district, as often claimed, but hastened it by wrapping the area in a confusing mall and arterial road configuration. Neighborhood business districts were probably undermined less by renewal, however ill-conceived, than by the emergence of suburban shopping malls, as well as substantial depopulation, poverty, and crime.

The city later made amends and restored some of the original traffic patterns, according to the *Pittsburgh Post-Gazette*, so "bit by bit, East Liberty is trying to undo its 1960s face lift that community leaders say nearly destroyed the business district."[1] Ironically, the now much-maligned East Liberty project was the first to involve extensive citizen participation.[2]

Neighborhood passivity ended in the 1960s in a growing resistance to large-scale clearance as a means of neighborhood renovation. The civil rights movement was expressed, partly, in demands that predominantly

East Liberty Mall, 1970s. *Photo: Carnegie Library of Pittsburgh*

black neighborhoods—the Hill District, Manchester (North Side) and Homewood-Brushton (East End) acquire greater control over their destiny. ACTION-Housing launched its Neighborhood Urban Extension experiment in 1963. Going beyond earlier concepts of advisory citizen participation in urban renewal, the ACTION-Housing program, as conceived by James Cunningham and ACTION director Bernard Loshbough, aspired to "the conversion of the mass of apathetic urban dwellers into a fully participating citizenry, taking responsibility for their own environment—physical, economic, and social."[3] The emergence of historic preservation through the Pittsburgh History & Landmarks Foundation also contributed to neighborhood assertiveness in the 1960s and later.

Neighborhood consciousness and organization were stimulated by such federal initiatives as community action in the 1964 antipoverty program and the model cities program (1966). Mayor Joseph Barr's staff was quick to bring antipoverty funding to Pittsburgh. It helped that Barr was friendly with Lyndon Johnson and that David Lawrence, along with the Pittsburgh congressional delegation, had influence in the executive office.[4] Barr's assistant executive secretary, Morton Coleman, was given responsibility for organizing a planning coalition to develop an antipoverty program.[5] This led to the creation of the Mayor's Committee on Human Resources in 1964 (an independent, nonprofit agency). ACTION-Housing was chosen to coordinate antipoverty operations in four of the eight neighborhoods selected by the mayor's committee (Homewood-Brushton, Hazelwood-Glenwood, South Oakland, Lawrenceville); a settlement house directed the antipoverty strategy in each of the other four. The twenty-two-person board of the Mayor's Committee on Human Resources included a citizen representative from each neighborhood, and a citizen's committee (including the poor) in all neighborhoods participated in formulating and operating the program. Not surprisingly, ACTION-Housing's urban extension influenced the design of the antipoverty program and its community action component. Cunningham had participated in Coleman's task force, and urban extension had provided the only local experience in large-scale neighborhood organization.[6]

An offshoot of neighborhood assertiveness and antipoverty in the 1960s was the creation of Citizens Against Slum Housing (CASH). It was founded by Dorothy Richardson, a Northside resident, assisted by an organizer provided by the mayor's committee. CASH members traversed the eight poverty neighborhoods, investigating complaints about housing conditions. Protests were carried to the homes or offices of alleged slumlords. CASH advocacy led to the creation of a city Housing Court; its first magistrate, Sholom Comay, an attorney, had worked closely with Richardson.[7] This "new spirit of protest" dramatized the contradiction in ACTION-Housing's role as neighborhood organizer. The agency had, after all, been created by the Allegheny Conference, and it was controlled by the established corporate, civic, and political elite. But the "controversy and turmoil" surrounding neighborhood organization in the 1960s "spread consternation [among] many of the leaders of the Renaissance civic agencies and in the mayor's office." ACTION-Housing thus ended its participation in antipoverty and neighborhood organizing by 1967–1968.[8]

Meanwhile, Cunningham, who had been director of neighborhood programs at ACTION-Housing since 1959, left in 1966 to join the faculty of the University of Pittsburgh's School of Social Work. Coleman had arrived there a year earlier, although he served on a part-time basis until 1968. He continued to be the mayor's secretary for manpower retraining and poverty programs until 1966, and was responsible for developing the Model Cities program as well as the antipoverty program earlier. In 1967–1968, he became Barr's human resources coordinator.

At the School of Social Work, Coleman and Cunningham joined Meyer Schwartz, a social planner on the faculty. Schwartz was instrumental in developing a curriculum that emphasized training students in neighborhood organization.[9] David P. Epperson, who became dean of the School of Social Work in 1972, provided another link to the neighborhood organizing and antipoverty programs of the 1960s; he had succeeded David Hill, a lawyer, as director of the mayor's Committee on Human Resources (1967–1969). Finally, Roger Alhbrandt, who had been ACTION-Housing's director of research (1973–1976) also joined the Social Work faculty in 1976 and collaborated with Cunningham on a number of research projects designed to strengthen neighborhood life in the 1970s.[10]

These included the preparation of a Pittsburgh Neighborhood Atlas. This was sponsored in 1972–1973 by the Pittsburgh Neighborhood Alliance, a federation of thirty organizations formed in 1969 out of frustration over the unresponsiveness of city government to neighborhood concerns. Through Cunningham and Ahlbrandt, the University of Pittsburgh contributed significantly to the project. Cunningham was a member of the Neighborhood Alliance, and Ahlbrandt served on the governing board of the atlas. They enlisted the University Center for Urban Research and its Office of Urban and Community Services to join with the alliance in designing the Atlas methodology. Funded by a $5,000 grant from the university in the summer of 1973, a pilot study was done for the Garfield neighborhood. Combining survey information with research data, investigators developed an information system for defining the condition of a neighborhood. The indicators included transaction prices for residential real estate, tax delinquency on real estate assets, mortgage loans and building permits, and welfare assistance. Preparation of a citywide atlas began in January 1976 and was completed in June 1977. It encompassed seventy-eight neighborhoods (the City Planning Department in 1990 counted ninety neighborhoods) and was distinctive in combining hard data with attitudinal information.

The atlas project, involving widespread citizen participation, helped maintain the momentum of the neighborhood movements begun in the 1960s. Cunningham and Ahlbrandt expected that neighborhood groups, armed with more exact information than ever before, could organize effectively and deal more confidently with city government. They also anticipated that municipal agencies would benefit by incorporating the expanded data base into their service system. Not least, the atlas might contribute to the neighborhood empowerment that Cunningham hoped would emerge from a new city charter.[11]

Pennsylvania had enacted home rule legislation in 1972 authorizing election of local charter commissions. Pittsburgh's neighborhood groups and other civic organizations petitioned to have the issue of home rule placed before the electorate. Following approval by the City Council, the referendum and election of the eleven commissioners were set for the November 1972 general election. Overwhelmingly approved by the voters, the City Government Study Commission appointed Cunningham as its executive director. Extensive yearlong public hearings were held beginning in the fall of 1972, and a charter discussion draft was released in September 1973.[12]

Cunningham viewed the Charter Commission as an instrument through which citizens could "gain access to and participate in our city government." Urban renewal projects of the 1950s, he believed, revealed the consequences "when local government operates without formal communication and access" and people had "no way to get up close to the decisions that drastically affected their lives."[13] The discussion draft, accordingly, contained several proposals to bring participatory democracy to Pittsburgh:

- Expand City Council from nine members (elected at large) to eleven (nine elected by district).

- Increase the authority of the city controller to enable him to act as an ombudsman.

- Enable city residents to hold a public meeting with the mayor if a petition is presented with fifty qualified signatures.

- Enable city residents to require a public hearing on any pending City Council ordinance or resolution following a petition signed by at least twenty-five voters.

- Permit the voters of any neighborhood or district of 10,000 to 60,000 population to elect a Neighborhood Study Commission to prepare a plan for a Neighborhood Service Board that would advise city government concerning social and physical conditions or development proposals, and could veto any city recreation program for the neighborhood.

Of these proposals for increased citizen access to city government, only two survived to be included in the new charter, which took effect in January 1976. One was the prerogative of any twenty-five citizens to request a hearing concerning pending council legislation. The other was the provision for Neighborhood Service Boards which, in fact, never came into existence. Neither the Democratic party establishment nor business interests were keen on the prospect of a new and unpredictable force in city government.[14] Others, like Robert Pease, objected to the clutter that would result from requiring the mayor and council to respond to easily obtained petitions, and to the parochialism inherent in district election of council.[15]

At ACTION-Housing, Cunningham had helped develop Pittsburgh's first model of comprehensive neighborhood organization, one that involved both extensive citizen participation and service delivery. From 1966 to the present, he has helped train a generation of community organizers at the University of Pittsburgh School of Social Work. He has advised numerous community groups and has sought to promote neighborhood organization and consciousness through projects like the Neighborhood Atlas and Charter Commission of the 1970s. His neighborhood theory has combined a strain of utopian idealism and earthbound practicality. The former, fortunately, has been peripheral, more rhetorical than operational: "Our God-given dignity is maintained, not through the pursuit of pleasure, but through service to other human beings. When we say that the neighborhood is the center of social life, we mean that for many of us our opportunities to respond to other people's needs arise largely in the daily life of neighborhood community."[16] In the same vein, Cunningham would like to believe that if citizens are consulted and educated about issues, then goodwill, rationality, and benign outcomes are likely to prevail in urban life.[17]

For the most part, however, Cunningham recognized that neighborhood organization has more to do with self-interest, coalition building, focused issues, and power relationships than with the spirit of service to others. The ultimate purpose is to endow ordinary citizens with a measure of self-determination and a sense of control over their own destiny. In the absence of participatory democracy, there is alienation and anomie. History, according to Cunningham, was largely a story of elite domination, or an ongoing struggle between the elite and commoners for control. The latter had to organize in order to "assert interests which have been neglected through the years." Mobilization should occur at the level of the block and neighborhood where a countervailing power could be created.[18]

There is, however, a dilemma inherent in any theory that sees neighborhood organization as an antidote to powerlessness and alienation: given the increasing tendency of the federal government to ooze over the life of the society under one pretext or another, given its remoteness and given the inability of individual citizens to avoid its impositions, how do neighborhood advocates respond to policies that expand the authority of the federal leviathan at the expense of localities and neighborhoods? In June 1993, for example, the Pittsburgh mayor's office decreed that the 1988 amendments to the federal Fair Housing Amendments Act required a redefinition of the zoning law controlling single-family residences. The definition of *family* would be changed to include "two or more persons with disabilities . . . who need not be related by blood or marriage or adoption, living together as a single housekeeping unit." If enacted, the zoning revision would virtually abolish the power of City Council to control the placement of group homes in residential districts. In any case, it demonstrates how the federal government can inhibit the autonomy of communities and neighborhoods. Alcoholism and drug addiction, of course, are included in the expansive federal definition of disability. Indeed, the Clinton administration, acting through HUD, seems to have instituted a police state–style enforcement of the Fair Housing Act, attempting to stifle citizen protest against the location of group homes for various varieties of "disabled." The bureaucratic zealots in Secretary Cisnero's HUD apparently skipped class when the First Amendment was discussed.[19]

In another vein, the Southwestern Pennsylvania Growth Alliance complained that "the federal and state governments, through legislation and regulation, mandate specific actions by local and county governments. These mandates, often not accompanied by the funding necessary to implement them, can pose an onerous burden on local and county governments." The commission cites environmental regulations, the Americans with Disabilities Act, low-income impact requirements in community development and other programs, bridge design requirements. It seems, for the most part, that local communities and neighborhood advocates take what they can get and ignore the broader issues of federalism and freedom.[20]

The Shadyside Action Coalition (SAC), established in 1973, exemplified for a time Cunningham's concept of neighborhood as a foundation for citizen activism. A coalition of thirty-four organizations, churches, and block clubs, the SAC "sought to be the instrument through which Shadyside could control its own destiny, mainly by generating sufficient power to influence forces such as government planners, larger property investors, banks and school boards." Its early success hinged, to a large degree, on avoiding mushy idealism in favor of aggressive mobilization around selected concrete issues. One of the first, and most contentious, was a successful three-year battle against the Fantastic Plastic night club. Prevented from acquiring a liquor or dance permit, the club was forced to close. To strengthen and dramatize its case, whatever the issue, the SAC thoroughly researched the facts and tried to identify an "enemy." This would, ideally, be some impersonal external institution (like Mellon Bank in connection with Fantastic Plastic). For Cunningham and Milton Kotler, the SAC and its counterparts in other neighborhoods and communities demonstrated that "city governments can and will respond to organized groups of neighborhood people . . . and that influence with city government gives a neighborhood organization some control over economic forces."[21]

Although Cunningham had become disillusioned with the federal antipoverty program as early as 1967—the Office of Economic Opportunity (OEO) had started out "brash and cocky" but "aged early and retired into a comfortable system of deals with mayors and prepackaged programs"—he concluded that the federal government should nonetheless create an agency to nurture "local democracy."[22] This would be something like a federal Office of Citizen Participation. The logic seemed to be that local democracy would flourish if clasped in a federal bear hug.

Meyer Schwartz had also been critical of OEO-inspired community organization: "Whatever the rhetoric of the Anti-Poverty Program may have been in the past three years," he declared in a 1967 speech, "it cannot by its very nature be *other than a coalition of City Hall, the established agencies and organizations, and lower middle class and middle class leadership in the neighborhoods.*" A somewhat anachronistic voice of 1930s-style radicalism, drenched in the rhetoric of class conflict, Schwartz in 1967 portrayed the trickle-down economics of Renaissance I in barnyard language—"harsh as it is to say so, the poor, the black and white sparrows, get what the horses leave on the ground." The effective assertion of the interests of the poor, Schwartz maintained, required an independent mechanism of advocacy and technical support for indigenous organizations. This would enable the poor to avoid cooptation and pursue their *"naked self-interests"* (though on the higher moral plane of equal opportunity and justice).[23]

As counterpoint to the technical and planning resources of the corporate sector embodied in the Allegheny Conference, Schwartz proposed the establishment, possibly under university auspices, of a Center for the City and Region. This would act as an advocate, strategist, and technical resource for those indigenous organizations representing the true interests of the poor. The future might even witness the emergence of a local Peoples' Conference on Community Development that would be "a match for the Allegheny Conference on Community Development." In short, idealism and commitment would not suffice to achieve social justice; they had to be supported by "organizational and technical know-how."[24]

More moderate and practical-minded than some of their rhetoric might suggest, neither Cunningham nor Schwartz reflected a 1960s New Left concept of community organizing. In a latter-day (1980s) expression of New Left hallucination, Robert Fisher, author of *Let the People Decide: Neighborhood Organizing in America*, minimizes self-interest in neighborhood organization compared to a "class- or race-based vision of something worth fighting for which was larger and more important than simply member self-interest." In fact, the larger purpose would be defeated if neighborhood groups were successful in winning services and material rewards because such progress would *"undermine* the organizing by 'proving' that the existing system is responsive to poor and working people and, therefore, in no need of fundamental change." Neighborhood was not even a basis for meaningful change in a society whose political and economic structure could not respond to concerns rooted in the sacred trilogy of race, class, gender. What was needed, therefore, was a "federated national organizing or national political coalition, noncapitalist and egalitarian in vision, formed and guided from above and below."[25]

Although Cunningham and Schwartz recognized that neighborhood organization would require external support, it would come from neither a federal agency nor a local "people's conference." It would develop in the spirit of Ben Franklin, whom Daniel Boorstin called "the man with a business sense and an eye on his community. For Franklin, doing good was not a private act between bountiful giver and grateful receiver; it was a prudent social act."[26] An elaborate national and local machinery of governmental, foundation, and corporate patronage has evolved to provide financial and technical assistance to neighborhood groups. The favored form of neighborhood organization is the community development corporation (CDC) in Pittsburgh and elsewhere. Both the CDC and its support system make clear the commanding role of nonprofit organizations in shaping contemporary social and cultural policy. National and local foundations, in particular, have became a major force for community development in the last quarter century. Answerable neither to voters nor shareholders, they can innovate, experiment, subsidize, or penalize with relative freedom.[27]

Although many community development corporations provide social services, their distinctive feature has been neighborhood housing betterment and economic revitalization. Housing has been the most common enterprise, supplemented by commercial and industrial development. The idea of a neighborhood organization taking the form of a legal corporation for purposes of economic development emerged in the 1960s, supported by federal antipoverty "special impact" funds and the Ford Foundation. The latter, in 1968, launched a social investment experiment whose major beneficiary was the Bedford-Stuyvesant Restoration Corporation in New York City—the prototype community development corporation. In the late sixties and seventies, the Ford Foundation would pour more than $100 million into community development.[28] The most significant Ford Foundation undertaking, however, was the creation of the Local Initiatives Support Corporation (LISC) in 1979–1980.[29] A year later James Rouse formed his Enterprise Foundation to support neighborhood development. Thus a potent national machinery emerged in the early 1980s to funnel vast foundation and corporate funding into local CDC networks. This would be supplemented by such national advocacy organizations as the National Congress for Community Economic Development and the Council for Community Based Development.

Rouse's Enterprise Corporation cooperated with more than 130 neighborhood organizations in 60 cities over the decade, helping to produce or rehabilitate some 14,500 housing units. It provided technical and financial assistance, including loans and grants. Influential in the founding of the Enterprise Foundation was the example of Jubilee Housing in Washington, D.C. It had rehabilitated two apartment buildings for low-income families and provided them with a support system. Rouse saw this as a model for a national network of neighborhood groups.[30]

The Jubilee Housing model, combining low-income housing development with social services, was exemplified in the Enterprise Foundation's ambitious Neighborhood Transformation Demonstration Program, launched in Baltimore in 1990. Working closely with Mayor Kurt L. Schmoke (elected in 1987), the foundation hoped to transform the blighted Sandtown-Winchester neighborhood on the west side of the city. An area of seventy-two square blocks with a population of 12,000, it was an archetype of inner-city decay by every statistical measure: with 44 percent unemployment, 40 percent of households on welfare, and the out-of-wedlock birth rate at 90 percent, it was among the city's highest crime areas and had hundreds of vacant dwellings. Besides working closely with the Schmoke administration, the Enterprise Foundation sought the cooperation of residents and two organizations. The New Song Community, an urban ministry of the Presbyterian Church, established a clinic, day care center, and after-school programs. Habitat for Humanity managed housing rehabilitation and sales (230 two-story row houses by 1992). The experiment included other services—job training, employment counseling, substance addiction treatment—hoping to attain a high degree of coordination among them.[31]

The already formidable resources of the Enterprise Foundation and the Local Initiatives Support Corporation swelled in 1990 as a result of the National Community Development Initiative. Seven foundations and corporations pledged $62.5 million to the two organizations. They would, in turn, distribute the funds to local community development corporations, leveraging (it was hoped) at least $500 million more and producing 7,500 housing units in twenty cities.[32]

The emergence of neighborhood CDCs in the last quarter century and the creation of national and local machinery for their support—financial and technical—has been a significant episode in the evolution of American social welfare. The CDC has been a vessel through which city government, corporations, and foundations have sought to influence

urban and social policy and, in particular, the mainstream of neighborhood or community citizen organization. CDCs depended upon external
funding and technical assistance, and by providing such aid the funding
agencies could nurture the spread of a new kind of social agency, one
that had to subscribe to business and market disciplines. Corporation
and foundation boards could feel comfortable with businesslike rationality in neighborhood organization. At the same time, the CDC movement could help train a corps of neighborhood workers in the skills
necessary for economic development and thus provide leadership for a
business-oriented strategy of urban revitalization. The result, according
to the development director of Pittsburgh's Bloomfield-Garfield Corporation, was the creation of "hybrid organizations" that "could elude
the grasp of governmental paternalism and forge an unlikely partnership
rooted in enlightened self-interest."[33]

Not least, the effectiveness of community development corporations
in revitalizing a local economy offered a great advantage over conventional redistributive welfare. Welfare generates widespread resentment
because of the ostensible lack of tangible benefits to society. In retrospect,
one looks back enviously to the New Deal relief programs that contributed so tremendously to the nation's infrastructure and its cultural capital. Similarly, the economic development function of the CDC gives its
sponsors material, measurable results in the form of housing and new
business enterprises. Thus the CDC contrasts with conventional welfare
or social service delivery systems where the return to society, if any, is
less visible and their efforts might even be seen as subsidizing undesirable
behavior. As Robert L. Woodson, founder and president of the National
Center for Neighborhood Enterprise, put it in 1992:

> Jesse Jackson doesn't get it. Neither do the mayors who marched on Wash-
> ington last month [May 1992], demanding more funds for cities. The an-
> swer . . . is a clear one, and one that is being voiced with astounding unity
> by citizens at our grass roots . . . "Don't send us social programs, send us
> capital."
>
> Rather than asking how many programs we have funded, we should ask
> how many new small businesses have come into being and how many new
> homeowners exist because of what we have done.

Woodson pointed to the strategy devised by Detroit's Twelfth Street
Baptist Church as an example of how development could thwart even

the drug pestilence. It created a company, Reach, Inc., which purchased crack houses and forced dealers to evacuate: "And, as those properties were renovated, job opportunities became available for community residents. Reach then sold the renovated properties to members of the congregation who needed housing." This contrasted sharply with the welfare paradigm that "focused on serving deficiencies, not buttressing capacities."[34]

Paul S. Grogan, president of LISC, compared the grass-roots economic development and self-help character of the community development corporation against the simple-minded and ineffectual guilt-stricken liberalism that followed Miami's Liberty City riots of 1980. The Miami Chamber of Commerce established a Business Assistance Center to support minority entrepreneurship. But millions in valuable capital were wasted, thanks to "unsound proposals made by blacks whose political ties were stronger than neighborhood ties." This top-down paternalism was succeeded by a neighborhood-centered strategy of community development embodied in the Tacolcy Economic Development Corporation; "visions of overnight transformation were replaced by a program that stressed creation of the community's own capacity to direct renewal and take responsibility for the results." In 1985, Tacolcy's Edison Plaza opened (with supermarket); other businesses and hundreds of housing units followed.[35]

Those who granted funds to community development corporations hoped they would provide neighborhoods with a mechanism to counteract disinvestment. They promised a greater measure of self-determination, initiative, and accomplishment, rather than a welfare or social service benefit. In addition, the CDC strategy was congenial to corporate and foundation funders because it reflected entrepreneurial and business values and produced visible, three-dimensional results. Not least, CDCs made it more likely that neighborhood or community organizations could be nudged toward a partnership, toward symbiotic rather than adversarial relations. No other concept of community organization linked citizens with leaders of city government, corporations, and foundations so effectively.

But CDC advocacy, such as Grogan's, can veer toward utopian expectations, creating a potential for disillusionment. CDCs are not all-purpose panaceas and, judging from the experience of New York and other large cities (Chicago, Philadelphia, Atlanta, Washington, D.C.), can become enmeshed in political and ethnic corruption. The result is "financial scams, cronyism and sheer ineptitude" and the transformation of the CDC into a latter-day patronage machine. Critics have been quick to attack.

> The money in New York . . . has established what amounts to a fourth level of government, one that operates in many ways like government did a hundred years ago, without civil service tests, employee or vendor background checks, or ethics or bidding regulations. . . .
>
> The flow of billions of dollars to not-for-profits, operating in the poorest parts of the city, shifts political power to those who control their operations. The money translates into jobs and contracts that can support patronage empires comparable to those historically controlled by political clubhouses.[36]

What is suggested by this sorry spectacle, worthy of Tom Wolfe's *Bonfire of the Vanities*, is that competence is more important than democracy or representativeness for CDCs, and that external monitoring is vital.

According to a 1991 survey by the National Congress for Community Economic Development, about 2,000 community development corporations existed. Housing was the preeminent activity (88 percent), and CDCs had produced almost 320,000 units. Twenty-five percent were involved in commercial activities. The majority of CDCs, it is important to note, were also involved to some degree in conventional advocacy and service activities: homeowner and renter counseling, accommodations for the homeless, emergency food distribution, job training and placement, health care, teen pregnancy counseling, youth and aged services, antidrug and pregnancy counseling.[37]

As suggested earlier, the national intermediary organizations—the Enterprise Foundation and LISC—had been significant in the surge of the CDC to prominence in 1980s. The Ford Foundation, joined by six corporations, was the catalyst in the creation of the Local Initiatives Support Corporation in 1979–1980. Ford contributed half of the $9.5 million starting capital. By 1984, it had provided an additional $20 million.[38] Equally important, LISC was an outcome of Ford Foundation experience in supporting CDCs in the 1960s and 1970s.

> The local independent CDC had proved to be a powerful vehicle with which to draw new private and public resources into neighborhood revitalization

and to do so without squeezing out the poor or neglecting the values that attract and hold middle-income people.[39]

The favorable response of corporations and foundations to the LISC strategy of urban revitalization was expressed in generous funding; $70 million from 262 corporations, foundations, and other sources by 1984. LISC was now involved with 272 community development corporations in 93 communities (representing 132 housing, 76 commercial, and 36 industrial projects).[40] Like the Enterprise Foundation, LISC took advantage of the Low Income Housing Tax Credit of 1986, which allowed corporations to invest in rental projects. It created a National Equity Fund in late 1987 to pool business capital for nonprofit rental housing.[41] A significant new initiative announced by LISC in September 1994 was the commitment of ten national corporations (including Bank of America and Prudential) to a $24 million fund to aid CDCs in building retail shopping centers anchored by a supermarket.

By 1990, LISC had become a social investment agency of colossal proportions. It had raised more than $460 million from over 700 corporations and foundations, had assisted 777 CDCs, and helped leverage $1.6 billion of additional funding. The outcome was not only 28,800 housing units and 6.4 million square feet of commercial space, but also the nurture of "indigenous talent, leadership and influence."[42]

LISC operated through so-called areas of concentration (meaning communities) with an advisory committee representing local donors in each vicinity. The committees and community development corporations worked with a LISC program officer to develop proposals for the New York–based LISC board of directors. The board considered only projects recommended by the advisory committee and required that LISC funds be matched by local donors.[43] LISC recognized that a program of grants or loans limited to economic development would not ensure the success of the CDC as "quite simply the most promising antipoverty effort in America today."[44] It was necessary to nurture leaders with business sense who could win the confidence of corporations and foundations. Accordingly, LISC provided grants for staff and management development and in 1988 had launched a Neighborhood Development Support Collaborative in Boston. This provided intensive operations training, as well as operating funds, to five CDCs in that city (expanded to ten in 1989). Another major training experiment undertaken in Los Angeles reversed the CDC process and trained social service executives in the skills needed to build affordable housing. Supported by four California foundations, the program paired executives from thirteen agencies with housing experts.[45]

By the late 1980s, LISC was evolving toward a broader conception of neighborhood reconstruction and the community development corporation's role: "Physical rebuilding is a catalyst in altering the behavior and the expectations of individuals and institutions. But lasting change is based on more than renovated buildings." Social and public services, jobs and economic opportunities were "all part of reconstructing neighborhoods." East Harlem's HOPE Community, Inc., exemplified this broader, "multifaceted" kind of CDC.[46] Seemingly intractable problems like drug addiction, gang violence, and crime, and an epidemic of out-of-wedlock births undoubtedly contributed to this acknowledgment of the need for services as well as development.[47]

A Pittsburgh social movement of the 1960s was a bridge to community-driven rather than downtown-driven revitalization. This was the Neighborhood Housing Services (NHS) established on the North Side in 1968. NHS attempted to arrest neighborhood disinvestment and deterioration by linking homeowners, financial institutions, and local government in a comprehensive housing program. The program assisted homeowners in rehabilitating homes and worked for enforcement of housing codes and improved public services. The federal government promoted the program in other communities, establishing a Neighborhood Reinvestment Corporation in 1978. By 1980, a NHS program had been established in about 100 neighborhoods nationally.[48]

The federal Housing Act of 1954 (and subsequent legislation) had mandated that enforcing building codes should be part of a workable program, but it was not until the creation of NHS that code enforcement became the nucleus of neighborhood revitalization. The Sarah Scaife Foundation, beginning in 1968, provided the capital for the NHS revolving fund, which supplied the riskier loans and made stricter code enforcement feasible. Ironically, Pittsburgh's North Side, a victim of old-style demolition renewal, now became the laboratory for renewal by conservation, rehabilitation, and preservation. Supplementing the rehabilitation efforts of NHS in the central North Side beginning in the late 1960s were experiments in neighborhood revitalization (the Manchester section, the picturesque Mexican War streets) initiated by the Pittsburgh History & Landmarks Foundation. The implications of the neighborhood-saving efforts of these two organizations was profound: they nurtured the idea that renewal could occur without destroying the physical and social fabric of older, historic neighborhoods, and without the trauma of large-scale relocation.

The emergence of NHS also testified to the need for citizen initiative and involvement in reversing neighborhood decline. Operating through numerous civic organizations by the 1970s—NHS, Citizens Against Slum Housing, the Central North Side Neighborhood Council, North Side Civic Development Council—citizens were determined that the area would not be redeveloped out of existence, as had been proposed in a 1954 city master plan. According to Roger Ahlbrandt and Paul Brophy, the central North Side cycle of decline was reversed, and the area experienced significant improvement in several dimensions during the 1968–1974 period: property values and private sector investment increased, income levels rose, and property owners reinvested more than previously.[49]

By the time NHS was established in 1968, a network of neighborhood organizations had come into existence in Pittsburgh, and the Barr administration took the first (token) steps toward including them in the

North Side demolition for East Street Valley Expressway, 1972: neighborhoods in ruins.
Photo: Author

government process. The City Planning Department had begun preparation of a federally mandated Community Renewal Program in early 1961, which led to the division of the city into five planning districts. In each, an area committee was organized consisting of representatives of neighborhood organizations. Their purpose was to advise city planners as they developed renewal plans.

A Social Planning Advisory Committee was also established in May 1962 as part of the city's Community Renewal Program. It strongly endorsed citizen participation in planning and renewal, as well as the obligation of government agencies "to work with citizens in the development and the execution of planning programs."[50] But while the committee maintained that the government should encourage citizen organization, it insisted that financial and organizing assistance be provided through private sources to protect the independence of citizen groups. At least twenty-seven neighborhood civic and business organizations existed by the fall of 1963—before the stimulus provided by ACTION-Housing's Urban Extension (1963) and Community Action (1964); and they convened in September to form a citywide Community Organizations of Pittsburgh.[51]

In 1970, the Flaherty administration created a Community Planning Division within the Planning Department. Seven community planners were assigned to districts, where they served as technical advisers and advocates for neighborhood interests[52]—and provided a buffer for Mayor Flaherty, who did not wish to be viewed as captive to neighborhoods any more than to downtown interests.[53] Along with community planners (abolished by the Masloff administration in 1992 as an economy move), Flaherty increased spending for neighborhood improvements and redesigned the capital budgeting process in the early 1970s. The yearly capital budget would now be prepared by the City Planning Department within the framework of a six-year capital development plan (also prepared yearly by the Planning Department) in which neighborhood improvements were clearly itemized.[54] As the department's deputy director for transportation and community planning, 1975–1984, Raymond L. Reaves supervised both the neighborhood planners and capital budget and development process. Reaves became director of the Allegheny County Planning Department in 1984.

As a result of Flaherty's initiatives, the neighborhoods were firmly established as an interest group constellation that city government had to consult (no doubt partly because it was mandated by federal Community Development Block Grant requirements). They were now represented through their organizations, the City Planning Department's community planners, and the capital budgeting process. Equally important, whereas the Barr administration in the 1960s had concentrated city and federal resources on the eight poverty neighborhoods, Flaherty's programs encompassed all neighborhoods.[55] This fact helped moderate the resentment that had emerged in white ethnic neighborhoods by the late 1960s over their exclusion from the largesse bestowed by Community Action and Model Cities.[56] Still, for Richard Swartz and other exponents of the reality, not the facade, of neighborhood power, Flaherty, like his predecessors,

> was still wedded to the notion that technical expertise could only be found in government-controlled organizations and initiatives. The proposition that such expertise might be nurtured in community organizations themselves was viewed by many at the URA and City Planning to be a fantastic notion, a sentiment that would prevail through the end of the decade.[57]

In the ten years after Caliguiri became mayor in 1977, a combination of pressure from neighborhood groups, the availability of federal block grant funds, the initiatives of national and local foundations, and the need to develop a neighborhood economic development strategy would lead to the emergence of a community development corporation network and increased city funding for neighborhood organizations. One of the most important neighborhood organizations to emerge was the Working Group on Community Development in 1983. It was created following workshops sponsored by LISC and the recently organized Community Technical Assistance Center (CTAC). The workshops had "allowed neighborhood groups and representatives from the City, the private sector and foundations to get away together" and discuss the prospects for neighborhood-based community development in Pittsburgh.[58] These workshops, followed by the establishment of the Working Group, helped educate the leadership of the CDCs and create a sense of common purpose. David Brewton of Breachmenders, Inc., for example, first grasped the potentialities of community-based development as a result of the workshops and his participation in the Working Group.[59]

The Working Group became a strong and effective advocate of city funding for CDCs and other neighborhood organizations. It also urged that public officials consider the implications of policy decisions for the city neighborhoods. Strategy 21, university research, advanced technology, suburban industrial parks, the explosive growth of the North Hills and western airport corridor either drained population and business from the city or failed to "ensure that benefits go to low and moderate income families or accrue to distressed neighborhoods." It was imperative, according to the Working Group, that neighborhood revitalization be incorporated into the city's economic development strategy.

> It means continued concentrated investment in streets and sidewalks, retaining walls, sewer lines, water lines and other public infrastructure. It means delivering City services effectively. It means the encouraging of entrepreneurial activities in neighborhood commercial areas. . . . Investment of public dollars must return benefits to low and moderate income persons and to needy neighborhoods.[60]

The neighborhoods had not been incorporated into the post-steel economic development strategy, yet they could not be allowed to sink as a result of population loss, disinvestment, ghost town commercial centers, deteriorated and abandoned housing, crime, or the incursions of the underclass. Advocates and funders of the CDC hoped it would contribute significantly to neighborhood revitalization, thus compensating for a conspicuous oversight in post-steel economic development strategy.

James Cunningham discerned a "communal power model for the future" coming not from the CDC but from the coalition of labor, neighborhood groups, churches, city and middle-class professionals who fought to save the East Liberty Nabisco plant in the fall of 1982. They formed the Save Nabisco Action Coalition, which threatened a national boycott of Nabisco Brands, USA, solicited support from city government, pressured local banking interests involved with Nabisco, and enjoyed local and national media coverage. The campaign was successful: Nabisco dropped its plans to close the plant, saving 650 jobs. The episode suggested to Cunningham that jobs as well as neighborhoods could be a basis for effective community organization.[61]

There was a second, more ambitious, labor and community-based effort in the early 1990s to save the jobs of Braun Bakery workers by financing their effort to establish a new City Pride Bakery. The failure, despite much determination and sacrifice by the workers, and despite extraordinary community support, suggested that job-based coalitions for economic development were at a disadvantage compared to CDCs. They had to meet the test of market success and profitability; unlike neighborhood-based CDCs, they could not remain subsidized indefinitely.

This experiment in employee-community job preservation was precipitated in the spring of 1989 when Continental Baking (a division of Ralston-Purina International) decided to close down the North Side Braun plant (maker of Town Talk bread) and ship its product from Philadelphia. Local 12 of the Bakery, Tobacco, and Confectioners Union (which also represents Nabisco workers) was advised by the Steel Valley Authority to establish an Employee Stock Ownership Plan Committee. The committee then pursued the possibility of establishing an employee-owned bakery with the help of grants from the URA, the city, and the county. Daniel Curtis, hired first as a consultant and then as project manager, urged that the workers should serve the local Giant Eagle supermarket chain rather than enter the national market. The agreement of Giant Eagle in the fall of 1990 to buy the product led to the formation of City Pride Bakery and served as the catalyst for an extraordinary fundraising campaign. Throughout, the SVA provided support and guidance.[62]

By the fall of 1991, City Pride had received $2.7 million in loans from the major Pittsburgh banks; $1.1 million from state agencies; $200,000 from the URA; $315,000 from religious and religious-affiliated organizations. Pittsburgh-based Point Venture Partners and Zero Stage Capital of State College, Pennsylvania, organized a $2.1 million investor group, which included the Lawrenceville CDC and the Bloomfield-Garfield CDC. Other sources—government agencies, foundations—completed the $8.3 million package.

City Pride's 120,000-square-foot plant, dedicated in the fall of 1991, was located in the Lawrenceville Industrial Park at Thirty-eighth Street along the Allegheny River. The URA and the Lawrenceville CDC had been instrumental in persuading the Buncher Company to build and lease the plant to City Pride. During the summer, $5 million in equipment had been hauled in from a defunct bakery in San Jose, California.

By early 1992, City Pride was nationally acclaimed as "the nation's first start-up of a major manufacturing company intended to be owned in full eventually by its employees, almost all of whom are being hired from welfare rolls and long-term unemployment lines."[63] The bakery employed about 170 workers upon start-up, with employment expected to rise to 300 after a few years (50 more than the 250 lost jobs upon the shutdown of the Braun Bakery in 1989). Employee ownership (applying to 40 original Braun workers), starting at 10 percent, was to rise to 30 percent by 1996. At the outset, wages would run nearly 30 percent less than prevailing union scales. Besides the worker-oriented employment policies, the social agenda included subsidized child care and a lunch-room as well as educational programs.

The production date of July 1992 was delayed until September be-cause of a faulty oven. This began to raise credibility problems that intensified as the year progressed, and the bakery lost money despite increasing sales. In December, Integra Bank announced an additional investment of $1.1 million to help stabilize the operation. Despite this additional funding and an expanded customer base (Shop n' Save and Food Gallery markets), City Pride's cash flow could not overcome the high start-up costs and undercapitalization. In March 1993, Michael Carlow, owner of the Iron City Brewery and Clark Candy Bar Company, purchased City Pride with the blessings of the URA and city (along with a URA loan of $250,000). Carlow also experienced difficulties keeping City Pride afloat in 1993. The Company was losing $100,000 a month and was having trouble satisfying creditors. It finally closed down again in February 1994.

In the fall of 1991, the URA's Center for Business Assistance had promised that Pittsburghers would soon "begin smelling the warm, fresh scents of rising bread (and profits) for this exciting new business."[64] It was an expensive aroma, forcing the agency to write off a total of $700,000 in loans.[65]

The federal Community Development Block grant program became the major source of city funding for the most durable neighborhood organizations.[66] Block grant money, for example, sustained the Com-munity Technical Assistance Center. Established in 1981, it provided neighborhood organizations with guidance on management, organiza-tional development, finances, computerized accounting, and economic strategy. The center had been created in response to community concerns and advocacy. Two citizen groups independently pursuing a technical assistance center in 1979 merged in January 1980 into a TAC Planning

Committee. The City Planning Department was drawn into the deliberations, and the proposal was supported by David Bergholz, assistant director of the Allegheny Conference. CTAC's first director, David Feehan, would later head East Liberty Development, Inc.[67]

The citizen groups originally promoting CTAC had proposed that it serve as a funding as well as a technical assistance agency. Indeed, funding community-based organizations was, at the outset, the primary emphasis of the citizen groups. But Feehan, who had directed a comparable agency in Minneapolis (Minneapolis Communications Center), strongly objected to funding and technical assistance on the grounds that the combination was "fraught with the potential for conflict." Bergholz agreed and strongly urged that the City Planning Department be included in the discussions immediately, since the city was expected to fund the proposed organization. Bergholz's influence with the Caliguiri administration, including David Matter, the mayor's Cardinal Richelieu, helped win city support.[68]

CTAC established a community organization program in the late 1980s. Originally, this was supposed to focus on public housing tenants, but it received no cooperation from the housing authority. It then switched to tenants in private subsidized housing. The program had no appeal for neighborhood organizations, which recognized that funders were interested in projects and not in organizing.[69]

The evolution of the neighborhood support system should not be conceived as a top-down process—a gift from the mayor, the City Planning Department, or URA. As the origins of the CTAC reveals, initiatives frequently came from citizen groups who had to deal, at times, with uncomprehending bureaucracies.[70] Planners, after all, were exhilarated by prospects of traffic counts and zoning arcana, not demands to transfer initiatives and power to neighborhoods. And the URA was even less a hotbed of community organization. Not all city and county politicians embraced the prospect of an independent, neighborhood-based power structure.[71] The emergence of a city-neighborhood partnership, including a community development corporation network, involved a step-by-step learning experience for government officials and the stubborn determination of citizens to have a voice in developing their neighborhoods—beyond token funding or the advocacy of planners who were also city employees.

Block grant money also helped support the Community Design Center of Pittsburgh, originally established in 1968 as the Architects' Workshop.[72] It provides neighborhood groups with architectural and design assistance. This includes a Design Fund, which supplies grants to neighborhood groups to cover architectural fees for feasibility studies and design concerns. Under contract with the city, the center provides design assistance through the Neighborhood Business District Revitalization Program. The Pittsburgh Partnership for Neighborhood Development, which also provides funds for local organizations to hire a consulting architect for predevelopment services, contributes to the support of the Design Center.[73]

Another neighborhood support organization, Neighborhoods for Living Center, was established by the city Housing Department in 1978. Now a nonprofit marketing, promotion, booster organization known as NeighborFair, it is a useful source of information about Pittsburgh neighborhoods—so long as nothing negative or critical is involved. It also sponsors a variety of public services: litter pickup, graffiti removal, and "Paint Your Heart Out, Pittsburgh," an event during which volunteers paint the homes of the elderly, disabled, or poor.[74]

The creation of a financial and technical support system for neighborhood organization between 1979 and 1983 culminated in the Pittsburgh Partnership for Neighborhood Development. The Partnership embodied the characteristic Pittsburgh approach to economic, social, and cultural policy: a city, corporate, nonprofit alliance.[75] The role of foundations was especially prominent in the origins of the Partnership and exemplified more generally their pervasive influence over social and cultural policy in Pittsburgh.[76] Yet—important as foundation initiatives and support were in creating the Partnership and in legitimizing the CDC as a technique of neighborhood of revitalization—the actual funding of CDCs was, according to Jane Downing, former director of the City Planning Department, "a new and fairly small component of their overall philanthropic mission."[77]

The Pittsburgh Partnership for Neighborhood Development (PPND) originated in discussions among three foundation officials at a 1982 Minneapolis conference on neighborhoods. Participants included G. Mehreteab, program officer, Ford Foundation; Henry Beukema, Howard Heinz Endowment, Pittsburgh; and Sylvia Clark, Mellon Bank Foundation, Pittsburgh. Mehreteab explained the desire of the Ford Foundation to expand the impact of its community development program by creating local networks. Follow-up discussions between the Ford Foundation and Pittsburgh city and foundation officials extended from September 1982 to April 1983, when the Partnership was established.[78] Its initial funding of $1 million was supplied by the Ford Foundation, Howard Heinz Endowment, Mellon Bank, and the city of Pittsburgh (represented by City Planning and the URA).[79] By 1990, new partners included the Vira I. Heinz Endowment, Pittsburgh Foundation, R. K. Mellon Foundation, and Westinghouse Foundation. Like LISC, the Partnership functioned as an intermediary or clearinghouse between funders and CDCs. Funders got the benefit of investing in a promising new social invention, a kind of nonprofit capitalism. CDCs got operational and project funding, as well as technical and training assistance.[80]

The operating support was vital to the stability, effectiveness, and professionalism of the CDCs. Without stable funding, they would not be able to recruit or retain competent staff (the Partnership did not acquire its own professional staff until 1989 when Sandra Phillips became executive director). In this connection, the participation of the city was significant. It contributes $35,000 a year of block grant money for each CDC's operating expenses.

The Partnership's project development support in the first few years was supplemented by LISC contributions. The Allegheny Conference in 1981 had taken the initiative in contacting LISC, viewing this connection as "the Pittsburgh test of a new model of public-private, national-local partnership"; within a year, the Conference had raised $400,000 of mainly foundation money, matched by LISC.[81] This helped support development projects by CDCs in Manchester, North Side, and Oakland. These three organizations (Manchester Citizens' Corporation, North Side Civic Development Council, Oakland Planning and Development Corporation) were among the first group of five Partnership affiliates.[82]

The Partnership launched its own development fund in 1989 with grants from the Howard Heinz Endowment, Vira Heinz Endowment, and Pittsburgh Foundation. The following year, the Ford Foundation added a $2 million PRI (program related investment) loan, bringing the development capital up to more than $3.4 million. Partnership Development Fund loans and grants totaled over $2.5 million in 1989–1990;

it distributed $1.1 million from its Operating Support Program in 1990.[83] To no small extent, the Partnership was the creation of the Ford Foundation. The latter had been instrumental in the conception and funding of the Partnership in 1982–1983, had a major voice in the choice of the first CDCs supported by the Partnership, had been the catalyst in the creation of LISC, and then provided the Partnership with a large capital infusion for its development fund in 1989. Locally, the catalyst was Henry Beukema. He helped persuade the several Heinz Foundations to support neighborhood development and solicited city backing for the prospective partnership. More generally, he has been one of the foundation community's most consistent advocates of neighborhood empowerment.[84]

The PPND exemplified the tremendous enthusiasm for the community development corporation that had emerged in the 1980s. Here was a social invention that combined neighborhood empowerment (a potentially disruptive force) with businesslike, nonprofit capitalism and tangible neighborhood improvement. The CDC was in essence the basis for a constructive alliance between neighborhoods (including significant minority participation) and foundations, corporations, and the government.

According to the chairman of PPND, Edward V. Randall, Jr., in 1990, "we have seen approaches to urban renewal come and go, and we believe that community-based development provides by far the best possible return on investment. . . . Its hands-on position is the best way to identify opportunities and needs, and to manage projects successfully." No group, whether public or private, "rebuilds urban neighborhoods as sensitive to local needs, as creatively, and as cost-effectively as CDCs."[85] The Partnership also hopes to encourage better links between CDCs and community social agencies, particularly in connection with employment opportunities.[86]

The PPND began life with a constituency of five CDCs. Mehreteab of the Ford Foundation was impressed by the housing rehabilitation accomplishments of the Manchester Citizens' Corporation; and its inclusion would ensure black neighborhood participation.[87] Mehreteab also advocated adding Homewood-Brushton, a second black neighborhood, to the alliance; it would be represented by the Homewood-Brushton Revitalization and Development Corporation. The founders of the Partnership had been impressed by the potential of the Oakland Planning and Development Corporation (headed by Sandra Phillips); North Side Civic Development Council (Thomas Cox), and East Liberty Development, Inc. (David Feehan). These CDCs were known locally as the "fortunate five." They received nearly $3 million of the $3.5 million in PPND funding through 1985.[88] By the end of the decade, the fortunate five had increased to a fortunate ten: added were Bloomfield-Garfield Corporation; Breachmenders, Inc. (West Oakland); Hill Community Development Corporation; South Side Local Development Company; Garfield Jubilee Association.[89]

Beukema's discussions with prospective participants in the Partnership had included Cox, Phillips, and Feehan.[90] According to Jane Downing, their organizations, along with Manchester and Homewood, had received city funding prior to 1983 for a "community planning process."[91] In other words, city funding (and that of LISC) had enabled them to hire staff, gain planning experience, or pursue development possibilities. The first block grant for support of a full-time CDC staff person went to Bloomfield-Garfield in 1981.[92]

Following the establishment of the Partnership in 1983, the city expanded its funding for less favored neighborhood organizations. It created the Neighborhood Fund, Inc., in 1984 to provide operating support for these groups.[93] The Neighborhood Fund distributed over $300,000 in small grants (up to $10,000) to thirty-two organizations by 1989. Recipients had to represent block grant–eligible neighborhoods and provide a feasibility plan or study for economic development. A second funding source, the CBO Fund, was established by the City Planning Department in 1986. Administered by the Neighborhood Fund, it distributed over $1.2 million in block grant money to seventeen organizations by 1989. This went to groups that might want to encourage but not necessarily undertake development.[94]

The Neighborhood Fund was dissolved as a result of conflict of interest problems and was succeeded in 1989 by the Advisory Commission on Community-Based Organizations (ACCBO), which took over the CBO Fund. Under ACCBO, the grant maximum increased to $35,000.[95] An additional ACCBO fund was established in the early 1990s for public and assisted housing groups; it offered an identical $20,000 for each recipient.[96] One other program—the Neighborhood

Economic Development Investment Fund—was financed through re-payments for URA loans.[97] A founder and chairman of the Neighbor-hood Fund and ACCBO (as well as CTAC) was Robin Jones, coordi-nator of the University of Pittsburgh Urban Studies Program since 1977. She had been active in neighborhood advocacy since the 1970s with the Central North Side Neighborhood Council and the citywide Pittsburgh Neighborhood Alliance (as president).

The federal Community Reinvestment Act (CRA) of 1977, along with the Home Mortgage Disclosure Act of 1975, became the basis for a new aggressive strategy of neighborhood revitalization in 1988 (one that both involved and benefited CDCs). The Pittsburgh Community Reinvestment Group (PCRG) was created to encourage local lenders to increase credit to low- and moderate-income and minority neighbor-hoods for mortgages or commercial development. Consisting of seven-teen neighborhood organizations at the outset, it had expanded to thirty by 1993.[98] The PGRG was midwifed by the Manchester Citizens Cor-poration and the Pittsburgh History & Landmarks Foundation.[99] The prime mover was Stanley Lowe, director of both the Manchester Citizens' Corporation and Landmarks' Development Fund. Working with Land-marks in Manchester as a young organizer in the 1960s and 1970s, Lowe recognized the utility of historic preservation in conserving and rehabil-itating older city neighborhoods. "Government at that time," he later reflected, "had the idea that redevelopment meant tear down Manchester. The only problem was, we live here."[100] For Lowe, the PCRG, preser-vation, and the CDC were all tools serving a single purpose—the revi-talization of older city neighborhoods without wholesale displacement of the low- and moderate-income population.

The Home Mortgage Disclosure Act had required lenders to issue annual reports documenting by census tract their mortgage and home improvement loans. The Community Reinvestment Act required fed-erally chartered or insured lenders to meet the credit needs of the entire community. Compliance would be evaluated by regulators or agencies reviewing applications for mergers, branch offices or new charters. Frus-trated by the "diminishing level of mainstream lending by financial in-stitutions for neighborhood housing and other real estate projects" in lower-income areas, Lowe launched the PCRG and, in a classic organ-izing technique, focused on a single bank whose petition for a merger made it vulnerable to the provisions of the Reinvestment Act and, therefore, to community pressure.[101]

In early 1988, Union National Corporation (now Integra Bank) announced a prospective merger with Pennbancorp. Manchester Citizens' Corporation analyzed its lending record based upon the Home Mortgage Disclosure Act and determined that it had been redlining. The formation of the PCRG followed, and within a year Union National agreed to a five-year $109 million lending program for mortgages, rehabilitation, and commercial activity. Cooperation was encouraged by the "threat to file a public protest against the merger application and release information on the bank's lending record and status of negotiations to the press."[102] The PCRG's leverage was enhanced by its partnership with the city of Pittsburgh, which saw a way to increase investment in poorer neighborhoods without making expenditures of its own. The Masloff administration thus announced in the fall of 1989 that city deposits would be determined in part by neighborhood investment. Lowe was appointed to a committee that would do the ranking.[103]

The PCRG focused on Dollar Bank in the early winter of 1991, complaining that Dollar had made only ten conventional mortgage loans in low-income areas through most of 1990. Dollar was initially recalcitrant, declaring it chose not to serve as a depositor for the city; but the combination of negative publicity and PCRG's charges of Reinvestment Act violations, led to an accommodation mediated by the URA.[104] A prototype of PCRG tactics was the spring 1993 offensive against Lincoln Savings Bank and Laurel Savings Association. These were suburban banks (Carnegie and Allison Park, respectively) with only one branch in Pittsburgh. Using the leverage provided by each bank's request to regulators for an organizational change, PCRG charged them with discriminatory practices and demanded a hold upon their application. Specifically, PCRG charged that Lincoln had not serviced a single loan in twenty-five of thirty-four Pittsburgh lower-income neighborhoods between 1985 and 1992, and that Laurel had made thirty-five mortgage loans outside its service area in affluent neighborhoods, compared to six in lower-income neighborhoods in its service area between 1984 and 1991. The chairman of Lincoln protested that all of Pittsburgh could not be considered the bank's service area when it only maintained a small downtown branch. Lowe, however, contended that the banks operated in the city and were "bound by the rules just like anybody else. And the rules say you will have lending programs and products for all the customers of an institution's lending area."[105]

The pressure tactics were supplemented by a more constructive strategy of meticulous research and documentation of lending practices, as well as an ingenious repackaging of those tactics into a service system for lenders. An experienced financial manager, Lowe ensured that PCRG operations would not degenerate into irresponsible complaints, demands, or expectations. It examined banking practices from every conceivable angle before reaching conclusions: considering total mortgage loan applications, approval rates for loans to lower-income neighborhoods by dollar totals and percentage of all mortgage dollars, loan applications received from blacks, the percentage of those loans approved compared to loans to other groups, and reasons for rejecting mortgage applications. The statistical findings were then translated into changes in banking practice through services offered by the PCRG. Progress was monitored through Community Development Advisory Groups formed with eleven banks by the beginning of 1992.

The services provided by the PCRG included review of compliance with the Reinvestment Act, support of banks needing federal regulatory approval if they satisfied reinvestment criteria, the design of reinvestment programs for lower-income and black neighborhoods in consultation with the neighborhood affiliates, advice to banks concerning marketing of mortgages and services, credit counseling for prospective home buyers, training for bank staff, and establishment of a PCRG Minority Business Development Committee. Mulugetta Birru, executive director of the Homewood-Brushton Revitalization Corporation in 1989 (later executive director of the URA) declared, "In the past, it was like going to war. Now, the bankers talk with us."[106] As a result of the talking, bank lending in lower-income neighborhoods for mortgages and home improvements increased from $6 million in 1988 to $15 million in 1989 and almost $19 million in 1990. Lending to community development corporations jumped from $4.3 million in 1989 to $7.7 million in 1990.[107]

The PCRG was significant, not because of its pressure tactics, but because it exemplified self-help and business values in the pursuit of social goals.[108] Its credibility depends upon avoiding any impression that the Reinvestment Act is used to undermine responsible banking procedure.[109] This is occurring in the Clinton administration, which seems to view banks as social service agencies under a different name. Taking advantage of banks' dependence upon federal regulators, including HUD zealots, officials of the Clinton administration are ready to perceive discrimination in lending behind every finding of statistical disparity. And in August 1994, the Justice Department invented a new concept of discrimination in banking—the fact that Chevy Chase Federal Savings bank of Chevy Chase, Maryland, had established its branches only in affluent suburbs; it would therefore have to establish branches in minority sections of the D.C. area as well implement other penitent measures (such as purchasing advertising in minority media). The more indiscriminate these tactics become, the more likely that "banks will find that the path of least political resistance is simply to shovel enough money into minority projects to make the regulators go away." Losses and costs will be passed on to the creditworthy, and the CDRA will degenerate into a system of straightforward extortion.[110] And should one assume that "under this bizarre view, restaurants, convenience stores and all other businesses that locate outside of black communities also could be said to be racist?"[111]

6

Community Development
Corporations

The following two chapters examine the financing and operations of the major community development corporations (CDCs) in Pittsburgh. They emphasize the vital role of the URA in the broader funding system that makes community development possible. CDC staff have little interest in (or time for) theory and ideology—much of their time is consumed in the pursuit of operating and project funds and building funding coalitions to support specific housing, commercial, or service projects. The analysis also emphasizes the variety and diversity of activities that characterize the CDC network. Although development is their distinctive characteristic, they are involved in many different endeavors on behalf of neighborhood betterment. These include social services, advocacy, leadership training, planning, neighborhood image building and promotion, and historic preservation. Thus an understanding of CDC operation must be rooted in the specific and concrete, not generalizations. The detail conveys the reality. Perhaps the best description of the CDC as it has evolved in Pittsburgh is that it is an all-purpose neighborhood advocate with development capacity.

In mid-1989 the URA, in alliance with the Pittsburgh Community Reinvestment Group (PCRG) and Pittsburgh National Bank, revised and expanded its Housing Recovery Program. Designed to encourage the rehabilitation of vacant, vandalized, or severely deteriorated houses, the program depended upon community organizations in fourteen targeted neighborhoods to identify sites and prospective loan recipients. It had been urged upon the URA by the PCRG and neighborhood organizations. They recognized the need for a program that could expand the supply of affordable housing by enabling individuals or families of moderate income to acquire homes needing extensive repairs. A key feature was folding rehabilitation costs into the total mortgage package. By the end of 1990, eighty units had been rehabilitated with URA financing of more than $1.1 million.[1] This was one of sixteen housing subsidy programs operated by the URA for the benefit of low- and moderate-income populations by 1990. Many of them originated in the 1970s, during the Flaherty and early Caliguiri administrations. When the URA absorbed the City Housing Department in 1982, funding and administration of the housing programs were totally centralized.

The URA also assumed control of the city's economic assistance programs in 1982 when it swallowed the Department of Economic Development. Its functions were consolidated into the URA's own newly christened Economic Development Department. If an organization like the Pittsburgh Partnership funneled foundation and corporate funds into neighborhood housing and economic development, the URA channeled state and federal funds by the millions each year into the neighborhoods. Hardly a unit of "affordable" housing is built or rehabilitated in Pittsburgh neighborhoods without URA financing; similarly, its Economic Development Department is a key funding resource for neighborhood real estate projects, commercial districts, and small businesses loans. Not surprisingly, being a development agency itself, the URA has established a close relationship with the neighborhood CDCs, "both in procuring tax-delinquent or abandoned real estate and bringing a significant share of debt and even equity financing to the table for CDC initiated projects."[2]

The need for URA cooperation with nonprofit neighborhood development organizations increased after 1986, when federal tax code changes discouraged private developers from participating in lower-income rental housing as well as in older or historic commercial property.[3] CDC sponsorship of rental development helped compensate for the exodus of private developers. But CDCs also served as developers of new or rehabilitated housing for sale to moderate-income families who would otherwise would be excluded from homeownership. CDCs also provided housing for "special population groups such as the homeless, the handicapped, the frail elderly, single parent households and victims of domestic violence" (supplementing the more extensive program of ACTION-Housing on behalf of these groups). Between 1986 and 1990, Pittsburgh CDCs provided fifty-five single-family, rental, and special population housing developments comprising 895 units.[4]

The CDCs operated within the comprehensive framework of URA housing assistance programs that encompassed four major categories: homeownership, multifamily rental, rehabilitation, and energy conservation. These were financed by federal grants (Community Development Block Grants, Urban Development Action Grants, HUD), the Pennsylvania Department of Community Affairs, URA revenue bonds, and project paybacks.[5]

The Pittsburgh Homeownership Program, established in 1979, provided mortgage rate subsidies and assistance grants to cover down payments and closing costs. By the end of 1990, it had provided over $125 million in financing for 4,025 units. Like the other URA housing programs, it imposed eligibility limits according to income, neighborhood, or purchase price.[6]

The major URA rental or multifamily offering was the Rental Housing Development and Improvement Program. Created in 1976, it funds developers for construction or rehabilitation of rental housing (filling the gap between total development costs and the sum equal to the equity contribution and conventional debt). By the end of 1990, it had financed the rehabilitation or construction of 4,614 rental units at a cost of $25.6 million.[7]

The URA rehabilitation and conservation programs were significant because of the age of Pittsburgh housing—as of 1980, over 63 percent of nearly 180,000 units were built prior to 1939. Supplemented by URA-financed new housing, the rehabilitation programs helped maintain the housing stock in older, poorer neighborhoods.[8] URA funding also leveraged private investment in lower-cost housing and increased the city property tax base. Not least, the housing programs facilitated homeownership—with its positive implications for neighborhood stability.[9] Taken together, the housing assistance programs had affected 46,052 units (about 25 percent of the total city housing stock) and involved $378,386,452 in URA financing by the end of 1990.[10]

Paralleling the URA's housing assistance efforts were its economic development programs. Together, they provided a cushion for neighborhoods buffeted by depopulation, job loss, and declining business districts as Pittsburgh evolved from a manufacturing to a diversified, professional, service-oriented economy. According to the Pennsylvania Economy League, the URA's neighborhood economic investments had "attracted additional private investment, created jobs within the City's neighborhoods, created business successes that would not have occurred without the URA's assistance, and provided tax revenues to the City."[11]

The citywide Business Investment Fund supported small nonretail businesses that exported goods or services such as manufacturing, wholesale, or advanced technology enterprises. In 1990, the URA's Center for Business Assistance dispensed over $1.3 million in loans to fourteen businesses (leveraging an additional $13.5 million of private funds).[12] Another citywide program, the Minority and Woman Owned Business Fund, financed seventeen loans totaling over $770,000 in 1990 (this was discontinued in 1991 because of a HUD complaint that it was discriminatory).[13]

The URA and City Planning Department jointly administered the Neighborhood Business District Revitalization Program. This included the Neighborhood Economic Development Investment Fund, which supported mostly small retail and service businesses in designated commercial districts.[14] The revitalization program also encompassed the popular and successful Streetface, which offered matching grants for facade improvements in targeted neighborhood business areas.[15] A third component, Top Shops, provided marketing and merchandising advice to individual merchants. Launched in 1985, the Neighborhood Business District Revitalization Program had poured more than $3.3 million into twenty neighborhood business districts through 1990; this investment leveraged over $7.3 million in private funds.

Also focused on neighborhood economic development was the Community Development Investment Fund. Established in 1985, it assisted CDCs with gap financing grants up to $75,000 for commercial or residential projects. In addition, CDCs received a commission (7 percent up to a maximum $5,000, as of 1988) for arranging loans under the Neighborhood Economic Development Investment Fund. In 1985 CDCs obtained a commitment from the URA to apply loan repayments from its Urban Development Action Grants to CDC real estate development.[16]

The origin of two of these funds illustrates the role of neighborhood organizations in initiating improvements in the financing system. What became the Neighborhood Economic Development Investment Fund was conceived at a spring 1983 conference sponsored by the Pittsburgh Neighborhood Alliance. The CDCs rejected Mayor Caliguiri's proposal to capitalize it at $500,000 and succeeded in getting City Council to raise it to $1 million. The Working Group on Community Development was responsible for the city's creation of the Community Development Investment Fund in 1985. Both use funds provided by the Pennsylvania Department of Community Affairs.[17] The Working Group also participated in the URA's establishment of a new fund in 1992. This was EFFORTS (Enterprise Fund for Trade and Services). It provides loans to entrepreneurs up to $100,000, or 60 percent of project cost (at 50 percent of prime interest rates).[18]

In 1986 the URA proclaimed, "The orientation of local urban planners and development officials for over the past decade has been toward working with Pittsburgh's communities, helping develop neighborhood strategies and fostering community-based organizations that could be relied on to carry out development projects with local support." Pittsburgh at that time harbored about 120 neighborhood organizations, of which eleven were CDCs; and the URA was now "closely working with these [latter] organizations on a variety of important projects." They included the Pennsylvania-funded Enterprise Zones in Lawrenceville, North Side, and East Liberty; in each case, the "URA worked with an active community development organization on comprehensive revitalization projects."[19] Enterprise Zone status provided, among other things, tax credits and low-cost public financing for businesses.

The URA's participating CDC in the Lawrenceville Enterprise Zone was the Lawrenceville Development Corporation (LDC), established in 1984.[20] A large East End neighborhood, extending from about Thirtieth to Sixtieth Streets, and a mile inward from the Allegheny River, Lawrenceville had been devastated by the shutdown of its industrial base in the 1970s. The community's major cultural asset, consuming a large chunk of its 1,300-acre land mass, is the 300-acre Allegheny Cemetery (established in 1844), a legacy of the mid-nineteenth century vogue of the rural or romantic cemetery.[21] Other than the permanent and expanding population residing there, Lawrenceville had hemorrhaged population every decade since 1940. A 1950 total of more than 25,000 persons had dwindled to about 12,000 by 1990.[22]

Like other nonaffluent and working-class Pittsburgh neighborhoods, Lawrenceville is amply endowed with many blocks of modest but handsome corridor rows of Victorian homes. The texture of these blocks is tight, urban, and on a pedestrian scale; their expressiveness lies in the buoyant rhythms of the rows rather than any lavish detailing. Examples are seen in the area near Butler Street close to Allegheny Cemetery. Attracted by this picturesque and historic environment, a number of young professionals have lately begun to repopulate Lawrenceville.[23] At Fortieth Street and Penn Avenue is a second cultural resource claimed by Lawrenceville; this is the Allegheny Arsenal, in its prime a Greek Revival complex (1814) of a dozen buildings, but reduced to barely three today.

The URA's revitalization efforts in Lawrenceville centered on two projects. In 1988, it acquired the ten-acre former CSX railyard (along the Allegheny River, from Thirty-sixth to Fortieth Streets), converting the site into the Lawrenceville Industrial Park. Within three years, it was fully leased. At about the same time, the URA planned a redevelopment of the Doughboy Square section (at the intersection of Penn Avenue and Butler) in collaboration with the LDC. The URA anticipated that Doughboy Square (named for a statue honoring WWI soldiers) would "serve as a catalyst for growth throughout the Enterprise Zone."[24] With substantial URA assistance, the LDC launched a ten-unit townhouse development. The successful sales by the summer of 1993 encouraged the LDC to plan six more.[25] The LDC also acquired the nearby Pennsylvania National Bank Building, a 1902 Beaux-Arts structure that had been vacant for many years and is vital to the rejuvenation of the Doughboy Square section.[26] One of the most important roles of CDCs in Pittsburgh, which has lost so much population, resulting in empty—vacant, abandoned, derelict—residences or commercial facilities, has been to reclaim these structures and put them back to productive use. If ignored or taken over by human predators, vacant buildings undermine efforts to upgrade a neighborhood. And since they are often of older vintage and may possess architectural merit, CDCs function as de facto historic preservation agencies.

The Lawrenceville Development Corporation's initial tribulations in acquiring URA funding for the Pennsylvania National Bank Building illustrate one element of the financial monitoring system for CDCs in Pittsburgh. The URA denied the LDC's first proposal because the price was too high, too much had to be paid the owner at time of sale, and there were no tenants. A second proposal was denied because the sale price of $200,000 was still too high. Finally, the owner reduced the price to $130,000 in 1991, and LDC purchased the bank building in September.[27] There are other safeguards besides URA scrutiny. The Pittsburgh Partnership undertakes yearly performance evaluations, and the Advisory Committee on Community-Based Organizations (ACCBO) also has an evaluation machinery.[28] Finally, Richard Swartz, development director of the Bloomfield-Garfield Corporation, emphasizes the role of the Community Technical Assistance Center that "helps CDC's and CBO's set up strong financial controls and operates a year-round training program to build organizational competence and legitimacy."[29]

Like East Liberty, the North Side had been traumatized by earlier roadway and renewal programs. Indeed, residents with historical memories would argue that the community's decline began when it was hijacked by Pittsburgh in 1907 through a devious annexation procedure.[30] Many now resented being used by Pittsburgh as a dumping ground for problem populations. According to one exasperated resident, " 'Put it on the North Side, be it the halfway house, the housing for abused women . . . some ass always comes along and accuses us of being insensitive to the social needs of society.' "[31] Nancy Schaefer, director of the Northside Conference, a coalition of thirteen neighborhood organizations, complained, " 'We're becoming the dumping ground for poverty problems' "; drug addicts or alcoholics could roam the North Side, knowing they could claim shelter and food. The conference urged action to clean up the once flourishing intersection of Federal Street and North Avenue, now the province of the X-rated movie palace, empty houses, alcohol and drug addicts. Several shelters for homeless men were located on the North Side—Pleasant Valley, Light of Life, Harbor Light. And the Salvation Army operated day programs near Light of Life. In the winter of 1991, the East Allegheny neighborhood was incensed over plans to convert Saint Wenceslaus Church into a homeless shelter.[32]

Embattlement had long been a way of life for the North Side. Residents of North Side neighborhoods—the Mexican War streets area,

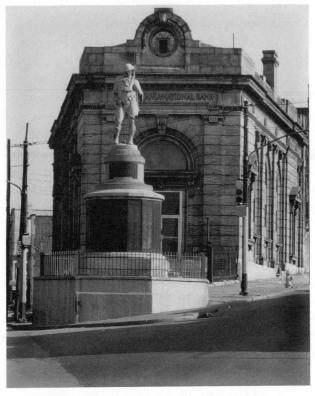

Doughboy Square, Lawrenceville, with the Pennsylvania National Bank in background, a major CDC project. *Photo: Author*

Manchester, Allegheny West—had battled the city in the 1960s and 1970s to be spared from redevelopment. Supported by the Pittsburgh History & Landmarks Foundation, they resisted the desire of the City Planning Department to convert their Victorian ambience into something closer to suburban tract-and-lawn. Nor did they wish to suffer the fate of the East Street Valley community. As construction of the expressway to the North Hills lurched and stumbled to completion over many years, homes, stores, playgrounds, and schools gave way to vacant lots that coalesced into "vast areas of nothing."[33] When completed at last, the expressway (Interstate 279) helped created a boom in the North Hills while contributing to the depopulation of Pittsburgh. Locating Three Rivers Stadium (built in the 1970s) and the Carnegie Science Center (1990s) on the Lower North Side had a serious drawback; such facilities require extensive parking areas, thus transforming large expanses of the North Side into more nothingness.

The changes in renewal policy that favored rehabilitation and preservation, as well as the financial and technical support for neighborhood organizations that evolved in the 1970s and 1980s, enabled North Side residents to exercise more control over their environment than had been possible earlier. The North Side in the vicinity of the Allegheny River was designated an Enterprise Zone. One of the original Pittsburgh Partnership's Fortunate Five, the North Side Civic Development Council (NSCDC), was the URA's collaborating CDC. The council represented fourteen North Side neighborhoods. Its director until 1988, Thomas Cox, along with Stanley Lowe, are singled out by Richard Swartz of the Bloomfield-Garfield Corporation as key figures in efforts "to chart the course of the CDC's emergence as a vital force in saving the inner-city from complete collapse." Cox, Lowe adds, "was something of a mentor to many of us." Their battles to get the URA to see the light in the 1970s (during the tenure of Stephen George as executive director) in the realm of neighborhood policy were "legendary."[34]

The Enterprise Zone program led to the creation of an Equity Capital Seed Fund to encourage business to locate on the North Side. The NSCDC, through the Enterprise Zone, had a prominent role in the creation of two business incubators beginning in the late 1980s. The Brewery Innovation Center featured a (now popular) pub and micro brewery as well as the incubator, and it demonstrated the practicality and economic benefits of historic preservation—the recycling of older buildings for contemporary uses. The site was the Eberhardt and Ober Brewery, an attractive Romanesque structure from the 1880s, located at the edge of the German-flavored Troy Hill neighborhood.[35]

Riverside Commons involved the restoration of the former May-Stern warehouse, a two-building, six-story complex. Conceived by Cox and William Strickland, director of the Bidwell Training Center, Riverside Commons reserved about one-third of its space (20,000 out of 65,000 square feet) for minority and women-owned businesses. After financing and leasing hurdles, it opened in the spring of 1992. The URA provided $325,000 of the $5.74 million total development cost (as well as $150,000 in Enterprise Zone funds). Along with the URA-NSCDC partnerships in Enterprise Zone and incubator development, the

NSCDC was involved in marketing Washington's Landing. In addition, the URA largely financed the NSCDC's Fineview Crest housing complex (twelve single-family units, begun in 1991).[36]

In the third Enterprise Zone, East Liberty, the URA worked with East Liberty Development, Inc. (ELDI), another of the Fortunate Five. As in the case of the two CDCs already discussed, commercial revitalization in East Liberty encompassed the reclamation of vacant properties and historic preservation– recycling. Any evaluation of the CDC role in neighborhood revitalization cannot be narrowly limited to purely quantitative criteria. CDC intervention is often strategically significant, saving architecturally notable commercial structures, returning vacant, perhaps dilapidated houses to productive use, or ridding a neighborhood of a demoralizing force like a problem bar. The reclamation of empty properties was explicitly defined as the core ELDI strategy by its president: "The entire revitalization effort has been to reuse, fill and to reinvest in vacant buildings and sites."[37]

East Liberty's population peaked in 1950 at nearly 15,000, but dropped to under 8,000 by 1990. The decline was particularly sharp in the 1960–1970 decade: 12,000 to 8,600.[38] Towering over its commercial center at the intersection of Penn and Highland Avenues (the main tower soars 300 feet high) is the East Liberty Presbyterian Church, designed by Ralph Adams Cram—a 1930s Gothic Revival gift from R. B. Mellon. There are several other notable church structures in the neighborhood— Eastminster United Presbyterian Church, Emery United Methodist Church, Pittsburgh Theological Seminary, and B'Nai Israel Synagogue.[39]

The controversial street mall, apart from the issue of its effect upon local businesses, was a curious design concept. A circular transportation pattern and a maze of one-way streets were imposed on what had been a conventional grid formation dominated by Penn Avenue, a traffic-choked artery linking downtown and eastern suburbs. I recall, upon first viewing it in the 1960s, a sense of disorientation. Oddly, the spatial flow led one around and away from the center of the mall complex. In effect, one was invited to avoid rather than enter the business section.

ELDI was established in 1979. In 1983 it became one of the Pittsburgh Partnership's original "fortunate five." A merchant-driven organization at the outset,[40] it concentrated on revitalization of East Liberty's Penn-Highland-Broad business district. The URA helped finance the

ELDI recycling of the Mansmann Building on Penn Avenue into a Showcase Outlet Center Mart in 1987 (now a Department of Public Welfare Office). That same year, ELDI acquired the Penn Highland–Regent Theatre complex, viewed by the URA as "one of the keys to successful revitalization of the business district."[41] This consisted of the vacant May-Stern Building at Penn and Highland, along with four storefronts and the Regent Theatre (a 1915 movie house unused since 1979). The two organizations also collaborated on the acquisition and rehabilitation of the Hiland Hotel. A four-story, broad-cornice, unflamboyant classical structure, it was reincarnated into 100 Sheridan Square, offering office and retail space. Like the three-story, art deco Mansmann Building, the former Hiland Hotel demonstrated the tendency of CDCs to constructively recycle a neighborhood's historic architecture and in this way reinforce a community's sense of continuity and identity.

ELDI completed renovation of the Penn-Highland group in 1990 (May-Stern became the Penn-Highland Building), and continued its pursuit of funding for the recycling of the Regent Theatre into a performing arts center for the East End. ELDI hoped that restoring a historic neighborhood theater in this way might do good things for East Liberty's image and prospects for revitalization.[42] As this project suggests, CDCs can link cultural progress with preservation as a strategy for neighborhood development. Preservation values are also expressed in the city's Streetface program. In East Liberty, ELDI has worked with the URA to administer Streetface, which encourages storefront renovation in neighborhood commercial districts.[43]

One ELDI project involving a genuine landmark structure generated considerable controversy. The thirteen-story Highland Building (1910), located behind the East Liberty Presbyterian Church, was designed by Daniel Burnham. It exemplified the renowned Chicago commercial architecture of the period. ELDI wanted to convert it into a 120-unit facility for low-income senior citizens. Several dozen owners of small businesses objected; they favored commercial-retail use so as to keep white-collar workers in the area, and feared that housing for the aged signaled that East Liberty had been written off as a commercial center. ELDI's director, Karen La France, maintained that the building was obsolete for modern office use and that they had long tried to find office and retail tenants without success. City Council supported ELDI, reasoning that a project for the elderly was preferable to a vacant structure.[44]

Even though it involved the aged, Karen La France viewed the plan in the broader context of efforts to repopulate East Liberty:

> In the last five years, ELDI has engaged fully in community organizing, community planning and housing renovation issues in East Liberty's residential neighborhoods. . . . This is because as residential areas go, so goes the commercial area and the businesspersons on the Board understand this. Thus the Highland Building re-use for seniors' housing was not really anomalous—rather, because the health of the community depends upon its residents, bringing 24-hour residents to the business distict could strengthen it.[45]

One great disappointment in pursuit of East Liberty's resurrection was the failure of Motor Square Garden as an upscale indoor mall. Located on Baum Boulevard a short distance from the commercial center, Motor Square had opened in 1900 as a marketplace. It then became a sports arena and a car dealership. When the latter folded, it remained vacant until ELDI launched a search for a developer in 1985. The Massaro Corporation, an experienced landmark restorer, agreed the following year to undertake the building's conversion into the mall. It opened in 1988 to considerable acclaim, but was repossessed by the mortgage holder (Equibank) in the spring of 1989. It was then acquired by West Penn AAA for its offices in May 1992.[46]

Motor Square Garden was one of the most spectacular indoor spaces in Pittsburgh. Roman-classical in design, it was capped by an enormous skylight dome. Exposed steel trusses produced a unique roof configuration.[47] Although it failed as a mall, devolving into the banality of a AAA office,[48] it at least stands as a vital component in Pittsburgh's architectural heritage. ELDI recognized its value for East Liberty's identity, once again highlighting the role that neighborhood organizations can play in protecting their architectural and cultural heritage—a recognition that had formed the basis for revitalization in Manchester at an early date. This heritage is often of no concern to commercial developers, political leaders, bureaucrats, and—not least—nonprofit institutions in an expansionary mood.[49]

As much as any CDC, East Liberty Development has been conspicuous in contesting the perception of its neighborhood as crime infested. This problem confronts other CDCs and is probably the most serious threat to their capacity to revitalize their neighborhoods. It discourages new residents from coming, undermines property values, and limits patronage of the area's commercial and cultural enterprises. ELDI thus urges residents to "point out the positives about East liberty to friends, acquaintances, and business associates. Help dispel false perceptions about the area." Exaggerated perceptions of crime are a source of constant frustration and exasperation for ELDI, which militantly challenges such views when expressed by the media or others.[50]

In 1987, the West End–Elliott Joint Project, Inc., published an *Urban Design Plan, West End Valley.* Pittsburgh History & Landmarks Foundation supported its claim that the South Main and Wabash area possessed "historically significant" structures. Accordingly, the plan's authors proposed that this "major positive feature" become the "foundation for continued development and revitalization." The plan also contained a protest: "The West End Valley is saturated with billboards. The entrances to the valley are dominated by billboards. Billboard advertising overpowers any efforts the valley businesses may make to establish a message to potential customers."[51]

A determined effort to curb the billboard blight was undertaken by Councilman Jim Ferlo beginning in the spring of 1992. Although the coalition backing Ferlo included Preservation Pittsburgh, Smokefree Pennsylvania, and other substance abuse organizations, the billboard lobby was experienced and well organized. Not least, it had the support of a city administration hostile to the most nominal of billboard controls. At City Council hearings, Martin Media mobilized its own work force to argue that jobs would be lost, lauded its alleged economic benefits to the city, got a number of nonprofit organizations to testify in favor of billboards, implied that small businesses in Pittsburgh would virtually have to close down without this source of advertising, and had several advertising executives testify that clients would not use billboards limited to 378 square feet, as Ferlo's legislation proposed. Not least important, local billboard companies could depend upon the financial and strategic support of the Outdoor Advertising Association, the national trade association, as well the tobacco and alcohol companies.

The only CDC administrator to bother testifying before City Council was Richard Swartz, development director of the Bloomfield-Garfield Corporation. Swartz had once suggested that efforts at economic development would be "pointless . . . if the neighborhood looks like a pig sty."[52] Swartz and his organization (joining with the Polish Hill Civic Association and Bellefield Area Citizen's Council) had spearheaded an earlier conflict over the prospect of billboard infestation. This was in 1986, when these neighborhood organizations "banded together and beat back . . . efforts to clog the intersection of the [Bloomfield] Bridge and Bigelow Blvd. with new pole-mounted boards."[53] Although it cost them over $5,000 in legal fees, these neighborhood groups thwarted a potential disaster. The approach to the Bloomfield Bridge from Bigelow Boulevard, which provides a spectacular view across the ravine to Bloomfield, would have been virtually blotted out if billboards had been erected. Although the City Planning Department attempted at that time to devise a stronger regulatory code for billboards, it was defeated in City Council. Ironically, in the midst of the arduous efforts by ELDI to resurrect East Liberty, a large weed in the form of a monopole billboard in the spring of 1993 sprouted over the business district. A provision of Ferlo's legislation, rejected by the City Council, would have prevented new billboards in commercial zones.

The domain of Swartz's Bloomfield-Garfield Corporation (BGC) includes the diminutive Friendship section. Bloomfield and Garfield border Lawrenceville; Friendship is surrounded by Bloomfield, Garfield, and East Liberty, and a small wedge touches Shadyside. Typically, all three neighborhoods suffered considerable population losses in the postwar decades. Bloomfield's 20,000 in 1950 was halved to 10,000 by 1990. Garfield's population of 11,000 dropped to 6,300 in the same period. Friendship's 2,800 fell to slightly under 2,000. The minority populations of Bloomfield in 1990 (9.1 percent) and Friendship (36.7 percent) contrasted with the predominantly minority population of Garfield (78.9 percent).

Bloomfield is Pittsburgh's Little Italy. One of its two main arteries, Liberty Avenue (Penn Avenue is the other) accommodates Italian restaurants and groceries as well as many small retail stores. Traffic can be slow moving because Liberty Avenue is also a route to the Strip and downtown, and two major hospitals are located in the area—West Penn and Saint Francis. Although the streets of Bloomfield and Garfield are lined with tightly lined, modest working-class housing, Friendship is endowed with the spacious Victorian homes reminiscent of better days.

The Bloomfield-Garfield Corporation was born in 1975 through the efforts of Rev. Leo G. Henry, pastor of Saint Lawrence O'Toole parish.[54]

Swartz, who had worked for Housing Opportunities, Inc. (a McKees-port-based nonprofit that devised homeownership programs for low-income populations), became its development director in 1981.[55] BGC has always retained a reputation for vigorous advocacy, owing to the early influence of confrontational tactics inspired by Saul Alinsky and the Industrial Areas Foundation. According to Swartz:

> The B.G.C. drew on [Alinsky's] philosophy for its inspiration, not Bobby Kennedy. It was Saul's work in Chicago's ["Back of the Yards"] that made common folk believe in the power inherent in the freedom to associate. As the old saying goes, when you enter a voting booth, you don't gain power, you cede it. Just look at Washington or Harrisburg today.[56]

Members of the BGC attended Industrial Area Foundation leadership seminars.

Established in part to fight crime, the BGC in its first year successfully blocked Veteran Administration plans to establish a methadone treatment center in the community. It pressured the city intensively to increase the police presence and install lighting along Penn Avenue. The BGC monitored criminal trials and worked to discourage drug traffic. It worked to have abandoned houses rehabilitated or demolished and to get streets and lots cleaned up. It acted to improve the business climate, particularly along Penn Avenue.[57]

Unfortunately, neither the BGC nor any community organization was equipped to deal with the urban curse that reached Pittsburgh neighborhoods by the early 1990s: drug-related crime, gangs, carjackings, casual shootings, convenience store robberies, graffiti-drenched walls, and prostitution. Garfield had become a main battlefield. Gang activity, centered on the cocaine trade, defied solution and undermined efforts at community betterment.[58]

In its advocacy role, BGC exemplified what James Cunningham and other exponents of neighborhood empowerment had long argued: that far from being an obstruction, neighborhood organizations could provide city officials with information they needed to perform their jobs effectively (and, if necessary, could exert pressure to force action). Thus Richard Swartz, in the winter of 1986, brought to the attention of the Caliguiri administration certain unwholesome trends in the Friendship district that undermined revitalization efforts. Some landlords, for example, failed to maintain their properties and then petitioned for assessment reductions because of the buildings' rundown condition. Swartz also complained about ineffectual code enforcement and the increase of scattered-site Section-8 housing. The Housing Authority subsidized rents for low-income families but failed to monitor the concentration of these units in certain buildings or blocks. Word would spread that a way existed to get tenants and guaranteed rent payments, but since rents were regulated, maintenance suffered and blight increased. Finally, Swartz objected to the city's delay in acquiring or disposing of tax-delinquent property. This also contributed to blight as properties lingered in limbo for years.[59]

Swartz gives much credit for the BGC's advocacy efforts to such longtime neighborhood residents as Agnes "Aggie" Brose. More than anyone, they have a stake in neighborhoods free of drugs or crime or dilapidation. In the early years of the BGC, Aggie Brose and others worked for small things that nonetheless provided a sense of accomplishment. " 'People ask for very little—getting a pothole fixed, a tree pruned, a stop sign installed." Brose remembered how destructive the city could be when it acted out of ignorance, a not uncommon feature of government. Simple-minded code enforcement dictates in the 1970s, requiring more expenditure than owners could afford without assistance, led to mass abandonment. In Brose's words, " 'At least 250 homeowners left Garfield. . . . They just walked away. The empty houses were demolished. Then we had empty lots.' "[60]

To prevent such actions by government or institutions that undermine neighborhoods, Swartz insists that ordinary citizens must have the power to make decisions and devise solutions.

> The CDC has become a vessel through which the corporate world and the citizens who make up the social and economic fabric of the inner city could elude the grasp of governmental paternalism and forge an unlikely partnership rooted in enlightened self-interest. For the corporate world, CDCs represented a nonideological and often nonpartisan response to two decades of mostly failed federal policies. For inner-city residents and businesses, the corporate world provided a source of help that looked at their communities not as wastelands for the poor, but as markets of largely untapped potential.[61]

BGC supplements its neighborhood-generated development work with a variety of youth-oriented social service programs. These include a reading center, a family health center in cooperation with Saint Margaret

Memorial Hospital, public school health services, and a youth development center.[62]

A neighborhood agency like the BGC can help eliminate threats to neighborhood well-being when the police or city are incapacitated or indifferent. It launched an aggressive campaign against troublesome taverns (in alliance with Patricia Scanlon of the South Oakland Citizens' Council and others) in the mid-1980s. This involved lobbying in Harrisburg to strengthen enforcement codes and encourage revocation of licenses if necessary. In the BGC neighborhood, four bar licenses were revoked between 1986 and 1992; enforcement authority had been transferred to the state police in 1987 to the acclaim of neighborhood leaders.[63]

Garfield had been plagued by the Pub & 10, a Penn Avenue bar outside of which fights, shouting, and drug dealing were commonplace. The tactics devised to deal with the problem embodied the kind of constructive, self-help initiatives that are the antithesis of paternalism. BGC acquired the property in July 1990 and worked with a minority entrepreneur, Simeon Johnson, to convert it into a family restaurant (in a similar vein, the Northside Tenants Reorganization had acquired two neighborhood bars with the assistance of the Pittsburgh History & Landmarks Foundation). Kayla's Place opened in March 1992.[64] The funding coalition for the project—the URA, Pennsylvania Department of Commerce, Integra Bank, McCune Foundation, Pittsburgh History & Landmarks Foundation, Pittsburgh Partnership—exemplified the public-private-nonprofit partnership that sustains neighborhood revitalization in Pittsburgh.[65]

The BGC's economic development efforts, in cooperation with the Friendship Preservation Group and Garfield Jubilee, have concentrated upon the Penn Avenue business district. It has linked entrepreneurs and merchants with financing sources and has conveyed their concerns to government and the police.[66] In the late 1980s, BGC embarked upon a vigorous housing program encompassing forty-six rental housing units, six condominiums, and twelve townhouses for sale.[67] Thirty-six of the rental units were located in Laurentian Hall, a vacant Catholic school converted into a facility for the frail elderly (including a clinic managed by Saint Margaret Hospital). The other ten rental units were in a rehabilitated three-story brick structure on South Millvale Avenue. The condominiums were also on South Millvale, and the twelve townhouse units, named Mossfield Court, were located in Garfield. The BGC also maintained an ongoing program of in-fill housing for first-time home buyers in Garfield (seventeen units over ten years).[68]

These BGC projects, indeed every CDC undertaking, involved the creation of an ad hoc funding coalition or partnership. This was the essence of the Pittsburgh system of subsidized neighborhood empowerment and encompassed the city (the URA and other departments), the private sector (banks), and nonprofits (the PPND, foundations, and churches). For example, the funding coalition for Mossfield Court ($1,233,026 in development costs) included the URA, Pittsburgh Water and Sewer Authority, Mellon Bank, and Pittsburgh Partnership. In addition, the URA provided $900,000 in permanent financing through its Pittsburgh Homeownership Program and Neighborhood Housing Program. In the case of the ten-unit South Millvale rehabilitation (with development costs of $656,652), the funding coalition included the URA (Rental Housing Development and Improvement Program, $292,402, and Community Development Investment Fund, $75,000); Pittsburgh National Bank ($230,000); the Pittsburgh Partnership ($50,250 grant); the BGC, $9,000.

A third example of the funding coalition mechanism upon which community development depends is the Montana Building in Garfield (1993). BGC joined with the East End Cooperative Ministry and Friendship Development Associates to form the nonprofit Montana Development Corporation. It acquired the vacant building for conversion into sixteen moderate-income residential units. The URA supplied most of the funding ($789,470 out of a total development cost of more than $1.1 million). Other participants included the Pittsburgh Partnership and the Pittsburgh National Bank Foundation.

In 1992, Richard Swartz served on the jury for a international competition addressed to inner-city housing design (although it was sponsored by the Community Design Center, not the BGC). The site was in Garfield (at Evaline and Kincaid), a forlorn, steep-sloped area of dilapidated houses and empty lots. Eight units were scheduled for completion in spring 1994. Swartz views the housing as an opportunity to get people to visit the community and see it in a positive way.[69] A few architects in the early twentieth century had been interested in a strategy of improved low-income housing through innovative design, as were model tenement companies, and a number of competitions for better tenement architecture had a substantial impact on architects and housing reformers.[70]

Like the BGC, the Garfield Jubilee Association was a second-wave Pittsburgh Partnership affiliate. Its program featured an interlocking emphasis on housing and social service. Rehab for Resale (R4R) enabled low-income applicants to lease a rehabilitated home in the East End for eighteen months. They could then apply for a mortgage, having benefited meanwhile from the Jubilee Counseling Assistance Re-Education Effort ("credit, mortgage, and budget counseling, advice, and assistance"). Jubilee's Christian Housing Partnership Program enlisted area churches to provide funding or labor for home rehabilitation. Youth Rebuilding Our Communities for the Future used vocational students from the Pittsburgh public schools to rehabilitate housing under the guidance of school instructors. The Community Maintenance Program educated homeowners in home repair and upkeep and in reducing energy costs. And the Garfield Heights Public Housing Counseling Program prepared tenants for homeownership through credit and budget counseling.

What is significant about the Jubilee program is the combination of housing, individualization, and coordination—housing improvement joined with counseling, vocational training, and appeals to the church community. Here again a neighborhood organization can accomplish what government cannot.[71] In the spring of 1993, Jubilee launched its most ambitious housing effort—the Vision of Hope or Black Street Revitalization Project. This will reclaim through rehabilitation at least eighteen homes on the main thoroughfares of Garfield (Black Street, Broad Street, Penn and North Aiken Avenues). The project was launched with a de facto historic preservation: the rehabilitation of two turn-of-the-century structures on Black Street.

7

Community Development Corporations, II

Like Garfield Jubilee, Breachmenders, Inc., in West Oakland is a Pittsburgh Partnership affiliate, has religious roots (Friendship Presbyterian Community Church), and combines housing rehabilitation with counseling and employment opportunities. Its diminutive four-square-block domain claimed a peak population of 7,900 in 1950. It declined to nearly 5,300 in 1980, and then fell dramatically to little more than 1,900 in 1990 (72.7 percent minority).

Hemmed in between Carlow College and the University of Pittsburgh Medical Center, the neighborhood had organized the No. 4 Block Club in 1978 to defend its interests. Pitt students established a home improvement company two years later, leading to the creation of Breachmenders through the initiative of Friendship Church. Breachmenders defined its commitment to better housing, employment, and neighborhood development as a "*partnership with* its neighbors as a demonstration of Christ's reconciling love."[1] But like any community development corporation (CDC), it was also a partnership with funding sources.[2] Its first and only executive director, David Brewton, views improved housing as a way to offer people independence and self-respect through homeownership and employment opportunity, and, therefore, a means to neighborhood stability.[3] A native of the Pittsburgh area, Brewton discovered while in college at the University of Virginia that his religious convictions inspired a commitment to social service. A visit to Jubilee Housing in

Washington, D.C., in 1980 convinced him that a campaign for better neighborhood housing could be the basis for the applied Christianity he embraced. In Brewton's view, nothing better illustrates the Breachmender ideal ("encouraging residents to help themselves and make positive changes to improve their lives")[4] than to employ and train neighborhood residents for office and rehabilitation work.[5]

Breachmenders' labor-free housing repair program provides job training for local residents. Breachmenders also operates JobLinks with the Oakland Planning and Development Corporation (OPDC). Launched in 1989, JobLinks attempts to find employment for participants, usually in Oakland area institutions, after three weeks of intensive training. It was first inspired by recognition of the employment opportunities offered by the development boom in Oakland.[6]

Breachmenders joined with OPDC in 1988 to acquire and restore Aliquippa Place (Robinson and Aliquippa Streets) for $1.4 million. The extensively renovated property consisted of twenty-four apartments in six buildings.[7] In 1991, Breachmenders launched the Carlow Community Advancement Project.[8] Seven houses were donated by the Sisters of Mercy, and an eighth was acquired from the city for $3,000. By 1993, three of the houses were sold, and five operated on a lease-purchase arrangement. Part of the monthly payment was applied to an escrow account (for up to three years) that would serve as a down payment. The URA then offered an interest-free mortgage for half the selling price, and a deferred mortgage for the second half. Breachmenders provided credit counseling.

The Carlow project was financed primarily by the URA ($400,000 out of total renovation costs of $618,000). Joining the other familiar participants in the funding coalition—Pittsburgh Partnership, PNC Bank—were the First Presbyterian Church of Pittsburgh, and the recently established Community Loan Fund of Western Pennsylvania. The latter consisted of Southwestern Pennsylvania religious organizations. This was its first loan ($21,000, at 7 percent interest for three and a half years).[9] Like other CDCs, Breachmenders mobilizes a coalition of public, private and nonprofit funders for neighborhood improvement. In turn, its focused program concentrates those resources upon housing rehabilitation projects that provide training and employment for neighborhood residents, and that make homeownership possible for a low-income population. In the process, it helps stabilize the neighborhood by increasing homeownership and eliminating vacant or dilapidated housing.[10]

Supplementing the Breachmender programs in housing and employment is community organizing. It supports People on the Move, a public housing tenant group in Terrace Village, and also the No. 4 Block Club. In addition, Breachmenders co-sponsors an annual Community Festival. Concerned about youth crime, Breachmenders declared Summer Youth Training its top priority for 1994. This resulted in an increase in the number of job placements for teens from eight to forty-two, along with extensive mentoring.[11]

One of the first five Pittsburgh Partnership CDCs, the Oakland Planning and Development Corporation (established in the same year as Breachmenders) was created to execute an Oakland Plan released in 1980 by Oakland Directions, Inc. (ODI).[12] Sandra Phillips, its first director, left in 1989 to become the first executive director of the Pittsburgh Partnership. She had helped found Oakland Directions in 1972, as well as an earlier group called People's Oakland.[13] ODI serves as an umbrella discussion and planning forum for Oakland civic groups and representatives of its institutions. It has close relationships with OPDC, which provides space and administrative support.[14] OPDC possesses an unusual financial resource. Its Oakland Development Fund was created in the 1980 by the Ford Foundation, Oakland institutions, and OPDC (which fills 51 percent of board positions).[15]

The issues confronting OPDC are radically different from those of other CDCs. Oakland has low-income residents, unemployment, and substandard housing, but the area is unique. It contains two major research universities, Carlow College, the medical complex (with seven hospitals, a medical school, clinics, medical offices and research facilities, Cancer Center, Nuclear Magnetic Resonator). It also encompasses two national- and city-designated historic preservation districts—the institutional civic center, and the residential Schenley Farms. Bordering on Schenley Park, one of the city's largest, Oakland is a cultural hub that contains the Carnegie—a complex of museums and public library—the University of Pittsburgh's Frick Art Museum, and Phipps Conservatory. Oakland is the third largest employment center in the state of Pennsylvania, including a large professional and educated component.[16] Nonetheless, three of its four neighborhoods lost population between 1950 and 1990.[17]

Like other community development groups, OPDI has been active in housing, filling niches ignored by commercial developers. Its first two projects, for example, were devoted to vulnerable populations. Atwood Apartments (1982) converted a dilapidated rooming house into a five-unit apartment building that accommodated former mental patients. This was followed by Parkview Manor (1984), fifteen units for the disabled and elderly at the converted Saint Regis School. Housing development for the remainder of the decade served moderate-income populations. Saybrook Court (1985), done jointly with a National Development Corporation subsidiary, consisted of fifty-six townhouse condominiums on the site of a burned-out apartment complex (Craft Avenue and Kennett Square). Close by was Niagara Square (1986, also with National Development), a forty-six-unit condominium constructed on open space that had caused trouble for the neighborhood. Holmes Place (1986) was built, in part, to thwart the prospect of transient commercial rental housing on the site (the closed Holmes School); it consisted of forty townhouses and twenty-four condominium units. Soon after, OPDC produced twenty-four additional condominium units at Holmes Court (1991).[18] Adjoining Holmes Place, it replaced burned-out buildings.[19]

OPDC's commercial operations include the Western Portal–Playhouse Square complex (1988–1990, also in partnership with National Development). It is located near the Greek Revival architecture of the Pittsburgh Playhouse on Craft Avenue and includes a 128-room Hampton Inn hotel, a garage, a RIDC-owned office building, and a school for the Playhouse. OPDC need not worry that the development will ever generate a historic preservation battle. OPDC also established a real estate office staffed by agents who lived in Oakland (1986), and it helped organize the Oakland Business and Civic Association to promote the interests of local retail merchants. Other commercial operations include consulting services for the University Medical Center in connection with retail space in its office buildings. As mentioned previously, OPDC operates JobLinks in cooperation with Breachmenders.[20]

OPDC is the object of criticism from some neighborhood residents who believe it has abdicated a meaningful advocacy role. It is not just the major emphasis on development that precipitates this complaint; more particularly, it is the business relationships that OPDC has established with the University of Pittsburgh and the National Development Corporation. (Seymour Baskin, head of National Development, had advised Sandra Phillips on real estate operations.) There is a legacy of mistrust between some Oakland residents and those institutions. It was reinforced in 1991 when Presbyterian University Hospital, through National Development, bought and permitted the demolition of the venerable Syria Mosque—one of the nation's leading expressions of City Beautiful design ideals in the early twentieth century—ripping a hole in the fabric of Oakland's Civic Center. After the structure was destroyed in September 1991, the site became (and remains) a parking lot.

In the spring of 1993, the University of Pittsburgh aroused another wave of concern in Oakland over its plans for a 15,000-seat basketball arena and convocation center. This is part of a more extensive, state-assisted capital development program for the university called Operation Jump Start. Concerns over Jump Start, the convocation center in particular, precipitated the creation of the Oakland Community Coalition in the spring of 1993. In 1994 Oakland residents vehemently opposed a University of Pittsburgh proposal to locate an undergraduate business school on a section of Schenley Park.

Neither OPDC nor ODI contributed to efforts to save Syria Mosque from demolition. It dispatched a staff member to testify before City Council in favor of stronger billboard regulations in the spring of 1993, but its contribution was minimal in light of the provocation—the approach to Oakland from downtown via the Boulevard of the Allies is a forest of billboards, as is the entry to Oakland from Forbes Avenue. But advocacy does not have a fixed meaning. According to the OPDC's ten-year report, OPDC-ODI considers itself a neighborhood advocate.

> With support from OPDC staff, ODI undertakes advocacy on issues as diverse as a threatened grocery store closing, the location of Oakland's post office, illegal commercial parking and various transportation issues. It provides the opportunity for most major developments and ideas proposed for Oakland to be reviewed from multiple perspectives, but particularly for their impact on residential areas.[21]

Moreover, OPDC's monthly newsletter, *Oakland*, is perhaps the most substantial publication by a local neighborhood group and could be considered an advocacy tool. And OPDC's former director, Caroline Boyce, had been hyperactive throughout 1993 in educating and organizing the neighborhood to deal with a variety of complex and potentially controversial issues: preparation of an Oakland 2000 master plan, revision of the city's zoning code, the location and impact of the University of Pittsburgh's proposed convocation center and other Operating Jump Start projects, and the University's five-, ten-, and twenty-year planning documents required by the City Planning Department.

It might be desirable to redefine the issue of advocacy. The Pittsburgh CDCs operate in a pluralistic universe. They all differ according to the character of their neighborhoods, the kinds of problems they confront, their resources, their leadership, and their mix of economic development, social service, and neighborhood betterment activities. This pluralism, providing variety and opportunity to experiment, is desirable. It includes a pluralism of advocacy; the CDC concept cannot be squeezed into a single format or a single conception of advocacy. In the case of OPDC and other CDCs, advocacy can even be defined simply as all the undertakings that improve the neighborhood quality of life. Traffic congestion, for example, is a pressing issue for Oakland. OPDC is closely involved through participation in the Oakland Transportation Management Association, incorporated in the spring of 1993. OPDC did the initial preparation for the organization, one of two in Western Pennsylvania.[22] Similarly, residents of Oakland would interpret OPDC's leadership in successful efforts to save the Giant Eagle supermarket near the university as an example of significant advocacy.[23]

Before becoming director of OPDC in 1992, Caroline Boyce had been director of "Main Street on East Carson" (1985–1987), sponsored by the South Side Local Development Company (SSLDC, 1985–1987), and then its executive director (1987–1990).[24] A Partnership affiliate, SSLDC exemplified a CDC that adopted an historic preservation strategy to promote economic revitalization. Its territory, the South Side flats and slopes ("Old Birmingham"), fronts on the Monongahela River and presents a dramatic scene as the slopes rise steeply off the flats in a panoramic sprawl of old-fashioned, modest, working-class homes. As in Lawrenceville or the North Side, the shutdown of factories had generated outmigration, unemployment, and an aging population. The population of the flats, 17,940 in 1950, had plummeted to 6,170 by 1990; similarly, the slope population, nearly 13,000 in 1950, dropped to 5,670 in 1990.[25] In 1980 the average age of the South Side population was forty-eight years, compared to a citywide figure of about thirty-five. It had also long been a quintessentially ethnic—East European—neighborhood where life centered on home, church, and ethnic social connections. The shutdown of the LTV plant in 1986 represented for the South Side the kind of opportunity for radical transformation that was occurring throughout the Pittsburgh region. According to one realtor, " 'Ever since the mills have been down and there aren't streams of orange smoke belching into the skies, inquiries about South Side houses have gone up.' "[26]

As early as 1968, four years after its creation, the Pittsburgh History & Landmarks Foundation recognized the potential for South Side revitalization centering on East Carson Street, a treasure house of Victorian commercial architecture. Landmarks joined with the South Side Chamber of Commerce and South Side Community Council to create the Birmingham Self-Help Community Restoration Program. This enabled property owners to get advice about facade restoration from Landmarks.[27] Reflecting the degree to which consciousness about historic preservation (nationally and locally) was precipitated by urban renewal, Landmarks asserted, "We do not want the Urban Redevelopment Authority to bulldoze the South Side in order to build our future. We have the future in our historic properties with their distinctive architecture."[28]

A Sarah Scaife Foundation grant in 1970 permitted the creation of a revolving fund for South Side restoration, and Landmarks acquired an Italianate building on East Carson Street for a demonstration project. By 1974, Arthur Ziegler, Landmark's president, anticipated that "we could have the longest restored Victorian shopping area in the country—twenty blocks of really great old buildings." He likened the future South Side to Ghirardelli Square (San Francisco), Trolley Square (Salt Lake City) or Savannah's waterfront section.[29] A former steelworker, Charlie Samaha, helped push Carson Street in this direction (antique shops, art galleries, specialty shops) in the decade after 1973 by acquiring properties and keeping rents low for these kinds of tenants.[30]

The Birmingham Union for the Restoration of Pittsburgh's South Side joined Landmarks, the Chamber of Commerce, and the South Side Community Council in advocating historic preservation, defining it as the key to revitalization. The Birmingham Union compared the South Side's Victorian row house and commercial architecture to antiques whose value grew over time.

Top: **Historic preservation and economic revitalization along East Carson Street.** *Photo: Author*
Above: **East Carson Street.** *Photo: Author*

The old, whether it be in furniture, or glassware, or architecture, today commands a high price. People are looking back to the age when craftsmanship prevailed, craftsmanship which cannot be duplicated today. The resale value for a building restored properly is far greater than for a building that has been "covered up." [31]

There were many historic assets on the South Side off East Carson Street: churches such as the Romanesque Saint Michael the Archangel that stood on the slopes at Pius Street, or the multidomed Saint John the Baptist Ukrainian Catholic Church at East Carson and South Seventh Street; the pedestrian-scale nineteenth-century row houses on the side streets of the flats; the South Side Market House (now a recreation center) at Bedford Square and Bingham Street; the Carnegie Library, South Side Branch; the Henry W. Oliver Bathhouse at Tenth and Bingham.

An historic preservation consciousness was thus well established when SSLDC, working closely with the South Side Planning Forum, adopted East Carson restoration as the core of its revitalization program. SSLDC had been organized in 1982 through the initiative of the Chamber of Commerce. The Planning Forum came into existence in 1985 as an umbrella organization for South Side community groups. A planning process addressed to key demographic, economic, and social issues culminated in the Planning Forum's adoption of an official South Side Neighborhood Plan in 1990.[32] Meanwhile, in 1985, an eighteen-block section of East Carson Street's commercial district was selected as the urban demonstration project sponsored by the National Trust for Historic Preservation and the National Main Street Center. It was administered by the SSLDC through its "Main Street on East Carson" division. This program included an agreement to have proposals for facade improvement reviewed by the URA's Main Street design committee to ensure quality. (Such design review proved to be desirable generally for Streetface and other URA-supported projects.)[33]

According to SSLDC figures, the Main Street program between 1985 and 1990 resulted in 110 new business starts and 28 expansions (against 52 closed or moved). Facade renovations totaled 131, along with 64 rehabilitation projects. A total capital investment of over $12 million generated nearly 400 jobs.[34] In effect, the community development process on the South Side in the 1980s helped the neighborhood survive the loss of its economic base and, indeed, defined its character in the post-steel era.

The South Side Planning Forum and SSLDC assumed stewardship over the community's historic architecture; this, in turn, led to exceptionally aggressive initiatives on behalf of structures to be designated worthy of historic preservation by the city. In 1991, the Planning Forum proposed historic status for two venerable factory buildings at Bingham and Ninth Streets. Once known as the Mackintosh-Hemphill Foundry, these structures were representative of late nineteenth-century factory architecture and belonged to the industrial history of Pittsburgh. The problem was not that a Dallas developer, William Grant, proposed to erect a $7.5 million, three-building office and warehouse complex in the vicinity, but that he intended to destroy the old buildings for a 250-space parking lot. SSLDC urged the developer to reduce the parking area by only thirty spaces in order the save the buildings on the nearly four-acre site. Rebecca Flora, its executive director, explained that "economic revitalization and historic preservation not only coexist on the South Side, they thrive on one another." "Adaptive reuse of our built environment," she maintained, "presents a cost-effective means of injecting life into both the market for small-scale commercial real estate and the fabric of our cities."[35] Despite the opposition of the Masloff administration, the City Council voted to designate the properties historic in October 1991 (overriding a mayoral veto). Grant then sued the city and the South Side preservation advocates for damages.[36]

As much as any civic organization, the SSLDC expresses a post-steel ideology concerning the role of historic preservation in the reconstruction of Pittsburgh. Preservation is not at all antidevelopment; rather, it is an economic development force that protects those qualities of a neighborhood or community that made it attractive in the first place—thus encouraging investment and increasing property values. By conserving its historic character, a community becomes more competitive in attracting population, business, and cultural institutions. As an example: many of Pittsburgh's historic churches—Protestant as well as Catholic—are threatened by closure and abandonment as their parishioners dwindle. The contribution that a CDC can make toward creative recycling of ecclesiastical architecture was illustrated when the SSLDC negotiated the transfer of City Theater from Oakland to the former Methodist Church at Thirteenth and Birmingham Streets.[37]

In January 1993, the South Side Planning Forum nominated much of the East Carson Street commercial section for designation as a historic district. The proposed area extended from South Sixth Street to South Twenty-seventh Street. The nomination followed years of discussion culminating in several months of educational seminars for business people, property owners, and others conducted by John DeSantis, chairman of the city's Historic Review Commission, and representatives of the City Planning Department. As part of this well-orchestrated and educational program (sponsored by the Planning Forum and staffed by SSLDC), Integra Bank representatives explained the economic benefits of preservation to property owners. They were informed that banks looked favorably at a preservation district because it stabilized an area and protected property values. The owner of an antique gallery affirmed, "[Historic designation] would bring more people here. . . . It would also help me because I feature antiques and fine art."[38]

At hearings before the Historic Review Commission on March 5, 1993, representatives of the Planning Forum and SSLDC described the extensive community education, the degree of local support, and, most emphatically, the economic benefits that historic designation would bring. According to Michele Reginelli, SSLDC director of the Main Street Program, preservation was a strategy for community economic development, one that both protected and encouraged investment. Executive Director Rebecca Flora testified that many were attracted to the South Side as a place of business or residence because of its historic character. That legacy, which enabled the South Side to maintain a sense of place and encouraged investment, had to be protected. And a representative of the South Side Community Council also affirmed that designation was needed to help preserve the community's identity—an identity that contributed greatly to the area's economic revitalization.[39] Approved by City Council in August 1993, East Carson Street became the eighth and largest historic district in Pittsburgh, encompassing about 475 buildings.

The SSLDC, like other CDCs and neighborhood organizations, tends to assume an all-purpose stewardship over conditions in its area. The many threats to a neighborhood's well-being include the behavior of public and nonprofit organizations, as well as of profit-making ones. Thus one of Pittsburgh's greatest assets is its extensive riverfront. The South Side benefited greatly from its eleven-acre riverfront park; built by the city in the mid-1980s, it extends from Seventeenth to Twenty-sixth Street. In 1992 the SSLDC attempted to purchase a 2.6-acre parcel owned by USX adjoining the Monongahela River near Seventeenth Street. But the Pittsburgh Board of Education offered twice as much ($600,000). The board intended to use this choice riverfront site for a maintenance garage, warehouse, and the inevitable parking lot. Flora, reflecting the SSLDC's characteristic emphasis on enhancing the quality of life as an economic asset, complained that the Board of Education reflected the mentality of a bygone era: "The industrial past of South Side's riverfront is not one that we hope to continue into another generation of uses. This site is pivotal to reversing this trend."[40] Board president Barbara Burns suggested, however, that the community should be indebted to the board because a possible third party had even more disagreeable industrial uses in mind.[41]

A much greater issue concerning land use, one that will have a decisive impact on the future of the South Side and the city of Pittsburgh, emerged by the mid-1980s. This concerned the development of the defunct LTV steel mill site (discussed in chapter 1). A second major prospective development, the expansion of Landmarks' Station Square, will also greatly influence the future of the South Side. In the case of the LTV site, one-third of the steel works had been cleared by 1990, and demolition of the remainder was in progress the following year. Near the end of 1990, SSLDC was asked by LTV to advise the company about how the site would be redeveloped. This resulted in the publication by SSLDC of a comprehensive planning strategy in the spring of 1992. At stake was 110 acres between the Monongahela River and East Carson Street running for over a mile eastward from Twenty-fifth Street. This constituted more than 10 percent of the South Side's land area, 30 percent of the flats, and it spanned 1.4 miles of riverfront. The site expanded from a pinched 400-foot width at the eastern end to 1,100 feet at the western edge, where it encountered Riverside Park.

The LTV site development represented a threat as well as a rare opportunity to exemplify postindustrial riverfront and land-use policies. The threat, according to the SSLDC, was the possible transformation of the character of the South Side:

> The South Side is essentially a fragile community which cares about its past as well as its future. . . . A major development of the type that is possible on the LTV property threatens not only the sensibilities of the people who live and work on the Side but also the structural underpinnings of the community itself.

The ultimate nightmare was any prospect of giantism: thousands of housing units, millions of square feet of office space, or light industrial use. This would generate something akin to an isolated island that "contributes little to the life and vitality" of the community.[42] Another grim prospect was suburbanization of the site—buildings amid a sea of parking lots or suburban low-density subdivisions. The South Side's character was quintessentially urban, both on the flats and on the slopes.

SSLDC offered recommendations concerning housing, retail, office, industrial, institutional, riverfront, and recreational development, as well as parking, access, and regulatory controls. In all cases, the objective in redevelopment of the LTV site was to "strengthen and revitalize the area without substantially altering it so as to retain a sense of its historical cohesion, identity, and self-sufficiency." Redevelopment should not lead to consequences that would undermine the "fundamental identity" of the community and the revitalization already in progress (such as the rejuvenation of the East Carson Street business district).

Revitalization policy for the South Side had been generated in a context of population loss, age imbalance, low incomes, economic decline, and environmental deterioration. In attempting to reverse this cycle, the SSLDC proposed a "basic strategy" designed to nurture the evolution of a balanced population. This in turn would stimulate local markets for revitalizing the business district, employment, and economic development. The SSLDC's vision for the LTV site, compatible with this goal and the existing historic, residential, and commercial world of the South Side, encompassed the following:

> Housing, stores, restaurants; courtyards, plazas and open space; entertainment and recreational facilities; maybe a museum. People and activity at the riverfront. Connections across the river. . . . Something new; something different; something we don't have now; and something we may never again get as good an opportunity to have.

Of transcendent importance to the future of the South Side, and of Pittsburgh, would be the treatment of the riverfront. Still prominent examples of industrial use, a legacy of the past, were "increasingly obsolete, uneconomical, and dysfunctional in terms of community character and potential."[43] The South Side wanted the riverfront to be viewed as a postindustrial amenity. New development should ensure public access to the water and opportunities for recreation as well as any commercial use.

The site proposals advanced by the SSLDC and the Planning Forum, along with their neighborhood and riverfront plans, testify to the potential role of CDCs and neighborhood groups in community planning.[44]

This is a vital function that would otherwise be controlled entirely by commercial developers and government agencies. Although not officially recognized by the city, these plans made it clear that the South Side wanted development that would, according to Rebecca Flora, "complement and co-exist with the residential core of South Side" and preserve its prized sense of community.[45]

An unexpected threat to the plans of South Side community groups, and to the entire future of the area, arose suddenly in the winter of 1994. The Murphy administration worked out an arrangement with Hospitality Franchise Systems (HFS), a gaming and hotel syndicate, to receive $10 million with which to purchase the 130-acre LTV site (for $9.5 million). In return, HFS will get an option for fifty acres on which it hopes to establish a riverboat gambling complex, assuming gambling is legalized following the retirement of Governor Casey from office in January 1995. More generally, the planning for riverfront revitalization has already been affected by the riverfront gambling mania. Numerous sites are being eyed by potential investors (Station Square, the Strip District, North Shore), thus diverting development interest into a single channel and bidding up the price of riverfront property. The LTV site, however, is the only one that would border a residential environment. All the effort expended on site and riverfront planning by South Side community groups would go down the drain if it were used for riverboat gambling.[46]

Located at the western edge of Pittsburgh, far from the antique and art galleries of East Carson Street, is the Fairywood neighborhood. A onetime picturesque rural village near Chartiers Creek, Fairywood still contains considerable open space. From a peak population of 4,490 in 1950, it had declined to 2,950 in 1990. The minority population, 10 percent of the total between 1950 and 1970, zoomed to 87 percent by 1980 and nearly 90 percent in 1990. These changes were attributable to the city's acquisition of Broadhead Manor in 1946 and the building of Westgate Village in 1970.[47] Broadhead Manor had been a low-rise World War II military housing project that was converted into 448 units of public housing. Westgate Village, privately owned, consists of 434 units (population 1,700) of Section 8 rent subsidy housing. Average household income for the neighborhood was below $10,000.

The geographical isolation of Fairywood was reinforced by the lack of a commercial center, or direct public transit to service areas. Few tenants of public housing owned an automobile. The last market had closed in 1983, and the Crafton-Ingram Shopping center was four miles distant. A Fairywood Citizens' Council, Inc., had been established in 1980 as an advocacy and social service organization. In 1984 it created the Westside Community Development Corporation (WCDC); its board of directors consisted mainly of residents of Broadhead Manor and Westgate Village.[48] Along with the WCDC's counterparts in Manchester, Homewood-Brushton, and the Hill District, CDCs had become significant forces for revitalization in minority neighborhoods—focal points for public, private, and nonprofit funding.

Progress in neighborhood revitalization is often measured by the ostensibly small, mundane, and undramatic—a Rite-Aid pharmacy in Garfield or Homewood-Brushton, a laundromat for Broadhead Manor and Westgate Village. But such facilities have disproportionate symbolic and practical significance for neighborhoods seeking to reverse a long cycle of decline. The opening of the Rite-Aid along the Penn Avenue section of Garfield was described by Richard Swartz of Bloomfield-Garfield Corporation as " 'a real boost from a quality-of-life standpoint. People are loath to want to live in a neighborhood that lacks the kind of basic services that a Rite Aid provides.' " Similarly, Helen Hurst, executive director of the Homewood-Brushton Revitalization and Development Corporation (HBRDC), viewed the establishment of another Rite-Aid on North Homewood Avenue as a stimulus for existing and new businesses. Located in the shopping center created by the HBRDC, it might improve the financial prospects of that facility.[49]

The WCDC's proposed laundromat was conceived as part of a larger $1.5 million development that included a credit union and convenience store and would be known as the Ujamaa Commercial Service Center.[50] The laundromat opened in the spring of 1992, followed by the grocery in the fall. Broadhead Manor and Westgate Village tenants were not only directors of the WCDC, but also the primary employees and customers of the facilities. This narrow base led to financial problems by 1993. It turned out that some tenants continued to launder at home to save money and that the difficulties of lugging heavy bags of groceries or laundry also deterred potential patrons. Administrative chaos afflicting the WCDC in early 1993 also proved damaging. The URA, the leading investor at more than $814,000 (other funders included the Pittsburgh

Partnership, Housing Authority, banks), found it difficult to review records at the grocery because of careless and inept bookkeeping. Evan Stoddard, URA development director, announced there would be no "receptivity" from the URA for funding of a proposed shopping plaza until there was more "history" to the Ujamaa complex.[51]

In light of the inexperienced management and faulty revenue projections (which did not fully anticipate the spending and behavior patterns of potential customers), the funding of Ujamaa seems to have represented a considerable act of faith on the part of the funding agencies. Yet, even the better-established Manchester Citizens Corporation had found itself in similar disarray in the mid-1980s; however, it was able to overcome its administrative and financial problems.[52]

Inexperience in management did not characterize the Homewood-Brushton Revitalization and Development Corporation (HBRDC). Mulugetta Birru, its executive director from 1983 until appointed to head the URA in June 1992, held a Ph.D. in public and international affairs. Included in his administrative experience was service as vice-president and director of business development for the Florida-based Seminole Economic Development Corporation. One of the original five Pittsburgh Partnership affiliates, the HBRDC presided over a once-fashionable neighborhood that shriveled in the post–World War II era. As in other neighborhoods, the CDC became a primary (if not the only) source of commercial and residential revitalization for Homewood-Brushton. The demographic profile was dominated by falling population and intensifying minority concentration. The population of Homewood North, 13,300 in 1950, had declined to 5,330 by 1990; the minority population in the same period went from 32.8 percent to 98.5 percent. Comparable figures for Homewood South were 12,600/4,800 and 20.4/98.2 percent; and for Homewood West, 4,300/1,370 and 11.2/98.5 percent.

HBRDC originated in a community renewal plan coordinated by the Department of City Planning in 1979–1980 that advised creation of a CDC.[53] Moreover, the Pittsburgh Partnership wanted to work with a CDC in that neighborhood. The revitalization strategy emphasized a combination of housing and commercial development. The housing was needed to provide customers and pedestrian traffic for local businesses; and the commercial development would focus on a limited area— Homewood Avenue between Hamilton and Frankstown Avenues—to dramatize the fact that the neighborhood was changing for the better.[54]

HBRDC housing developments by 1990 included the twenty-seven-unit Gateway Townhomes, and the nineteen-unit Bennett Street row house rehabilitation (scattered-site, two-bedroom, multifamily dwellings). Funding in each case was provided by the URA, supplemented by the Pittsburgh Partnership and a bank. A highlight of the HBRDC commercial revitalization program was the opening in April 1991 of a farmer's market in a former post office on Hamilton Avenue. It planned to acquire fresh produce from African-American farmers for sale by twenty vendors who were mostly from the Homewood neighborhood. The URA, through its Homewood South Development Fund, provided more than one-third of the $900,000 cost. For Birru, the farmer's market was more than just a convenient neighborhood source of high-quality fresh produce:

> It's an alternative way of shopping that connotes freshness in the minds of people—freshness in food, of course, but also freshness in Homewood. In that way, it's one of the most important developments in the revitalization of Homewood.[55]

The market was also a link in the HBRDC effort to bring business back to the commercial strip on Homewood Avenue, long desolate with abandoned and boarded-up properties. It had claimed success with several franchise operations—a Dairy Queen (for a time), a Kentucky Fried Chicken outlet, a Subway sandwich shop, and an Athlete's Foot shoe store. In 1993, HBRDC opened a mini-mall at Homewood Avenue and Bennett Street. Like other CDCs, HBRDC supplemented its development efforts with employment and business assistance programs. The latter—Top Shops, franchise skills, financial packaging—were meant to expand the neighborhood's pool of entrepreneurs and potential employers.[56]

Birru viewed the housing and commercial efforts as " 'all part of the community learning to take pride in itself again.' "[57] It meant the restoration of a sense of community (and keeping money circulating within the neighborhood). In pursuit of community, HBRDC launched its own newspaper, the *Informer*, and an AM radio station. And in the spring of 1992 Birru hoped to make Homewood the cultural center of Pittsburgh's black community by acquiring the 2,000-seat Greater Pittsburgh Coliseum—formerly a trolley barn and skating rink—and transforming it into a multipurpose entertainment facility.[58]

By 1993, a decade after its creation, the HBRDC's experience represented in microcosm the difficulties and challenges of revitalization of
some inner-city neighborhoods. Determination and optimism are probably as necessary for leadership as any other qualities. In Homewood,
the solid progress made by HBRDC was threatened by "a surge of robberies, shootings and gang feuds in 1991 and 1992 [that] frightened
both local residents and outsiders, reducing foot traffic on the streets of
the neighborhood." Since inner-city neighborhood revitalization is so
dependent upon retail operations, which are highly vulnerable to criminal incursions, it follows that curbing crime, especially juvenile and
drug-related offenses, would greatly improve the prospects of revitalization.[59]

The Dairy Queen at Homewood and Frankstown Avenues closed in
the fall of 1992 and, more seriously, the farmer's market almost failed.
Crime was not the only problem; undercapitalization and inexperience
take a high toll of small retail businesses even under the best of circumstances. Community leaders hope that the Rite-Aid pharmacy that
opened in the summer of 1993 in the mini-mall, will encourage shoppers
and restore momentum—in combination with a reduced crime rate.

A determination to save the once elegant North Side neighborhood
of Manchester from further damage from highway construction and renewal clearance had inspired the creation of the Pittsburgh History &
Landmarks Foundation in 1964. Landmarks then worked with Manchester residents to rebuild the community through conservation and
rehabilitation programs. This was accomplished by the creation of the
United Manchester Redevelopment Corporation in 1967, later the Manchester Citizens Corporation (MCC).[60] In 1979, the URA selected MCC
at its agent for managing renewal in the Manchester National Register
Historic District. Thus Manchester was a national pioneer in the strategy
of using historic preservation to reclaim a nonaffluent neighborhood on
behalf of the existing residents.

Manchester's revitalization efforts were, from the beginning, closely
identified with Stanley Lowe, an energetic young organizer who later
became director of Landmark's Preservation Fund and the catalyst for
the organization of the Pittsburgh Community Reinvestment Group.[61]
By 1990 nearly 280 units had been rehabilitated through the Manchester
Historic Housing Restoration Program—many of the homes in Man-

chester date from the 1870s–1890s. Another 109 single-family homes were built under the Manchester Neighborhood In-Fill Program. MCC had participated in the development of nearly 300 other rental units. Like other CDCs, the MCC attempted to revive the economic life of its neighborhood. It has been involved in the renovation or reuse of commercial properties such as the American Electric Plant and Chateau Shopping Plaza.[62] Meanwhile, the neighborhood's population of nearly 11,000 in 1950 had dwindled to barely 3,100 by 1990; the minority population increased from 17.2 percent to 86.9 percent in the same period.

As in Fairywood, Homewood, and Manchester, community development in the Hill District became a vessel through which city, private, and nonprofit funds flowed into minority neighborhoods. A center of eastern European immigration in the late nineteenth and early twentieth centuries, the Hill experienced a large black influx between the wars. This was the community's golden age; stable and culturally vibrant, it flourished as the Pittsburgh equivalent of Harlem during its Renaissance. As historian Laurence Glasco describes the scene:

> Wylie Avenue, Centre Avenue, and side streets . . . "jumped" as blacks and whites flocked to its bars and night spots. The Collins Inn, the Humming Bird, the Leader House, upstairs over the Crawford Grill . . . attracted some of the nation's finest jazz musicians. . . . Claude McKay, leading poet of the Harlem Renaissance, labeled the intersection of Wylie and Fullerton Avenues—in the heart of the Hill—"Crossroads of the World."[63]

After the Second World War, conditions deteriorated. Poverty, unemployment, the dispersal of the Hill's middle-class population, demolition renewal of the Lower Hill, dilapidated and abandoned housing, drugs, and crime created a purgatory. The population of the Upper Hill (the area closest to Oakland) dropped from 5,880 in 1950 to 2,590 in 1990. The already substantial black population, 73 percent in 1950, reached nearly 90 percent by 1990. Comparable figures for the Middle Hill were 14,900 in 1950, and 2,800 in 1990; the minority percentage from 95.1 percent to 98.9 percent. The Lower Hill (now termed Crawford-Roberts by the City Planning Department) claimed a population of 17,330 in 1950; it dropped to 2,450 by 1990; the minority population of 80.6 percent in 1950 rose to 95.5 percent by 1990. Two large public housing projects are included in the Hill's demographic profile: Bedford

Dwellings (2,300 residents in 1990), and Terrace Village (5,970 in 1990).

Strategically located between Oakland and Downtown, endowed with a hilly, picturesque terrain, lined with two- and three-story red brick rows dotted with dormers, the Hill has potential for renewal—retaining the pedestrian-scale, low-rise urban village flavor, if possible. The URA has invested heavily there in recent years, often in partnership with the Hill District Development Corporation (HillCDC), a Pittsburgh Partnership affiliate. Active in the character-building dimension of Hill District revitalization is the Hill House Association. Akin to a contemporary social settlement, it offers a wide variety of educational, social, and recreational programs. There is also a Hill District Civic Association.[64]

A newly formed organization (1990), the Uptown Community Action Group, exemplified the need for neighborhood citizen organization to compensate for the inability of public agencies to cope with serious problems. In the spring of 1991, neighborhood residents, fed up with the prostitution soliciting centered on the intersection of Forbes Avenue and Gist Street, as well as drug trafficking, occupied several street intersections to dramatize their concerns. They succeeded the following year in getting a state liquor store on Fifth Avenue closed; it had been a focal point for intoxication, drugs, and criminal elements.[65]

Those concerned with the fate of nations or ultimate causes of antisocial behavior often cannot be bothered with the mundane forces that undermine the quality of life on the level of the block—the nuisance bar or liquor store, the long-abandoned building, the vacant lot serving as a refuse dump, the delinquents and vandals, the unsupervised group facility, the troublesome subsidized housing project, graffiti, and litter. A novel strategy of neighborhood revitalization was undertaken by Councilman Jim Ferlo—two initiatives in one week—on behalf of his constituents in Stanton Heights and Lawrenceville. Fed up with the long vacant Stanton Heights Shopping Center on Mossfield Avenue, a repository for garbage and abandoned cars, Ferlo persuaded City Council to demand its demolition by the Bureau of Buildings. In the case of a Lawrenceville crack house on Leech Street, he entered and proceeded to toss out the furniture. He contended that he was justified in such action if landlords ignored their responsibility. Leech Street residents had attempted to get the city to act for two years without success. According to one resident, " 'It's been a nightmare living here. . . . You have drug trafficking going on all day and all night.' " While the neighborhood was delighted with Ferlo's initiative, city officials could only express their puzzlement and concerns about procedure.[66]

A different kind of initiative on behalf of the Hill was launched by the URA in the summer of 1991. This was Phase I of Crawford Square in the Lower Hill, a residential area overlooking the Civic Arena near the handsome Saint Benedict the Moor Church. It was one of the largest residential developments ever undertaken in Pittsburgh. The URA was gambling not only that it would be successful, but that it would trigger a wave of additional revitalization. Thelma Lovette, chairman of the HillCDC, had no doubts: " 'We're confident that it will spark even more development of a diversity of housing—low income, affordable and market rate. This will also attract more retail development, something our community sorely needs.' "[67] The HillCDC formed part of the development group along with the Hill District Project Area Committee. The latter's past president, Jeanette Poole, had long urged such a project (to five directors of the URA).[68] But the prime catalyst for Crawford Square (and the Hill Tuberculosis Hospital complex) was the late councilman Jack Milliones; without his leadership, "it might not have happened." Milliones chaired a task force organized by the Allegheny Conference. Consisting of Hill District residents and representatives of the URA, the city, the University of Pittsburgh, and the Conference (Pease and Bergholz), it "spearheaded the developments."[69]

The principal developer was McCormack Baron & Associates of St. Louis, a specialist in large-scale urban residential villages. The company's Lexington Village in Cleveland consisted of fifteen acres of apartments and townhouses in the Hough District. According to a McCormack Baron executive, the success of Crawford Square depended upon a changed perception of the Hill, and this in turn would be possible only through "sudden and massive change." In fact, it meant creating a total community and doing everything necessary "to make the area drug-free and crime-free."[70] Some, like Rev. Gregory Greene, pastor of the Powerhouse Church of God in Christ, believe that " 'the development will offer nothing at all to poor blacks in the Hill.' "[71] This is not entirely true; some units will rent at less than market price. Still, Crawford Square is not designed as a low-income complex. Its purpose is to act as a catalyst

Crawford Square, Hill District, a major URA project. *Photo: Pittsburgh Urban Redevelopment Authority*

for the Hill, attracting business, middle-class, and professional populations, raising property values, changing the image of the neighborhood.

Eighteen acres in size, Crawford Square is projected to cost $55 million and provide nearly 500 housing units. Phase I, launched in August 1991, consists of 203 rental and 27 sale units. The financing package for Phase I, $19 million, included $5 million of equity from the sale of tax credits. This made possible the leasing of nearly 50 percent of the rental units to lower-income households. As projected in the late summer of 1993, Phase II will consist of seventy-three rental and thirty sale units. Market rate rents for garden apartments and townhouses (one to three bedrooms) ranged from $450 to $695. Sale prices ranged from $89,500 for a small townhouse to $127,500 for a detached unit.[72]

A second large-scale development undertaken by the URA in cooperation with the HillCDC and other nonprofit agencies was the Western Restoration Center. A former Tuberculosis League Hospital on Bedford Avenue, not far from Crawford Square, it consists of a campuslike cluster of six buildings and courtyard spread over six acres. When completed, it will provide 120 units of housing for the low-income elderly along with a health care clinic.[73] Another HillCDC project, small but with historic preservation value, was the recycling of an old firehouse into five units of housing for low-income single mothers.[74] In the winter of 1992, the HillCDC eyed the possibility of acquiring the boarded-up New Granada Cinema on Centre Avenue with the intention of restoring it as a theater, but adding parking and a new building for retail and office use.[75]

Along with the major CDCs, other groups in Pittsburgh also engaged in community development on a modest scale in the early 1990s. The East Side Alliance and the Polish Hill Civic Association undertook the construction of three single-family homes in Polish Hill in 1993.[76] At the same time, the East Allegheny Community Council (North Side) built four townhomes on Avery Street; these were two-and-a-half-story brick structures built in conformity with the historic rowhouse architecture in the area.[77] Elsewhere, the Friendship Development Associates converted three vacant units on Roup Avenue into condominiums in the early 1990s. And in Homewood Brushton, Operation Better Block, with the assistance of ACTION-Housing, was developing eighteen single-family homes.

One of the best examples of the strategic impact of community development in neighborhood revitalization occurred in Allegheny West—a small North Side historic preservation district. An area of spacious Victorian homes and gardens, it was cursed with a troublesome bar and twenty-four-hour convenience store at its main intersection of Western Avenue and Galveston. To rely on the city for help, as in many other matters, was useless. In 1987, therefore, a coalition of the Allegheny West Civic Council (its president, John DeSantis, would later become chairman of the city's Historic Review Commission), the North Side Civic Development Council, and the Allegheny Court Associates acquired the property. With funding from the URA, Union National Bank, and Pittsburgh History & Landmarks Foundation's Preservation Fund, they proceeded to create Allegheny Court, an office facility with courtyard and terrace. Through a single community development project, a neighborhood blight was eliminated, property values increased, and a structure was remodeled to conform to the historic character of the neighborhood.[78]

8

Community Development in Allegheny County

Community development in Pittsburgh in the 1980s had been preceded by two decades of experience in neighborhood organization and advocacy. Pittsburgh also possessed an Urban Redevelopment Authority and City Planning Department experienced in channeling federal and state funds to neighborhood groups. With the emergence of the Local Initiatives Support Corporation (LISC) and the Pittsburgh Partnership for Neighborhood Development in the early 1980s (both discussed in chapter 5), public resources were supplemented by funds from foundations and corporations.

Circumstances in the Monongahela River Valley inhibited the creation of a comparable, internally generated system of community development. The tax base of the mill towns was shattered; their public services and infrastructure had so long been adapted to the needs of steel production that there was little experience in community organization; and hope persisted well into the 1980s that steel production could be revived. Organized response to the economic devastation was mainly labor-based and expressed in committees of the unemployed, food depots, mortgage relief, the radicalism of the Denominational Ministry Strategy, or the reindustrialization aspirations of the Tri-State Conference on Steel and the Steel Valley Authority. The major responsibility for economic redevelopment in the Mon Valley was assumed by the Regional Industrial Development Corporation (RIDC) in East Pittsburgh, Duquesne, and McKeesport. A private developer, the Park Corporation, acquired J&L's Homestead Works.

Given the lack of resources and the incongruous institutional and political structure, the impetus for widespread, community-based development came from outside. The catalyst would be the Allegheny Conference, which now encouraged LISC, foundations, and corporations to support community development in the former steel communities. Following its fundraising drive for Pittsburgh CDCs in 1982, the Conference launched a second drive (LISC II) in 1985. It invited LISC to support Mon Valley revitalization, and LISC responded by declaring the Mon Valley to be an official area of concentration. A Mon Valley Fund was established when LISC contributed $325,000 to supplement the $340,000 provided by Pittsburgh corporations and foundations.[1]

At the suggestion of Michael Eichler, a community organizer, the Allegheny Conference would oversee the creation of a Mon Valley Development Team (MVDT) to stimulate community-based revitalization. A native of Buffalo, New York, and a graduate of the University of Pittsburgh School of Social Work, Eichler had gained organizing experience on Pittsburgh's North Side and had helped organize the Homestead Credit Union.[2] In 1985 Eichler received a summons from Pease and Bergholz to discuss a position at the Allegheny Conference. They told him that the Conference had received a grant from the Heinz Endowment and "wanted to do something for the Mon Valley." His staff position had no job description, and the Conference had no plan of its own for the demoralized region. Eichler then visited Mon Valley communities, interviewed many residents, and decided that they should determine their own future. This would be the only enduring basis for reconstruction. What was needed from the foundations and LISC was funding for a community organization staff to find the potential local leaders and then help create the organizations through which those leaders could operate.[3]

The exact strategy was devised by Eichler and a group of advisers that included David Bergholz, Henry Beukema, H. J. Heinz II, Michael Sviridoff (of LISC), and Morton Coleman.[4] According to Jo DeBolt, although alternatives to Eichler's program were offered, "the MVDT concept appealed to the Heinz family because it spoke to their belief in the need for systematic change from within."[5]

Consisting of organizers and technical advisers recruited by Eichler, supported by operating funds from the Allegheny Conference and project funding from LISC, the Development Team was launched in January 1987.[6] The challenge, as defined by the formulators of the MVDT strategy, was "a lack of organized local leadership."

> Existing institutions did not have the energy, expertise, or mandate to take on new economic development activities; linkages between the Valley and Pittsburgh, for private investment, and Harrisburg, for public investment, were weak or non-existent; and the entrepreneurial environment needed to attract investment was not evident in the Valley and would have to be created.[7]

CDCs had been established in four communities prior to the creation of the MVDT: Homestead, Duquesne, McKeesport and Wilmerding.[8] Within a year, nine more were created through its intervention: Charleroi, Clairton, Elizabeth, Glassport, Monessen, Monongahela, Rankin, Swissvale, and Turtle Creek.[9] These thirteen CDCs were spread over Allegheny, Washington, and Westmoreland Counties. The Homestead Economic Revitalization Corporation (HERC) successfully completed a project—the renovation of the Tindall Building on Homestead's Eighth Avenue in 1987–1988. Financed through a predevelopment grant from LISC, a grant from the Howard Heinz Endowment for equity, and a low-interest second mortgage from LISC, the Tindall Building testified to the key role of foundations and corporations in launching and funding community development in the Mon Valley. As in Pittsburgh, the CDC in the Mon Valley represented a kind of self-help, social capitalism that appealed to the business sector and foundations; and it could initiate revitalization that might not otherwise occur. Even a small-scale improvement had significant multiplier effects that benefited a community. Thus, evaluating the Tindall Building, the Allegheny Conference declared:

> The building is an attractive addition to the business district. HERC pays real estate taxes to local taxing bodies on the renovated value of the property. Nineteen people are working in the building—they eat at local restaurants, frequent shops in the business district, and many have become involved in the community.[10]

A second project by a CDC that had been established prior to the MVDT was the McKeesport Development Corporation's Business

Growth Center. This business incubator also involved renovating an existing structure, Union Hall, in the community's business district. Foundation support included the G. C. Murphy Foundation, the Pittsburgh Foundation, and LISC. Significant also was the support provided by Pennsylvania through the Department of Commerce's Small Business Incubator Program, the Ben Franklin Partnership, and the Southwestern Pennsylvania Economic Development District (SPEDD) Business Incubator Network.[11]

Despite these beginnings of community-based development in the Mon Valley, and its expansion in 1987–1988, future prospects were not good. Funding was uncertain. The only source of technical assistance to volunteer and inexperienced boards was the MVDT, compared to Pittsburgh's Community Technical Assistance Center, Community Design Center, and CDC staff. In the smaller localities, the political climate—city and county—was not always supportive. And the Mon Valley communities were individually too weak and unaccustomed to maximizing their political leverage through regional cooperation. Conscious of these limitations, a small number of Mon Valley residents met in the spring and summer of 1988 to consider ways to strengthen CDCs. This led, by August, to an agreement to create a federated, regional organization—the Mon Valley Initiative (MVI).[12] Incorporated in December, its charter members consisted of the four CDCs that preceded the MVDT and the nine it helped to create. Three more, representing Brownsville, Braddock, and East Pittsburgh, were added at the end of 1989.[13] Subsequently, North Braddock and West Newton were included, for a total of eighteen.[14] The communities served by the MVI at the end of 1991 totaled about 156,000 in population.

The MVI defined itself as a "grass roots effort made up of people who believe that those who live and work in the Mon Valley should play a major role in shaping their own future."[15] Member CDCs elected two delegates (and one alternate) to the MVI board of delegates. Officers and committee heads constituted the executive board. MVI organizers and development experts functioned as staff for the member CDCs. Along with providing staff expertise, the MVI also functioned as a funding intermediary, something akin to a combination of LISC and Pittsburgh's URA and Partnership. Public, private, and nonprofit funds would be funneled to the CDCs through the Mon Valley Initiative, which in turn would serve as a monitoring agency.[16]

The MVI was consciously structured to emphasize process as much as task, and board more than staff. A federated structure was favored over a more centralized or hierarchical system because it promised to nurture local autonomy and citizen empowerment, as well as regional consciousness and cooperation. Cooperation was inherent in the operation of the board of delegates (two from each CDC). Board members, in the quest for funding and in making policy, were obliged to transcend parochialism and consider the interests of communities other than their own. This regional commitment was dramatically expressed in the summer of 1993 when the MVI board voted to expel the McKeesport Development Corporation. The precipitant was McKeesport's unapproved application for funding from the Pittsburgh Foundation. According to Jo DeBolt, the MVI's executive director from its inception, there had long been tension deriving from McKeesport's unwillingness to work as " 'part of a coalition of communities. They don't want to work with other groups. Our strength is in working together.' " To this, she added that it was impossible to cooperate with the noncooperative: " 'Some people in the Mon Valley have believed for decades that parochialism and isolationism is the best way to go.' "[17]

If CDC autonomy is not absolute, it is substantial. Just as the MVI was deliberately structured to serve as an incubator of regional consciousness, it was also engineered as an incubator for local and citizen empowerment. This was accomplished by the shared staff arrangement, which necessitated more citizen involvement and decision making and less dependence on staff. Compared to Pittsburgh's CDC ratio of approximately one staff person to four board members, the MVI ratio is twenty-seven board members to one staffer. This structure, DeBolt argues, leads to greater interaction among ordinary citizens in contrast to the more staff-driven Pittsburgh system.

> Look, for example, at the composition of the Working Group on Community Development or PCRG [Pittsburgh Community Reinvestment Group]. Communication among Mon Valley CDCs is at the Board level, not just through the MVI, but in joint projects and sponsorship of programs, etc. What fosters citizen empowerment and citizen action? I'd say the interaction and decision-making of Board members rather than staff.[18]

In addition, several CDCs have non-MVI staff, and not all depend on the MVI for publications or promotion.[19]

As in Pittsburgh, the reach of a CDC beyond the board or staff, and into the community, varies. The Bloomfield-Garfield Corporation, for example, tries harder than most to build a membership base. But there are other ways to connect with the community—coalition-building, project development, sponsorship of events, services.

The planning and creation of the MVI released a stream of funding from Pittsburgh banks and foundations that were already familiar with CDC operations in Pittsburgh neighborhoods and comfortable with the blend of business and social values they embodied. The Howard and Vira Heinz Endowments joined with the Pittsburgh Foundation in December 1988 to provide the MVI with a $1.1 million, three-year commitment for operating funds. At the same time, the major Pittsburgh commercial banks (Mellon, Pittsburgh National, Union National [Integra], Equibank [Integra]) established a "development partnership" to help finance up to $10 million worth of project costs.[20] Prior to the creation of the MVI, bank lending for Mon Valley CDCs was difficult to obtain. According to a MVI report: "Three years ago, Pittsburgh National Bank was the only bank willing to lend to CDCs, and even PNB was slow to come to the table on both the Tindall Building project in Homestead and the First and Cedar project in Duquesne."[21]

The MVI confronted a Herculean task in bringing community-based economic revitalization to the region. Apart from small population, limited local resources or tax base, and citizens' inexperience with community development, the MVI had to deal with old resentments based on class and political divisions, misconceptions about its operations and objectives, and the indifference of Allegheny County to its revitalization strategy. The MVI found the Allegheny County Department of Development difficult to deal with; financing decisions, it complained, were made subjectively and politically, without attention to funding cycles. Attitudes of county housing officials "ranged from annoyed to hostile."[22] The county Department of Development seemed, in essence, to subscribe to 1950s urban renewal patterns: large-scale projects conceived at the top with minimal citizen initiative or participation. Development meant a new international airport, highways, or reclamation of an industrial site by the RIDC. Joseph Hohman, former director of the Department of Development, explained the basis for the unfriendly relations with the MVI.

We're interested in building homes for low-moderate income [persons] and we're interested in putting projects back on the tax rolls and we're not interested in developing some capacity at [the community] level to do it. If that happens as a side benefit, fine. But that's not the major objective.[23]

The Steel Valley Authority (SVA) apparently considered itself a more authentic voice for the region and its workers, viewing the MVI as an interloper and competitor. Formed in 1986, amid the final death throes of the steel industry, it had embodied the bitterness and anguish of the Mon Valley in that period. Frustrated in its original strategy to preserve or revive the steel industry, it changed course following the appointment of Tom Croft as executive director in 1988—although it clung to the belief as late as 1991 that the LTV plant on the South Side could be revived.[24] It increasingly emphasized the need to retain the existing manufacturing base, however unglamorous, as the way to preserve jobs. This involved creating an early warning network to work with troubled companies to prevent their shutdown.[25] SVA enjoyed a measure of national acclaim for its role in the City Pride Bakery coalition: "The SVA has provided communities and industrial neighborhoods around the country with a model for economic revitalization,"[26] announced its progress report. It turned out to be, of course, a failed model.

Drawing an implicit comparison to the MVI, Crofts described the SVA as a movement that " 'was born with a lot of hostility. It came out of the mill towns and neighborhoods and grew out of aspirations to revitalize the mills. It wasn't a Downtown-driven organization.' "[27] The SVA seemed to view the MVI with the calculated indifference and disdain expressed by the movie industry toward television in its early years. Thus it announced in 1992 that it was exploring the establishment of exactly the kind of "Mon Valley Partnership" that the MVI had embodied since late 1988. According to the SVA, its proposed partnership would

fill a vacuum in the Mon Valley to broaden the participation of banks and local foundations in the valley, planning cooperatively with local community development and milltown leaders, for our economic future. The approach would target jobs and enterprise and community development investments. . . . Many of the milltown municipal leaders are interested in this idea.[28]

In keeping with this community development agenda, the SVA is seeking to broaden its constituency and perhaps shift its structure away from a municipality base and toward a nonprofit development corporation.[29]

A controversial newspaper article in the fall of 1991 provided a glimpse of the resentments harbored by the old political order in the Mon Valley. The MVI, with its ties to Pittsburgh foundations, banks, and civic organizations, did not fit into the Democratic party–labor alliance that had reigned in the Pittsburgh region since the Great Depression. Indeed, journalist Wes Cotter reported that "development officials in the area interviewed in this story requested that their names not be used for fear that foundations, banks and the Initiative itself would decide not to provide funding to their communities."[30]

The article precipitated a storm of criticism from Mon Valley citizens and officials. They complained that Cotter relied upon anonymous informants and two mayors, Betty Esper of Homestead and Louis Washowich of McKeesport; although the president of MVI was interviewed, none of the staff was, and—more important—not a single CDC board member or citizen in the seventeen communities. They objected to the portrait of the MVI as an inert, bureaucratic organization, hoarding its pile of gold and generating studies and surveys rather than jobs and development. " 'I get upset," said Esper, "when I see all the money brought in for studies when I can't get funding to keep my borough running. . . . All these organizations are there to keep themselves on the payroll.' " As for efforts by the Steel Industry Heritage Task Force and MVI to create a steel heritage park in Homestead, she again complained of money wasted on studies and hoped to see the buildings blown up. Washowich complained that McKeesport had not received any funding, that the administrative overhead of the MVI was excessive, and that job creation was more important than its emphasis on housing.[31]

A year later Cotter published a second article featuring critics of the MVI, notably the Steel Valley Regional Planning Commission (SVRPC)—which, in turn, was closely allied to the Steel Valley Council of Governments (a service sharing organization). Again, the MVI was resented as an interloper. Indignant over the distribution of MVI surveys at council meetings, thus allegedly duplicating its activities, the SVRPC condemned MVI efforts to revitalize the economy and become the dominant force in Mon Valley reconstruction. The commission declared that

" 'Allegheny County recognizes the SVRPC/Steel Valley Council of Governments as the lead agency, or 'one voice' of the Steel Valley Region. We intend to stay in that position.' "[32] Commission Chairman Melvyn Achtzehn, mayor of Duquesne and a board member of MVI, supported the claim that the MVI was trying to become the region's megadevelopment force and promised to oppose it.

Cotter's articles provided a limited understanding of the MVI's operations, but they did reveal the Mon Valley to be a hornets' nest of organizations competing for funds, power, and influence. Many of them—the Steel Valley Authority, the Steel Valley Regional Planning Commission and Council of Governments, Allegheny County officials, old-line machine politicians, and unionists—viewed the MVI as an alien importation. The MVI has always been exasperated by efforts to discredit it as the creation of Pittsburgh's foundation, banking, and corporate elite. While the MVI did indeed come about because of the initiative of this elite, its director insisted that decisions about how resources would be used "came from the volunteer community leadership that set the agenda for the MVI." She considered it cynical and insulting to assume that citizens were incapable of setting their own agenda and could only pursue one devised by the Pittsburgh elite. To the contrary, the MVI agenda was devised by ordinary citizens and expressed their needs and desires.[33]

There was no doubt about the commitment of Jo DeBolt to a new civic order. A University of Pittsburgh MBA, she had worked in Beaver County and elsewhere in the Pittsburgh area as a development consultant before becoming director of the MVDT development staff in 1987 and director of the MVI in 1988. At the outset, in the late 1980s, she saw the Mon Valley as a region whose controlling institutions—corporations, churches, unions—had diminished in authority. Change, therefore, was inevitable.[34] "What we are doing is creating a civic infrastructure in the Mon Valley," DeBolt writes. "Community development corporations are vehicles for empowerment. In that process we are employing a different style of community organizing that is typically used in community development. Our style is based in coalition building through consensus rather than through conflict."[35]

Equally important, it would be a regional civic infrastructure. Jo DeBolt defined the MVI mission to be in part the creation of a regional identity. For too long, Mon Valley communities had suffered from a tradition of isolation and competition. When added to their many other economic and demographic liabilities, the lack of regional consciousness and cooperation thwarted the prospects for revitalization. DeBolt claimed that the MVI, by 1992, was indeed changing attitudes among those participating in the emergent civic infrastructure. A new leadership for the Mon Valley was surfacing. Some were even running for public office, DeBolt observed approvingly.[36] And, according to the MVI,

> many of these novice office seekers were women or African-Americans. Their success in winning primary elections . . . is significant because they will come to office outside the traditional white male dominated party system. Involvement in a CDC became a way to build or to expand the political base that took them to victory. . . . The Mon Valley sorely needs public officials who understand development, believe in cooperation and collaboration.[37]

Political activism, however, could backfire. Should CDCs become identified with partisan politics, their support might unravel.[38]

The MVI had been created at the climax of the steel plant shutdown cycle. Its leaders believed that its economic, participatory, and civic goals depended greatly on instilling pride in a demoralized population.

> In the local and national press, the Mon Valley is repeatedly portrayed as an economic and social wasteland. One of the first steps toward economic revitalization has to be the establishment of the image that the Mon Valley is a good place to live and do business; . . . a sense of pride has to be cultivated among residents. This stronger self-image then has to be projected to those outside the Valley.[39]

This emphasis upon pride building has always characterized the MVI. It helps explain the organization's distinctive emphasis on historic preservation and other quality of life concerns such as cultural development, beautification projects, and recreational use of the river. Although preserving the area's architectural heritage brought economic benefits, including prospects of state and federal funding, it also instilled pride in what the steel communities and what their work force had accomplished. Pride, in turn, might be translated into greater commitment to community betterment.

Along with economic development (housing, jobs, commercial district revitalization, or manufacturing opportunities), and enhancing citizen power and pride, the MVI espoused a new conception of community, or civic culture, in the Mon Valley. It was one in which economic development, participatory democracy, and quality of life concerns converged. Throughout the steel era, economic imperatives predominated. Workers took refuge in their institutions—church, family, union, fraternal society—and left community issues to the steel companies and municipal officials. Manufacturing plants monopolized the riverfronts and community amenities consisted of whatever the companies might contribute, like a Carnegie library or a small park.

The MVI conception of community development is unique in the annals of the Mon Valley. The other claimants to revitalization leadership—Allegheny County officials, the RIDC, labor-based organizations such as the Steel Valley Authority—embodied the traditional view in which economic development and jobs—any jobs—were the primary concerns. The problem with this one-dimensional strategy is that it might leave the Mon Valley communities in a permanent state of drabness and marginality. The demographic profile is unpromising: too old, too poor, too undereducated. The valley's terrain and riverfronts provide a spectacular setting—but for what? Can the redevelopment process create communities that can expand and diversify the population, creating a younger, better-educated mix? Can this occur in a predominately low-tech economy and in communities hitherto indifferent to quality of life concerns, or the economic and civic benefits of amenities such as scenic riverbanks, restored old buildings and historic industrial structures, a vital cultural life, a rejuvenated commercial district—meaning more than few clothing or shoe stores and fast food outlets. The MVI attempts to confront these broader concerns of civic renewal, recognizing that the future of the Mon Valley depends on community building as well as jobs:

> As we look to the future, the quality of life in the Mon Valley will be determined by the extent to which we . . . are able to retain or redefine the institutions and traditions by which we identify ourselves. Community arts and performance groups, events and festivals, and preservation of key civic and institutional sites will build the quality of our lives and become the legacy we create for our children.[40]

An indifference to what kind of economic development occurs, just as long as jobs are created, contrasts sharply with Pittsburgh's emphasis on advanced technology and professional services as well as support for cultural institutions. It also contrasts with the brave new world of "high performance manufacturing" advocated in 1993 by economist Richard Florida for the Pittsburgh region.[41]

Consider, for example, the prospects for the city of Duquesne. Nearly 40 percent of its residents lacked a high school diploma, and only 5 percent had a college degree. The slow-moving RIDC reclamation of the 270-acre former U.S. Steel plant is the major economic development activity. According to state representative Tom Michlovic, Mon Valley communities could manage without high-tech economies: " 'They should be able to employ people who don't have a college degree.' " The RIDC's "City Center of Duquesne" will replicate the steel era's industrial domination of the riverfront (although a path will be cut through the property to enable pedestrians to reach the river). Also on the former plant site will be a landfill (12.5 acres, 30 feet deep) made of foundry sand from casting molds.[42]

The broader citizen participation and community improvement goals that characterized the MVI strategy of revitalization were conspicuous from the outset. Its advocacy efforts in the first half of 1989 included historic preservation and "community pride." Both purposes were served when the MVI assumed "primary responsibility for community education and support building for the Steel Industry Heritage Task Force." Preservation for the MVI became a technique for community organization and nurture of a regional consciousness:

> Community organizing has focused on linking local groups and professional organizations through participation in Task Force Committees and activities. Over 60 presentations have been made to Mon Valley and Pittsburgh based organizations. The MVI has also coordinated lobbying efforts to increase support among elected officials.[43]

MVI encouragement of "clean-up days" was another technique for building community pride, expanding the realm of citizen participation in civic affairs, and publicizing the CDCs. Thus the Rankin and Swissvale CDCs jointly "enlisted the help of community residents, and solicited donations of materials and equipment from several businesses to clean-up an area. . . at the border." The East Pittsburgh Economic Development Corporation successfully persuaded Conrail to deal with a pigeon roost on an overpass. In Braddock, the Housing Task Force engaged volunteers to clean up the Carnegie Library Music Hall. Downtown West Newton, Inc., sponsored a Green Thumb Day (for summer plantings in the business district).[44]

Unlike most of the MVI affiliates, Monongahela is a nonindustrial community with a substantial middle-class and Victorian ambiance. Located in Washington County, its 1990 population (the towns of Monongahela and New Eagle), was about 7,000. The Monongahela Area Revitalization Corporation was unusually active in promoting live entertainment ("event programming"), heritage consciousness, and neighborhood beautification as a development strategy. These would help create an image of Monongahela as an "attractive, historic community." Thus, MARC produced the "Monongahela Scrapbook," a program that depicted the area's "rich history." It planned to develop an "overall beautification strategy," in order to "improve the local quality of life and increase civic pride." Such enhancement of the community's residential and commercial areas would "make Monongahela more competitive as a location for new businesses and more attractive to new residents."[45]

Clean-up days, pigeon control, heritage programs, and beautification efforts were not at all trivial undertakings in the view of the MVI. What Jo DeBolt envisioned in a successful clean-up day, for example, was a dynamic process of community organization:

> Successful planning and implementation of such an event is a demonstration that the group is functioning, has gotten support and involvement from the larger community, has found a way to get its name in front of the general public, and is building a sense of identity and accomplishment within the group.[46]

More generally, concern with amenities encompassed all the elements of the MVI strategy of community revitalization: spurring economic growth, citizen empowerment, and a better quality of life. At the heart of the MVI's vision of a new civic order in the Mon Valley was the proposition that economic development, although vital, should not be separated from the rest of community life.

The criticisms cited earlier of the MVI's role in stimulating economic development conveyed the impression that it was hoarding money and had accomplished little in nearly three years (1989–1991). In fact, its production was substantial, measured by the standard of recently formed CDCs. New housing units were in progress or had been completed in Braddock, Duquesne, East Pittsburgh, Rankin, and Turtle Creek. Homestead had successfully renovated the Tindall Building, while McKeesport had completed a business incubator and another was in the works in Monessen. The Clairton Economic Development Corporation had opened a recycling plant.[47] Equally important, the MVI was an intermediary organization responsible to its funders. It could not casually dole out money to CDCs that had not developed the ability to successfully undertake a project. It was created, in part, to help local CDCs achieve that capacity. Neither nonprofit status nor a social investment ethic created a license to squander funds and discredit the CDC concept. Equally important, the criticism did not take account of the many non–real estate activities of the CDCs, a vitally important dimension of the MVI strategy. As in Pittsburgh, quantity was not the only or the most valid measure of CDC achievement.

Along with technical and organizing assistance, the MVI operated three funds in support of the affiliated CDCs. The Program Activities Grants, totaling $13,000 in 1992, went to eleven CDCs for such diverse projects as a tool lending library in Clairton, a walking trail in Monongahela, and a mural project in Homestead. The Pre-Development Grants, totaling $101,450 in 1992, enabled CDCs to conduct feasibility studies and other preliminary tasks (also, in 1992, the MVI funneled $1,725,000 in bank loans and $1,055,000 in public money to the CDCs). The third fund, the revolving Community Investment Fund (CIF), was capitalized at $2.5 million contributed by the Heinz Endowments and had loaned more than $2 million by 1992.[48] The two smaller funds are managed by the MVI. The CIF, however, is controlled by an independent board consisting of three MVI delegates and eight outside members—an arrangement designed to reduce the possibility of dissension or political manipulation.[49]

Housing, nationally, was the favored CDC enterprise. It was visible and faster to produce and less complex than commercial or industrial development. But it was also a form of strategic intervention with desirable ripple effects, according to a MVI report:

> Mon Valley CDCs see housing as an important aspect of community revitalization; a healthy residential community rebuilds the tax base, supports the commercial business districts . . . as well as . . . important community institutions, including churches, social clubs, volunteer organizations, and schools. New and rehabilitated housing attracts new residents, encourages investment on the part of other home owners.[50]

Particularly beneficial was the CDC's recycling of abandoned houses, tax delinquent but undemolished and unsellable, taken over by crack users, arsonists, and rats.

In the sphere of commercial revitalization, the MVI assisted Homestead and Glassport in encouraging local merchants and other business interests to form downtown revitalization committees under CDC auspices. It also encouraged communities to pursue the possibility of participating in the Pennsylvania Department of Community Affairs Main Street Program.[51] Early in 1993 the MVI launched an ambitious, three-part regional Partnership for Jobs and Industry. The Manufacturing Center, housed in RIDC's Keystone Commons (East Pittsburgh), will provide shared manufacturing facilities, training, and technical services to smaller manufacturers. An Entrepreneur's Center in the Monessen Business Development Center will support new enterprises. And a Jobs Center in Braddock will provide basic education and skills and will work with employers to provide jobs. Significantly, the MVI viewed the Partnership as an opportunity to lift the Mon Valley out of the low-tech rut: "The project will . . . demonstrate the capacity of the regional work force to rise to the challenges of high performance manufacturing methods that require more decision-making on the shop floor and higher-skill level among workers."[52]

These housing and economic development programs, although important to the resurrection of the Mon Valley, are not what makes the MVI unique. What is novel in that part of the world, as suggested earlier, is a new conception of community, or civic culture, that combines economic revitalization with born-again citizenship and commitment to improving the quality of life. The citizenship part, according to the MVI, is the fountainhead:

> Probably the most difficult to explain, but most satisfying to experience, is the empowerment of individuals. Seeing someone speak at a public meeting for the first time, or press an elected official for an answer, or demand action on a community problem is something that has happened over and over again in the past few years.
>
> The lesson learned here is that the key to success in rebuilding the Valley is in developing people. Everything else flows from that.[53]

Like the MVI, ACTION-Housing was a nonprofit organization with a distinctive program centered on "developing people." Operating in

Pittsburgh and Allegheny County (including the Monongahela Valley) since 1957, it was totally committed to the Renaissance I principle of civic partnership, coalition building, and consensus as the basis for community development and progress. The partnership ideal was not simply an article of faith or ceremonial rhetoric; ACTION-Housing was the quintessential nonprofit entrepreneur, involved in a wide variety of programs, packages, and projects, all of which required cooperation with other nonprofit and public agencies. Equally important, partnerships increased the resources available for dealing with social problems.

By the 1980s, these partnerships and entrepreneurial skills were focused upon the "vulnerable populations"—the low-income elderly and disabled, long-term unemployed, teenage mothers and other women and children in crisis, the homeless, low- and moderate-income families, victims of mental illness or retardation, public housing dwellers. The connecting thread has been to combine finding housing for these groups with extensive social service support. The goal is to help each individual to achieve the highest possible degree of self-sufficiency or independence. ACTION-Housing's systematic coordination of housing and social services on behalf of the most marginalized populations represents a unique development policy. Director Jonathan Zimmer believes that this coordination of living environment and social service is the direction toward which community development, generally, will grow.[54]

Established by the Allegheny Conference to cope with renewal dislocations, ACTION-Housing's first fifteen years, 1957–1972, produced a succession of widely acclaimed housing experiments and programs: East Hills; the Cora Street (Homewood-Brushton) housing rehabilitation demonstration followed by the formation of the Allegheny Housing and Rehabilitation Corporation (AHRCO) for large-scale rehabilitation; and the pioneering experiments in Neighborhood Urban Extension. During those fifteen years, ACTION-Housing helped generate 2,833 new and rehabilitated housing units, while AHRCO between 1967 and 1972 rehabilitated another 1,600 units.[55]

By the late 1960s and early 1970s, ACTION-Housing projects were popping up like rabbits out of a magician's hat: East Hills, phases II, III, and IV, and nearby East Gate; Liberty Park in East Liberty; Allegheny Commons East; Greenway Park, West End; Palisades Park, Rankin (its first housing outside Pittsburgh).[56] At this point, in the early 1970s, major changes were taking place in ACTION-Housing's staff. Bernard Loshbough retired as executive director in January 1973 and was succeeded by William Farkas, and then Paul Brophy in 1975. Roger Ahlbrandt became Director of Housing Research and Development, 1973–1976, followed by twelve years as board member and president. Jonathan E. Zimmer, who become director of supportive services in 1972, became executive director in 1978.[57] Along with other key longtime staff—Lawrence A. Swanson, director of housing and research, and Terri F. Gould, director of human services and community affairs—Zimmer and Ahlbrandt would provide continuity and cohesion. Not least important, ACTION-Housing under Zimmer would demonstrate that a large organization could remain creative, nimble, and free of administrative pretentiousness and bloat.

Yet, it was not even certain that ACTION-Housing would survive when Zimmer and Ahlbrandt joined the staff.[58] The agency almost self-destructed because it had come to depend on federal subsidies for its development program by the late 1960s. But it had underestimated the real costs and overheads of nonmarket housing resulting from rent delinquency, vandalism and crime, and the need for security measures. Simultaneously, the federal government in 1973 imposed a moratorium (lasting eighteen months) on federal housing subsidies. Finally, inflation was driving the organization's operating costs up faster than its income.[59]

Throughout the 1970s, ACTION-Housing had to cope with these problems, including the prospect of HUD's foreclosure of nine projects. It drained its Development Fund of $600,000 in 1972 to rescue the properties. Finally, it salvaged seven projects through a syndication that combined private funds with operating subsidies from the new Section 8 rental assistance program. East Hills Park III and Greenway Park were converted into cooperatives, also with Section 8 subsidies. To keep afloat during this period, ACTION-Housing avoided development and concentrated on technical services for nonprofit developers and research leading to an Allegheny County Neighborhood Preservation Program. ACTION-Housing, ever inventive, could perceive an upside to the debacle. The experience put it in "a unique position to research management strategies and to become a pioneer in testing cooperative conversion and syndication as alternatives to foreclosure."[60]

Adding to the disarray was the realization in the early 1970s that East Hills—the nationally acclaimed experiment in moderate-income, large-scale, cluster-design row housing—was a failure socially as well as economically. The original vision of a racially integrated, multiclass community never materialized, partly because of delays in opening the promised East Hills Elementary School, as well as other recreational and community facilities. ACTION-Housing conceded, by 1974, that East Hills, "like many inner-city rental developments, suffered from slow rent-up, rent delinquency, and an alleged crime rate high enough to warrant security guards."[61] The nearby East Hills Shopping Center was economically sabotaged by the opening of Monroeville Mall in 1969. By 1980 East Hill's shopping center was described as a wasteland of boarded-up storefronts and graffiti that invited crime and vandalism.[62] A decade later it came to an ignominious end when plans for conversion into a light industrial center failed.[63] ACTION-Housing had previously concluded that a "concentration of large numbers of newly constructed federally subsidized housing, such as East Hills" might not be desirable because it could "lead to serious economic and social problems." If attempted at all, it should be accompanied by all necessary city services—police, schools, recreation, refuse collection—as well as social services.[64]

When Zimmer became director in 1977, he had to devote much time over two years to correcting financial problems, including working out the syndication expedient.[65] The agency continued to avoid undertaking development, but participated in several county and federal programs between 1977 and 1982 that led to new or improved affordable housing (6,342 units in fifty Pittsburgh and Allegheny County neighborhoods at an investment of $40.5 million). Three of the programs (Section 8 Technical Assistance, Section 8 Moderate Rehabilitation, and the Allegheny County Neighborhood Preservation Program) were funded through the county's Department of Development. The Pittsburgh URA funded Operation Paintbrush in which ACTION-Housing assisted homeowners (1766) in twenty-three neighborhoods to paint their house exteriors. Project Fresh Start, funded by the county Department of Development, resulted in fresh paint for 177 homes in Braddock. The URA also funded Rent Brake, a weatherization improvement program in which ACTION-Housing participated: over six years, $1.7 million in improved weatherproofing benefited 861 rental units, while landlords agreed to freeze rents for two years. Finally, the Farmers' Home Administration used ACTION-Housing to fund repairs or purchase of homes for 215 families in four western Pennsylvania counties.[66]

These activities exemplified two of the four ACTION-Housing strategies favored by Zimmer. The agency, as always, worked through partnerships and coalitions during this period. And, in contrast to the "demonstration" projects in the early years of ACTION-Housing, Zimmer wanted the organization to have a widespread impact and to benefit large numbers.[67] The other two policies would evolve in the 1980s: the creation of a coordinated housing development and social service program and a focus on the most vulnerable populations.

Beginning with Neighborhood Urban Extension and the federal antipoverty program in the 1960s, ACTION-Housing had always incorporated some social service component. Its Homemakers' Services Program continued into the 1970s in Homewood-Brushton and the North Side. The troubles of the 1970s, especially at East Hills, affirmed the need for a concentrated and coordinated a social services program to accompany housing development.[68] The evolution of such a program in the 1980s, and its focus on vulnerable populations, was not really planned. It developed in an ad hoc way as ACTION-Housing responded to opportunities as they arose (in its characteristically entrepreneurial fashion). The objective was never mere caretaking; it was to provide a living environment and supportive services that would empower individuals to live as full and independent lives as possible.

As a nonprofit entrepreneur, ACTION-Housing responded to the market for its services in a variety of ways. The agency might serve as sponsor, developer, consultant, coordinator, technical advisor, advocate or, not least, funding conduit and packager. Like Pittsburgh's URA, ACTION-Housing channeled millions in federal and state money into Allegheny County. It had the confidence of the foundation world and private corporations as well. The city and county benefited, especially, from ACTION-Housing's links to Pennsylvania's Department of Community Affairs and Housing Finance Agency. It also worked closely with county officials and was often funded by the Allegheny County Department of Development. ACTION-Housing's effectiveness and flexibility derived, in part, from United Way support; this helped cover operating expenses and spared the agency the necessity of a yearly scramble.[69]

ACTION-Housing's entrepreneurial style was expressed not only in responsiveness to nonprofit market opportunities and mobilization of economic resources; its partnership principle was also synonymous with the mobilization of community and political support. It attempted to create as broad and potent a coalition as possible in a universe of competing demands for resources. This was especially important in connection with the vulnerable populations who lacked both visibility and influence.

The focus on vulnerable populations had its beginnings in the massive Mon Valley dislocations and increase in homelessness in the early 1980s. It all started with a suggestion by Roger Ahlbrandt to Zimmer in 1982 that the agency meet with the Mon Valley Unemployed Committee and try to do something about the growing tragedy of home mortgage foreclosures in Allegheny County. Zimmer met not only with the committee, but also with bankers on the board of ACTION-Housing.[70] The Unemployed Committee wanted ACTION-Housing to undertake a survey to document the magnitude of the problem. This was done in the fall of 1982 (351 unemployed persons were surveyed), leading to the creation of a twenty-member Mortgage Delinquency Task Force that included representatives of lending institutions. This kind of research project or survey as a prelude to participation was characteristic of ACTION-Housing. It provided the documentation to justify the proposed program and served as a basis for coalition building.

A moratorium on foreclosures in Allegheny County reduced the pressure on the Task Force, which released its report in January 1983. It recommended, among other things, that lenders work out partial payment plans and refinancing options and that a $250,000 Mortgage Foreclosure Prevention fund be created. Between 1982 and 1985, this program helped save the homes of 2,500 unemployed workers in Allegheny County.[71] ACTION-Housing in 1983 also assisted the state in establishing a Homeowners' Emergency Mortgage Assistance Program. Initially funded at $30 million, it authorized the Housing Finance Agency to extend loans to homeowners confronting foreclosure. ACTION-Housing, under contract with the Housing Finance Agency, administered the program in a six-county area of Western Pennsylvania (assisting more than 3,500 unemployed families to save their homes).

Research and coalition building were also ACTION-Housing's initial contribution to helping the homeless. The agency had participated in an Emergency Shelter Task Force in early 1983 along with the URA and Urban League of Pittsburgh. A year later, in February 1984, the county (with funds from the state Department of Public Welfare) requested ACTION-Housing's assistance in devising an emergency shelter plan. Typically, Zimmer preferred to seek more lasting solutions—prevention or rehabilitation—and the opportunity arose the next month when the URA, the Allegheny County Office of Long Term Care, and an anonymous donor agreed to finance a comprehensive plan under the direction of ACTION-Housing. Mayor Caliguiri and County Commissioner Tom Foerster then appointed (in April 1984) an Advisory Committee on Housing for the Homeless. Following publication of the plan in June 1985, the Advisory Committee would oversee its implementation with the assistance of ACTION-Housing.

The key policy recommendations included helping the homeless to achieve the greatest possible degree of self-sufficiency and, where this was not possible, to provide satisfactory shelters with support services. By the end of the decade, most of the plan's recommendations had been implemented. A comprehensive system of accommodations had been established that included nineteen emergency shelters (376 beds); twelve bridge facilities (180 beds); and five single-room occupancy facilities (443 beds). An additional program, responding to the problem of evictions from public housing, authorized direct rent payments from welfare checks in four projects.[72]

If Allegheny County confronted problems of unemployment, mortgage foreclosures, and homelessness in the 1980s, it also had to deal with an aging population. Toward the end of the decade, the county claimed the highest percentage of aged persons outside the St. Petersburg–Tampa area (20 percent of Allegheny County's population, 285,000 persons, were sixty years of age or older). Early in the decade, ACTION-Housing undertook a study of personal care facilities for the frail elderly and contributed to the creation of hundreds of personal care units. It participated in developing major projects, beginning with the Sweetbriar Apartments on Mount Washington in 1985 (fifty-six units for the low-income elderly and handicapped). The Bennett Place Apartments in Homewood-Brushton and the Laurentian Hall Extended Care Apartments in Bloomfield were significant expressions of the ACTION-Housing strategy of coordinated housing and social services to help individuals maintain a sense of autonomy and independence.

Bennett Place (in partnership with Operation Better Block and the Retirement Housing Foundation of Los Angeles) was a seven-story, fifty-two-unit apartment that opened in 1990. Five units were specially designed for tenants with physical disabilities. Operation Better Block, a Homewood organization, was responsible for providing supporting services and helping the aged participate in community life. The conversion of the former Saint Lawrence O'Toole parochial school in Bloomfield into Laurentian Hall was a collaborative effort linking the Bloomfield-Garfield Corporation, Saint Lawrence O'Toole Church, and Saint Margaret Hospital. It was conceived, in part, as a demonstration project, an example of housing for the aged that falls between the boarding home and completely independent living. Opened in 1989, with thirty-six units, it included a health care center operated by Saint Margaret. BGC was responsible for incorporating the residents into the community, and Saint Lawrence O'Toole parish would supply volunteers for housekeeping services.[73]

ACTION-Housing's policy toward the low-income frail elderly, applied to the entire range of vulnerable populations:

> to create supportive, but non-intrusive, living environments which: (1) enhance the quality of their lives; (2) avoid or defer institutionalization; and (3) strengthen the individual's sense of independence and self-sufficiency to the maximum extent possible within the limitations imposed by advancing age, declining health and limited financial resources.[74]

Thus it pursued practices that avoided or minimized the warehousing of any social group.

Between 1970 and 1987, Pennsylvania had released 8,780 retarded and 15,700 mentally ill persons from state institutions. ACTION-Housing's consistent response to this problem was to "develop housing on a scattered site basis and to link more effectively the community's housing and supportive service systems."[75] When Pennsylvania in the early 1980s closed local state mental institutions, releasing 400 patients, ACTION-Housing assumed responsibility for placing 30 in personal care facilities and then monitoring their condition. During the 1980s, ACTION-Housing participated in several projects to create scattered-site, small-scale accommodations for the retarded and mentally ill.[76]

ACTION-Housing's first encounter with the problems of the handicapped occurred in the early 1980s. Staff members had been meeting with representatives of agencies serving the disabled, leading to the creation of an Accessibility Coalition. Significant also in triggering

ACTION-Housing's awareness of the disabled was a needs assessment undertaken for the Harmarville Rehabilitation Center in 1982. The most dramatic accomplishment on behalf of the handicapped was Allegheny Independence House (AIH). Developed in collaboration with Harmarville Rehabilitation Center and Three Rivers Center for Independent Living, AIH was a twenty-five-unit home for those with multiple and severe disabilities. Every element in the design was carefully calculated and tested in advance at Harmarville. The Three Rivers Center for Independent Living assumed responsibility for the extensive supportive services: attendants; personal, educational and vocational counseling; and self-maintenance training ("life skills").[77]

ACTION-Housing's strategy of empowerment through coordinated, comprehensive housing and social services also encompassed women in crisis. This included unwed mothers, victims of domestic violence, and those with drug and alcohol problems. It was an issue closely related to public assistance issues. ACTION-Housing reported in 1988 that women (56,459) and children (50,956) comprised 80 percent of county assistance caseloads. More than 6,000 out-of-wedlock births were reported in Allegheny County in the previous five years. Over 80 percent of public housing families in Pittsburgh and the county were headed by single women. And women and children were populating the emergency shelters in unprecedented numbers.

ACTION-Housing first addressed this issue in 1981–1982. It assisted the Women's Center and Shelter, previously confined to the basement of the Pittsburgh Theological Seminary, in finding its own permanent facility. Its contribution to the development of Debra House for teenage mothers in Braddock enabled ACTION-Housing to pursue the creation of bridge housing, its major interest. Bridge housing provides shelter for a specified period, together with support services designed to help individuals gain economic independence. Debra House, operated by Bridge to Independence with the assistance of fifteen social agencies, opened in early 1989 in the renovated Saint Brendan's convent building. It enabled twelve single-parent families to reside there six to eighteen months. Beneficiaries had to devise a plan for self-sufficiency, including participation in job training or an educational program. An on-site counselor helped monitor their progress.

ACTION-Housing also assisted McKeesport's Womansplace Shelter to acquire a larger emergency refuge for abused women and children.

This opened in 1990, as did Womanspace East. The latter was both an emergency shelter (ten single rooms) and a bridge facility (six apartments). Located in a handsome, three-story brick-and-stone building in Pittsburgh's Hill District, near downtown, it contained a group living and dining room and child care center. ACTION-Housing also helped Corpus Christi Church in the Lincoln-Larimer neighborhood to develop the Dorothy Day Apartments. Completed in 1990, it was another transitional (or bridge) project. Located in the converted Corpus Christi School, it accommodated seventeen single-parent families and a day care center operated by the University of Pittsburgh's Right Start Program. Characteristically, participants had to sign a contract mandating a self-sufficiency plan over a one-to-three-year period.[78]

Closely related to ACTION-Housing's involvement in guiding single mothers to self-sufficiency was its participation in the world of public housing:

> Today, public housing in Pittsburgh and Allegheny County and other large urban areas is populated primarily by single-parent families on public assistance. Public housing means permanent housing to most of these families because they lack the resources, opportunities and skills to achieve greater levels of self-sufficiency.[79]

The problem was compounded by the isolation of public housing projects in the Pittsburgh area's hilly terrain.

Leon Haley, former director of the Urban League, proposed that ACTION-Housing join in a Public Housing Improvement Program.[80] Established in late 1986 in cooperation with the Allegheny County Housing Authority, the program provided an elaborate array of services in six public housing communities in Braddock, Rankin, and McKees Rocks.[81] It included casework to help participants define their problems, the encouragement of outreach services by local agencies, and "comprehensive life skills training" such as classes in financial management and child care. By 1992–1933 the program was serving more than 1,000 residents in the six projects with assistance from forty-five public and nonprofit agencies.

A related program, also established in 1986, was Project Self-Sufficiency (Partners in Self Sufficiency). It reflected the characteristic ACTION-Housing strategy of coordinated housing and social services to promote competence and the capacity for independent living. Funded by the county Department of Development and United Way, sponsored by the county Housing Authority, and administered by ACTION-Housing, it offered improved housing to low-income single parents through HUD's Section 8 rental subsidies as well as extensive counseling, job training, and educational opportunities.[82]

The ACTION-Housing program that reached the largest number of low- and moderate-income residents of Allegheny County was energy conservation and home weatherization. In the best entrepreneurial tradition, ACTION-Housing recognized a shift in market circumstances and adapted accordingly. As a result of "significant retrenchment by the federal government in the fields of housing and community development" by 1984, the agency realized that it was necessary to "make some fundamental changes" in low-income housing policy.[83] One such change was to help maintain existing housing through a cost-effective method like weatherization.

ACTION-Housing's role in energy conservation in the 1980s also reflected its coalition-building strategy. The agency operated the Pennsylvania Energy Center, which helped with the payment of utility bills. Through the center it coordinated the Energy Resources Group, a coalition of consumer representatives, utility executives, and public officials concerned with the problem of utility bills:

> The Energy Resources Group follows the same model of community-based problem solving that ACTION-Housing has used to address other major issues such as mortgage foreclosure and the homeless—the bringing together of leaders in the community who can directly contribute to solving a problem and then creating an environment where this network develops and implements the needed solution.[84]

Besides operating a variety of conservation and weatherization programs in the 1980s that benefited several thousand homeowners and renters, ACTION-Housing also organized three National Affordable Comfort Conferences in Pittsburgh.[85]

The most dramatic undertaking on behalf of homes for the non-affluent, and the largest in scale since East Hills, was the development of Century Townhomes in Clairton. In June 1987, ACTION-Housing acquired 300 of the 450 units of Woodland Terrace, a row house project built by the federal government in World War II for workers in the U.S. Steel coke plant. ACTION-Housing acted as developer, contractor, and manager through its subsidiary AHI Development, Inc. Improving the property required a new water system, repairing and repaving of all roads, and extensive landscaping. With the East Hills experience in mind, perhaps, ACTION-Housing planned a system of support services modeled on the Public Housing Improvement Program.[86]

ACTION-Housing, the MVI, and the CDCs of Pittsburgh illustrate varieties of nonprofit, community-based development in Allegheny County. (Although ACTION-Housing, strictly speaking, is not community based, it works closely with many community groups.) Another sphere of nonprofit development in Allegheny County centers on quality of life improvements. In the post-steel era, encouraging cultural activities, capitalizing on the city's scenic rivers, and the preservation of historic old buildings were seen as promoting economic development. As in the case of socially oriented community development, charitable foundations have made a conspicuous contribution to these efforts.

9

Amenities and Economic Development

In 27 B.C., Augustus, having defeated Antony and Cleopatra and pacified much of the known world, was busily consolidating the new Roman emperorship. This new Rome needed an arts policy to match its grand self-image. Augustus, therefore, set up a virtual Imperial Endowment for the Arts under the suave Etruscan magnate Maecenas. It was Maecenas' luck to hire some of history's greatest poets — Virgil and Horace — as enthusiastic propagandists for the First Citizen.[1]

In the 1980s many American cities, large and small, enlisted culture as a weapon in the Darwinian competition for economic survival and transformation. As never before, culture became enveloped in the rhetoric of jobs and economic development. Political scientists and sociologists spoke of community arts coalitions or strategies designed to promote downtown revitalization and, more generally, urban growth and renewal. Government, developers, corporations and banks, foundations, arts organizations, and advocates coalesced to build cultural centers, large-scale mixed-use developments, and cultural districts. In some cases, these projects doubled as a form of adaptive historic preservation.

Underlying the transformation of perspective in the industrial Northeast and Midwest—culture or amenities as a cause rather than a consequence of economic growth—was the conviction that economic revitalization depended upon the nurture of a diversified service and professional economy. This post–heavy industry universe revolving around advanced technology, educational and health services, financial and business services, or clean, high-performance manufacturing depended not so much on classic locational factors as on a literate, educated labor force. The latter, in turn, was more oriented than a blue-collar labor force to a community's quality of life—its recreational and aesthetic as well as cultural assets. Thus investment in quality of life would improve a community's chances of attracting desirable economic investment and new residents.[2]

Less speculative, perhaps, was the proposition that the traditional concentration of cultural facilities and organizations in the city center was to give cities their greatest single competitive advantage over the suburbs—to which could be added the cities' educational and medical institutions, historic architecture, zoos, aquariums, botanical gardens, arboretums, waterfronts, specialty shops, and variety of night life attractions. In this sense, a strategy to develop a city's amenities was economically defensible and compatible with the proposition that *"cities with strong, distinctive identities are more likely than others to negotiate a successful economic transition. Each city must identify its strongest and most distinctive features and develop them or run the risk of being all things to all persons and nothing special to any."*[3] In the Pittsburgh region, these amenities are monopolized by the city and are central to its identity; whatever the advantages of the suburbs in other respects, they are cultural deserts. The eastern suburb of Monroeville, for example, is free of museums or art galleries, but it has a "miracle mile" and a smoke-infested mall of transcendent banality dominated by the usual chain outlets and a fast-food court (which long ago superseded a more engaging ice skating rink). Yet, as San Diego's Horton Plaza demonstrates, good design can transform even a mall into a visually life-enhancing experience.[4]

Pittsburgh's suburbs need not fear an invasion of tourists. Tourism, the third largest industry in the United States, is one of the concrete economic benefits of a city's improvement of its cultural resources, scenic assets, waterfronts, and historic districts. Tourists do not invade communities like Savannah, Charleston, San Diego, Baltimore, Boston, Lowell—and, for that matter, Cleveland or Pittsburgh—to see billboards, tasteless office towers, insipid malls, or barren concrete retail sheds. They do go to Cleveland, however, for its symphony, art museum, and performing arts center at Playhouse Square, to Baltimore for the museums, festival market, and other features of the Inner Harbor complex, to Pittsburgh for its Station Square, Carnegie Museum, the East Carson Street commercial district, and the Penn-Liberty Cultural District.

Along with improving the central city's competitive status, in relation to its own suburbs as well as distant communities, and promoting tourism, Pittsburgh's enhanced quality of life has contributed particularly to the downtown's resurrection. In the cities mentioned above, and in many others, developing the city's cultural facilities involved large-scale real estate operations, often associated with office, hotel, and retail development. The arts organizations, in turn, supported downtown businesses, as did their patrons. The performing arts helped sustain the downtown's nightlife. Not least important, downtown cultural complexes, as in Pittsburgh, could trigger an assault against urban sleaze.[5]

One of the earliest examples of support for culture as a large-scale economic development tool was New York City's Lincoln Center, built in the 1960s. The success of this project proved that the performing arts could become the basis for the rejuvenation of an entire district—in this case the city's Middle West Side. One of the earliest and most successful demonstrations of mixed-use revitalization is Baltimore's Charles Center–Inner Harbor complex. Charles Center, launched in the 1950s, included the Morris Mechanic Theater and two performance plazas, along with standard commercial facilities. The Inner Harbor project, launched in the mid-1960s, combines waterfront ambience, gardens and landscaping, a science museum, and a nationally acclaimed aquarium, marina, and the Rouse Festival market.[6]

Cleveland's Playhouse Square, conceived in the 1970s, was notable not only as the nation's largest theatrical restoration, but one in which a foundation—the Cleveland Foundation—took the initiative, along with the Playhouse Square Foundation. The restoration of three historic theaters (the State, the Palace, the Ohio), beginning in 1982, precipitated additional downtown office, retail, and restaurant development—partly to ensure a benign environment for the theater audiences.[7] A possible rival to Playhouse Square is Grand Center in St. Louis. A formerly seedy eight-block district is being transformed into a mix of performing arts facilities (six), galleries, artist studios, and restaurants. The area in its prime, from the 1920s to the 1940s, had claimed over a dozen film and performance theaters, but had degenerated into a "symbol of urban decay" by the 1960s.[8] A smaller community that utilized an arts strategy for downtown revitalization is Louisville, which built the Kentucky Center for the Arts to house the opera, ballet, and symphony.[9]

The creation of Heinz Hall in 1971 foreshadowed Pittsburgh's more extensive plunge into a culturally based economic development strategy in the 1980s. It meant, as in other communities, that cultural institutions would now be increasingly wrapped up in the world of high finance and real estate, of foundations, corporations, government, professional marketing, and would find themselves on a funding treadmill.[10] Spearheading the cultural (big project) development strategy in Pittsburgh were organizations like the Carnegie,[11] the Historical Society of Western Pennsylvania, and the Pittsburgh Cultural Trust.

Presiding over the Carnegie's expansion in the 1980s was Robert C. Wilburn, its president from 1984 to 1992. He not only promoted major development projects like the Science Center and Warhol Museum, but also initiated a Second Century Fund of $125 million to finance the Science Center and physical improvements to the Oakland complex. Wilburn also favored outreach programs that contributed to a near tripling of membership (11,000 to 32,000).[12] The Carnegie Museum was no longer merely a library, music hall, art museum, and natural history museum housed in one massive structure. It came to represent the nonprofit cultural institution in the new guise of expansion-minded entrepreneur. What Wilburn and other cultural administrators realized was that they had leverage in the worlds of government, corporations, and charitable foundations. They could deliver (or at least promise) economic payoffs to communities hungry for jobs and economic development in return for an investment in culture. In the case of the Science Center, built on the city's North Side, the payoff (after construction expenditures) would come in tourist dollars and in popular science education.

Construction of the $40 million Carnegie Science Center began in October 1989 and it opened in October 1991. The center grew out of a merger in 1987 of the Carnegie with the earlier (1939) Buhl Planetarium and Institute of Popular Science located in the North Side's Allegheny Center.[13] The Science Center overlooks the Ohio River and a slice of Roberto Clemente Memorial Park. It is separated by a large parking lot from Three Rivers Stadium. Along with four floors of exhibits, it claims a domed 350-seat Omnimax Theater (one of twelve in the United States)[14] and a domed Henry J. Buhl, Jr., Planetarium—both state of the art. The architectural style, much favored by local government and corporations, might be termed Pittsburgh safe modernist. The exterior of concrete, glass, and metal is dominated by a drab gray trimmed with red. The two domed wings enclose a predominately horizontal flow of interlocking building segments. There is no exterior ornamentation to enliven the facade.[15] Indeed, the only element to relieve the monotony is the World War II submarine parked along the river shore.[16]

One reporter anticipated that the Science Center would be a stimulus "for making this city a major tourist attraction." Jane Downing, former director of the City Planning Department, viewed it as a "great amenity," which might be part of a group of "tourist-related" attractions. Another reporter observed, "One large goal of the new Carnegie Science Center is to become a major tourist attraction in Pittsburgh—and a big enough attraction that people will come to Pittsburgh just to see it—as people now travel to see the National Aquarium."[17]

But advocates of a modern science center anticipated educational benefits as well as tourism. The idea of an institution for popular science meshed with visions of post-steel Pittsburgh. "In a city that is switching from heavy industry to a high-tech economy, interest in science must be cultivated, especially among the young. And there's nothing that can accomplish that more quickly than a hands-on science center."[18]

According to Alphonse DeSena, the center's first director, science education has three objectives: acquaintance, enrichment, and the pursuit of excellence.[19] The last two defined the purpose of the old Buhl complex, now termed the Carnegie Science Center at the Allegheny Square Annex.[20] Thus the new facility was fated to become a kind of first-level technological amusement park that presented science as "fun." Fun meant, first and foremost, as many "interactive" exhibits as possible (including the planetarium). The museum world, generally, seems to have become infected with the interactive virus, as if solitary contemplation were unwholesome. It may be the consequence of an egalitarian, lowest-common-denominator ethic combined with marketing imperatives. A closely related phenomenon is the mania for "outreach." This undoubtedly has marketing implications, but it also might reflect the expectations of funders—government, foundations, corporations— leery of any taint of elitism or lack of commitment to the cliches of multiculturalism. Thus DeSena explained that the Science Center was a place where the culture of science was accessible to all.[21] It is so accessible, in fact, that science and technology are reduced to the level of games and distractions for young children and their adult equivalents. A Science Center promotional piece entitled "An Amusement Park for the Mind" proposes that "Science is Kids' Stuff" and offers this "Food for Thought":

> We're cooking up lots of tasty experiments for our hall of eating. Discover how food manufacturers get all those tomatoes in those little tiny cans. Improve your appetite for nutritious eating. Even nibble on our guest chefs' yummy creations.[22]

One might well question whether this approach to science has any educational value at all.[23] Nor has the dumbing-down strategy of cultural presentation succeeded in breaking attendance records.[24]

Thanks to the Carnegie, pop art joins pop science on the North Side in the form of the Andy Warhol Museum. This also was predicted to be "a major tourist attraction."[25] A museum dedicated to Warhol—a native of Pittsburgh and a Carnegie Tech graduate—was originally conceived by the DIA Art Foundation of New York. Established in 1974, it specialized in mounting exhibits of the work of individual artists. Its executive director, Charles Wright, decided in 1988 to honor Warhol by finding a permanent exhibit facility for its Warhol holdings. Unable to acquire support in New York City, he turned to Pittsburgh, where the Carnegie enthusiastically embraced the project. The Andy Warhol Foundation, created in 1987, also agreed to support a Warhol museum in Pittsburgh.[26] Conceived as an international attraction that will seek support beyond Pittsburgh, it is the largest, most ambitious single-artist museum in the United States; it represents an experiment among three cultural institutions "to create a cultural resource that none of them could have attempted individually."[27]

The DIA Foundation wanted the Carnegie to find a structure that could accommodate research and archival facilities (preferably a nineteenth-century commercial building like its own on Twenty-second Street). After looking at about 100 possibilities throughout Pittsburgh, Wilburn and his administrators decided upon the old Volkwein Music

Building on Sandusky Street (North Side) near the Seventh Street Bridge.[28] This seven-story, 70,000-square-foot terra cotta structure was built over a decade beginning in 1911. Now reborn as a museum, it houses about 1,000 Warhol paintings and drawings, film prints, sculptures, video and audio tapes, all donated by the two foundations. Originally scheduled to open in 1992, construction did not start until that year, and it opened in the spring of 1994. Its director, Thomas N. Armstrong III, had presided over the New York Whitney Museum for fifteen years and had been an early Warhol advocate.[29]

The Carnegie, in the 1980s, exemplified the nonprofit cultural entrepreneur. It aggressively mobilized financial resources and political-public support for two major North Side projects—becoming, in the process, a major North Side developer. It responded, in classic entrepreneurial fashion, to the demand for culture as a source of jobs, tourists, and a way to enhance the city's image.[30] This was true, also, of the Mattress Factory (on the North Side), which linked art to neighborhood development.

The Mattress Factory (named for the six-story building where mattresses were manufactured early in the century) had been established by sculptor Barbara Luderowski in 1977. Located in the vicinity of the Mexican War streets (Sampsonia Way), it specialized in installation art— art designed for a specific site.[31] The Mattress Factory acquired four more properties in 1985, a nuisance bar on Monterey Street and three slum buildings. It redeveloped these into seven moderate-income housing units, a business office, and additional gallery space on Monterey Street, which opened in 1988.

The Mattress Factory's request to the Kresge Foundation and the Pittsburgh Partnership for additional funding to expand its original facility on Sampsonia Way was strongly endorsed by neighborhood organizations. Indeed, the funding proposal was framed as much in terms of neighborhood revitalization as cultural development. The Mattress Factory, according to the president of the Central Northside Neighborhood Council, "has become a major force in redeveloping a significant portion of the Central Northside neighborhood. Low-to-moderate-income housing, creative reuses of 'problem' buildings and the positive image projected for the neighborhood by the world-renowned exhibitors have done much to complement all of our efforts to rebuild our community."[32]

Similarly, an executive of the Northside Civic Development Council urged the Partnership to grant the requested $100,000 loan because the Mattress Factory had contributed significantly to neighborhood improvement.[33] In her proposal to the Kresge Foundation for $107,800, Barbara Luderowski suggested that the proposed renovations of the building at 500 Sampsonia Way would be a model of "creative partnership" linking a nonprofit cultural institution, nonprofit funding agencies, and community development organizations.[34]

Another partnership of government, foundations, corporations, and a nonprofit cultural institution led to the creation of a Pittsburgh Regional History Center. Midwifed by the Committee on Pittsburgh Archaeology and History (CPAH), it was established by the Historical Society of Western Pennsylvania. A small, informal group of volunteers dedicated to preserving Pittsburgh area architecture, artifacts, and archives, CPAH had sponsored a conference in November 1985 to explore the prospects for establishing a city history museum (following up a March 1985 workshop organized by Landmarks to discuss the same subject).

Like other large-scale cultural projects in the 1980s, the history museum was defined as both an economic investment and a way to salvage the region's disappearing heritage in an era of economic transformation: "As a complement to other existing cultural and entertainment resources, the museum would strengthen the city's tourist economy. At the same time it could instill local pride and reinforce the city's image as a first-class city." By way of invidious comparison, CPAH noted that such cities as Baltimore, Cincinnati, and Kansas City had forged ahead of Pittsburgh "in preserving their urban past." Baltimore's Industrial Museum had "become a tourist attraction," and history had also "played an important role in Philadelphia's center city revival." A Pittsburgh history museum would foster pride in the industrial past and "advance the tourist and academic attractions of the region."[35]

The prospect of spearheading the creation of a Pittsburgh history museum was eagerly embraced by the Historical Society. It needed a focus as it underwent a radical transformation in the mid-1980s. Established in 1879, the society had been a largely antiquarian, old family–oriented backwater that reeked of gentility and cobwebs. In 1986 the board hired John Herbst, a museum professional, as executive director to transform the society from a marginal into a major cultural force in Pittsburgh. Within five years, the society's staff, membership, corporate and foundation funding, and budget increased significantly.[36] Equally important, the Historical Society's relationship to the Pittsburgh community changed in the new era. It organized exhibits and collections that celebrated the city's ethnic and working-class heritage and embodied the new social history (history from the bottom up).[37] The society's journal, edited by Paul Roberts, changed from a drab antiquarian format to a pictorial magazine style. But the key to the society's future role in the community was embodied in the creation of the Regional History Center.

The site selected in 1989 was a seven-story, 160,000-square-foot warehouse bounded by two four-story buildings in the Strip District. Located on Smallman Street close to the David Lawrence Convention Center, the warehouse had originated in 1898 as the home of the Chautauqua Lake Ice Company (later Adelman Lumber Company). It was acquired by the Public Auditorium Authority in December 1991 for $3.1 million and was transferred on a long-term renewable lease to the Historical Society.[38] This was a critical event because it inspired confidence in corporate and foundation circles. Of the total projected cost of more than $22 million, $7 million was provided by the state through a Strategy 21 grant in June 1994. These public contributions were supplemented by substantial corporate and foundation grants.[39] The Historical Society has thus has thus joined a small charmed circle—including the Carnegie Museum, Pittsburgh Symphony, and Pittsburgh Cultural Trust—generously supported by the civic, social, corporate, and political elites of Pittsburgh.[40]

The History Center exemplified the emergence in the 1980s and early 1990s of the new political economy of culture. Culture was legitimized as an economic asset rather than a liability with limited appeal. According to Tom Foerster, chairman of the Allegheny County Commissioners, the History Center would be " 'a great selling tool for companies who want to locate here and a great tool for tourism.' "[41] The figure predicted by the Historical Society was at least 400,000 visitors annually. The Center would, presumably, pump nearly $5 million a year into the local economy and inspire new development in the Strip District. Close to the Convention Center and Allegheny River, it would attract conventioneers and might form part of a boat link to other tourist attractions.[42]

Neither the History Center nor the Carnegie Science Center could have been funded without an economic, utilitarian rationale. But there is a potential Faustian bargain involved. The formidable capital investment and operating expenses associated with nonprofit cultural entrepreneurship necessitates mass patronage. The latter, in turn, requires the adoption of corporate-style marketing methods and exhibition techniques that would not overtax the intellect or the attention span of a heterogeneous audience. At all costs, any hint of elitism or intellectual strain has to be avoided in favor of interactivism and outreach. Indeed, Herbst declared that the History Center "would not be an 'elitist museum,' but a growing, living demonstration of . . . life in Western Pennsylvania." As at the Science Center, the Historical Society anticipated that "designers and exhibit staff will find ways to excite and involve visitors through recreated environments, interactive computer displays, full-screen video dramatizations and mini-theatrical presentations." There might also be live dramatic presentations bringing "history to life" and "hands-on" activities for children. There is even the threat of an Alcoa-funded training program for actors who would assume the attire and character of historical figures such as Henry Clay Frick or an East European peasant.[43]

Perhaps all this is the price to be paid for the more solid purposes of a Regional History Center: providing archival and research facilities, sponsoring academic scholarship and conferences, the quiet display of artifacts from the past. At least one can hope.

The most ambitious Pittsburgh effort to use culture as an economic stimulus involved the creation of the Pittsburgh Cultural Trust in 1984. Incorporated by the Allegheny Conference, its mission was to nurture the growth of a cultural district in the Penn-Liberty corridor and thereby contribute to Pittsburgh's economic vitality. The Cultural District was "planned to provide a critical mass of arts and entertainment activities in order to draw commercial investment and thereby expand the tax base and employment base of the city and the region."[44]

Bounded by Fort Duquesne Boulevard, which borders the Allegheny River, Liberty Avenue, Stanwix Street, and Tenth Street, where it joins the Convention Center and Liberty Center, this large fourteen-square-block section of downtown had been ignored during Renaissance I. The major exception was the creation of Heinz Hall in 1971 (and Heinz

Penn-Liberty cultural and historic district, a Pittsburgh Cultural Trust project. *Photo: Author*

Plaza in 1979). The Heinz family, acting through the Howard Heinz Endowment (in alliance with the public and corporate sectors) was instrumental in the renewed effort to fulfill the thwarted Renaissance I dream of creating a Pittsburgh cultural center.[45]

The catalyst for a culturally centered revitalization program for the Penn-Liberty district was a consultant report sponsored by the Allegheny Conference. Prepared by Llewellyn-Davies Associates and released in 1979, its recommendations included the creation of a cultural district. The proposal was enthusiastically endorsed by the Conference; a cultural district would "be a positive selling point for attracting and retaining businesses for the region and holds the potential for sparking a new arts/ entertainment industry that would create jobs and add dollars to the regional economy."[46] The Trust, similarly, maintained that "a lively arts and entertainment district in downtown Pittsburgh can enhance the city's image as a place to live and work."[47] Guided in its first decade by its president, Carol Brown, the Cultural Trust was perhaps unique in its combination of functions—as real estate developer, facilities manager, service provider for local arts organizations, and booking agent.[48] The first two roles explain the need for subsidies—to cover costs associated with development and theater deficits.[49]

More than any cultural institution in Pittsburgh, the Trust has been favored by city government and the Heinz Endowment (with the strong personal support and involvement of the late H. J. Heinz II).[50] Indeed, as cultural organizations go, it occupies an extraordinarily high niche in the local power structure. This status derives from key role it is assigned in preserving the vitality of downtown. When the Trust was established in 1984, Pittsburgh's downtown had become "increasingly desolate" at night. The streets had been a mess in the early 1980s because of construction on the subway system. Landmark's Station Square on the South Side had, since the late 1970s, siphoned off nighttime crowds. Within five years, three major movie houses—the Gateway, the Stanley, and the Warner—had folded. Attendance had even dropped at Heinz Hall. Restaurant and retail activity was not too vibrant, either.[51] The Trust and the cultural district strategy were devised, in good measure, to prevent the downtown from becoming a graveyard at night. A cultural district might also attract business to the Convention Center.[52]

The first step, occupying the Trust from 1984 to 1987, was the conversion of the old Stanley Theater into the Benedum Center for the Performing Arts (located at Penn Avenue between Seventh and Eighth Streets) and the construction of the CNG Tower (on Liberty Avenue behind Heinz Hall). This twin project involved an extraordinarily complex and convoluted series of real estate transactions featuring the Trust, the Heinz Endowment, the Public Auditorium Authority, and the city of Pittsburgh (through the URA). The important consideration was to structure the project so that the Trust received financial subsidies in the end.

The role of the Heinz Endowment extended beyond taking the usual foundation initiatives or funding. Operating through a Penn-Liberty Holding Company, it acquired the land that made the CNG and Benedum projects possible.[53] The Heinz Endowment retained ownership of the land on which the CNG Tower was built, and about $400,000 in rental income went to the Trust annually for operating and development expenses ($200,000 for the first couple of years).[54] The Heinz Endowment, on behalf of the Trust, also acquired a 2.3-acre site across from

Benedum Center for the Performing Arts. *Photo: Dennis Marsico. Courtesy of MacLachlan, Cornelius, and Filoni, Inc.*

the Benedum at Penn and Seventh for later development (Theater Square). Another foundation, the Claude Worthington Benedum, also played a vital role in funding the Benedum Center. It contributed $8 million toward the total $42 million cost of converting the Stanley into a performing arts center.[55]

A side effect of the Benedum–CNG Tower complex was the loss of the 1915 Moose Building on Penn Avenue. One of Pittsburgh's most gracious Beaux-Arts structures, its decorative facade included engaged fluted columns, rustication, light-colored terra cotta tiles, dentils, ornamental spandrel carvings, a row of upper-story windows capped by segmental arches. The Pittsburgh History & Landmarks Foundation inherited chunks of the facade, but was never able to display them. About to be auctioned off by Landmarks in October 1993, they went instead, ironically, to the Cultural Trust for possible display in its planned park and plaza.[56]

The city of Pittsburgh's desire to increase tax revenues from its central business district was translated into unqualified support for the cultural district strategy. A URA Urban Development Action Grant of $17 million was divided into $8.5 million in low-interest loans toward the development of the CNG Tower and the Benedum Theater. But the Trust's payback of its share would take the form reduced ticket prices or free performances for special groups such as senior citizens, the poor, or children. In addition, the city and county split the cost of retiring the bonds issued by the Public Auditorium Authority to cover the $7,500,000 cost of the Stanley Theater, purchased from the Penn-Liberty Holding Company.

The city has also invested heavily in street and facade beautification for the Cultural District. With the assistance of the Trust, it launched a three-year, $3 million project, beginning in 1990, involving lighting, trees, and sidewalk and crosswalk improvements in the vicinity of Penn Avenue between Ninth and Tenth Streets. Contained within the fourteen-block Cultural District is a historic preservation subdistrict of six blocks located on Penn and Liberty Avenues, between Seventh and Tenth Streets. Officially designated historic by both the National Register and the city (1987), it consists of about sixty buildings dating from the late nineteenth and early twentieth centuries. Four to ten stories in height, they originated as warehouses or light manufacturing facilities and exhibited a wide variety of revival styles: Italianate, Queen Anne, Romanesque, neoclassical. The URA and the Heinz Endowment launched a three-year, $1.5 million facade renovation program in this area that provided generous loans subsidizing 30 to 50 percent of the cost—at no interest and demanding no payment unless the property was sold. In addition, participants were eligible for federal historic preservation tax credits and local tax abatement.

The city's support for the cultural district strategy was also motivated, in part, by the expectation that it would undermine the unsavory complex of prostitution, X-rated movie houses, massage parlors, and adult book stores arrayed along Liberty Avenue. This would emulate the transformation of Boston's notorious combat zone by the creation of a Midtown Cultural District. An important step was the Cultural Trust's acquisition of the Art Cinema (which was anything but) on Liberty Avenue early in 1990. The 200-seat facility will be a showplace for foreign and specialty or experimental films and smaller live performances.[57]

The Pittsburgh Cultural Trust represents a unique cultural experiment. It has been delegated significant responsibility for the economic and cultural development of the city's downtown, for managing several major performing arts facilities, for overseeing a historic landmark district, and eradicating sleaze from the Penn-Liberty corridor.[58] It is attempting, in its role as cultural catalyst, the difficult task of bringing the visual arts to the downtown desert.[59] A recent initiative by John Robin (in cooperation with Carol Brown) enabled the Trust to establish an art gallery. An odd triangular space bounded by Sixth and Liberty Avenues and Wood Street had been the site for a five-story building erected in 1928 to house Max Azen Furriers. Acquired by the Port Authority Transit for about $1 million in 1981 in connection with the Wood Street subway station, it was transferred to the Cultural Trust in 1990 at the urging of Robin on a dollar-a-year, ten-year lease. It opened in October 1992 as the Trust's Wood Street Galleries, joining a smidgen of other commercial galleries in downtown.[60] The Trust also plans to commission site-specific art for the cultural district.[61]

Within its first ten years, the Trust's most substantial accomplishment has been the expansion of downtown performing arts facilities. Heinz Hall and the Benedum, each holding about 2,800 seats, were too large for many local or touring groups, and each was already committed to resident organizations—the Pittsburgh Symphony at Heinz Hall, and the Pittsburgh Opera, Pittsburgh Civic Light Opera, Pittsburgh Ballet Theater, and Pittsburgh Dance Council at the Benedum. To fill the gap, the Trust acquired the Fulton Theater in the fall of 1988. The oldest of the performing arts theaters, the 1,370-seat Fulton was launched in 1904 as the Gayety, a vaudeville and burlesque house. It became a movie theater around 1930, when it was renamed.[62] Located on Sixth Street between Penn Avenue and Fort Duquesne Boulevard, it reopened in the spring of 1991 after Trust supervised remodeling. Lacking resident companies, and thus flexible in scheduling, it accommodated such local groups as the Pittsburgh New Music Ensemble, Pittsburgh Dance Alloy, Bach Choir, Renaissance and Baroque Society, and Three Rivers Lecture

Series. In the interest of affordability, the Trust maintained a tiered rental system (reduced rates for nonprofessional arts groups, and higher rates for profit-making organizations).[63] Adjoining the Fulton Theater is the 200-seat Fulton Mini, a movie house leased by the Trust to the Pittsburgh Filmmakers for exhibiting quality films.

The Trust's plans for a fourth downtown theater were viewed with dismay by North Side civic organizations. Having lost the Buhl Planetarium in 1991 and then the Sears store in Allegheny Center Mall in the winter of 1992, Northside residents confronted the loss of the Pittsburgh Public Theater, which had been housed since the mid-1970s in the 450-seat Hazlett Theater in the Carnegie Library's Allegheny Regional Branch. The Trust had been negotiating with the Public Theater since 1989, and its offer in January 1992 to provide a new 650-seat theater as part of an office complex in the cultural district was irresistible.[64] A larger facility would permit the Public Theater to earn more revenue for shorter runs, thus making it possible to hire major artists who had hitherto avoided the Public Theater because of its extended rehearsal and performance requirements. Another problem with the North Side site was the lack of appealing restaurants in the vicinity, thus making a night at the theater less than a total experience.

The new theater, expected to cost $17 million, will adjoin a fifteen-to-twenty-story office tower in a continuous fifty-foot facade at Penn Avenue and Seventh Street. Included in the development, called Theater Square, will be a parking garage and green plaza.[65] The plan to include a first-run movie theater was dropped for lack of a commercial operator. The city and county have committed $2.5 million each for the theater complex, and in the spring of 1993 the state legislature approved a Strategy 21 grant of $17.75 million. The funds were released by Governor Casey in January 1994 (along with $6 million for the Warhol Museum). Michael Graves will be the architect of the project, which has been stalled for lack of a prime tenant.[66]

The Trust envisioned the cultural district as a place where, one day,

concerts, Broadway shows, and theater are playing almost every night of the week. A place where late-hour diners relax in restaurants and romantic outdoor cafes . . . where window shoppers stroll tree-lined streets past art galleries, boutiques, and ice cream parlors . . . where fountains, outdoor sculptures, and small parks nestle among beautifully restored 19th-century buildings.[67]

Obstructing the fulfillment of this vision are the incompatible institutions that operate in the cultural district—social and government
agencies, miscellaneous retail outlets, fast food operations.[68] At present,
strangers to Pittsburgh wandering in the Penn-Liberty corridor would
probably not realize they were in a cultural district. In time, perhaps, the
critical mass will be in place and "an influx of new art and business life
. . . could literally turn the area around."[69] What is greatly needed is
encouragement for the kind of small entrepreneurs who have established
the colorful, quirky shops that pop up on East Carson, who open cof-
feehouses, antique stores, small galleries, and restaurants. Meanwhile, the
Trust has been the catalyst for significant economic and cultural development in the Penn-Liberty section of downtown.[70]

If cultural vitality could provide a competitive advantage in a new
economy based on providing services, amenities, and information, so
also could natural or scenic assets make "certain cities distinctive and
attractive and . . . offer untapped development opportunities." Pittsburgh's industrial history had, however, obscured the city's "striking and
distinctive" natural features—its topography and rivers.[71] Even though
the success of Renaissance I had been based, in part, on the creation of
Point State Park at the confluence of the three rivers—the Allegheny
and the Monongahela, which form the Ohio—the rivers played no further role in the development program.[72] It was not until the 1980s that
a significant river consciousness emerged in Pittsburgh, an awareness for
the first time in over a hundred years that the rivers, no longer append-
ages to industry and rail traffic, could enter into the life of the city.

One of the earliest expressions of the rediscovery of the rivers as a
civic asset occurred at a historical geography conference held in September 1982. In a report to the URA following the conference, "Pittsburgh's
Waterfront Lands," Edward Muller, a University of Pittsburgh historian,
called for a "more regionally comprehensive, functionally balanced, and
people oriented plan for the future." To accomplish this, however, it was
necessary to overcome a century of negative perceptions and actively
promote the rivers to the community as something better than "work-
places, barriers, and foul pools." They had to become "part of our *daily*
lives, enhancing the quality of life to the degree to which water resources
have in many other cities."[73]

Muller regretted the failure of Renaissance I to incorporate the rivers
into the city's fabric; to the contrary, the era's redevelopment program

divorced the public from its rivers by fronting them with highways and parking areas. The best view, in fact, was from "empty cars stored in vast parking lots." Beyond the downtown was the industrial debris of the past, including the rail systems that hugged the river edge. There were, however, activities that hinted at the rivers' potential for both economic development and recreational use. These included weekend boating, tour cruises on the Gateway Clipper fleet, and summer events like the Three Rivers Arts Festival, the Regatta, Wind Symphony performances from a floating barge—all of which drew people downtown and toward Point State Park. But there was virtually no residential housing, and few res-taurants, entertainments, or marinas for the boaters. The waterfronts were largely depopulated on weekdays, and "large areas remain unde-veloped or deteriorating, while the rivers still seem separate from the surrounding city life."[74]

Muller advocated the creation of an Allegheny Conference–like or-ganization to overcome the many obstacles to riverfront consciousness and development: lack of coordination and planning, government frag-mentation, the tangle of public and private interests and ownership, fi-nancial constraints. His proposals for a comprehensive river policy en-compassed residential and commercial development (including specialty retail outlets and marinas), opportunities for leisure activity along the rivers for neighborhood residents, and nurture of vegetation and wildlife to add to the rivers' allure.

In the decade following the conference and Muller's early formulation of a riverfront policy, Pittsburgh's rivers received more attention from government and civic groups. But the results have been uneven, limited, fragmentary, and in some cases undesirable. Government and citizens' groups have issued reports that testify to their recognition that the rivers could become a civic asset, but nothing much has come of them. River development is something of a casual free-for-all in which government, nonprofit and commercial interests operate independently. Development lacks coherence and, apparently, any design criteria. The zoning of the riverfronts even permits billboards to enrich the river scene.

The director of the Allegheny County Planning Department declared in 1988 that " 'now, with railroads and industries declining, we have to try to recapture and make better use of the riverfronts.' " And the 1991 *Allegheny County 2001* statement proposed that the county's 170 miles of riverfront offered abundant opportunities for "recreation, conservation, historic preservation, transportation, and quality mixed use development. With careful planning, the rivers can again be an integral part of the everyday life of our communities."[75] In October 1993 the county commissioners adopted a riverfront plan that recommended a conservation and development classification system, identified "opportunity areas" or prime development parcels, and proposed a regional river access system that included a riverfront trail.[76]

The plan was advisory in nature because the Planning Department had no authority over local zoning ordinances. The most dramatic contribution of the county commissioners to riverfront development, in fact, was authorizing the construction of a massive new county jail on former CSX property. Scheduled for completion in 1995, the seventeen-acre site on the fringe of the Golden Triangle, between Second Avenue and the Parkway East, claims a superb river view. Consisting of seven units or "pods," the structures range from five to nine stories in height, and totally dominate the view of the city from the Parkway.[77] Admittedly, a prison is an appropriate symbol for the quality of life in the United States at the century's end, but is it desirable to build it on a prime riverfront site?

The city of Pittsburgh had made a feeble, inconclusive gesture toward river planning in the 1950s,[78] but it was not until 1989 that the City Planning Department issued a riverfront plan. A dry, fairly technical document enveloped in bureaucratic prose, it was less than inspirational and aroused minimal community interest or response. This was unfortunate, because it did embrace values and policies compatible with post-industrial river development:

> Connection of residents to their riverfronts for the first time in the history of the City or the first time in this century will help create the environment of a 'River City' that will distinguish Pittsburgh from other cities. . . . An attractive environment with a high quality of life is essential to attract quality economic development.[79]

The general policies proposed for riverfront development included a balanced mix of land uses, greater public access, and a concern for "environmental quality" along the river edges. Concrete recommendations included creating or enhancing six large parks (only three would be new); building neighborhood parks; protecting outstanding views through zoning restrictions (Riverfront District Regulations, View Protection Reg-

Allegheny County Jail. *Photo: Author*

ulations); and the creation of a special taxing district for a regional recreation system to which the riverfront parks would be assigned.[80] The Department of City Planning, cognizant of fiscal constraints, proposed no development timetables.[81]

Oddly, the mayor's office responded to this report by appointing a Mayor's Working Group in March 1990 to prepare another report. Issued in January 1991, this report reiterated several of the Planning Department's recommendations—a regional recreational agency, greater public access, zoning protection for scenic views. To these it added the appointment of a Riverfront Project Coordinator within the Planning Department, a rails-to-trails program to transform the railroad corridors into public recreation areas, and a water taxi system.[82] Still another report, issued by the Citizens' League of Southwestern Pennsylvania in November 1990, similarly endorsed greater public access to the riverfronts, a regional authority or special-purpose district, more parks, and riverfront trails.[83]

Tom Murphy (elected mayor of Pittsburgh in November 1993) had been a member of the Mayor's Working Group. He had complained in 1991 that despite all the rhetoric about the importance of the riverfronts, " 'there's no sense of urgency and no sense of who's in charge.' " Mayor

Masloff did not even convene a news conference to release the group's report, Murphy observed.[84] In charge of river development in the 1980s and early 1990s, it seems, were the URA and a variety of entrepreneurial nonprofit cultural organizations. The city had been relatively inactive on this front since the construction of South Side Riverside Park (1983) and Allegheny Landing (1984). Allegheny County, as just noted, contributed a jail whose inmates will command choice Mon River views. Private development was limited to the restaurant complex called "The Strip—Down by the Riverside," an architectural embarrassment, and to whatever will happen to the cleared LTV site on the South Side. The Armstrong Cork project in the Strip, which would have provided over 300 housing units and preserved attractive historic commercial architecture, failed to find a developer who could get financing or avoid bankruptcy. On the other hand, the effort by a private developer to obliterate the historic Mackintosh-Hemphill factory buildings on the South Side for an expanded parking lot was thwarted by a historic landmark designation.

The only evidence of a comprehensive, programmatic development vision that has emerged since Muller's 1982 call for a river renaissance is the Three Rivers Heritage Trail undertaken by the Friends of the Riverfront.[85] The Friends were an outgrowth of the Three Rivers Task Force, a coalition of environmental and civic groups that in December 1990 announced a plan to create an eleven-and-a-half-mile walking-hiking-biking recreational trail. It would begin at Washington's Landing, two miles from the Point, cross the West End Bridge to the South Side, and continue along the Monongahela past the South Side Park and Birmingham Bridge as far as Sandcastle.[86] But this plan is only the beginning. Robert Gangewere emphasizes the group's connection to broader regional and national policy:

> The Friends envision not only a riverfront trail within the city limits but connecting trails to other regional hiking and cycling trails in Allegheny County and Western Pennsylvania. The ultimate vision is to connect Pittsburgh to Washington, D.C., and to Lake Erie by rail-to-trail conversions . . . made possible by federal "railbanking" legislation and financing through state administration of ISTEA monies.[87]

Disappointment over the lack of initiative by the Masloff administration, and the leaden report by the City Planning Department, triggered the creation of the Friends.[88] The prime mover and catalyst was the late Martin J. O'Malley, a onetime California environmental organizer.[89] Tom Murphy was strongly committed to the Friends' goals. Also prominent in the group's formative years were R. Jay Gangewere, editor of *Carnegie Magazine*; John Stephen, who abandoned a corporate law career to become executive director in 1992; and R. Todd Erkel, a freelance writer.[90] Later, its board of directors would include Larry Ridenour, the County Planning Department's coordinator of trails; Rob Thomson, chairman of the Rails-to-Trails Conservancy; and Edward Muller.

A combination "land trust . . . Rails-to-Trails [and] citizens riverfront advocacy group," the Friends of the Riverfront solicit cadres of volunteers for cleanup days (always during Earth Day weekend in April) and Heritage Trail preparation.[91] Besides volunteer recruitment, practical challenges confronted by the Friends include fundraising and acquiring rights-of-way from various property owners. The city government does not provide material assistance, but is otherwise cooperative.[92] This had not been true at the outset, when O'Malley's confrontational style had pushed the group toward an adversarial relationship with the city. It reached a climax in a heated encounter over the city's intention to use asphalt instead of softer crushed limestone for a section of South Side trail.[93] The incident, however, turned out well for the Friends: it gained them public attention. Asphalt was not used on the trail. And a meeting between the Friends and city department heads led to better relations.[94] The "missing player in the riverfront drama," complains Turkel, "has been Pittsburgh's philanthropic and corporate community. With minor exceptions, this powerful group . . . has ignored the riverfront issue."[95]

The ultimate goal is, through citizen initiative and involvement, to transform the rivers into a source of community identity and cohesion. The Friends believe that the trail will have a powerful impact on the city's quality of life, providing a focal point for river-oriented social interaction:

> We invite a new kind of participation in the city's rivers and riverfronts. We envision a very social riverfront: a place for evening river walks, and morning bike rides. We want residents to reclaim a sense of ownership of this valuable natural resource. Pittsburgh's riverfront . . . can become a memorable and invigorating place—alive with community gardens, playgrounds, vendors, stages, and a range of commercial interests.[96]

In addition to creating a new kind of social landscape, Muller believes that the trail will serve to "link up many institutions and places, which are today disparately placed." The Three Rivers would be transformed, "accessible at multiple points and with multiple points of destination."[97] The reorientation of the Pittsburgh river system to accommodate recreational and social uses has been difficult, not only because of the historic legacy of domination by industry and the railroads, but also because of the extent of river frontage. Unlike Baltimore's Harborplace, which is a contained space, Pittsburgh's sprawling rivers are difficult to visualize as a whole. The effort to exploit their beauty and possibilities for recreation did not even begin until 1989–1990, and the Friends of the Riverfront were the first to conceive a unifying development plan.[98]

Historic Preservation and Industrial Heritage in the Pittsburgh Region

And when the heavens rolled away and St. John beheld the new Jerusalem, so a vision of a new London, a new Washington, Chicago, or New York breaks with the morning's sunshine upon the degradation, discomfort, and baseness of modern city life. There are born a new dream and a new hope. And of such is the impulse to civic art.

—Charles Mulford Robinson, 1903

There is a New York lady who had a Tuscan father and an English mother and has been married to an American for most of 50 years. She has seen the old buildings go down and the new buildings go up. Observing a typical apartment house rising on York Avenue recently she asked a workman, in Italian, "How do you build them so fast?"
"Senza rispetto," he replied, "without respect."

—Ada Huxtable, 1986

One of the great American pastimes of the late nineteenth century, and well into the twentieth, was the Pittsburgh joke. In an issue of the New York *Daily Graphic* in 1882, for example, we learn that "Pittsburgh is a place where the inhabitants breathe, move and have their being in soot

---

The first part of this chapter originally appeared in "City Beautiful, City Banal: Design Advocacy and Historic Preservation in Pittsburgh," *Pittsburgh History* (Historical Society of Western Pennsylvania), Spring 1992, 26–36. Reprinted by permission.

and grime"; it is a city "where the smoke is so dense that a cyclone would only scare the people by making the sun visible for a few minutes." Willard Glazier, in *Peculiarities of American Cities* (1885), describes a night approach to Pittsburgh as a "scene so strange and weird that it will live in the memory forever. One pictures . . . the tortured spirits writhing in agony, their sinewy limbs convulsed, and the very air oppressive with pain and rage"; in truth, he adds, "Pittsburg is a smoky, dismal city, at her best. At her worst, nothing darker, dingier or more dispiriting can be imagined." An article in the *Century Magazine* in 1901 speaks of the "smoke and steam that hang in a heavy black canopy close above the roofs" of Pittsburgh, "the dirtiest city in America." And the author of *The Personality of American Cities* (1913) relates the woes of a New York girl "who has been living in Pittsburgh for the last four years" and complained "that she had never seen but two sunsets there."[1]

Finally, in this same spirit of defamation, Edward Muller explored H. L. Mencken's uncomplimentary portrait of America's Inferno: "There is good reason to doubt," Mencken asserted, "that pansies would flourish along the Monongahela, particularly within sight, sound or scent of Pittsburg. The soil there is of a peculiar quality, being composed of almost equal parts of coal dust, grease and garbage, and is plainly too rich for small plants."[2]

One can date architectural and design advocacy to the first decade of the twentieth century and local defensiveness over the findings of the Pittsburgh Survey of 1907–1908. The repercussions of that wholesale condemnation of Pittsburgh's social institutions included the creation of the Pittsburgh Civic Commission in 1909 by Mayor George W. Guthrie. It was a kind of early version of the Allegheny Conference on Community Development—a cooperative endeavor by the mayor's office and the civic elite—whose mandate was to "plan and promote improvements in civic and industrial conditions."[3] The fourteen committees through which it operated included one on city planning and another on municipal art and design. Civic Commission publications included a report on *City Planning for Pittsburgh*, published in 1910, whose three authors included Frederick Law Olmsted, Jr.[4]

Completed the same year was Olmsted's masterful *Pittsburgh: Main Thoroughfares and the Down Town District*, which outlined both a philosophy of civic design and many concrete proposals for improvement.

He condemned the indifference to Pittsburgh's waterfront potential "for recreation and as an element in civic comeliness and self-respect" and challenged the ethic behind that attitude:

> One of the deplorable consequences of the short-sighted and wasteful commercialism of the later nineteenth century lay in its disregard of what might have been the esthetic by-products of economic improvement; in the false impression . . . that economical and useful things were normally ugly; and in the vicious idea which followed, that beauty and the higher pleasures of civilized life were to be sought only in things otherwise useless.

Olmsted cited European cities as models for civic use of riverfronts. Wherever people could sit and walk near the water, he noted, "the result has added to the comeliness of the city itself, the health and happiness of the people and their loyalty and local pride."[5]

Olmsted also had constructive suggestions about another dramatic but ignored asset in the Pittsburgh environment. He complained that the area's steep slopes were neglected, unsightly, and slatternly, and recommended that the city assume the burden of their maintenance, converting them from public nuisances to park assets of value to the community.[6]

Events beyond Pittsburgh also influenced the emergence of a design awareness. Most important was the vision embodied in the City Beautiful phase of American urban culture. The City Beautiful ideal, which flourished in the early twentieth century, was a compound of several environmental and cultural developments affecting urban life: an emphasis on parks, open spaces, and boulevards characteristic of the post–Civil War generation of landscape architects; the tradition of village and municipal improvement societies that embraced betterment schemes ranging from tree-planting to underground utility wires and billboard control; the striking vision of neoclassical architecture, civic centers, and coordinated planning expressed in the Chicago World's Fair of 1893; the concrete embodiment of those visions in the McMillan Commission Plan for Washington, D.C., in 1902 (with Daniel Burnham a connecting link between the Chicago Exposition and the Washington plans); the aspirations of architects and other trained professionals to exert greater influence over urban development.[7]

It would be a mistake to dismiss the City Beautiful ideal as a superficial or cosmetic approach to urban design. One of its leading advocates,

Charles Mulford Robinson, argued that "civic art" stood for more than beauty and ornamentation: "On how many sides—moral, physical, intellectual, political, and economic—does an effort for beauty in towns and cities touch the welfare of mankind!" The economic argument lay "in the attraction of the wealth and culture of the leisure class and the transient trade of tourists"; the philanthropic "in the brightening of the lives of the poor"; the educational "in the instructive possibilities of outdoor art"; the political "in the awakening to civic pride." Although elite-inspired and elite-guided, the City Beautiful was, nonetheless, an inclusive vision. Robinson, for example, argued that it was not enough to provide tenement districts with "clean and well paved streets and frequent playgrounds" in the name of hygiene: the spirit of "aesthetic renaissance" had to descend into the slums and nurture "artistic impulses." Until then, the civic renaissance would be incomplete.[8]

The inclusiveness of the City Beautiful vision extended to the past, thus linking it to latter-day historic preservation:

> Splendid public structures and refined and costly private work give, of course, new glory to the visible city life; but we would not have our villages or cities merely new. There is a beauty of age hallowed by history, since art is undying. We must save what is good from the legacies of earlier days if we would secure the completest beauty and interest."[9]

Robinson praised the preservation of New York's beautiful but outgrown City Hall and was pleased by the storm of protest in 1896 that thwarted destruction of the Bulfinch front of Boston's State House. Robinson educated contemporaries about historic preservation in Europe: the London Society for the Protection of Ancient Buildings; the French legislation of 1887 that required the Ministry of Public Instruction and Fine Arts to designate all ancient or classical remains that would be in the national interest to preserve and protect, and also in France, the municipal and national historical commissions including the Commission du Vieux Paris, established in 1897. There was also the Royal Commission of Monuments in Belgium that protected public buildings, while local voluntary historical societies attempted to protect privately owned dwellings.

In the City Beautiful vision, every detail of the built environment had to be judged by the test of civic art: "If drinking fountains, for man or beast, band stands, or lavatories have the conspicuousness in site of a public statue, their artistic character should be scrutinized as rigidly. Utility Should Not Excuse Ugliness."[10]

A significant expression of these City Beautiful ideals in early twentieth-century Pittsburgh was embodied in "A Plan for the Architectural Improvement of Pittsburgh" prepared by the Committee on Civic Improvement of the Pittsburgh Chapter of the American Institute of Architects. It envisioned for Pittsburgh one of the key design objectives of the City Beautiful—the grand public square. It had in mind a downtown location "in the heart of the municipal and business district." The civic complex would include a colossal monument to "one of Pittsburgh's heroes or benefactors" and would be bounded by Richardson's great Allegheny County Courthouse and Jail on one end, and a proposed new city hall balancing it on the other end on Sixth Avenue.[11]

It is significant that the local architectural society attempted to strengthen and document its case by citing the ambitious plans of other cities, suggesting an effort to persuade Pittsburghers to overcome the negative image of their community by sponsoring an architectural and design renaissance. It informed local people of Cleveland's intention to create a civic center that would ensure that city's status as "one of the most distinguished and artistic cities in America." Chicago was developing its lake front park so as to include "an harmonious group of beautiful buildings." Buffalo was working on a new railway terminal and waterfront. The Pittsburgh civic center, however, materialized not downtown but in Oakland, two miles east, where it would expand to include a residential section, Schenley Farms. Conceived by F. F. Nicola, the Oakland Civic Center was conceived as a model multinucleated suburban community that included residential, civic, cultural, and educational institutions. It was an archetype of responsible capitalism and entrepreneurship, expressed in the neoclassical architecture that had dominated the Chicago Exposition. The Oakland complex received high praise from Montgomery Schuyler, America's leading architectural critic of the era. More than any other city, he declared, Pittsburgh had created a "real civic center." It possessed an "architectural excellence and . . . architectural impressiveness" that filled a visitor with "admiring astonishment."[12]

The City Beautiful was an experiment in transcendence. A broad stratum of middle- and upper-class Americans from coast to coast was engaged in a kind of crusade to recreate the American city as a work of art. The controlling insight, expressed by Robinson, that "utility should not excuse ugliness," inspired improvement-minded Pittsburghers of the period and, not least, its architects:

> The ugliness of the majority of American cities is the first thing which strikes a foreigner. The ugliness is not only offensive to the eye, but it is repellent to the soul. Its influence upon education is disastrous to the last degree. Men need beauty precisely as they need fresh air and clear skies. To condemn them to live among ugly surroundings, under skies blackened with smoke, is to deaden their sensibility to the beautiful and to rob their lives of one great element of interest and dignity.[13]

For exponents of the City Beautiful, high-quality civic architecture and design, in all aspects of city life, was not a mere cosmetic to cover a leper's sores. Environmental comeliness was endowed with moral and social significance, and in this sense was supremely practical or utilitarian.

Clearly, there was a tradition of design advocacy in Pittsburgh, one rooted in the national urban culture of the early twentieth century. This context makes comprehensible the creation of a municipal Art Commission in Pittsburgh in 1911. The act creating the commission gave it the authority to approve any work of art, ornamentation, or commemoration involving the city. This included the design of any municipal building, bridge, lamp, or other structure. The commission could also volunteer advice to private property owners. The kind of submissions on which the Art Commission acted for the year 1912 included the Murray Avenue Bridge in the East End, the pumping station at Aspinwall, Bloomfield Bridge, a *Maine* memorial monument (which was disapproved), a municipal tuberculosis hospital. The commission also addressed broader issues akin to city planning, like advocating a plan for renewing the Point, zoning and districting regulations, and calling for a design for the section of Schenley Park that lay between Carnegie Library and Forbes Field.[14] George Baird, executive secretary of the Art Commission from 1920 to 1933, maintained that it saw in bridges the opportunity to make its mark, encouraging the county as well as the city to submit bridge plans for evaluation. He believed that its outstanding contribution to civic design in the 1920s involved approving designs for the ten major river spans and the land bridges that were built in that decade.[15]

Another manifestation of the City Beautiful vision, incorporated into city government, was a Shade Tree Commission. It was established in 1909 and included the formidable director of public works, E. M. Bigelow, as one of the three commissioners. Its view of Pittsburgh's future was the quintessence of City Beautiful idealism: "The coming generation will behold the wonderful transformation of the desiccated scarred hills of Allegheny County reverting to their former glory of forested crown of green, and traversed not by wagon roads of former days but by miles of boulevards and broad avenues lined with symmetrical rows of fruit and shade trees."[16] Programmatically, the Shade Tree Commission assumed a surprisingly broad mandate for civic betterment and beautification— again reflecting the City Beautiful agenda. It determined that since its jurisdiction extended from curb to property line, then all sidewalks would be laid in place as specified by the commission. It intended to have ornamental lights placed on residential streets, to oppose the erection of unsightly poles and signboards along streets where trees had been or would be planted, and it favored taking over small, ugly unused plots where streets converged and beautifying them with trees and shrubs.

There was significant design advocacy in the interwar period, but it was advocacy by example. There was no national cultural or design movement comparable to the City Beautiful. In Pittsburgh, handsome structures like the Grant, Gulf, and Koppers Buildings perpetuated the revivalist tradition and incorporated a mix of Gothic, neoclassical, and art deco styles. The most important illustration of design advocacy of the era is Chatham Village on Mount Washington. Here a group of creative architects and landscape architects blended design, ecological, and social considerations in its planning. Using a sophisticated superblock plan, designers were able to consolidate the green space to form large interior parks, toward which the homes faced, as an alternative to the conventional neighborhood design in which small private plots are divided by streets, alleys, driveways, and parking areas. A differentiated road system was created for purposes of economy and to protect residents, especially children, from the hazards of through traffic. The Chatham Village plan exemplified a commitment to ecological values: the area's natural topography was regarded as a precious asset to be protected and used for scenic and recreational purposes, among others. And consideration was given to incorporating civic as well as recreational facilities for residents.[17]

Modernism, or the international style, made limited progress between the wars, but it would define a new architecture and a new urban design system after World War II. Renaissance I in Pittsburgh possessed an implicit design philosophy: it was international-style architecture expressed in Le Corbusier's Radiant City, executed through the Urban Redevelopment Authority's large-scale clearance projects. At the outset, perhaps, architectural modernism as promulgated by figures like Loos, Mies, Le Corbusier, and Gropius was liberating and innovative. It aspired, at its inception, to liberate the architect and designer from the constraints of the past, to encourage the use of new materials and technology, and to express this liberation in new environmental forms appropriate to the life of contemporary society. But modernism degenerated into a suffocating formalism and radical reductionism. The first generation of modernists, in the initial flush of idealistic enthusiasm, revolted against history, nature, and organic continuity: no traditional styles, no ornamentation, no complex social fabrics to consider—and, most pertinent, no sensitivity to the cultural dimensions of nature and open space in the urban fabric. Life, in effect, would adapt and live up to a conception of art and form—language rooted in a machine-inspired, puritanical architectural aesthetic. The straight line, right angle, and cube, the barren, unornamented facade, and the concrete, windswept plaza were endowed with moral properties: they expressed the architect's and society's liberation from historicism and from nature. Ultimately, the reductionist aesthetic of modernism was well suited to the needs of the most banal contemporary development.[18]

So defined, there is a fundamental conflict between modernism and preservation. This conflict was intensified in Renaissance I because Pittsburgh's redemption was conceived in terms of liberation from the past, including an unsavory environment: liberation from smoke, from floods, from blighted residential and commercial structures, from a top-heavy, aging industrial economy. In essence, Pittsburgh's very survival depended on dissociation from its history, including an architecture that no longer symbolized progress but instead clutter that had to be eliminated.

The last chapter in the original (1964) edition of Lorant's *Pittsburgh: The Story of an American City*, was entitled "Rebirth" and was presumably written by David Lawrence as told to John Robin and Stefan Lorant. The following passage does capture the essence of Renaissance I as it concerned the past and approaches to preservation:

Pittsburgh's great effort has been to remake itself, to change as fast as it can from the environment of the old nineteenth-century technology into the sleek new forms of the future. The city is racing time. It has no inclination to look back; it has no nostalgia for the past.

The city welcomes tomorrow, because yesterday was hard and unlovely. Pittsburgh likes buildings that glisten with stainless steel and aluminum, and it has little time for the niceties of architectural criticism when it compares what it gained with what it lost. The town has no worship of landmarks. Instead, it takes its pleasure in the swing of the headache ball and the crash of falling brick. It will tear down bridges without a second thought.[19]

This antihistorical, antinaturalistic bias and the Radiant City utopia of Le Corbusier would find expression in such projects as Gateway Center, East Liberty's mall, the clearance and rebuilding of the Lower Hill, and projects all across the Lower North Side, notably Allegheny Center and the concrete spaghetti of I-279 slashing through the East Street Valley.[20] Boulevards and parkways usurped the riverfronts bordering the Golden Triangle, and the rivers as sources of recreational or cultural or residential development were generally ignored. The problem continued up to the era of the Convention Center and Three Rivers Stadium—an arena that might as well be situated in the Mohave Desert as in a city defined by its rivers.

It was in this inhospitable environment that the Pittsburgh History & Landmarks Foundation was established in 1964. The immediate stimulus came from the Urban Redevelopment Authority, which apparently viewed the North Side as a laboratory for the realization of Le Corbusier's sterile utopia—the city of high-rise concrete slabs set in a wasteland of suburbanlike open space and highways. Thus the Allegheny Market House was destroyed in 1965 for the high-rise apartment complex in Allegheny Center. Nor could Landmarks save several Greek Revival homes in the area, or Pittsburgh's only example of the model tenement era—the Phipps apartments on General Robinson Street. In the downtown area, the spectacular Fourth Avenue Post Office was lost in 1966, and Landmarks could not save the Pennsylvania Railroad engine roundhouses at Liberty Avenue and Twenty-eighth Street.

On the other hand, it not only saved the 1300 block of Liverpool Street (where it all started in the course of a stroll taken by Arthur Ziegler and James Van Trump one winter day in 1964) but played a significant part in preventing a URA rampage in the North Side's Manchester, its Mexican War streets section, and Allegheny West. Along with these neighborhoods, Landmarks in its early years concentrated on creating a historic preservation consciousness among merchants on the South Side's East Carson Street through a facade restoration program.

The character of Landmarks was largely shaped in these early half dozen or so years, when urban renewal was still doing to American cities what bombs and artillery did to European cities during World War II. Landmarks embodied the concept of a local preservation agency that was all-inclusive. This was partly a matter of necessity. There was no other preservation-minded organization in Pittsburgh; it was Landmarks or nothing. One should remember also that no machinery of municipal landmarking would exist until the creation of the Historic Review Commission in 1979 (except for a limited 1971 ordinance). Under the circumstances, a multidimensional strategy was necessary. It would encompass advocacy and negotiation, often with the URA; preservation projects funded and managed by Landmarks; educational programs in the schools; membership, publicity, and tours for consciousness raising; surveys such as the first-ever county survey of historic structures, published in 1967; and through its architectural historians—James Van Trump originally, then Walter Kidney—a continuing series of attractive publications that could only enhance preservation consciousness in the community.[21]

Within this framework of an all-encompassing preservation organization, Landmarks signified a vital shift in the theory and practice of historic preservation in the United States. The 1960s marked a transition from the older tradition of pietistic preservation to advocacy and then developmental preservation. Pietistic preservation arises from an attitude long associated with house museums commemorating social or political notables, patriotic sentiment expressed in military parks and memorials, historical restorations of entire communities such as Williamsburg, Old Sturbridge, or Deerfield, and a partiality for the colonial era.

Advocacy preservation refers to all activities that promote preservation consciousness as well as efforts to protect districts and buildings (both those of architectural significance and those in the vernacular style) through protective legislation. Such advocacy has recently expanded to encompass preservation of an area's industrial heritage.

Developmental or practical preservation signified a radical innovation in practice and was central to Landmarks' preservation policy (too much so, some would later claim). But Landmarks was never a conventional advocacy organization. Development was always central to its program. It favored an economic growth strategy of preservation: recycling buildings for new commercial uses, as at Station Square, or maintaining the viability of old neighborhoods through preservation-oriented rehabilitation, as in the North Side neighborhoods where Landmarks acquired, remodeled, sold, and rented property. Although Landmarks accepted the necessity of city-imposed preservation, it has always been most comfortable with practical, market-oriented preservation. In its 1975 publication, *Revolving Funds for Historic Preservation,* Landmarks maintained that "architecture is an art wholly based upon continuing utility, and that utility is in turn grounded in the market place. When you accept that circumstance and apply the techniques of finance, real estate, and construction to the problems at hand, you compete on equal terms with the forces that destroy buildings. . . . You must demonstrate that the buildings are workable as well as beautiful."[22]

Station Square was Landmarks' large-scale demonstration in practical preservation. Like its neighborhood reclamation efforts, Station Square was conceived as an alternative to conventional urban renewal projects. By the early 1970s, however, Landmarks wanted to move beyond neighborhood revitalization and find a major property to demonstrate that communities could pursue economic revitalization without destroying their architectural heritage. In other words, preservation-based renewal could be commercially successful.[23]

While exploring several downtown possibilities, including the Colonial Trust Building, Arthur Ziegler, president of Landmarks, received a call from Donald Collins, an official of Richard Scaife's Allegheny Foundation. He conveyed Scaife's interest in a Ghirardelli Square–like project for Pittsburgh. Ziegler examined (and rejected) the possibility of using a complex of bank buildings on Wood Street (later turned into an indoor mall that soon failed) for the experiment in adaptive recycling of significant architecture.[24]

Landmarks then attempted in 1973 to negotiate for the Pittsburgh & Lake Erie Railroad's passenger terminal on the South Side. The P&LE had started operations in 1879 as a freight and (short-haul) passenger

Station Square from the Smithfield Street Bridge; in foreground is the old Pittsburgh and Lake Erie Railroad Station (1901). *Photo: Jim Judkis*

line. After World II, like most railroads, it experienced a sharp decline in both freight and passenger service and had essentially closed down passenger operations by 1970.[25] Ziegler thought the passenger terminal might be transformed into an attractive riverside restaurant, but railroad officials refused to negotiate. They were skeptical about Landmarks' ability to finance the transaction. Ziegler then contacted Scaife for permission to reveal that he was backing the project.[26] This disclosure not only ended the stalemate but also enabled Landmarks to pursue a forty-one-acre site (later fifty-two acres) sandwiched between the Monongahela River and West Carson Street.

What the Heinz Foundation was to become to the Cultural Trust, Richard Mellon Scaife and his Allegheny Foundation were to Landmarks. Scaife had already supported the neighborhood work and the acquisition and remodeling of the old North Side Post Office in Allegheny Center. He now provided $350,000 for predevelopment studies for Station Square, followed by $5 million in 1976 (when the project was launched), and another $1.5 million in 1978 for landscaping and artifacts. Ultimately, Scaife contributed over $12 million in equity capital.[27]

A critical decision, vital for the success of Station Square, was the choice of restaurant to occupy the passenger waiting room of the terminal building. This was settled when Ziegler visited and was impressed by Engine House No. 5 in Columbus, Ohio, operated as a restaurant by the C. A. Muer Corporation of Detroit.[28] Muer's 550-seat Grand Concourse seafood restaurant opened in 1978. It became a spectacular demonstration of preservation remodeling in a spectacular setting. High above the main dining room is a barrel vaulted ceiling whose ribs enclose stained-glass panels. It is supported by rows of two-story Corinthian columns. Arched stained-glass windows, pedimented doorways, and decorative wall mouldings are plentiful. A grand staircase terminates one end of the dining room. The Gandy Dancer saloon, specializing in shellfish, adjoins the main dining room (it had originally been a baggage section of the terminal). One edge of the dining room offers a choice view across the river to the Golden Triangle. The entire passenger terminal became the Landmarks Building in the mid-1980s, when the P&LE departed, liberating six floors of office space above the restaurant.

Grand Concourse Restaurant, Station Square. *Photo: Jim Judkis*

The passenger terminal was one of five buildings that constituted the historic core of Station Square. The first to open had been the Express House. Dating back to around 1900, it became a three-story office building in 1977. Following the Grand Concourse in 1978 came the Freight House shops in 1979. A steel-framed shed (vintage 1897), it was reborn as the Shops at Station Square, offering visitors a variety of retail stores and restaurants. A seven-story warehouse built in 1917 was transformed into Commerce Court in 1982. The ground level, which flowed into the Freight House, contained more shops and restaurants. The upper stories, used for offices, overlooked a newly created atrium. The last of the original buildings, the six-story 1916 annex at Smithfield and Carson, reopened as an office building, the Gatehouse, in 1984. An important event was the transfer of the Gateway Clipper excursion fleet from the Mon Wharf to Station Square in 1982. It represented the first use of the riverfront setting beyond passive looking.

A variety of nonhistoric, but commercially successful enterprises rounded out the Station Square complex. These included the architecturally bland, bulky, and visually obtrusive 297-room Sheraton Hotel (1981). The same could be said of the nearby four-story 1982 parking garage. The less said the better about a Pittsburgh Sports Garden that appeared in 1989 and closed in 1994. A miniature golf course opened in 1989, and there is a Melody Tent whose 19,000 square feet are rented out for ethnic celebrations, concerts, and similar events. A Station Square Transportation Museum opened in 1985 (and moved to larger quarters in 1992), and there is a Bessemer Court with a small display of local industrial machinery.

Station Square, by its fifteenth anniversary, was receiving more than 3 million visitors a year. Landmarks claims it has created jobs for 3,000 persons in 134 enterprises and has contributed about $6 million annually in taxes. It represents private investment of $87 million, $12,250,000 in philanthropic and public funds, and repaid Urban Development Action Grant loans of $5 million. Station Square thus exemplifies Landmark's concept of practical preservation: buildings "must be made to operate consistent with the requirements of economics before they can help to revitalize human beings, to give them more pride or more pleasure."[29]

The success of Station Square had encouraged Landmarks to launch Phase II, a fifteen-year master plan for expansion (1993–2008). It proposed expenditures of $150 million of private capital, supplemented by another $12 million in philanthropic and public funds (including a $4 million city road project already approved). Another $5.5 million contributed by the Allegheny Foundation and Scaife Family Foundation was to go for the centerpiece of Phase II—a 1,500-foot-long terraced linear Riverpark of two and a half acres designed by Oehme, van Sweden, and Associates. Containing a restaurant and gardens, it would form part of the Three Rivers Heritage Trail. Supplementing Riverpark, and already in progress, is a Riverwalk of Industrial Artifacts. This will display machinery representing Pittsburgh's historic industries, as a kind of mammoth sculpture ensemble in an illuminated and landscaped setting adjoining the Monongahela River. There is only one building on the future development site. This is the Lawrence Paint Building, owned by Landmarks along with the entire fifty-two acres of Station Square.[30] A large brick building, long vacant and dilapidated, topped by a cupola, it dates back to 1897. Landmarks hoped that Riverpark and the Riverwalk of Industrial Artifacts would "create a fine landscaped setting for the private development of hotels, housing units, offices, restaurants, and cultural and entertainment facilities."[31] But the future of Station Square suddenly became uncertain when Landmarks announced its sale in June 1994.

The purchasers were the Promus Companies, Inc., of Memphis and Forest City Enterprises, Inc., of Cleveland. The former, which acquired a 75 percent interest, operated several hotel chains—Embassy Suites, Hampton Inns, and Homewood Suites—and thirteen Harrah's casinos. Forest City Enterprises, which acquired a 25 percent interest, is the developer of Tower City in Cleveland and has invested locally in the Vista Hotel and office building at Liberty Center as well as at Robinson Town Centre. Its assets total more than $2 billion and include shopping centers, office complexes, hotels, and apartments.[32]

As on the South Side LTV site, gambling prospects powered the transaction. Ziegler had been approached by numerous potential purchasers, all of whom made any sale contingent on legalization of gambling. Promus originally investigated Station Square on the same basis, but decided that investment could be justified even without riverboat gambling. The $25.5 million sale price seems reasonable when compared to the $26.5 million paid by Oxford Development Corporation (five times market value) for only 12.3 acres on the former steel supply facility owned by U.S. Metalsource. The only definite commitment by the joint venture at the time of sale was to build a 200-room hotel. The fate of the linear park is unclear. (In any case, the $5.5 million of Scaife Foundation funds will be withdrawn, since development will now be controlled by a commercial venture.) The Riverwalk of Industrial Artifacts will proceed as planned.[33]

Landmarks' motive in selling Station Square (although it will remain involved in several capacities) was to strengthen its preservation operations.[34] The income received from investment of the sales proceeds will about equal what it gained as owner and landlord of Station Square. But that income can go entirely into preservation rather than Station Square development. Priority projects include assisting inner-city neighborhoods in restoration planning and property acquisition through an augmented Preservation Fund; creation of a Religious Properties Restoration Program;[35] exploring the possibilities of housing in downtown historic buildings; making possible computer access to Landmarks' 50,000 slides and photographs; an expanded educational and publications program; and development of a preservation plan for historic parks and gardens.[36]

Landmarks' success in practical preservation was rooted in a combination of audacity (Ziegler staked the reputation and future of Landmarks on a project many considered a likely failure), the creation of a Revolving Fund in 1966 (succeeded by the Preservation Fund in 1985), and links with the social and economic elites of the community, especially the ability to win the confidence of the foundation sector. Ziegler and his associates recognized this at an early date. It was Sarah Scaife Foundation money that established the Revolving Fund in 1966, and Richard Scaife's Allegheny Foundation that provided the millions to support Station Square.[37] Encouraging Landmarks' practical and development orientation was the conviction, from the outset, that Pittsburgh foundations and corporations would not respond to "vague cultural, historical, and 'heritage' appeals." They would respond to demonstrations that preservation improved neighborhoods, the business climate, or the cash flow for businesses in historic commercial districts.[38] Landmarks would not succeed, then, if identified as the province of dreamers or unworldly purists.

From the beginning, Landmarks recognized the neighborhood organization and revitalization potential of preservation—its communitarian as well as economic possibilities. Although one might differ on details of Landmarks' role in the North Side and South Side neighborhoods, there is no doubt that Landmarks believed that it was pioneering in a new kind of urban renewal, using architectural preservation as a means to neighborhood social revitalization and cohesion. Ziegler, in 1972, for example, explained that the neighborhood work was meant to develop "in all these people a new sense of neighborhood, with restoration of the houses as the unifying denominator."[39] Preservation, in essence, becomes the basis for a new strategy of community organization: "The old architecture will be an attractive and binding element that brings people from different backgrounds and income groups together in the quest to create a special neighborhood. . . . Their only common denominator will be their devotion to their historic buildings."[40]

This was an important insight in the early years of the modern phase of historic preservation in Pittsburgh and nationally. Preservation is not just about old buildings; it is equally about the sense of community which they nurture. The objects of preservation elicit affection and commitment. This promotes a greater sense of identification with a neighborhood or community. People thus care more about the community and its future precisely because they care more about its past. A source of urban decay in American life is the sense of alienation many have come to feel. There is little identification with the community. Historic preservation counteracts this alienation.

The 1300 block of Liverpool Street in Manchester ("in its own solid bourgeois way the finest surviving Victorian street in Pittsburgh")[41] had inspired the creation of Landmarks in 1964, and Manchester would be a site of Landmarks' early experiments in preservation-based neighborhood renewal. There was a sense of urgency. The angel of death hovered in the form of the renewal bulldozer and wrecking ball. Arthur Ziegler remembers:

> The next day we checked and learned that not only was Liverpool Street listed for demolition but so was the entire Manchester neighborhood, and much of the Central North Side and the Mexican War Streets area were under similar threats.[42]

Before intervention was possible, Manchester was chopped up by the Chateau Street Expressway and the ninety-eight-acre Chateau West renewal project, which eliminated blocks of houses and stores in favor of

Recycling of historic firehouse, Penn Avenue, Strip District. *Photo: Author*

a suburban shopping plaza that ultimately failed.[43] Thus the expressway severed the neighborhood, commercial activity was relocated to the plaza, but the plaza failed and retail stores on the other side of the expressway evaporated. The neighborhood shrank to fifty blocks, and its population dropped from 8,500 in 1960 to under 5,000 in 1970 (3,000 in 1990). Total housing units, 2,766 in 1960, fell to 2,012 by 1970 (and 1,500 in

Liverpool Street, North Side, inspiration for the founding of the History & Landmarks Foundation. *Photo: Pittsburgh History & Landmarks Foundation*

1990). The minority population, 17.2 percent in 1950, zoomed to 44.2 percent in a single decade (largely owing to population evicted by the Lower Hill renewal).

Renewal plans for the North Side and elsewhere in Pittsburgh suggested to Ziegler that city leaders intended to annihilate "our compressed urban cores."[44] Dense urban textures, like those of older North Side neighborhoods, would be loosened up in favor of a more suburban design. John DeSantis, current chairman of the Historic Review Commission, agrees that planning and renewal programs in this era suggested a determination to reshape the city as a central core of commerce and culture surrounded by garden suburb–like neighborhoods.[45] Federally funded highway development was as devastating to older urban neighborhoods in this period as federally funded renewal had been. Highway planning for the lower North Side does suggest the image of a scythe sweeping across the landscape. Ziegler found that "an elevated highway had been proposed to run through the Allegheny Commons, up Monterey Street, and across the back of the Mexican War Streets to the proposed East Street Expressway, which would slice through East Allegheny."[46]

Landmarks redefined the relationship between preservation, renewal, and the population of inner-city neighborhoods like Manchester. As important to Landmarks as the great work of architecture or opulent great mansion was the residential and commercial vernacular of older city neighborhoods. Their buildings and textures were also a significant part of the local and national heritage. But while Savannah and Charleston had pioneered in preservation-inspired neighborhood redemption, it was usually at the expense of the original inhabitants. What Landmarks wanted to achieve in Manchester or the Mexican War streets was not only renewal by preservation, but preservation of the nonaffluent residents as well.

Within a year of its organization, Landmarks' staff walked the streets of Manchester, talking with the people about the distinctive quality of the neighborhood and how preservation might both save and improve it.[47] Landmarks acquired two houses on Liverpool Street to demonstrate preservation techniques.[48] In 1967, Landmarks and Manchester residents organized the United Manchester Redevelopment Corporation (which became the Manchester Citizens' Corporation in 1979) to spearhead the revitalization effort. A close working relationship developed between Landmarks and Stanley Lowe. For many years Tom Cox (later director of the North Side Civic Development Council) was associated with Lowe and Landmarks in the Manchester community revitalization efforts.[49]

Frustrating on-and-off-again relationships with the URA, as well as a period of federal funding cutbacks, prevented large-scale revitalization in Manchester for a decade and a half. What was left of the neighborhood was removed from the prospective demolition list, and Landmarks and the community had worked out a renewal agreement with the URA by 1971. But the Nixon administration abruptly suspended the 312 program for rehabilitation loans, and for the next four years a deterioration took place characterized by vacancies, vandalism, and dilapidation. Worse still, the URA retrogressed; Landmarks was excluded from participation, 150 buildings were demolished and replaced by mock-suburban homes, and brick sidewalks were replaced with concrete.[50]

With the restoration of the 312 subsidy program, Landmarks and the community renewed their efforts to devise a development program. A marketing scheme was worked out with the assistance of Leopold Adler II, Savannah's preservation leader. Landmarks attempted to get all fifty blocks of Manchester listed on the National Register of Historic Places.

Liverpool Street, North Side. *Photo: Pittsburgh History & Landmarks Foundation*

The city administration wanted only two. At the suggestion of the state preservation official, a compromise was reached at twenty-four blocks. Most important, the URA in 1979 launched the nation's first large-scale neighborhood renewal program (1,200 homes) based on preservation. It included a unique facade easement feature. The URA purchased (at one-tenth appraised value) the right to restore a house facade; the owner, in

North Side vernacular. *Photo: Pittsburgh History & Landmarks Foundation*

turn, was obliged to maintain it for twenty years. Interiors had to be raised to renewal standards, but the burden was eased through grants and the 312 rehabilitation loan program. Overseeing the program was a Project Area Committee composed of Manchester residents. Stanley Lowe headed the URA field office.[51]

Landmarks' neighborhood policies achieved national attention and acclaim by the 1970s. The National Trust for Historic Preservation described Pittsburgh as a "preservation laboratory" where Landmarks' program would "help relieve the preservationist conscience—the fact that often in our efforts to save historic areas, we have unintentionally shunted off the poor to faceless projects." Pittsburgh, said another observer, "was perhaps the prime example of rehabilitation without dislocation." A staff member of the National Park Service praised the "remarkable achievements of the Pittsburgh History and Landmarks Foundation, especially with revitalization projects as that in the city's famous Mexican War Streets district."[52]

This sixteen-block North Side neighborhood had been surveyed in 1848 and named for Mexican War battles. Like Manchester, it was built up in the last three decades of the nineteenth century and inhabited by middle-class merchants and professionals. Also like Manchester, it displayed a variety of Victorian residential styles—Greek Revival, Italianate, and Second Empire, Romanesque and Queen Anne. These neighborhoods declined in popularity with the coming of the automobile and the greater mobility it provided. Many large older homes were subdivided into rooming houses and apartments, maintenance deteriorated, a poorer population moved in.[53] By the time Landmarks arrived in 1966, the neighborhood had become 50 percent absentee-owned, and "people were in exodus." A 1954 city plan had proposed total demolition of the district.[54]

Meeting with residents, Landmarks developed a strategy designed to rehabilitate the area without extensive dislocation. A $100,000 grant from the Sarah Scaife Foundation in 1966 made possible the creation of Landmarks' Preservation Revolving Fund and the implementation of its program beginning in 1967. It would: (1) buy absentee-owned houses in poor condition, thus demonstrating commitment to improve the neighborhood in a material way; (2) renovate the houses for different income levels, providing an alternative model for the URA; (3) encourage

Landmark members to acquire houses either as homes or investments; (4) nurture pride and optimism among residents, thus encouraging them to improve their properties; and, more broadly,

> bind together this mixture of people—young, old, well-to-do, black, white—in the cause of preserving and restoring this unique architecture and conducting an experiment in urban neighborhood renewal.[55]

By 1980, Landmarks had invested $500,000 in the Mexican War streets and owned twenty-five houses, but residents had spent over $3 million. More than fifty new families had purchased houses and thus reduced the number of absentee owners. Residents followed Landmarks' suggestion to form their own citizens' organization—the Mexican War Streets Society.[56]

Landmarks, of course, never redeveloped Manchester, Birmingham, or the Mexican War streets. The residents of the neighborhood did.[57] Landmarks' role, and a vital one, was to serve as a catalyst. It saw beauty, an urban heritage worth protecting, and the possibilities of community revitalization through preservation renewal where no one else had—in ostensibly drab, outmoded, and expendable working-class and poor neighborhoods.[58] With the emergence of community development corporations and other forms of neighborhood organization by the 1980s, Landmarks was less needed as either an organizing or development force. It thus sold off its neighborhood properties and converted its Revolving Loan Fund into the Preservation Fund in the mid-1980s.

Preservation Fund assets totaled $2 million by the end of 1994. Managed by Stanley Lowe (followed by Howard B. Slaughter in December 1993),[59] the Preservation Fund was designed to assist nonprofit organizations in historic or low-income districts with bridge financing and technical assistance. Many loans have gone to CDCs, thus increasing their financial resources. Since its inception, the fund has supported a wide and significant range of preservation and neighborhood projects. Examples include the conversion of Saint Mary's Church Priory (North Side) into an attractive bed-and-breakfast, resurrection of the Eberhardt and Ober Brewery on the North Side into an incubator and popular brewery-pub, acquisition by the Steel Heritage Task Force of the Homestead plant's forty-eight-inch rolling mill, acquisition and renovation of the Hollander Building by a North Side neighborhood coalition, and a loan for renovating the reading room in the historic Carnegie Library of Braddock.[60]

Another major contribution of Landmarks to neighborhood development had been its role as catalyst-midwife to the Pittsburgh Community Reinvestment Group. Indeed, throughout its history, Landmarks has been responsible not only for saving significant buildings like the North Side Post Office or the P&LE passenger terminal, or protesting plans to demolish major structures like the Pennsylvania Railroad terminal; it has also served as a stimulus for other developments important to preservation. These include the Steel Industry Heritage Corporation and the creation of the Allegheny Cemetery Historical Association to act as restoration agent for Pittsburgh's 300-acre nineteenth-century romantic cemetery.[61] Landmarks' impact on preservation has been reinforced by its educational, research, and publications programs as well as its extensive consulting activity.

Landmarks also helped prepare Pittsburgh's first historic preservation ordinance in 1971.[62] This was a limited measure that authorized City Council to designate buildings and districts. Administered by the City Planning Department, it permitted a six-month delay if the Planning Commission opposed a proposed development affecting a historic property.[63] A stronger preservation ordinance emerged from the City Planning Department in 1979.[64] It was initiated by Mark Bunnell, a planner who had been on the staff of New York City's Landmarks Preservation Commission. He believed that preservation was becoming a significant dimension of urban planning and that the city government should be able to exercise greater control. Planning director Lurcott agreed, as did Mayor Caliguiri. Bunnell drafted a rough draft for an ordinance, based in part on the New York City legislation.[65]

The landmark ordinance authorized the creation of a seven-member administrative agency, the Historic Review Commission (HRC), and established the nomination procedure. After an initial hearing before the HRC to determine the suitability of a proposed nomination, hearings were required before the HRC, City Planning Commission, and City Council. Council had the final authority. If either the Planning Commission or HRC voted against a nomination, or if the mayor vetoed a Council nomination, Council could overrule the veto by a six-to-three majority. HRC members, appointed by the mayor, included a representative of the Planning Department and the Bureau of Building Inspection (ordinarily the directors).

The first chairman of the HRC, Joan Ivey, served from 1979 to 1990. She confronted significant obstacles that compromised the effectiveness of the agency. For one thing, it was not taken seriously by the Caliguiri administration. And while Ivey had some administrative experience, she had no background whatever in planning or preservation. She was surprised to be nominated, and even more so to be appointed chairman, but she became a committed preservation advocate.

The attitude toward preservation of Robert Lurcott, director of the Planning Department, ranged from indifference to hostility. He did not inform the commission of prospective developments like the demolition of Jenkins Arcade for Fifth Avenue Place, or of the Moose Building for the Benedum and CNG Tower. These came as a surprise. And he opposed historic district nominations for the Oakland Civic Center and Allegheny West (both of which succeeded in the early 1990s). Yet commission members looked to him as an authority and arbiter. Another problem was the tendency of commission members to frame the discussion of issues not in terms of merit, but whether City Council would approve of a decision.

One of the most serious structural flaws in the design of the commission was its dependence on the Planning Department for staff. This placed the staff in the position of serving two masters. They were planning department employees but were assigned to the independent HRC, and Ivey became embroiled in conflicts with Lurcott over their use.[66] Lurcott would find his proper niche later in the decade as vice-president for district development of the Pittsburgh Cultural Trust.[67]

Another problem confronting the HRC in the 1980s was a lack of community support for preservation. No one contested the debt owed to Landmarks for creating a preservation consciousness in Pittsburgh and for the buildings and neighborhoods it had saved. But the sentiment was growing that Landmarks was drifting away from advocacy as Station Square and development objectives began to take precedence. Although Landmarks was viewed by the community as the voice of preservation, some complained that its voice was diminishing to a whisper as advocacy conflicted with development.

A second source of concern over Landmarks' role was centered in the historians, archivists, preservationists, and museum staff associated with the Committee on Pittsburgh Archeology and History, an informal volunteer organization born in 1983. They were disturbed over Landmarks' reputation in the community as steward of historical documents and artifacts (such as fragments from demolished buildings). Landmarks, they complained, had neither the resources nor expertise for this role; thus objects too often were stored away, auctioned off, or inappropriately exhibited. These concerns were instrumental in the committee's pursuit of a regional history center under the auspices of the Historical Society.

In reality, Landmarks had not abandoned advocacy or evolved from militant advocate to developer. Station Square was really a large-scale embodiment of the practical preservation always espoused by Landmarks. What happened was that a different conception of preservation advocacy emerged in the 1980s which clashed with that of Landmarks. Concern that an advocacy vacuum existed in Pittsburgh, that Landmarks no longer spoke for the preservation community, reached a climax in 1989–1991.[68] In those few years, a series of dramatic setbacks precipitated a new political and organizational alignment on behalf of preservation. In addition, the Masloff administration, which succeeded Caliguiri after his death in 1988, was not so much indifferent as antagonistic to preservation. The mayor's key advisers, notably executive secretary Joseph Mistick, viewed preservationists as an obstacle to development (any kind of commercial development, anywhere).

Always concerned that Landmarks should never be identified as impractical or indifferent to economic realities, Ziegler in the early 1970s warned that preservationists

> frequently become identified as starry-eyed idealists without a notion of practicality, or as contrary minded, progress stopping intransigents, or at best well meaning but uninformed and vaguely dizzy Romantics. . . . Preservationists always have enough obstacles to overcome without conveying an image of general perversity and light-mindedness.[69]

The message never changed. Two decades later, Landmarks acknowledged that it was "less disposed than some preservation groups toward freezing structures and places in time." Some preservationists acted "as if the world owes them whatever they want to keep, the mere property owner being an unpaid curator who has to be kept up to the mark." Landmarks thus viewed itself as a kind of mediator working "to bring preservationists and owners into a relationship of trust and respect." A critical corollary was that government's coercive powers should not be casually imposed; preservationists had better "use any legal powers with a light touch."[70] In remarks to Preservation Pittsburgh, as it was organizing in October 1991, Ziegler provided a definitive statement of the relationship between preservation and economics:

> Our philosophy has generally been to try to advocate during early stages of planning if at all possible, and in crisis situations develop an alternative, feasible plan for the preservation of a building. If we cannot find an economical way to save a building, we then have difficulty advocating retention because a way must be found to pay for the preservation of a structure.[71]

This view of preservation stewardship was defensible, and critics of Landmarks were sometimes unrealistic in assuming that the organization was omnipotent—that historic properties were lost because it did not advocate vigorously enough or exercise its influence. The organization had no such power. In addition, like all social movements, preservation had its share of unreasonable zealots oblivious to economics. But critics of Landmarks were altogether realistic in their concern that a combination of development pressures and a hostile city administration (and City Council) could wreak havoc with the city's architectural heritage and texture.

The first major preservation controversy in the 1989–1991 period was over Saint Peter's Church in Oakland. It was originally constructed in 1851–1852 at Forbes Avenue and Grant Street, downtown. Its architect was the noted nineteenth-century Philadelphian, John Notman. Saint Peter's was Pittsburgh's oldest church and only example of fourteenth-century English Gothic. Henry Clay Frick had it moved from downtown to Oakland in 1901. The Episcopal diocese was anxious to dispose of it, and considerable controversy raged over whether it was salvageable. Although approved for landmarking by the Planning Commission and HRC, this was denied by City Council in November 1989. The church was quickly demolished by Oxford Development Corporation, and the site remained an empty lot toward the end of 1994. The Saint Peter's controversy revealed, among other things, a limiting condition for preservation in Pittsburgh—the willingness of City Council to obey the wishes of religious institutions for exemption from landmark ordinances. The Catholic Church maintains a blanket opposition to landmarking, on the grounds of religious freedom and property rights.[72]

In the following year, 1990, the diminutive, six-block Allegheny West neighborhood was finally designated a historic district (after two failed efforts in the 1980s). Michael Eversmeyer of the Historic Review Commission staff described the area as a virtual textbook of late nineteenth- and early twentieth-century revival styles.[73] Also, textbook examples of neoclassical and Beaux-Arts commercial architecture were to be found along Pittsburgh's Fourth Avenue between Market Square and Smithfield Street. It had once been the city's financial and banking center. In 1908 no fewer than twenty banks and the Pittsburgh Stock Exchange were housed in the vicinity. It had remained a superb example of "dense urban fabric and monumental scale."[74] Like other historic structures and districts, the Fourth Avenue complex provided a visual oasis, an alternative vision of city building.

The City Planning Commission in September 1989 overruled its own staff and voted against historic designation for Fourth Avenue. The newly appointed planning director, Jane Downing, reflecting the sentiments of the administration and building owners, declared that flexibility was needed for downtown development (meaning that Oxford Development was considering a mall project, never executed). The only support came from the Engineers Club; most owners probably were anticipating a buyout for the proposed mall.[75]

Finally, the campaign in 1989–1990 to landmark the western section of Shadyside also failed. Residents were divided. Here as elsewhere, opponents conveyed misleading information about the constraints imposed by designation upon property owners.[76] On the other hand, this tactic may have succeeded because proponents did not undertake an adequate educational campaign (in contrast to the South Side Local Development Company and the historic district nomination for East Carson Street). According to Michael Eversmeyer:

> The group of owners who nominated the district claimed to have talked to . . . their neighbors about the ramifications of the nomination, but so many of the owners stated that they had heard nothing of the nomination before it occurred that I have to doubt the effectiveness of the nominators' efforts. Once the nomination was in place, people started to take stands for or against it, without the proper information, and the opponents were able to play on owners' fears successfully.[77]

Although designation sponsors agreed to reduce the nomination area from 539 to 355 buildings, the Planning Commission staff had recommended denial, and proponents revoked the nomination.

Joan Ivey tried to meet with Mayor Masloff to discuss preservation issues, but never got past Joseph Mistick and another aide, Lew Borman. Mistick publicly expressed his displeasure with both the commission and historic preservation. Preservation, he asserted, was being challenged around the country as well as in Pittsburgh because government should not be allowed to confiscate property rights with impunity.[78] Ivey was deposed in July 1990 and replaced by John DeSantis. Only the second chairman in the history of the HRC, DeSantis was a surprising choice to some. He was not only a controversial figure in his Allegheny West neighborhood, but also a dedicated preservationist and prime mover in the Allegheny West Civic Council. Director of the Pittsburgh Home and Garden Show, he had moved into the neighborhood in 1977 and successfully pushed for the renovation of three townhouse rows threatened with extinction as well as several large old mansions. His nomination was opposed by the Allegheny West Merchants' Association and some residents, and he was in the midst of a battle with the county medical society over its intention to expand its headquarters on Ridge Avenue. He had contested the proposal by Mistick, Inc., in the mid-1980s for an eight-story apartment building at Brighton Road and Western Avenue. DeSantis had also filed the historic district nominations for Allegheny West.[79]

Increased dissatisfaction over the lack of effective preservation advocacy, the sense of thinning community support for preservation, the loss of architectural landmarks in the 1980s, beginning with the Moose Building and Jenkins Arcade,[80] the failure to designate Fourth Avenue—Pittsburgh's Wall Street—as a landmark district, and the presence of a city administration that disdained the city's extraordinary legacy of historic architecture resulted in a realignment of preservation forces in 1991. The catalyst was the Committee to Save the Syria Mosque.[81]

Syria Mosque (1915), a cavernous auditorium, was part of the Oakland Civic Center. Although not a great architectural achievement, it was significant as the area's only example of early twentieth-century Shriner Mideastern Revival style. A mocha-brick, cubelike structure of reductive simplicity, it was sparingly adorned with molded terra cotta Arabic characters, stained-glass windows, and guardian sphinxes. It was also Pittsburgh's link to the world of classical music—for many years before Heinz Hall it was home to the Pittsburgh Symphony and the Pittsburgh Opera—jazz, and popular music over many decades. Lately it had presented mostly rock concerts.[82] In the winter of 1991, the National Development Corporation announced that it had bought the building for $10 million. It later was revealed in a court hearing initiated by the Committee to Save the Syria Mosque that NDC was acting on behalf of Presbyterian University Hospital (University of Pittsburgh Medical Center), which intended to erect an office building in its place.[83]

Rather than accepting the announcement by National Development as a fait accompli, Scott Mervis, an editor of the weekly *In Pittsburgh*, decided to nominate it for historical landmarking toward the end of March. He notified the owners of the Mosque, as required, but was slow to deliver the nomination papers to the HRC. This proved fatal to the building. National Development rushed downtown and applied for a demolition permit two hours before Mervis delivered the nomination to the HRC. The demolition permit legally took precedence over the nomination, and no amount of effort was able to overcome this obstacle.

Nonetheless, a small group convened after the HRC held its initial hearing to determine the merits of the nomination. Underfinanced and unconnected to the financial or political power structure, but stubborn, it meet several times a week until September to devise ways to keep the Mosque alive and arouse the concern of the broader community. Its members testified at hearings before the HRC, Planning Commission, and City Council. It employed a lawyer to contest the demolition permit and forced the issue into the courts, tried to stimulate media attention, and held a fund-raising event. Most important, it tried to educate members of City Council to the importance of the building in the context of the Oakland Civic Center. By the time of the Council hearing in August 1991, several Council members had become committed to saving the Mosque, the Oakland Civic Center, and historic preservation.

The most persuasive argument, it turned out, was the need to protect a unique building in a unique civic complex that distinguished Pittsburgh from any other community in the United States. The Oakland Civic Center, Council members learned, was more than an agglomeration of stately institutional buildings. It was based on a far-sighted master plan for the Schenley Farms district by developer F. F. Nicola. He was much influenced by the City Beautiful movement of the late nineteenth and early twentieth centuries—a vision of cities resplendent with civic centers, monuments, grand neoclassical commercial and civic architecture, and majestic boulevards, parks, and horticulture. But the City Beautiful ideal also had a social dimension. An antidote to the squalid industrial city, the architecture of the City Beautiful would, it was hoped, produce better citizens because they would translate its message into their own lives: aesthetic and cultural aspiration, discipline, rationality, and order, and pride in the community. The Oakland Civic Center stands witness to a time when architects and their clients had the vision, self-respect, and sense of civic obligation to believe in architecture as a moral and social force. Under the circumstances, the Civic Center, including the Mosque, was not just a vital part of Pittsburgh's heritage, but a national stewardship as one of the few examples of the City Beautiful dream. The Civic Center's fabric would be significantly compromised without the Mosque. It would leave a conspicuous gap.

Although the Shriners abruptly ordered the dismantling of the Mosque in the dead of night early in September, preservation now had a political base. Several City Council members had gained insight into the local and national significance of the Oakland Civic Center and the communitarian value of preservation. The Mosque issue demonstrated to them that Pittsburgh possessed an architectural heritage that many citizens considered worth fighting to save. Was it not better to have citizens who identified with Pittsburgh through its legacy of historic architecture, than citizens who could not care less about the community's environment and heritage? The ideal, they now realized, was preservation and economic development. In Pittsburgh and other American cities, there were many examples of creative recycling—a strategy that served the need for economic development and simultaneously expressed a stewardship commitment that linked past, present, and future generations.[84]

Councilman Jim Ferlo, who (to his later regret) had voted against the Saint Peter's designation in 1989, took the initiative in empowering the preservation movement. He was consistently supported by three other Council members—Dan Cohen, Gene Ricciardi, and Michelle Madoff (who left office at the end of 1993). Never before in the history of Pittsburgh had preservation benefited from this kind of political commitment. In the fall of 1991, after the destruction of the Mosque, Ferlo nominated the Oakland Civic Center as a historic district and organized Preservation Pittsburgh as an advocacy group with no development aspirations to create possible role conflicts. Its first responsibility was to mobilize community support for the Civic Center landmarking. The owners or managers of every institution in Oakland were visited. The University of Pittsburgh and other institutions had successfully opposed designation in the early 1980s (and were supported by Lurcott in the HRC). This time the community mobilization achieved by Preservation Pittsburgh, and Council support, ensured its landmarking in 1992. The Committee to Save the Mosque was also indirectly responsible for saving the Mackintosh-Hemphill factory on the South Side in the fall of 1991 (discussed in chapter 7). The preservation-conscious Council not only landmarked the structures but also overrode the mayor's veto.

The Mosque–Civic Center drama illuminated Landmarks' organizational and advocacy style. It has a large membership, but members have no formal voice in the governance. From the beginning, it has successfully cultivated the support of community (social) and foundation leaders and has reflected Ziegler's zeal for practical preservation.[85] The soft-spoken former English teacher turned out, somewhat unexpectedly, to have a talent for high finance and large-scale development. Co-founder Jamie Van Trump, an incorrigible dreamer and romantic, a gifted architectural historian, was something of an anomaly. The combination of exclusivity in governance and apotheosis of economics-driven preservation discouraged a populist style of preservation advocacy—one involving a general public or political mobilization. Thus Landmarks speaks softly and operates behind the scenes in a more controlled environment. This was exemplified in the Syria Mosque case. Ziegler met with architects in the spring of 1991 to explore the feasibility of constructing the proposed new building on the Mosque parking lot. He agreed that the Mosque possessed a " 'magnificent auditorium with a long association in Pittsburgh' " and hoped it would live on. But economics controlled the situation. One had to find a way to save a building. A journalist commented: " 'Buildings must have owners, and must have money in order to sustain themselves.' "[86]

Preservation is a dialectic between two desirable values that sometimes conflict: community stewardship and private property rights. The ideal reconciliation would come through enlightened developers and owners, whose enlightenment would be encouraged by financial and tax incentives and the many examples of successful recycling of historic properties. But there are times when the stewardship principle must be asserted in the hope that the valued landmark will find an owner, and because the ostensibly practical is not always practical or economically advantageous. The tragedy of Penn Station in New York City is instructive.

In 1968, five years after the practical, hardheaded, dollars-and-cents types who managed the Pennsylvania Railroad consigned their great structure to the New Jersey meadowlands, the railroad merged with the New York Central. Two years later, in 1970, the Penn-Central declared bankruptcy. No railroad and no station. Then in the early 1980s, New York had to bail out the Madison Square Garden Corporation whose sports palace had replaced Penn Station (and sat astride the loathsome remnant of a passenger terminal). New York got snake oil from the practical men who destroyed one of the world's great achievements in architecture and civil engineering. Now New York City regrets the loss of its magnificent terminal and contemplates its resurrection in the Post Office across the street.[87] The same practical individuals would have leveled not only Pittsburgh's Pennsylvania Station in the 1960s (now recycled into an attractive apartment complex), but also much of the vibrant Strip District if Penn-Central's development scheme had succeeded in the 1960s.

With no office, no staff, no money, no support from government or high society, the Committee to Save the Syria Mosque would nonetheless have saved the building if not for the fluke of the demolition permit. Asserting the stewardship principle and mobilizing both popular and political support against the trustees of the University of Pittsburgh, the City Council would have voted for designation if the Shriners had not themselves ordered demolition of the Mosque.[88]

Ferlo, backed by Preservation Pittsburgh and the same nucleus of Council members, continued to pursue preservation and broader quality of life objectives. Ferlo was able to get the historic King Estate in Highland Park (owned by the city but threatened with demolition) designated historic and to get bed-and-breakfast legislation enacted as a way of saving older mansions. He has also entreated city officials to stop playing

"The Pennsylvanian," formerly Pennsylvania Railroad terminal. *Photo: Author*

dead in the face of federal and state mandates that undermine the beauty and quality of life in the city. Thus he urged that more creative solutions be sought in response to the federal dictate that Pittsburgh's drinking water reservoirs be covered over. At issue, in particular, is the Highland Park Reservoir, a community walkway where park and water join. The cheapest solution, favored by the city, is a plastic condom. Similarly, Preservation Pittsburgh members have protested that the city's historic bridges are being blanketed with concrete Jersey barriers and cyclone fencing—another example of the cheapest, path-of-least-resistance response by the city to federal and state dictates; as in many other cases, the federal system of government does not seem alive and well in advancing civic improvements.[89] And despite the Masloff administration's opposition, Ferlo forced billboard control legislation onto the city's agenda.[90]

Pittsburgh's experience suggests that the best basis for preservation is a mix of public and private components: a development organization like Landmarks concerned with economic possibilities and concrete demonstrations to the business community that preservation-oriented development can be successful; an advocacy organization like Preservation Pittsburgh free of development responsibilities and constraints; a city ordinance and administrative agency like the Historic Review Commission to serve as a preservation advocate in city government; and a political base in city government, wherever possible.

Preservation efforts were temporarily thrown into disarray in July 1991 when the Pennsylvania Supreme Court unexpectedly declared that landmarking individual buildings without permission from owners was unconstitutional, analogous to spot zoning (presumably allowing historic district nominations). Since this decision was based on the Pennsylvania constitution, no appeal to the federal courts was possible. The Court then reversed itself in November 1993.[91]

Outside Pittsburgh, smaller communities in Western Pennsylvania also adopted preservation as a strategy for revitalizing and cultivating local community spirit. They, too, discovered that historic architecture of all kinds was marketable; it gave the community an image and identity that attracted visitors, enabled renewal to take place without obliterating the past, and nurtured pride among residents. The town of Brookville (Jefferson County seat, population 4,000), for example, formed Historic Brookville, Inc., in 1982 and in 1983 launched a Main Street Program to renovate the handsome Victorian-era commercial architecture in the town's center. Within less than a decade, more than $3 million was invested in this nine-block district. The program was designed, in part, to enable the downtown to compete with nearby malls. The Brookville

Penn Central Railroad's plans for the Strip District, 1960. *Photo: Pittsburgh History & Landmarks Foundation*

Area Business Association estimates that over 340,000 tourists pass through annually. This includes the 5,000–6,000 guests during Historic Brookville's Victorian Christmas weekend.[92]

Brownsville, a Mon Valley Initiative community in Fayette County, is host to an effort to transform the Monongahela Railroad Freight House into an art colony which, in turn, might precipitate revitalization as it has in other cities. " 'I've seen it done elsewhere,' " said Richard Grinstead, director of the Southwestern Pennsylvania Arts Network. " 'The artists come in and do renovations and next thing you know, other people are coming into town. Artists can play a major role in the revival of a town.' "[93] Even tiny Rice's Landing (Greene County) hopes that its attractive Monongahela River waterfront, historic buildings, and vintage 1900 W. A. Young and Son's machine shop will warrant historic preservation funding.[94]

Vandergrift (Westmoreland County, population 5,900) was established in 1895 through the initiative of George G. McMurtry, president of the Apollo Iron & Steel Company (now Allegheny Ludlum Corporation, after a period as USX). A century ago, the company developed a internationally renowned model industrial town designed by the firm of Frederick Law Olmsted, Jr., on 650 rural acres adjoining the Kiskiminetas River. Curved streets hugging the contours of the hilly terrain were planted with trees, and the company provided an extensive infrastructure in advance of lot sales to its workers. McMurtry hoped that workers would live up to their benign environment. Residents are conscious of this history and the distinction it confers upon the community.[95]

Historic consciousness and pride have recently been reinforced by efforts to restore Vandergrift's Casino Theater, vacant since the early 1980s, and transform it into a performing arts and community center for the Allegheny-Kiski Valley. Built in 1900 as a playhouse and vaudeville theater, the Casino became a cinema in 1927. A two-story, cream-colored Greek Revival structure, it consists of two setback wings (now used for municipal offices) that frame the Casino, the large center section. A dominant element is the portico—four fluted Ionic columns supporting the entablature and cornice. Behind the columns are three rounded-arch doorways. At the urging of the Vandergrift Museum and Historical Society, a major advocate of historic preservation and consciousness, the town council in 1991 established the Vandergrift Borough

Preservation Committee to organize the Casino project.[96] Vandergrift is an outstanding example of how history and preservation help nurture community identity and cohesiveness. In addition to the Casino restoration, a focal point for preservation commitment, the community also celebrates Vandergrift Community Spirit Day in the fall and holds an annual Historic Preservation Week banquet in the spring.[97]

A larger-scale kind of preservation in Pennsylvania (and elsewhere) is represented by the industrial heritage concept. One of the earliest, most influential examples was the conversion of a chocolate factory in San Francisco into the popular Ghirardelli Square in the mid-1960s. But the prototype was the heritage park strategy devised in Lowell, Massachusetts (population 100,000) in the 1970s. A visitor to Lowell in the early 1960s encountered a scene of desolation. Its campuslike mill complexes and canals were deserted and rotting away—it was an industrial ghost town. A few individuals perceived their potential for community revitalization. They included Patrick Mogan, superintendent of schools, who viewed the mills as a community asset because historic preservation could serve as an educational tool. Michael Southworth, an urban planner, devised the national urban park concept in the late 1960s and early 1970s on behalf of the Lowell Model Cities Education Component. In his words, "A design plan, done with Susan Southworth, incorporated my idea of reusing the abandoned mills and threatened canals as a cultural and educational resource."[98]

Support for the novel strategy solidified between 1972 and 1975. Business and government leaders formed a coalition to implement the first major experiment in preserving an area's industrial heritage as a basis for community revitalization. The public-private advocacy machinery included a Lowell Center City Committee, created in 1972, whose first priority was to advance the urban park concept. That same year, the Lowell City Council passed a resolution designating the park as the nucleus of all planning and redevelopment efforts. Paul Tsongas, elected to Congress in 1974, pressured local bankers to establish the Lowell Development and Finance Corporation in 1975 to provide low-interest rehabilitation loans for downtown historic structures. Elected to the Senate in 1978, Tsongas sponsored legislation establishing the Lowell National Historic Park. Three years earlier, the state had created the Heritage State Park in Lowell, recognizing the recreational potential of the canals and riverbanks, locks and gatehouses. The heritage park system encompassed two historic districts, both placed on the National Register of Historic Places. The City Hall district encompassed Lowell's rich legacy of nineteenth-century civic and commercial buildings. The Locks and Canals Historic District included the canal system, mill complexes, and boarding houses.[99]

The core of the heritage park was a 136-acre section defined by the Merrimack and Concord Rivers and Pawtucket Canal. The Market Mill, consisting of two brick structures once used for manufacturing, now houses the state and national park visitors' center. Tourist options include a canal tour provided by the National Park Service. It was not until the mid-1980s that redevelopment of the major mill complexes was launched. The $60 million renovation of the Massachusetts Mill created 420 rental units. The adjacent Boott Mills were converted into offices. Boarding House Park, containing sculptures suggestive of the industrial heritage, opened in 1990; nearby were the recycled rows of boarding houses that once accommodated mill operatives.[100]

Like Charleston, South Carolina, Lowell had the good fortune to have languished economically. Spared the renewal (demolition) pressures of more prosperous communities, it retained the unique architectural and industrial heritage that defined its identity and served as a basis for revitalization (along with Wang Industries after 1976 until the company's decline in the late 1980s). The transformation of that heritage into urban parks was made possible by the inventiveness of individuals like Mogan and Southworth and a cohesive alliance of local public officials and business and civic leaders who enlisted support and funding from the state and federal governments.

Pennsylvania's heritage programs, launched in the 1980s, exposed a problem that arises when many communities or regions, conscious of the Lowell archetype (and the $1 billion invested there between 1975 and 1990), pursue economic revitalization through industrial preservation.[101] The only access to major funding from the federal cornucopia seems to be political: funds go to an area whose congressman has leverage to open the funding spigot or win national park designation. One heritage project that provoked much controversy (and disdain) was Scranton's Steamtown. Championed by Rep. Joseph M. McDade, it involved the creation of a forty-two-acre theme park that was to recreate the steam locomotive era. Launched in 1986, Steamtown had received $56 million in federal appropriations by 1991 to develop a historic railroad restoration in a community that had little to do with railroad history. Robert M. Vogel, former curator of mechanical and civil engineering at the Smithsonian National Museum of American History, complained, " 'They are spending millions of dollars building a Walt Disney movie set that will be absolutely phony from the word go.' " Others, objecting to the creation of a "third-rate" collection where there was no railroad heritage, complained that the funding should have gone to Baltimore's B&O Railroad Museum or the National Museum of Transport in St. Louis. And the director of the National Park Service voiced dismay over the many pork-barrel restoration projects in the 1980s that were forced upon it. Conceivably, Steamtown can evolve into a substantial complex that combines a museum with excursions and a rolling stock and working railyard. The fallacy lies in presuming that Scranton can embody the age of the steam railroad. It is indeed as false as a Disney theme park, or as inappropriate as a collection of steel industry artifacts in a Boston heritage park.[102]

The Park Service joined the Southwestern Pennsylvania Heritage Preservation Commission in another railroad assignment—a $5.8 million visitors' center that opened in 1992 near Altoona at the site of the Pennsylvania Railroad's famed Horseshoe Curve. Completed in 1854, this dramatic section of rail line was an extraordinary engineering achievement, and Altoona became the Pennsylvania Railroad's main repair center between Philadelphia and Pittsburgh. Also in 1992 the Heritage Commission opened a $5 million visitors' center at Cresson, Cambria County. This memorialized the Allegheny Portage Railroad, which had been superseded by the building of the Horseshoe Curve.[103]

The Heritage Preservation Commission administered the generously funded America's Industrial Heritage Project (AIHP). This originated in a 1985 Reconnaissance Survey of Western Pennsylvania Roads and Sites by the National Park Service, followed by a 1986 congressional mandate to the Park Service to develop a regional preservation and heritage program. The federally legislated Southwestern Pennsylvania Heritage Preservation Commission was established in 1989 in the Department of the Interior. Encompassing nine counties in the Allegheny Highlands, AIHP was "to commemorate the significant contribution of the region's iron and steel, coal, and transportation industries. . . . The area's important contribution to the rich ethnic and social history of the nation is also an important part of the project."[104] Hardly an end in itself, commemoration would lead to economic development:

> the project will use related historic sites and cultural resources within the nine counties as focal points for a tourism promotion program. Tourism development efforts will also include the region's scenic, natural, and recreational areas in the overall AIHP plan. A series of heritage routes or tour routes will be designated.[105]

The AIHP's $63 million funding authorization between 1989 and 1993 was largely attributable to the persuasive talents of Rep. John Murtha of Johnstown. Indeed, Johnstown, although part of the nine-county AIHP territory, developed an ambitious, independent heritage plan designed to nurture community pride, to enhance the quality of life, and revitalize the economy. Famous for its 1889 flood of biblical proportions, Johnstown celebrated a Flood Centennial, out of which came a "new vision."[106] Expressed in *Johnstown: The Third Century*, the vision called for using the "heritage and cultural resources of Johnstown as a basis for community-wide revitalization." The specific goal was to "expand the economic base of the city through cultural tourism, while upgrading the environment." After a ten-month planning period in 1990–1991, a workshop entitled "Preservation: A Strategy for Community Revitalization" was held in December 1990. The keynote speaker was Representative Murtha, who "stressed the importance of Johnstown to the nation and to the evolving regional cultural tourism industry."[107]

The core of the Johnstown plan for revitalizing its industrial and cultural heritage was the proposal for a Cambria Iron and Steel National Historic Park whose focus would be Bethlehem Steel's Lower Works. Explicitly inspired by the Lowell prototype, it would be a Park Service unit funded separately from the AIHP. The park's larger heritage context would include Johnstown's downtown, along with the old working-class districts of Cambria City and Minersville. If "properly developed and marketed," hoped the Johnstown Heritage Association, such historic districts with their human scale architecture and eye arresting detail might "attract not only visitors, but also new residents, new investments, and jobs."[108] The establishment of an annual Johnstown Folkfest in Cambria City, nestled in a bend of the Conemaugh River, reflected hopes that the industrial and cultural heritage might "be recycled to curb a sagging economy and declining population."[109]

The catalyst for heritage planning in Southwestern Pennsylvania—the Pittsburgh region and Mon Valley—was the Pittsburgh History & Landmarks Foundation. Under contract to the Pennsylvania Historical and Museum Commission, Landmarks in 1987 surveyed thirty iron and steel production sites for possible listing in the National Register of Historic Places. Then, in February 1988, it sponsored an Allegheny County Steel Site Preservation Conference; this led to the creation of the Steel Industry Heritage Task Force in April.[110] Federal legislation in November authorized the National Park Service to help the Task Force plan for preserving and interpreting historically significant iron and steel resources in Allegheny and Washington Counties. Westmoreland and Fayette Counties were soon added to the project area, followed by Greene and Beaver Counties.[111] These six counties, along with other government units and agencies, signed a "Memorandum of Understanding" in September 1990, thus launching what was now designated the Steel Industry Heritage Project (SIHP). The memorandum stipulated that the MVI would provide staff and community organizing support. Jo DeBolt and Edward Muller served, respectively, as chairman and vice-chairman of the Steering Committee.

The SIHP was required to produce a Draft Concept Plan for a regional heritage program. Presented to the state and federal governments in January 1992, it was followed by a final Concept Plan in March 1993. Meanwhile, program development was turned over to the nonprofit Steel Industry Heritage Corporation. August Carlino was selected as executive director. In late 1993, work began on A "Management Action Plan," another requirement of heritage planning. This will select specific sites for heritage development, specify transportation strategies for linkage of sites, and deal with educational programs and community involvement.[112]

Steel heritage efforts in southwestern Pennsylvania from 1988 to 1995 were necessarily a study in process, since nothing could be developed during that period. What has occurred, besides planning and preparing a case for federal and state funding of a steel heritage corridor, has been much community organization and research.[113] Funding was something of a sore point. It grieved the editors of the *Pittsburgh Post-*

Gazette, for example, that the nearby AIHP had received $63 million in federal appropriations by the summer of 1993, compared to only $3 million for the Steel Industry Heritage Project. The fact that the Mon Valley was the fountainhead for the second industrial revolution in America was far less important, it seemed, than whether a site was located in Rep. John Murtha's district.[114]

Throughout these first six years of heritage planning, the themes most emphasized were similar to those of the Mon Valley Initiative: bolstering community pride, community organizing, and economic revitalization. The Mon Valley communities had become economically marginalized and their population demoralized. But they had a rich heritage which, if cultivated, could became a source of identity, cohesion, and economic renewal. According to the Steel Industry Heritage Task Force,

> Heritage initiative has the potential to preserve the most important elements of the region's history in a manner that stimulates local economic revitalization through tourism, creates a self-sufficient historic site, and develops a powerful array of educational experiences and materials for our local schools.[115]

Heritage advocates believed that nurturing self-help and participatory democracy were vital to the revival of the Mon Valley. Heritage involvement—town meetings, volunteer work for events and projects—would nurture a "community pride and self-worth" that would have the greatest "long-run economic impact."[116]

Heritage planning included conducting extensive surveys of people and communities reminiscent of the New Deal's Farm Security Administration photographic project. The Steel Industry Heritage Corporation, for example, launched an exploration of cultural life in the six counties. Fourteen field workers, including former steelworkers, spread across the region photographing, taping, interviewing, and collecting information about social, religious, and cultural organizations. They looked into "living traditions," or "skills, events, places and values that play a vital role in the ongoing life of the community."[117]

The SIHP heritage study area covered approximately 2,000 square miles and more than 600 communities. The Task Force initiated a massive community organization project to win support. Apart from the many individuals and groups affiliated with the Task Force Steering Committee and Planning Council, hundreds of community meetings were held to acquaint citizens with the heritage program.[118] By the early 1990s these had "evolved into a town meeting format" that featured slide presentations and efforts to involve the communities in heritage planning.[119] Like another New Deal precedent—the WPA arts and theater programs—these efforts created a new interest in the local heritage and a preservation consciousness that had not existed before. This, combined with extensive research and documentation, constitutes a significant achievement.

The SIHP Concept Plan of 1992 was an advocacy document designed to win federal and state funding and support for a proposed regionwide heritage park. It proposed the creation of a Steel Industry Heritage Center on the site of the former USS Homestead Works, supplemented by a Scottdale "core area" dealing with the coal and coke industries.[120] These would be supplemented by interpretive sites at other locations. The three rivers of the region would offer outdoor recreational opportunities and raise awareness of natural resource conservation, as well being as a water link connecting the interpretive sites. The Concept Plan also contemplated additional educational facilities like a Center for Cultural and Labor Heritage and an Environmental Education Center. The economic case for heritage funding rested on the prospect of attracting visitors to the heritage sites and programs, as well as increased business investment. The plan estimated that the Steel Industry Heritage Center itself could draw as many as 375,000 annually and revenues of more than $25 million. The increased appeal of the region as a place to live and work because of the heritage program would also attract new businesses. Not least, the "community awareness and pride stimulated by involvement in the program" would encourage further local revitalization efforts.[121]

In the context of U.S. history, the Pittsburgh region is unique. Its "capital intensive, mass production industries" made it the fountainhead of the second industrial revolution in the United States. The Concept Plan justifiably emphasized this basis for local heritage park designation. It related in detail the role of Andrew Carnegie and Henry Clay Frick in creating the Mon Valley empire of steel, the significance of the Connellsville coke district, the surplus capital accumulated in Pittsburgh (T. Mellon and Sons, banks, corporations), the contributions of George Westinghouse, the mass-production glass industry of the 1890s, and the aluminum company founded by Alfred Hunt and Charles Hall that became Alcoa. Examined also were the regional labor force and the cultural and ethnic traditions of working-class communities.[122] In all, heritage research uncovered 500 industrial sites and 600 religious, fraternal, and union locations that could be part of the heritage story. Many physical artifacts remain: coal patches, coke ovens, mill towns, and working-class neighborhoods, the landmark architecture of elite residences and commercial buildings, and the Carnegie libraries.

A central event in the story of the region's industrial development and its consequences for labor relations was the disastrous 1892 Homestead Strike. This made Homestead the logical setting for the heritage program's major museum and interpretive center. Unfortunately, an enormous obstacle arose in the form of the Park Corporation of Cleveland, which had purchased the USS Homestead Plant and Carrie Furnaces across the river in the spring of 1988. The heritage planners needed seventy-seven acres, including the area surrounding the Carrie Blast Furnaces Six and Seven (sixty-five acres) and twelve acres in Munhall that included the site where the Pinkertons landed as well as the water tower and pump house that played a role in the 1892 events.[123]

Carrie Furnaces Six and Seven, ca. 1910. *Photo: Steel Industry Heritage Corporation*

They expected also to preserve the "Hole in the Wall," a pedestrian underpass used by the workers to reach the mill, and the 1910 roll shop (the Big Shop). Both, however, were demolished by the Park Corporation. Although steel heritage advocates believed they had an understanding with the Park Corporation, they were appalled to find the Big Shop, 100 by 300 feet, suddenly undergoing demolition in January 1994. Ninety-five years old, it had contained the machinery to service the USS Mon Valley mills. The SIHC had planned to house the forty-eight-inch rolling mill stock and other artifacts in the Big Shop.[124]

Although the Park Corporation agreed to preserve the landing site as well as the Carrie Furnaces, and allowed the removal of the 1895 forty-eight-inch mill for storage, it would not budge in its conviction that the proposed heritage park clashed with its economic interests.[125] The company stubbornly insisted that the heritage program would not get the funds it needed and that the Carrie Furnaces were an unattractive safety hazard that would compromise its development plans. Yet the Carrie Furnaces were vital to the heritage program because the National Park Service wanted production facilities to be included in a heritage museum.

Carrie Furnaces, 1990. *Photo: Steel Industry Heritage Corporation*

More generally, company officials were convinced that they could not risk selling the property and then discover that the heritage program could not be funded.[126]

The SIHC was in an unenviable position in two respects. The Park Corporation was reluctant to complete the sale until it was assured that the state and federal governments would fund the project. But it was nearly impossible to get the money without owning the property. Similarly, the Howard Heinz Endowment in 1993, acting through the Western Pennsylvania Conservancy, ostensibly provided the money for the seventy-seven acres, but allocation of funds was again contingent on government designation and funding.[127]

The conflict between the Park Corporation and the heritage planners was similar to that between the MVI and its critics, and was rooted in differing views over post-steel economic and community development policy. To some mill town residents and labor interests, historic preservation appeared to be a " 'mild mannered, white-collar solution to urgent blue-collar problems.' "[128] Tom Croft, director of the Steel Valley Authority, objected to the spectacle of downtown money going into studies rather than jobs—at least blue-collar jobs. And Mike Stout, former steelworker and unionist, detected an intention to obliterate manufacturing in favor of tourism and yuppie carpetbaggers.[129] In contrast, the MVI and Steel Heritage advocates viewed preservation as a source of community pride and economic development that would create communities that would be magnets for new business investment and new jobs. From this perspective, the Park Corporation's obstructionism was myopic because a nearby heritage complex would enhance the value of its own investment.[130]

11

Conclusion

In November 1993, *Toward a Shared Economic Vision for Pittsburgh and Southwestern Pennsylvania: A Report by the White Paper Committee for the Allegheny Conference on Community Development* was released. The committee's chairman was Robert Mehrabian, president of Carnegie Mellon University. Conspicuously absent from the fourteen-member committee were representatives of labor, neighborhood organizations, or just about anyone not fairly high up the corporate ladder. The two academics, Richard L. Florida and Robert Gleeson, were, respectively, director and executive director of the Center for Economic Development of CMU's School of Public Policy and Management.[1] The committee's statement largely reflected Florida's views on manufacturing, especially high-performance manufacturing, as the basis of economic well-being: "Manufacturing is the primary source of wealth and prosperity in all advanced industrial economies."[2]

The report maintained that the economic problems of the Pittsburgh Metropolitan region (Allegheny, Beaver, Fayette, Washington, and Westmoreland Counties) "have reached crisis proportions." Nearly 157,000 quality manufacturing jobs were lost in the two decades ending in 1990. Service growth did not compensate in terms of employment rates (compared to other regions) or wage levels. Only 6 percent of employment derived from advanced technology in the five-county region. And the region ranked lowest in the nation in economic health indicators: value added, productivity, investment in manufacturing sectors; and changes in total earnings.[3]

As an analysis of Pittsburgh's economy, this report was flawed because of a methodological fault. Almost all the economic data and comparisons use the 1970–1990 period. This distorts the picture because it exaggerates the impact of the late seventies and early eighties, when the steel industry was dissolving, and minimizes the positive growth elements starting in the middle and late 1980s. Thus the Pittsburgh region experienced a 21 percent growth in service jobs from 1987 to 1992 and a 7.2 percent increase in total employment. And the region's unemployment rate in these latter years compared favorably with rates in the rest of the nation (the Mon Valley, in most cases, excepted).[4]

It has become a cliche to argue that service employment is dead-end work or pays less than manufacturing, and therefore does not compensate for the loss of manufacturing jobs. Yet a study for the Federal Reserve Bank of Cleveland concluded that "service-producing industries now offer wage opportunities very similar to those in manufacturing and construction." The major spread in wages between the goods-and-service-producing sectors concerned workers with only high school diplomas. The report concludes, "Policy that favors goods-producing employment is not necessarily a sensible strategy for generating high-wage opportunities for American workers."[5]

The White Paper was succeeded by a broader nine-month Regional Economic Revitalization Initiative (RERI), also propelled by the Allegheny Conference, chaired by Mehrabian and staffed by CMU's Center for Economic Development.[6] Although conceding improvements in the economy since 1990, the RERI report stressed the Pittsburgh region's comparative lag in job creation and entrepreneurship.[7] The six-county region would require 100,000 new jobs in the near future in order to keep pace with the projected national average. A report by the Enterprise Corporation was critical of the entrepreneurial climate. It maintained that about 3,400 companies were created each year in the region, but that the formation rate would have to increase by 90 percent (3,000 more new companies for a total over more than 6,500) in order to match the national average.[8]

To deal with the regional liabilities in job formation and entrepreneurship, the RERI proposed a wide range of initiatives.[9] These included:

- a frequent and strong emphasis on coordinating economic development organizations and efforts (defined as creating a "hub"). Coordination should include the creation of a Regional Business Financial Services Initiative; a Regional Business Retention Initiative; a Regional Business Market Development Initiative for small business; and an International Marketing and Business Recruitment Initiative.

- Better marketing of the region's cultural amenities as well as its economic opportunities.[10]

- Creation of investment funds and partnerships.[11]

- Launching an Entrepreneurship Vitality Campaign that would "build" $3–4 million annually in "adventure" capital for early start-ups; development of educational programs to encourage entrepreneurship; and improvement of the technology transfer process from universities to entrepreneurs.

- Nurture of five economic sectors or clusters in which the Pittsburgh region might emerge as a world leader. These five clusters employed 250,000 and produced 21 percent of salaries or wages: metalworking, chemicals and plastics, biomedical technologies, information and communication products and services, and environmental technologies.[12]

- Infrastructure improvements.[13]

- Better labor-management relations. Proposed is a worldwide recognition of Pittsburgh as a center for "visionary workplace relations." This would include the "Pittsburgh pledge," or a commitment to avoid strikes as much as possible.[14]

- A more favorable tax and business climate. Negative factors included environmental remediation costs, perceived poor labor relations and union problems, a splintered system of government, a tax structure characterized by high corporate and workmen's compensation taxes. Indeed, the report reads, "without bold action on the tax issue, no effort to improve economic development could be effective." The RERI proposed establishing an Independent Tax Review Council to revise the state tax code and turn the economy "once again into a competitive environment for business."[15]

- Improved economic conditions for the African-American population. Shortly before the release of the RERI in the fall of 1994, the University Center for Social and Urban Research reported that, according to 1990 census data for the nation's fifty largest cities and counties, Pittsburgh and Allegheny County "have the fourth highest black poverty rates, the fifth highest black unemployment rates, the fourth largest difference between black and white poverty rates, and the fourth and fifth (respectively) largest difference between black and white unemployment rates."[16] The RERI proposed that 20 percent of the $50 million Partnership for Regional Investment in Development and Entrepreneurship be applied to "business ventures which will enhance job and wealth creation for disadvantaged populations and neighborhoods."[17]

Surprisingly, the RERI did not deal with demographic problems. The population of the region cannot continue to hemorrhage without disastrous consequences. From a peak population of 676,000 in 1950, the number had fallen to below 370,000 by 1990. Since Pittsburgh's population had expanded to service the vast manufacturing sector, with its need for unskilled and semiskilled labor, it is not surprising that it declined substantially as economic circumstances changed. But unless the downward trend is halted or reversed, the tax base will shrink, as will the base of support for cultural and retail facilities. A related problem is the demographic mix. Within the shrinking population, the proportion of aged citizens increases (Allegheny County is second only to Tampa–St. Petersburg in its proportion of aged). In short, Pittsburgh needs not only more population, but more younger residents (preferably educated and tax-paying).[18]

A second issue—one that affects most American cities—overlooked by the RERI concerns crime. Efforts to stabilize, repopulate, or revitalize neighborhoods are often compromised by gang wars, drug problems, vandalism, and violent crime. These conditions discourage investment and demoralize neighborhoods. In the modern urban community, it is as true that crime causes poverty as the reverse. The prospects for neighborhood revitalization would greatly improve in many areas if criminal elements could be curbed.

Finally, the future-oriented findings and recommendations of the RERI obscure the significance and accomplishments of the Renaissance

II era. The civic coalition established economic diversification and modernization as a key regional objective; this, in turn, was translated into efforts to nurture advanced technology and other elements of a post-steel, post–heavy industry economy. Recent events in Pittsburgh (and the nation) dramatize the importance of economic diversification. One of the engines of growth in Pittsburgh has been the health industry. It is now shrinking, but there seems to be enough flexibility in the Pittsburgh economy to absorb the shock.[19]

Along with a commitment to economic diversification, the post-steel era in Pittsburgh has been characterized by the creation of economic support mechanisms for neighborhood organizations. In turn, these organizations served as advocates for their communities, as intermediaries between residents and the external world, and as countervailing influences against forces making for deterioration. CDCs, in particular, serve as conduits for funds from government agencies, foundations, banks.

Along with economic diversification and support for neighborhood revitalization through a system of subsidized empowerment, the civic coalition in the post-steel era agreed on the desirability of cultural progress. Cultural institutions were viewed as economic development forces in their own right and a draw for tourists. In the Mon Valley, the steel heritage project was likewise conceived by its advocates as a major community revitalization effort. Station Square and many smaller examples of creative recycling of historic structures supported the claims of preservationists that the local architectural heritage did not have to be destroyed in the name of development.

The future of Pittsburgh will be influenced by how well it maintains a stewardship over its unique environmental and architectural assets, and how generously it supports its cultural institutions, small as well as large. These give Pittsburgh its identity—not the look-alike malls, fast-food and retail chain outlets—and justify living in the city rather than the suburbs (or in another city). Protection of the city's environmental, architectural, and cultural resources requires an aggressive commitment because of multidimensional threats. State dictates are ruining the city's bridges as concrete Jersey barriers and cyclone fences appear and convey the image of a linear prison. Federal mandates threaten to force covering the reservoirs with protective sheets. Billboards touting tobacco products and alcohol tower over residential neighborhoods. The graffiti pestilence

McDonald's Restaurant at Fourth Avenue and
Wood Street: clash between old and new,
beautiful and ugly. *Photo: Author*

spreads. Historic architecture lacking official landmark status is vulnerable to destruction (where Oakland's Saint Peter's Church and Syria Mosque once stood are empty lots). Corporate mergers and downsizing and outmigration have diminished the base of support for cultural institutions and art galleries. One hopeful trend is the effort of some CDCs (East Liberty Development, Inc., Bloomfield-Garfield, South Side Local Development) to promote cultural growth in the neighborhoods.

In the post-steel era, Pittsburgh has moved constructively toward economic diversification and neighborhood and cultural revitalization. This has laid the foundation for a prosperous post-steel city, but nothing is guaranteed. A downtown McDonald's, capped by an ungainly, top-heavy, shedlike orange block whose corrugated facade is relieved only by sinister, narrow, vertical slits, could as well become the Pittsburgh icon as much as the three rivers.

Appendixes
Notes
Index

APPENDIXES

Appendix 1. City Landmarks

As of October 1993, the following structures have been designated landmarks by the Pittsburgh City Council. Dates indicate when they were so designated.

Allegheny Arsenal, Penn Avenue at Fortieth Street, February 22, 1977
Allegheny County Courthouse, 436 Grant Street, December 26, 1972
Allegheny County Jail, 400 block of Ross Street, December 26, 1972
Allegheny Library, Allegheny Center, North Side, March 15, 1974
Allegheny Post Office (now the Pittsburgh Children's Museum), Allegheny Center, December 26, 1972
Byers-Lyons House (now Byers Hall of Community College of Allegheny County), 808 Ridge Avenue, March 15, 1974
Calvary United Methodist Church, Allegheny Avenue at Beech Avenue, February 22, 1977
Cathedral of Learning, University of Pittsburgh, 4200 Fifth Avenue, February 22, 1977
Dower's Tavern (former Beck's Run School), 1000 Beck's Run Road, September 18, 1987
Emmanuel Episcopal Church, 957 West North Avenue, February 22, 1977
Engine Company Nos. 1 and 30, 344 Boulevard of the Allies, March 17, 1993
Stephen Foster Center (former Washington School), 286 Main Street, July 8, 1982
Garrison Foundry–Mackintosh Hemphill Company Offices, 901–11 Bingham Street, October 18, 1991
Howe-Childs-Gateway House, 5918 Fifth Avenue, April 16, 1986
John Wesley A.M.E. Zion Church, 594 Herron Avenue
B. F. Jones House (now Jones Hall of Community College of Allegheny County), 808 Ridge Avenue, March 15, 1974
King Estate (or "Baywood"), 1251 North Negley Avenue, November 12, 1992
Lowen-Shaffer House, 311 Lowenhill Street, February 10, 1992
Monongahela Incline, between West Carson Street, near Smithfield Street, and Grandview Avenue, March 15, 1974

Moreland-Hoffstot House, 5057 Fifth Avenue, February 22, 1977

Neill Log House, Serpentine Drive, Schenley Park, February 22, 1977

Old Heidelberg Apartment, 401–423 South Braddock Avenue, March 15, 1974

Phipps Conservatory, Schenley Drive, Schenley Park, December 26, 1972

Pittsburgh and Erie Railroad Station (now the Landmarks Building), One Station Square, Smithfield Street, near West Carson Street, March 15, 1974

Shrine of Saint Anthony of Padua, 1700 Harpster Street, February 22, 1977

Smithfield Street Bridge, Monongahela River, February 22, 1977

W. P. Synder House (now Babb Insurance Company), 854 Ridge Avenue, March 15, 1974

Soldiers and Sailors Memorial Hall of Allegheny County, 4201 Fifth Avenue at Bigelow Boulevard, February 11, 1991

South Side Market House, South Twelfth Street and Bingham Street at Bedford Square, February 22, 1977

Stanley Theater (now the Benedum Center for the Performing Arts), 207 Seventh Street, November 20, 1984

Ursuline Academy (former Lynch House), 201 South Winebiddle Street, and associated buildings, August 20, 1982

Woods House, 4604 Monongahela Street, February 22, 1977

Appendix 2. Pittsburgh Register of Historic Places

This list, compiled by the City Historic Review Commission, was adopted on December 10, 1993.

Historic Districts Designated by the City

Allegheny Commons Parks
Allegheny West
East Carson Street
Manchester Area
Market Square
Mexican War Streets
Oakland Civic Center
Penn-Liberty Area
Schenley Farms

Districts Designated or Eligible for Designation
by the National Register
of Historic Places

Abbot-Edgerton Area*
Allegheny Cemetery
Allegheny West
Alpha Terrace
Carnegie Tech*
Central North Side*
Deutschtown
East Carson Street
East Deutschtown*
Firstside Area
Fourth Avenue
Freindship Area*
Highland Park*
Lawrenceville*
Manchester Area
Mexican War Streets
North Point Breeze*
Old Allegheny Rows
Penn-Liberty Area
Pittsburgh Central Downtown
Robin Road*
Schenley Farms
Schenley Park
Shadyside (West)*
West End Valley*
Woodland Road*

*Asterisk indicates that the district is eligible for identification by the National Register
of Historic Places.

Appendix 3. Activities and Accomplishments of Preservation Pittsburgh, 1992–1993

The following list is taken from Preservation Pittsburgh, *Annual Report,* September 1992–August 1993.

• Accomplished City Historic Designation of the Oakland Civic Historic District.

• Participated in the Syria Mosque Settlement Agreement between the University of Pittsburgh Medical Center, National Development Corp., and city officials to assure that established guidelines for the historically designated district will apply to the new structure to be constructed on the former Mosque site.

• Co-sponsored a Religious Structures seminar.

• Combined a tour of the architecturally and historically interesting Berger Manor House with a slide presentation of endangered religious structures.

• Presented "An Open Town Meeting," with speakers addressing current preservation issues.

• Provided guidance, information, and expertise toward the preservation of the 1840s Murray House, Frazer Township.

• Established the Preservation Pittsburgh Jamie D. Van Trump Award to be awarded annually for outstanding performance in the area of preservation. Mr. James Van Trump was the first recipient.

• Participated in accomplishing Bed and Breakfast Legislation for the City of Pittsburgh.

• Participated in an architectural preservation program jointly with the AIA, PHLF, and HSWP.

• Held an educational slide program for members, presented by architect John Martine, on endangered Pittsburgh structures.

• Acquired (contributed) office space for our organization and engaged a consultant.

• Assisted in forming a coalition of Oakland neighborhood groups to create open dialogue with the University of Pittsburgh and the Medical Center regarding future expansion and development.

• Presented educational programs to other groups in Pittsburgh and the region.

• As a follow-up to our participation in the historic designation of the King Estate, celebrated the historic designation and preservation of this important landmark with a tour of the house and a garden party.

• Influenced sensitive restoration of two bridges. Participated in bringing the attention of area road and bridge designers the importance of retaining the original appearance of the historically and architecturally important Schenley Bridge and the Panther Hollow Bridge.

- Supported and pursued an advocacy role for more comprehensive legislative reform to limit the number, size, height, and location of advertising billboards.
- Brought to the attention of mayoral candidates the importance of preservation to the city of Pittsburgh.
- Assisted the City Historic Review Commission to coordinate "Preservation Month" (May 1993) by promoting activities in the city and region, producing a brochure, and notifying the media.
- Made a major contribution to the monthlong observance sponsored by the National Trust for Historic Preservation by coordinating a calendar of events and promising twenty-two regional activities.
- Cleaned 200-year-old Neill Log House (the oldest Pittsburgh residence), located in Schenley Park, and conducted free lectures and tours of the house.
- Advocated a more sensitive solution reconstructing the 1890s Schenley Park bridges than standard fences and barriers.
- Supported the city's historic designation of the South Side East Carson Street Historic District.
- Assisted the city's Historic Review Commission with the ongoing Historic Building Survey by photographing buildings identified in the survey.
- Was publicly commended and recognized by City Council, together with the Historic Review Commission, for "important work in maintaining our historic buildings and furthering the cause of the historic preservation of the City," May 11, 1993.
- Processed the following significant structures through our Architectural Assessment Committee for review and recommendations to the Board and Membership:
  1. Ursuline Academy, Bloomfield
  2. Scheibler Townhouses, Frankstown Road, Homewood
  3. King Estate, Highland Park
  4. Wabash Bridge, South Side to First Side
  5. Number One Fire Station, Boulevard of the Allies, Downtown
  6. Harder Mansion, Fifth Avenue and Amberson Street, Shadyside
  7. Hornbostel Buildings, University of Pittsburgh campus, Oakland
  8. Havard-Yale-Princeton Club, William Penn Way, Downtown
  9. Schenley Golf Course and Phipps Conservatory, Schenley Park (for more details, please refer to the annual report).

NOTES

Preface

1. An informative account of the Flaherty administration is included in Shelby Stewman and Joel A. Tarr, "Four Decades of Public-Private Partnerships in Pittsburgh," in *Public-Private Partnership in American Cities: Seven Case Studies,* ed. R. Scott Fosler and Renee A. Berger (Lexington, Mass.: Lexington Books, 1982), 89–94.

2. According to Roger Ahlbrandt, the term "Renaissance II" was a "politically motivated" effort to identify the new (1977) Caliguiri mayoralty with a program of CBD and neighborhood development. He adds: "I do not believe it was originally conceived to broaden the industrial base or create a new economy" (letter to author, August 30, 1991). This is technically correct. But I never felt that Caliguiri's CBD and neighborhood programs justified designation as a Renaissance; greater justice is done to history by conceiving of Renaissance II as a much broader convergence of the forces that reshaped the economy and culture of the Pittsburgh region.

3. I refer to an economic development strategy or consensus from an after-the-fact perspective. The leading participants in the economic revitalization process—city of Pittsburgh, Allegheny County, State of Pennsylvania, Allegheny Conference on Community Development, corporations, foundations, universities, the advanced technology community—did not actually convene and devise a strategy. But it seems clear that their disparate efforts in the 1980s amounted to a de facto consensus or strategy, rooted in pursuit of diversification and its components as I describe them. Roger Ahlbrandt, for one, emphasizes the desirability of avoiding any impression that terms like *strategy* or *consensus* imply anything more than a loose, informal orientation (personal interview, May 24, 1993).

4. G. Evan Stoddard to author, written commentary.

Chapter 1. Elegy for a Bygone World

1. *Economic Study of the Pittsburgh Region,* conducted by the Pittsburgh Regional Planning Association, vol. 1, *Region in Transition,* vol. 2, *Portrait of a*

Region, vol. 3, *Region with a Future* (Pittsburgh: University of Pittsburgh Press, 1963).

2. Along with the classic six volumes of the Pittsburgh Survey, the following provide insight into the way of life of the Pittsburgh working class: Francis G. Couvares, *The Remaking of Pittsburgh: Class and Culture in an Industrializing City, 1877–1919* (Albany, New York: State University of New York Press, 1984); S. J. Kleinberg, *The Shadow of the Mills: Working-Class Families in Pittsburgh, 1870–1907* (Pittsburgh: University of Pittsburgh Press, 1989); John Bodnar, Roger Simon, Michael P. Weber, *Lives of Their Own: Blacks, Italians, and Poles in Pittsburgh, 1900–1960* (Urbana: University of Illinois Press, 1982); Samuel P. Hays, ed., *City at the Point: Essays on the Social History of Pittsburgh* (Pittsburgh: University of Pittsburgh Press, 1989); Matthew S. Magda, *Monessen: Industrial Boomtown and Steel Community, 1898–1980* (Harrisburg: Pennsylvania Historical and Museum Commission, 1985); Curtis Miner, *Homestead: The Story of a Steel Town* (Pittsburgh: Historical Society of Western Pennsylvania, 1989); and Curtis Miner and Paul Roberts, "Engineering an Industrial Diaspora: Homestead, 1941," *Pittsburgh History* 72 (Winter 1989), 4–25; Dennis C. Dickerson, *Out of the Crucible: Black Steelworkers in Western Pennsylvania* (Albany: State University of New York Press, 1986). A fictional classic set in Braddock is Thomas Bell's novel, *Out of This Furnace* (1941; Pittsburgh: University of Pittsburgh Press, 1976).

3. Thanks to a $250 million investment in a continuous caster, opened in August 1992, the USX plant at Braddock is now a technologically advanced and competitive producer of steel slabs, which are shipped to the West Mifflin Irvin Plant for conversion into finished products. Jack Markowitz, "E. T. Plant Casts Steel Toward Third Century," *Tribune-Review*, August 16, 1992; Jim McKay, "Caster Puts Steel in Future," *Pittsburgh Post-Gazette*, August 15, 1993; Ron DaParma, "USX Unveils Continuous Caster," *Tribune-Review*, September 3, 1992. The new process resulted in a labor force reduction at Edgar Thomson of 200 (from 900), but assured the jobs at Irvin and the Clairton Coke Works (1,600 each).

4. "Clairton Pleads for Help," editorial, *Pittsburgh Post-Gazette*, July 16, 1991. See also Davidson Taylor, "Clairton: Another Weekend in Tough Times," *Pittsburgh Press*, July 15, 1991.

5. "The Rise and Decline of the Westinghouse Presence," in *Trouble in Electric Valley: Local Leaders Assess the Difficult Future of Their Community*, River Communities Project, School of Social Work, University of Pittsburgh, 1986, 40.

6. Jim McKay, "Banking the Fire," *Pittsburgh Post-Gazette*, Dec. 5, 1990. Also closed was the blast furnace of the Shenango Group on Neville Island. In 1993, Armco Inc. announced the closing of its Bowman Metal Deck facility in Heidelberg, southwest of Pittsburgh near Carnegie. The shutdown of the steel

fabricating plant, in operation for about half a century, will cost 125 jobs. Jack Markowitz, "Pittsburgh Area About to Lose Another Big Plant," *Tribune-Review,* January 20, 1993.

7. John P. Hoerr, *And the Wolf Finally Came: The Decline of the American Steel Industry* (Pittsburgh: University of Pittsburgh Press, 1988), 97, 105. According to David Ignatius, the federal government joined management and labor in undermining the capacity of the steel industry to compete: "In its dealings with the industry, the government has behaved like the worst sort of monopolist—remote, arbitrary and inefficient. By the 1970s, the federal government had a hand in virtually every aspect of the industry." David Ignatius, "How Steel Industry's Spirit of Progress Sputtered," *Pittsburgh Post-Gazette,* April 2, 1979 (rpt. from *Washington Monthly,* March 1979).

8. The loss of manufacturing jobs in southwestern Pennsylvania was already substantial in the 1970s, and accelerated between 1979 and 1983. According to the University Center for Social and Urban Research (UCSUR), manufacturing jobs in the region dropped from 303,600 in 1972 to 196,800 by 1983. These figures include a drop from 135,700 to 70,000 in primary and fabricated metals. On the other hand, employment gains in nonmanufacturing increased by some 100,000. Within the Pittsburgh SMSA, the manufacturing job loss totaled 88,000 during this decade. More than half, 49,000, was represented by primary metals. (The UCSUR database for the Pittsburgh SMSA encompassed Allegheny, Beaver, Washington and Westmoreland Counties; the southwestern Pennsylvania region added Armstrong, Butler, Fayette, Greene, Indiana, and Lawrence Counties.) See UCSUR, *The State of the Region: Recent Economic, Demographic, and Social Trends in Southwestern Pennsylvania* (Pittsburgh: University of Pittsburgh, 1984), 29, vi, 11, 2, 3.

In the period 1979 to 1990, the Pittsburgh SMSA lost 100,000 manufacturing jobs, but gained the same number in services. Manufacturing dropped from 25 percent of total employment to 13 percent, but services increased from 19 percent to 25 percent. See University of Pittsburgh Center for Social and Urban Research, *The State of the Region: Economic, Demographic and Social Trends in Southwestern Pennsylvania,* November 1990, 3.

Ralph Bangs of the University Center for Social and Urban Research summarized the dominant economic trends in 1983–1987: "The greatest number of jobs was created in services (37,000), wholesale and retail trade (33,300), finance, insurance and real estate (5,700), and construction (4,700). Among services, most growth occurred in health care (e.g., hospitals and physicians offices), business services (e.g., protective, building maintenance, computer and data processing services), social services . . . legal and personal services." Ralph Bangs, "Restructuring of the Regional Economy: 1983–1987," UCSUR, *The State of the Region: Economic, Demographic and Social Trends in Southwestern Pennsylvania,* April 1988, 3. In sum, Southwestern Pennsylvania by 1988 had been "transformed from a heavy industry manufacturing center to a services economy. Finance and corporate services, heath services, retail trade, government and education services are now major components of the regional economy" ("Preface," ibid., vii).

9. Hoerr, *And the Wolf Finally Came*, 8.

10. Jane Blotzer, "All They Ask for Is a Chance," *Pittsburgh Post-Gazette*, December 30, 1985; Blotzer, "Jobless Adrift, Cling to Hope," *Pittsburgh Post-Gazette*, December 30, 1985; Bryan Burrough and Carol Hymowitz, "As Steel Jobs Dwindle, Blue-Collar Families Face Vexing Changes," *Wall Street Journal*, August 8, 1986.

11. Hoerr, *And the Wolf Finally Came*, 4; Monica L. Haynes, "Council Fights as Braddock Crumbles,"*Pittsburgh Post-Gazette*, March 19, 1991; Bob Dvorchak, "From Boom to Bust, a Town Built of Steel," *Philadelphia Inquirer*, August 24, 1984; Mike Pellegrini, "The Rankin They Remember," *Pittsburgh Post-Gazette*, April 7, 1986.

12. Burrough and Hymowitz, "As Steel Jobs Dwindle"; Haynes, "Council Fights as Braddock Crumbles"; Dvorchak, "From Boom to Bust. See also Abby Mendelson, "Braddock: Is There Light at the End of the Tunnel?" *Pittsburgh*, November 1990, 27–28.

Braddock suffered a serious blow in 1993 when Braddock Medical Center, which had become a for-profit hospital in 1990, decided to return to nonprofit status. Braddock had received from the hospital over $400,000 annually in taxes, representing nearly a third of its annual budget. Ed Blazina, "For-Profit Tax Status Pales," *Pittsburgh Post-Gazette*, March 23, 1993; Jeff Griffin, "Braddock Hospital's Realignment Shoots Hole in Town Budget," *Tribune-Review*, May 10, 1993.

Homestead in late 1993 was still confronting budget problems. The council authorized an emergency loan of $512,000 from the Pennsylvania Department of Community Affairs to cover a year-end deficit. And the state had hired a consultant to assist East Pittsburgh cope with its "financial distress." "Homestead" and "East Pittsburgh," *Pittsburgh Post-Gazette*, October 19, 1993.

13. See Carnegie Mellon University, *Milltowns in the Pittsburgh Region: Conditions and Prospects*, Physical Technical Systems Project Report, Department of Engineering and Public Policy, School of Urban and Public Affairs and Department of Social Science, May 1983. This study examined Aliquippa, Clairton, and Homestead in detail along with a composite survey of thirty-two mill towns in Allegheny and Beaver Counties. A CMU study released four years later summarized the demographic transformation as "largely white and younger for most of the twentieth century" to black, female, and older. In Homestead, for example, a population of 13,303 in 1950 dropped in successive decades by 12.37 percent, 13.37 percent, 18.60 percent, and 13.10 percent from 1980 to 1986 (when it totaled 7,143). Females increased from 49.92 percent in 1950 to 55.10 percent in 1986. Minority population rose from 11.36 percent in 1950

to 29.01 percent in 1986. The proportion of the population seventeen years of age dropped from 21.76 percent in 1960 to 8.44 percent in 1986; those sixty-five years and older rose from 11.36 percent to 23.84 percent in the same period. As in other mill towns, steel industry employment in Homestead peaked in the early 1950s, but began to drop steadily (with occasional reversals) even before the cataclysm of the 1980s.

But while unemployment and dependency increased, revenues dropped precipitously. The later study found, for example, that Clairton's tax revenues fell by 61 percent from 1975 to 1987; in Homestead, it was nearly 75 percent; in Duquesne, 29 percent.

CMU, School of Urban and Public Affairs, *Milltowns Revisited*, April 20, 1987, 1–3, 26–28, 30.

Despite significant obstacles, the proportion of black steelworkers had increased to nearly 8 percent of the total by 1978 in a sample of Western Pennsylvania Steel Companies (Dickerson, *Out of the Crucible*, 246).

14. Denny Trombulak, "Steelworkers Lament from Beaver County," in *Overtime: Punchin'Out with the Mill Hunk Herald (Worker Writer Anthology, 1979–1989)* (Homestead, Pa.: Piece of the Hunk Publishers, 1990), 40; David Corn, "Dreams Gone to Rust: The Monongahela Valley Mourns for Steel," *Harper's Magazine* 273 (September 1986), 59, 60, 61.

Corn's article is based, in part, on attendance at a four-day workshop held at the Duquesne Job Center. Also relevant are: Matthew Kennedy, Lee Hotz, Lee Bowman, "Region in Economic Turmoil," *Pittsburgh Press*, December 5, 1982; William Serrin, "After Steel Dream Dies, Junk Cars Drive Streets," *New York Times*, February 5, 1986; Mary Kane, "Poll Shows Unemployed Still Have the Tools," *Pittsburgh Press*, March 1, 1990.

For a survey of unemployment programs, see Thomas J. La Belle and Christopher Ward, "Education and Training in the Mon Valley," prepared for the President's Conference, "Mill Towns: Despair, Hopes and Opportunities," May 5–6, 1988. The authors review the federally funded Job Training Partnership Act which in 1983 superseded the Comprehensive Employment and Training Act (CETA); the Trade Adjustment Assistance program, also federally funded; the Dislocated Worker Educational Training Program inaugurated in 1983 by Allegheny County and the Community College of Allegheny County; and California (Pa.) University's Mon Valley Renaissance, which included training and retraining programs.

An East McKeesport minister, summarizing discussions held by mid-Mon Valley Presbyterian clergy, maintained that "by and large, retraining served to prepare people to leave the area or was ineffective. . . . If you don't already have a job, retraining won't get you one." Gary W. Carson, "After Steel Bust Mon Remains Valley of Despair," *Pittsburgh Post-Gazette*, July 7, 1990.

15. Hoerr, *And the Wolf Finally Came*, 20, 35.

16. Eleanor Bergholz, "Some Retrain for New Careers," *Pittsburgh Post-Gazette*, December 30, 1985.

17. *Aliquippa: Struggle for Survival in a Pittsburgh Milltown 1984 and Before*, School of Social Work, University of Pittsburgh, with the Support of UCSUR, 1984; see also the following studies prepared for the School of Social Work's River Communities Project: Cathy Cairns and Jim Cunningham, eds., *Aliquippa Update: A Pittsburgh Milltown Struggles to come Back, 1984–86* (1986); *Trouble in Electric Valley: Local Leaders Assess the Difficult Future of Their Community* (1986); and Jim Cunningham and Pamela Martz, eds., *Steel People: Survival and Resilience in Pittsburgh's Mon Valley* (1986).

18. David E. Biegel, James Cunningham, Hide Yamatani, Pamela Martz, "Self-Reliance and Blue-Collar Unemployment in Steel Town," *Social Work* 34 (September 1989), 399–406; Hide Yamatani, Lambert Maguire, Robin Rogers, Mary Lou O'Kennedy, *The Impact of Social/Economic Change on Households Among Six Communities in Western Pennsylvania*, River Communities, Longitudinal Data Bank System, School of Social Work, University of Pittsburgh, November 1, 1989; *Evaluation of the Unemployed Council of Southwestern Pennsylvania*, River Communities Project, School of Social Work, UCSUR, January 1989; the following were also prepared for the River Communities Project: Martha Baum, Barbara Shore, Kathy Fleissner, *When Unemployment Strikes: The Impact on Women in Families*, June 1989; Mary H. Page and Myrna Silverman, *The Impact of Unemployment: The Elderly and Their Families*, December 1989; and Phillis D. Coontz, Judith A. Martin, Edward W. Sites, *Steeltown Fathers: Rearing Children in an Era of Industrial Decline*, December 1989.

19. Pamela Martz, *The Youth Enterprise Demonstration: A Critical Evaluation of Three Projects Carried Out in Southwestern Pennsylvania*, River Communities Project, School of Social Work, University of Pittsburgh, December 1990.

20. David Biegel, Jim Cunningham, and Pamela Martz, "Mon Valley People Speak," in *Steel People*, ed. Cunningham and Martz, 67.

21. James V. Cunningham, "The Role of Local Government: Present and Potential," in *Aliquippa: Struggle for Survival in a Pittsburgh Milltown 1984 and Before*, 84; Page and Silverman, "The Impact of Unemployment," vii.

22. Shannon Guy, "Human Services Network," *Trouble in Electric Valley*, 71; Biegal et al., "Self-Reliance and Blue-Collar Unemployment in Steel Town," 404.

23. Jim Cunningham and Joel Tarr, "The Communities of the Mon Valley: A Strategy for Recovery," prepared for the President's Conference, "Mill Towns: Despair, Hopes and Opportunities," May 5–6, 1988, 11.

24. James V. Cunningham, "The Role of Local Government: Present and Potential," *Aliquippa: Struggle for Survival*, 97, 101.

25. Most commentators were exasperated by the difficulties of achieving a unified, constructive response to deindustrialization and disinvestment in a con-

text of government fragmentation. There are seventy-four jurisdictions in the historic steel production section of the Mon Valley, an area stretching forty miles between Brownsville and Pittsburgh. These problems frustrated efforts to devise a common policy such as for riverfront use or economic development. Edward S. Kiely and Richard L. Conaway, "State of Local Government," in UCSUR, *The State of the Region: Economic, Demographic and Social Trends in Southwestern Pennsylvania* (University of Pittsburgh, November 1990), 75–85. The authors, both executives of the Pennsylvania Economy League, Western Division, maintained that government fragmentation has "rendered local government ... largely ineffective, inefficient, and static in the face of economic, social, and demographic change" (75).

26. The following references are to the River Communities Project, *Aliquippa Update*: "Introduction and Summary," iv; Mary Ohmer, "Response of Churches, Social Agencies and Community Organizations," 7; Sr. Carol Burger, "People Helping People," 9, 10.

27. "Retraining Steelworkers Tempered by Uncertainties," *Pittsburgh Press*, April 4, 1984; Gary W. Carson, "After Steel Bust Mon Remains Valley of Despair," *Pittsburgh Post-Gazette*, July 7, 1990.

28. River Communities Project, School of Social Work, UCSUR, *Evaluation of the Unemployed Council of Southwestern Pennsylvania*, January 31, 1989. The Mon Valley Unemployed Committee was active for many years in efforts to repeal the state law requiring liens upon the homes of welfare recipients. The committee and its allies succeeded in the summer of 1993." John Temple, "Overhaul of Welfare Lien Law Cheered," *Tribune-Review*, August 7, 1993.

29. *Aliquippa: Struggle for Survival*, 101; Jim Cunningham and Pauline Cooper, "Local Government Makes a Move," ibid., 58, 59, and "Conclusions by the Editors," ibid., 87; River Communities Project, *Aliquippa Update*.

30. Cunningham and Cooper, "Conclusions by the Editors," in *Aliquippa: Struggle for Survival*, 85.

31. This section is based on "General Alliance Thoughts," September 20, 1994, prepared for the author by Cairns. See also Cathy Cairns, "The Aliquippa Alliance for Unity and Development: An Organizer's Perspective of the Initial Effort," *Aliquippa Update*; Jun H. Yu, "AAUD Director Ministers to Aliquippa," *The Times*, December 14, 1988; Jeff Byko, "Alliance Produces Positive Outcome," *The Times*, September 29, 1988.

32. David L. Rosenberg, "Did the Collapse of Basic Industry Really Take the Allegheny Conference by Surprise?" *In Pittsburgh*, March 21–27, 1990, 18, 19, 20. Rosenberg's explanation for the economic changes of the 1980s is amplified in Dale A. Hathaway, *Can Workers Have a Voice? The Politics of Deindustrialization in Pittsburgh* (University Park: Pennsylvania State University Press, 1993). The author focuses on three groups that challenged corporate economic policy: the Denominational Ministry Strategy, Tri-State Conference

on Steel (and Steel Valley Authority), and Mon Valley Unemployed Committee. *Can Workers Have a Voice?* is advocacy history: "This book does not stop at merely discovering the potency of elite power; it seeks to undermine it. Exposing it at work in its hidden forms is part of that process" (24). It is also reductionist in defining community life and economic outcomes in the period as a struggle between workers and corporate elites (with nothing much in between).

33. No episode more dramatically symbolized the disinvestment process than U.S. Steel's acquisition of Marathon Oil in the early 1980s. David Roderick, who became chairman in 1979, was committed to major diversification because the company's 35 million tons of steelmaking capacity was excessive, "looking at profit margins and inflation." It was imperative, from his viewpoint, to seize a "growth opportunity" to compensate for the shrinking steel component. " 'We Had to Diversify' " (interview with David Roderick), *Pittsburgh Business Review*, August 1991, 12–17.

34. Patrick J. Kiger, "Steeltown Radicals," *Pittsburgh*, March 1984), 44–51; Larry Evans, "Prosperity in the Valley? Strategies for Saving Basic Industry," *In Pittsburgh*, July 2–8, 1986) 4; Johnna A. Pro and David Guo, "DMS Is Alive but Spotlight has Dimmed," and "Activists in DMS Take New Paths," *Pittsburgh Post-Gazette*, November 12, 1990.

A representative of the still-alive but shadowy DMS appeared at a hearing by the City Planning Commission in the fall of 1991 to protest a proposal to use a building in the East Liberty business district for senior citizen housing. The rhetoric of a press release was characteristic:

THE CITY (PAIDOFF RUBBER STAMP) PLANNING DEPARTMENT OF PITTSBURGH will give the OK for organized crime related owners, Lesher and Guttman, to continue the process of undermining the business community of East Liberty by taking the Highland Building out of commercial circulation and making it into a government funded high-rise residential facility (Section 8 money maker) for senior citizens.

Denominational Ministry Strategy, *Release*, November 19, 1991 To all of East Liberty & C4 areas/ City Planning Department/ criminal agencies.

35. Staughton Lynd, "The Genesis of the Idea of a Community Right to Industrial Property in Youngstown and Pittsburgh, 1977–1987," *Journal of American History* 74 (December 1987), 926–27. The Youngstown Sheet and Tube Company closed in 1977, LTV's Brier Hill Works closed in 1978, and USS announced the shutdown of all its area plants in the fall of 1979. Lynd credits Frank O'Brien as the originator of the idea of using eminent domain to acquire industrial properties. O'Brien was a former USWA official and member of the Pennsylvania state legislature (941–42).

36. The Park Corporation, which had purchased the Homestead plant from USX in 1988, had presumably studied the possibility of restarting some of the

mills, but nothing came of it. Edward Muller to author, written commentary, June 1991.

37. On Tri-State and the SVA, see, along with Lynd's article: John Portz, *The Politics of Plant Closings* (Lawrence: University Press of Kansas, 1990); Joan Fitzgerald and Louise Simmons, "From Consumption to Production: Labor Participation in Grass-Roots Movements in Pittsburgh and Hartford," *Urban Affairs Quarterly* 26 (June 1991), 512–31. Lynd recently concluded that neither private capital nor local-regional resources would provide the necessary capital for Mon Valley redevelopment. Fulfillment of Tri-State/SVA goals would depend on the federal government in the form of massive funding administered by "democratic" local authorities. See Lynd's review of Portz's book in *Pittsburgh History* 74 (Spring 1991), 40–41, 43. On the origins and development of Tri-State/SVA by a leading participant, see Charles McCollester, "Tri-State Conference on Steel: Ten Years of a Labor/Community Alliance," unpublished manuscript, n.d.; and McCollester, "Deindustrialization in the Mon Valley: 1979–1986: The Community and Labor Response," prepared for a meeting of the Pennsylvania Historical Society, October 19, 1990.

The struggle to save the Duquesne facilities was the specific precipitant for the creation of the SVA. According to Lynn Williams, president of the USWA since 1984, the Duquesne effort "taught ordinary people they can have an effect on their own lives," and it encouraged the USWA to initiate ESOPs (Employee Stock Ownership Plans). Lynn Williams, "The Culprit Was an Economic Sham," *Pittsburgh Business Review*, August 1991, 28–29. The original nine communities in the SVA were East Pittsburgh, Glassport, Homestead, McKeesport, Munhall, Pittsburgh, Rankin, Turtle Creek, Swissvale.

38. "Plant's Demolition Urged," *Pittsburgh Post-Gazette*, July 1, 1991. The councilmen were Gene Ricciardi and Jack Wagner.

39. Editorial: "Developing the LTV Site," *Pittsburgh Press*, July 3, 1991; "Steeling for a Farewell," editorial, *Pittsburgh Post-Gazette*, July 5, 1991.

40. Jim McKay, "Strike 3, and SVA Was Out," *Pittsburgh Post-Gazette*, July 3, 1991; Margie Romero, "Electric Furnace Restart Scrapped: Will Other Projects Fare Better?" *In Pittsburgh*, August 7–13, 1991, 4. Although Erickson conceded that there was little possibility of restarting the electric furnaces in the present economic climate, he questioned the economic logic of demolishing the facility in order to "import steel slabs from Brazil." More broadly, he reaffirmed the need for the United States to preserve its manufacturing base or "we will become increasingly poor." "Stealing Our Future from Blight," letter to the editor, *Pittsburgh Post-Gazette*, June 23, 1991. SVA advocates maintained that although the electric furnaces had been a huge investment and were highly productive, LTV intended to get out of bankruptcy by unloading steel. In addition, the company had built a major steel facility in nearby Cleveland. SVA believed for a time that German investors were a possibility, but the Berlin Wall

fell and the Germans lost interest. SVA was unable to acquire local capital. Charles McCollester, personal interview, December 8, 1993. SVA had prepared a fifteen-minute documentary, "Recharge South Side Steel," as part of its case for the feasibility of the electric furnace project.

41. Tri-State Conference on Steel, *Steel Valley Authority: A Community Plan to Save Pittsburgh's Steel Industry*, 1984, 2.42. Ibid., 3.

43. Charles McCollester, personal interview, December 8, 1993.

44. Tri-State Conference on Steel, *Steel Valley Authority*, 1; Tri-State Conference on Steel, *Will He Have a Future in the Mon Valley? United States Steel Corporation, 1980, Counter Annual Report*, n.p., 9.

45. David L. Michelmore,"'Valley Towns' Fortunes Still in Steady Decline," *Pittsburgh Post-Gazette*, November 29, 1993. Michelmore adds that these communties "are poorer; they have more old people; they have lost more families and more jobs; they have lost more income and more real wealth."

Chapter 2. Economic Development Strategy in the Post-Steel Era

1. Federal Reserve Bank of Cleveland, *Annual Report*, 1986, 8, 18.

2. Ibid., 4.

3. David B. Houston, "A Brief History of the Process of Capital Accumulation in Pittsburgh: A Marxist Interpretation," in Joel A. Tarr, ed., *Pittsburgh-Sheffield: Sister Cities* (Carnegie-Mellon University, 1986).

4. Roy Lubove, *Twentieth Century Pittsburgh: Government, Business and Environmental Change* (New York: Alfred A. Knopf, 1969), 62–63.

5. Morton Coleman and James V. Cunningham, "By-Passed Pittsburgh Cries Out for New National Economic Policy," in *Pitt*, February 1984, 14–15.

6. Stephen Goldsmith, "Bureaucracy Shackles the Urban Poor," *Wall Street Journal*, June 10, 1992. Goldsmith is mayor of Indianapolis. As the role of state government has increased, similar problems of mandates and controls has arisen in the eyes of local government officials. See Clarke M. Thomas, *State Mandated Services*, University of Pittsburgh, Institute of Politics, December 1991. Thomas cites a 1991 report of the Pennsylvania League of Cities which claims that 50 percent of all municipal expenditures derive from mandates (2).

7. Roger S. Ahlbrandt, Jr., "A Cry For Leadership," October 23, 1984, 6, 9; Roger S. Ahlbrandt, Jr., and Clyde Weaver, "Public-Private Institutions and Advanced Technology Development in Southwestern Pennsylvania," *Journal of the American Planning Association* 53 (Autumn 1987), 456–57; Ahlbrandt, "Economic Development in Southwestern Pennsylvania: Case Studies and Analysis," University of Pittsburgh, Center for Social and Urban Research, May 1988, 4.

Other surveys and interpretations of regional development issues and agencies by Ahlbrandt include: with James P. DeAngelis, "Local Options for Economic Development in a Maturing Industrial Region," *Economic Development Quarterly* 1 (1987), 41–51; "Adjusting to Changes in Traditional Markets: The Problems of Small Manufacturers in Older Industrial Regions," *Economic Development Quarterly* 2 (August 1988), 252–64; "Regional Responses to Structural Change," *The State of the Region,* University of Pittsburgh, University Center for Social and Urban Research, April 1988, 29–53; "The Revival of Pittsburgh—A Partnership Between Business and Government," *Long Range Planning* 23 (October 1990), 31–40; "Mill Town Decline Ten Years Later: The Limits of Corporate Civic Leadership," *Journal of the American Planning Association* 57 (Spring 1991), 193–203.

8. Barbara White Stack, "$3.6-Million Economic Pill Prescribed," *Pittsburgh Post-Gazette,* November 10, 1984; Don Hopey, "Conference Unveils Economic Revitalization Plan," *Pittsburgh Press,* November 16, 1984; "A Question of Leadership," editorial, *Pittsburgh Press,* November 11, 1984.

9. Timothy Parks,"Technology Slowly Finds Its Place in Pittsburgh," *Pittsburgh Business Times,* December 27, 1993–January 2, 1994. Parks cited Boston's acclaimed Route 128 corridor as another example of the economic difficulty caused by overdependence on a limited economic base—defense-related electronics and a certain segment of the computer market.

10. Report of the Allegheny Conference on Community Development, *A Strategy for Growth: An Economic Development Program for the Pittsburgh Region,* vol. 2 of *The Task Force Reports* (Pittsburgh, November 1984), chap. 3:2, 3; University Center for Social and Urban Research, *The State of the Region: Recent Economic, Demographic, and Social Trends in Southwestern Pennsylvania,* University of Pittsburgh, September 1984, 35. In contrast, basic steel employment in a four-year period, 1979–1983, dropped by 51.4 percent in the Pittsburgh SMSA (ibid., 45).

11. Mon Valley Commission, *Report to the Allegheny Board of Commissioners for the Economic Revitalization of the Monongahela, Youghiogheny, and Turtle Creek Valleys,* February 1987, 7, 8, 20. The commission's seven task forces included Manufacturing, Non-Manufacturing, Transportation, Education and Labor, Environmental Systems, Housing and Human Services, Local Government.

12. Allegheny Conference, *Economic Development Program,* chap. 2:2; Ralph Bangs, "Restructuring of the Regional Economy," University Center for Social and Urban Research, *The State of the Region: Economic, Demographic and Social Trends in Southwestern Pennsylvania,* University of Pittsburgh, April 1988, 2.

13. Allegheny Conference, *Economic Development Program,* chap. 2:8.

14. According to Ahlbrandt, SPEDD owned or managed seventeen incubators for small businesses by the early 1980s; they were occupied by some 150 companies. The largest incubator, 400,000 square feet, operated in Glassport

in what had once been the Copperweld Steel Corporation. Roger S. Ahlbrandt, Jr., "Bottoms-Up Way to Meet Region Woes," *Pittsburgh Post-Gazette*, December 4, 1989. In 1991, the state certified the Southwestern Pennyvania Regional Planning Association as the new manager of the local development district. "SPRPC to Designate Development Area," *Pittsburgh Post-Gazette*, Dec. 12, 1991.

15. Raymond Christman, personal interview, December 21, 1993.

16. Jeanne Molyneaux, "Funding Problems Stunt Mon Valley Expressway," *Pittsburgh Business Times*, May 28, 1990, 12s; "If We Don't Hang Together, We Will Most Assuredly Hang Separately," interview with Frank Mascara, University of Pittsburgh, Institute of Politics, *Report* 3 (Spring 1992), 3. The planning process has been slow and complex. A major problem centers on how it would enter Pittsburgh with minimal damage. Intense opposition exists in Jefferson Borough in southern Allegheny County over a seventeen-mile section running from Interstate 70 (eastern Washington County) to connect to Route 51. Dayna DiRienzo and Sue Gottlieb, "The Big Picture: The Mon Valley/Fayette Expressway," *Oakland* 7 (March 1993), 1, 4–6; Joe Napsha, "Expressway's Link to Area Economic Growth Debated," *Tribune-Review*, October 17, 1993; David Tessitor, "Don't Follow the Yellow Brick Road," *Pittsburgh Post-Gazette*, June 14, 1994.

Considerable controversy was stimulated by the negative comments by Raymond Reaves, director of the Allegheny County Planning Department. He was unconvinced that the proposed expressway would be a significant revitalization tool and suggested such alternatives as upgrading existing roads and improving the educational system in the region. Jim McKinnon, "Expressway Critic Sets Off Furor," *Pittsburgh Post-Gazette*, September 11, 1994.

17. Allegheny Conference, *Economic Development Program*, chap. 3:18, chap. 9:5.

18. Ibid., chap. 9:2–3; Mon Valley Commission, *Report*, 39.

19. Allegheny Conference, *Economic Development Program*, chap. 1:2. Examples of high-technology companies cited by the report included instruments, information systems, advanced manufacturing systems, communications, semiconductors, advanced materials.

20. Ibid., chap. 1:10, 12. Specific recommendations included establishing a regional seed capital fund and a corporate technical support program; endowing chairs at the universities, and strengthening the Western Pennsylvania Advanced Technology Center.

21. Penn's Southwest evolved out of the Area Development Committee of the Allegheny Conference. Created in 1971, the Committee and Penn's Southwest dealt with nine counties: Allegheny, Armstrong, Beaver, Butler, Fayette, Greene, Lawrence, Washington, Westmoreland.

22. Roger Ahlbrandt credits Aldridge with having been a key influence in promoting advanced technology in the Pittsburgh region (personal interview, May 25, 1993).

23. Timothy Parks, " 'Nurture the Entrepreneurial Spirit,' " Pittsburgh Business Times, *10 Years in Review, 1981–1991*, August 1991, 18–19.

24. Reddy, a member of the CMU Computer Science Department since 1969, was director of the Robotics Institute and founder of the Carnegie Group, Inc. The latter attempted to apply artificial intelligence to commercial production. Sangrey, chairman of the CMU Civil Engineering Department, was co-chairman of the Western Pennsylvania Advanced Technology Center. He left CMU in the mid-1980s to become dean of the School of Engineering at Rensselaer Polytechnic Institute. "From Research to Products in Pittsburgh," *Pittsburgh High Technology*, 1985, 20–21.

25. The articles by Roger Ahlbrandt cited earlier catalogue the various nonprofit high-tech and economic development agencies that evolved in the Pittsburgh region in the 1980s.

26. Angel Jordon of CMU and Jay Aldridge were prime movers in creating the Pittsburgh High Technology Council (Ahlbrandt, interview, May 25, 1993).

27. The Pittsburgh High Technology Council was a regional association comprised of high technology manufacturers, suppliers, firms which provided professional or commercial services, as well as academic, government and other support groups (*Pittsburgh High Technology*, 1985, 39).

28. Parks, " 'Nurture the Entrepreneurial Spirit,' " 19, 20.

29. Roger S. Ahlbrandt, "Regional Economic Restructuring: Partnerships Between the Public, Private and Nonprofit Sectors," November 2, 1989, 10.

30. Daniel Bates, "Christman Moves to Consolidate State-Funded Programs," *Pittsburgh Business Times*, December 2–8, 1991, 6; Clarke Thomas, "Pittsburgh Manufacturers Must Strive for Perfection," *Pittsburgh Post-Gazette*, March 14, 1990.

The Pittsburgh Biomedical Development Corporation operates as a subsidary of TDEC. It identifies and supports biomedical research that has commercial possibilities and hopes to "establish a critical mass of businesses which, in combination with adequate financing, will establish a major economic base for the Pittsburgh region."

The Industrial Resource Center services for small and medium-size manufacturers include operations review, plant layout analysis, and cost-of-quality studies, export trade assistance, a Manufacturing Technology Loan Fund, and educational seminars.

TDEC also operates an International Business Development Program, which assists manufacturers with market research analysis and strategic planning designed to increase export sales.

TDEC, finally, administers the regional Pennsylvania Youth Apprenticeship Program. This combines school- and work-based education and focuses on machining and engineering technology.

See *Pittsburgh Biomedical Development Corporation: A Catalyst for Biomedical Business in Western Pennsylvania*, n.d.; Southwestern Pennsylvania Industrial Resource Center, *SPIRC: Profile Report*, 1993.

31. "Sony to Build Color TVs in Westmoreland County," *Pittsburgh Press*, February 13, 1991; "Sony's Expansion," editorial, *Pittsburgh Post-Gazette*, February 14, 1991; Jim McKay, "Job Hunger Swayed Sony," *Pittsburgh Post-Gazette*, March 4, 1991.

32. Ray Christman, " 'Our Greatest Economic Triumph,' " Pittsburgh Business Times, *10 Years in Review, 1981–1991*, 25; Thomas Buell, Jr., "Chain Reaction: Officials Believe Sony Will Help Lure More Firms," *Pittsburgh Press*, February 14, 1991.

33. Joyce Gannon, "Return of the Native," *Pittsburgh Post-Gazette*, March 6, 1991.

34. Christman credits Casey with strongly supporting efforts to revive manufacturing in southwestern Pennsylvania (personal interview, December 21, 1993).

35. Thomas Buell, Jr., "Local Businesses Focus on Supplying New Sony Plant," *Pittsburgh Press*, March 3, 1991; Christman, " 'Our Greatest Economic Triumph,' " 24, 26. Although Sony launched production of large rear-projection TVs in the summer of 1992, the company put off production of the main job generator—the twenty-seven-inch TVs and picture tubes. Production was still limited to large-screen TVs by the summer of 1994, and employment remained at 400. Sony still planned to eventually produce twenty-seven-inch color tubes and TVs and possibly high-definition TVs. Ron DaParma, "Job Growth Remains Steady at Sony Corp," *Tribune-Review*, May 26, 1994.

36. James Rankin, "Casey to Ask for $2 Million for Area Maglev," McKeesport *Daily News*, May 28, 1992; Ron DaParma, "Casey Proposes $2 Million Push for 'Maglev' Project," *Tribune-Review*, May 29, 1992. As originally outlined, phase 1 of the competition, sponsored by the Department of Transportation, and funded by the "Inter-Surface Transportation Efficiency Act," would select five projects to continue with conceptual design. In phase 2, three projects would be selected to proceed with more detailed design work. Competitors included Atlanta, Orlando, and a Texas group.

Peter Stone, "The Faster Track: Should We Build a High-Speed Rail System?" *American Prospect*, Fall 1992, maintained that "over the last few years Pittsburgh has emerged as the nation's most ambitious effort to promote maglev through a private/public partnership called Maglev, Inc." (103). As of late 1993, the federal government has not made a choice for prototype funding. Maglev supporters remain optimistic and plan to establish a fabricating center and test site for Maglev components. Also under consideration was an extension of the nineteen-mile downtown-to-airport route to New Stanton (Westmoreland County) for a total of thirty-eight miles. Ron DaParma, "Maglev Center, Test Facility Planned," *Tribune-Review*, October 1, 1993; Joe Grata, "Longer Maglev Route Proposed," *Pittsburgh Post-Gazette*, May 20, 1993; Editorial: "Maglev Re-Routed," *Pittsburgh Post-Gazette*, May 21, 1993.

37. Ellen M. Perlmutter, "RIDC Off Course? Private Firms Charge Unfair Competition," *Pittsburgh Press*, February 17, 1991; Frank Brooks Robinson, "Testimony," Select Committee of the Pennsylvania House of Representatives Investigating Industrial Development Corporations, September 12, 1991, 3; Clarke Thomas, "Job Creation Issues Paper," University of Pittsburgh, Institute of Politics, June 1991, 6.

38. Perlmutter, "RIDC Off Course?"; Robinson, "Testimony," 4–6.

39. Tom Murphy, "RIDC Parks Turn into Unfair Competition," *Pittsburgh Press*, September 9, 1991.

40. The RIDC policy was to construct buildings when it had a commitment from a client to buy or rent the property. Sam Spatter, "RIDC Ready to Review Policy on Private Developers," *Pittsburgh Press*, February 22, 1991.

41. Robinson, "Testimony," 2, 7.

42. Thomas, "Job Creation Issues Paper," 5. The "usual rule" was "three acres of land for every acre of building."

43. Ibid., 1.

44. A valid criticism would be the failure of the RIDC to have issued an annual report since 1986.

45. Robert B. Pease, former executive director of the ACCD, criticized Murphy for getting the facts wrong (the RIDC had been created by the Conference in the mid-1950s, not by the state legislature), and because "over the years, RIDC has been responsible for close to 20,000 new and permanent jobs in our area, and it is the envy of organizations in many other cities. Mr. Murphy has his own agenda, and I hate to see him use the RIDC as his whipping boy" (Pease, "RIDC Still Major Asset to City, Area," letter to the editor, *Pittsburgh Post-Gazette*, September 26, 1991). The legislative investigation was published as *Sharing the Wealth: A Report on Pennsylvania's Industrial Development Corporations*, October 1992. The Select Committee recommended that businesses which chose to relocate from urban areas to prosperous suburban areas should do so at market rates; public subsidies should go to areas where the private market was not working (14).

A rabid and parochial protectionism has often characterized the jobs issue in recent years. This is as true locally as nationally (consider NAFTA). The Southeast Pennsylvania Transit Authority in 1993 was considering whether to award a contract for 220 rail cars to AEG Transportation Systems, located in

West Mifflin, or to ABB Traction, Inc., of Elmira Heights, New York. A letter to SEPTA by state representative Christopher McNally of Munhall threatened the agency's future prospects for state financial assistance if it made the wrong decision. "Uncompetitive Bidding," editorial, *Pittsburgh Post-Gazette*, October 1, 1993.

46. These included the Community Economic Recovery Program which provided funding to municipal agencies for feasibility studies; the Industrial Communities Site Program, which provided grants to developers for infrastructure; and the Industrial Communities Action Program which offered low-interest loans to developers of former industrial sites. Sam Spatter, "Creating Jobs: Old Plant Sites Attract New Manufacturers," *Pittsburgh Press*, March 15, 1991.

Another economic program, the Pennsylvania Industrial Development Authority (PIDA) was described by one business publication as the state government's "most innovative and effective economic-development program"; it originally provided low-interest loans for job creation, but as of 1992 also offered loans to assist in job retention. "In Praise of PIDA," *Pittsburgh Business Times*, August 10–16, 1992, 14; Wes Cotter, "State Offers Development Funding for Manufacturing Expansion Plans," ibid., 13; Wes Cotter, "Casey's 'Raid' On PIDA Funds Wasn't Debacle Feared by Many," ibid., 16–17.

47. Barbara White Stack, "State Aids Mills' Reuse," *Pittsburgh Post-Gazette*, February 2, 1990; Lydia Strohl, "Mills for Sale," *Pittsburgh Business Times*, June 10–16, 1991, 13, 22–23, 25. The state of Pennsylvania in February 1990 contributed $15.6 million to the RIDC projects, along with the private Park Corporation redevelopment of the former USX Homestead plant: Keystone Commons, $4.84 million; McKeesport Industrial Center, $4.97 million; City Center of Duquesne, $3.75 million; Homestead Industrial Park, $2.1 million.

48. Robinson, "Testimony," 8.

49. Cited in Thomas, "Job Creation Issues Paper," 5.

50. By spring 1994, about 650 were employed at Keystone Commons. The West Shop Industrial Mall accommodated thirty-two tenants, and another sixteen occupied the South Shops and other buildings. Despite state grants totaling $15 million, the project has operated at a loss. Robinson expects a break-even point by 1996. Eleanor Chute, "Keystone Commons at Five Years," *Pittsburgh Post-Gazette East*, April 7, 1994.

51. Local officials were exasperated by the extent to which state environmental laws obstructed site development in urban areas. Because the Department of Environmental Resources required the virtual elimination of contaminants on building sites, banks and other lending agencies were leery of investing in any project where environmental hazard liability was a threat. In response, the state Departments of Commerce and Environmental Resources launched a $1 million pilot program in March 1993 in which the state would help pay for

environmental assessments studies, and would limit liability for problems which were discovered. Nonetheless, F. Brooks Robinson, president of RIDC, complained vehemently about the "harsh, antagonistic attitude" exhibited by lower-echelon DER employees in connection with efforts to clean up the Duquesne and McKeesport mill sites. Don Hopey, "State Aims to Redevelop Old Mill Sites," *Pittsburgh Post-Gazette*, March 24, 1993; Ron DaParma, "Environment, Economy Mesh at Revitalized Industrial sites," *Tribune-Review*, March 28, 1993; Daniel Bates, "Environmental Management: City's Redevelopment Plan Hinges on Regulatory Relief," *Pittsburgh Business Times*, May 31–June 6, 1993, 12–14; Tom Barnes, "RIDC Chief Criticizes DER Staff Attitudes," *Pittsburgh Post-Gazette*, April 15, 1993. Greg Peterson, "State Environmental Laws Stall Urban Projects, Penalize Innocent Firms," *Pittsburgh Business Times*, November 8–14, 1993. See also Ron DaParma, "Environment Puts Choke Hold on Reindustrialization," *Tribune-Review*, March 7, 1994; Greg Peterson, "A Shot in the Foot: Change our Regulations for Brownfields or Watch Prospective Businesses Go Elsewhere," *Pittsburgh Post-Gazette*, December 11, 1993.

A useful overview is Clarke M. Thomas, *How Brown Is My Valley*, University of Pittsburgh, Institute of Politics, 1994. The issue, according to Thomas, had three dimensions: "Purity. (How pure is pure?) Clearance (When can there be a definitive sign-off by environmental agencies?) Liability (Who is financially responsible for cleanup, both for past and for future pollution?)" (2).

52. Rick Teaff, "Demolishing a Factory Can Prove Difficult Task," Pittsburgh Business Times, *Economic Development Report: Business, Mon Valley*, May 18, 1990, 2s, 12s; Tim Vercellotti and Christine Vorce, "One Step Forward, Two Steps Back," *Pittsburgh Press*, September 29, 1991; Tom Barnes, "Casey Visits Reclaimed Mill Sites," *Pittsburgh Post-Gazette*, April 15, 1992.

53. Rev. Pierre Whalon, Letter, "Mon Valley Needs Jobs, Not Beauty," *Pittsburgh Post Gazette*, July 13, 1989.

54. Mary Kane and Ellen M. Perlmutter, "Pipe Dream: Residents Skeptical About Mon Valley Plan," *Pittsburgh Press*, March 1, 1988; Michael A. Fuoco, "Give Up on Steel, Planners Tell Towns," *Pittsburgh-Post Gazette*, February 29, 1988. See also Michael A. Fuoco, "New Life Urged for Old Mills," *Pittsburgh Post-Gazette*, March 1, 1988; William S. Kowinsky, "Visions and Revisions," *In Pittsburgh*, March 16–22, 1988.

The report of the Mon Valley R/UDAT (Regional/Urban Design Assistance Team) is summarized in Pittsburgh Chapter of the American Institute of Architects, *Remaking Cities: Proceedings of the 1988 International Conference in Pittsburgh* (Pittsburgh: University of Pittsburgh Press, 1988), sec. 2, "Remaking the Mon Valley," 49–59. The flower and horticulture festival was conceived as a kind of glorious, ephemeral World's Fair—"a great event lasting one summer only, which will bring international interest and tourism to the Mon Valley." Its centerpiece would be the conversion a mill building into a latter-day "Crystal Palace" (56); Clarke Thomas, "Pittsburgh Manufacturers Must Strive for Perfection," *Pittsburgh Post-Gazette*, March 14, 1990.

Chapter 3. University, City, and Strategy 21

1. Allegheny County, *Our Future, 2001, Our Choice*, September, 1991, 8.

2. According to University of Pittsburgh data for fiscal year 1990, the university's business volume in Allegheny County totaled $752.4 million. This consisted of (1) direct expenditures of $476.2 million by the university, and university employees, students, and visitors; and (2) induced expenditures based on the above figures that totaled $276.2 million. The net expansion in the local credit base (bank deposits) attributable to the university was more than $55.3 million. Local government revenues attributable to the university were more than $59.4 million in real estate taxes, personal property taxes, sales taxes, public school and other per capita appropriations, wage and occupational privilege taxes; miscellaneous taxes and fees. The university supported about 35,320 jobs in Allegheny County that provided more than $720.9 million in personal income. University jobs totaled 9,685; the rest were estimated university-related induced employment. Eileen F. McLaughlin, *A Study of the Impacts of the University of Pittsburgh on the Local Economy*, University of Pittsburgh, Office of Management Information and Policy Analysis, Information Document no. 172, February 5, 1992, iii, *passim.*

3. Operation Jump Start also funded Penn State University ($67.6 million); Temple University ($1.9 million); Lincoln University ($12 million); State System of Higher Education ($102.9 million).

The University of Pittsburgh planned to use Operation Jump Start funds for nine projects. Six were designated for the Oakland, the remainder for the Greensburg, Johnstown, and Titusville campuses. The most controversial of the Oakland projects was a $35 million, 12,000-seat multipurpose convocation-sports-entertainment center—was it needed at all, and where could it be located without overloading Oakland? Also planned was a $30 million clinic and office complex for Western Psychiatric Institute; a $28 million complex of academic facilities south of Forbes Avenue; a $19 million university library addition; an $8 million renovation of Bellefield Hall for academic programs; and a $5 million safety system upgrade. "Major Pitt Building, Renovation Project Planned with State," *University Times*, October 15, 1992, 1, 3; Suzanne Elliott, "State's Millions Might 'Jump Start' Pitt's Ambitious Development Plans," *Pittsburgh Business Times*, November 9–15, 1992.

4. "Building, Renovation Projects Abound on University's Campuses," *University Times*, September 2, 1993, 5.

5. Karen De Witt, "Universities Become Full Partners to Cities in South," *New York Times*, August 13, 1991. See also Joseph N. Boyce, "Marquette University Leads Urban Revival of Blighed Environs," *Wall Street Journal*, February 1, 1994.

6. Alberta M. Sbragia, "Pittsburgh's 'Third Way:' The Nonprofit Sector as a Key to Urban Regeneration," in *Leadership in Urban Regeneration:Cities in*

North America and Europe, ed. Dennis Judd and Michael Parkinson, *Urban Affairs Annual Reviews*, vol. 37. Contrasting employment patterns between 1978 and 1988, Sbragia notes that while industry dominated in 1978, the universities and hospitals were the leading employers by 1988. In the latter year the figures for the leading seven industrial firms, the major institutions of higher education, and eight major hospitals were, respectively, 11,000, 37,000, and 23,400.

7. Susan B. Hansen, "State Governments and Industrial Policy in the United States: The Case of Pennsylvania," in *Regional Structural Change and Industrial Policy in International Perspective: United States, Great Britain, France, Federal Republic of Germany*, ed. Joachim Jens Hesse (Baden-Baden, 1988), 104–05.

8. "Ben Franklin Technology Center," Office of Research, University of Pittsburgh, *Continuum* 2 (January–February 1993), 2. Manufacturing 2000 also funded technical assistance offered through the university's Manufacturing Assistance Center.

9. "Technology Center to Offer Grants," *Pittsburgh Post-Gazette*, November 11, 1991; Daniel Bates, "Ben Franklin Center Doles Out Manufacturing Grants," *Pittsburgh Business Times*, June 15–21, 1992, 4; Daniel Bates, "Ben Franklin's $5. 7 Million Pot Attracts Startups, "*Pittsburgh Business Times*, September 30–October 6, 1991, 13. According to Lawrence T. McGeehan, president of the Ben Franklin Center, average project funding was $60,000. It ordinarily required a three-to-one match from a company and received royalties in the event of commercial success. The center's most significant role was to assist companies in the earliest or pre–venture capital stage when financing was difficult to attain. Examples of the kind of projects funded by the center include development of a device to improve patient balance; development of an advanced fluorescence microscope; development of molding processes in meta matrix composites; development of a superior enzyme for DNA research; development of an early warning fire detection system in coal mines; development of an acoustic brain aneurysm detection system. Dan Pollastrini, "Ben Franklin Technology Center," *Oakland*, February 1992, 1, 8. See also, "25 Largest Ben Franklin Challenge Grant Recipients," *Pittsburgh Business Times*, April 5–11, 1993, 15.

10. Ben Franklin Technology Center of Western Pennsylvania, *Commemorating Ten Years of Achievement*, 1993, 2.

11. Mary Niederberger, "Cyert Engineered Carnegie Mellon's Rise in Prominence," *Pittsburgh Press*, May 13, 1990.

12. Annette L. Giovengo, *Pittsburgh Universities and Regional High Technology Economic Development*, Western Pennsylvania Advanced Technology Center, 1986, 8.

13. Niederberger, "Cyert Engineered"; Giovengo, *Pittsburgh Universities*, 36. A flurry of other CMU research programs were established in the mid-1980s. As listed by Giovengo, they included the Center for Excellence in Optical Data

Processing, 1984; Center for Molecular Electronics, 1985; Center for Fluorescence Research in Biomedical Sciences, 1985; Center for Art and Technology, 1985, Engineering Design Research Center, 1986 (37).

14. James O'Toole, "CMU Wins Software War: Gets $103 Million for Research Center," *Pittsburgh Post-Gazette*, November 15, 1984; Jim McKay, "Jubilant CMU Sees Big Boost for Region," ibid. See also Mike Sajna, "Behind the Terminals," *Pittsburgh*, December 1989, 50, 52–53; 55, 78–81. Predictions for the spinoff potential of the SEI were overly optimistic. None had occurred by early 1990 although the institute was awarded a second five-year contract. Joyce Gannon, "Hopes Were Too High," *Pittsburgh Post-Gazette*, January 3, 1990.

15. Joyce Gannon, "Semiconductor Research Coming to Carnegie Mellon," *Pittsburgh Post-Gazette*, January 12, 1990; "Sematech Taps CMU for Chip Product," *Pittsburgh Press*, ibid. In July 1993, CMU established a technology transfer office to help link university researchers with entrepreneurs. Its director, Benno Bernt, was an experienced business executive (as president and CEO of Rayovac).

16. Michael Romanello, "NASA Locates Space Technology Transfer Center in Pittsburgh," *Eastside Observer*, May 1994, 1; Micheole Fanzo, "The Once 'Steel City' Is Set to Lead America into the Robotic Age," ibid., 17–19; and Fanzo, "Eastsider Heads Up NASA/CMU Technology Transfer Consortium," ibid., 20–21; Michael Romanello, "URA Approves Purchase of Lawrenceville Property for NASA Robotics Facility: Bodack Guides $6.5 Million Through Budget Process," *Eastsider Observer*, August 1994, 1, 12 (a reference to state senator Leonard J. Bodack); Patty Tascarella, "Boston Robotics Firm Drawn to City's NASA Alliance," *Pittsburgh Business Times*, May 9–15, 1994, 6; Steve Creedy, "Movable Beasts: Consortium Puts Lawrenceville in Vanguard of Advanced Robotics," *Pittsburgh Post-Gazette*, August 11, 1994.

Prime movers in the creation of the robotics consortium were David Pahnos, assistant director, CMU Robotics Institute Field Robotics Center, and director of the new organization; and William "Red" Whittaker, principal scientist for the consortium.

17. For a partial survey of sponsored research at CMU and the UPg in 1994, see "Largest Ongoing Sponsored Research Projects at Pittsburgh-Area Universities," *Pittsburgh Business Times*, August 22–28, 1994, 18.

18. Bill Zlatos, "Posvar Pushed Economic Rebirth at Pitt, Growing Pains and All," *Pittsburgh Press*, May 13, 1990; Tommy Ehrbar, "Posvar," *Pitt Magazine*, February 1991, 14, 17, 18.

19. Giovengo, *Pittsburgh Universities*, 43; Ehrbar, "Posvar"; "U-PARC: Where Business and Research Meet," full-page advertisement, *Allegheny Business News*, September 25–October 8, 1991.

20. Byron Spice, "Pitt Gets $5 Million from Air Force," *Pittsburgh Post-Gazette*, October 15, 1991; Mary Niederberger, "Pitt Gets Grant for Technology Research Center," *Pittsburgh Press*, October 15, 1991; "Pitt Gets $5 Million for Materials Center," *University Times*, October 24, 1991, 1.

21. Hilary Stout, "Soaring Health Costs Have a Silver Lining: A Host of New Jobs," *Wall Street Journal*, September 6, 1991.

22. Ibid.

23. Ellen M. Perlmutter, "North Side Relying on AGH, Once an Adversary, to Save It," *Pittsburgh Press*, November 18, 1991; Andrew Sheehan, "Allegheny General Planning Expansion," *Pittsburgh Post-Gazette*, April 15, 1992. Perlmutter points out that hospitals had become the "driving force" in economic development in several Pittsburgh neighborhoods: Bloomfield-Garfield, Lawrenceville, Polish Hill, Hill District, Uptown.

24. Courtney S. Walston, "Oakland: Moving into the 1990s, " *University Times*, July 20, 1989, 3–6; "University Medical Center Continues to Break New Ground," *Oakland*, April 1992, 3. Other Medical Center projects include a pedestrian tunnel connecting Presbyterian Hospital with Western Psychiatric, a pedestrian bridge connecting Presbyterian and Montefiore, a conference center built over a section of Scaife Hall, two parking garages, and the acquisition of several Oakland office buildings for administrative purposes. Under construction in 1994 was the UPMC's Iroquois development in Oakland. A $55 million, ten-story structure, it will house the School of Health Related-Professions, Western Psychiatric Institute's outpatient programs, and various administrative functions. In response to community concerns, the Medical Center will provide space for retail uses. The preservation of retail space also characterized the Medical Center's highly praised renovation of the historic Iroquois Building, completed in October 1992. Sue Gottlieb, "Iroquois Development to Expand Oakland Business District," *Oakland*, December 1993, 1, 12; and Gottlieb, "Sensitivity to Neighborhood Needs Earns UPMC Award for Iroquois Building," ibid., 1, 12.

25. Alta Rusman, "Ventures Capital," *Ventures*, March 1991, 17. 18.

26. A new graduate program in bioengineering, linking the life sciences and engineering, jointly managed by the Schools of Medicine and Engineering, has been established. Interdisciplinary research at the center encompasses "molecular and cellular biology, bioengineering, and clinical practice," biocatalysts (enzymes), biomolecular materials (synthesis of potentially unique materials), biosensors (antibodies, bioreceptors), metabolic modeling and control (alter enzyme concentrations in cells), tissue engineering, artificial organs, viral therapeutics and vectors for gene transfer" (University of Pittsburgh, *Center for Biotechnology and Bioengineering*, brochure).

27. Udayan Gupta, "Hungry for Funds, Universities Embrace Technology Transfer," *Wall Street Journal*, July 1, 1994.

28. Raymond Christman, personal interview, December 21, 1993. Up until 1992, the University of Pittsburgh was mainly concerned with patent protection and lacked any system for technology transfer. It now maintains an "Office of Technological Transfer and Intellectual Property."

29. Robert Pease, personal interview, July 9, 1993.

30. This account of the origins of Strategy 21 is drawn from Morton Coleman, "Public/Private Cooperative Response Patterns to Regional Structural Change in the Pittsburgh Region," in *Regional Structural Change and Industrial Policy in International Perpsective*, ed. Joachim Jens Hesse, 141–45. By 1988, the Pennsylvania had budgeted over $286 million for Strategy 21. City of Pittsburgh, County of Allegheny, University of Pittsburgh, Carnegie-Mellon University, *Strategy 21 Update: Progress Report and Proposed Amendments*, January 1988, 9.

31. Coleman, "Public/Private Cooperative Response Patterns," 125.

32. City of Pittsburgh, County of Allegheny, University of Pittsburgh, Carnegie Mellon University, *Strategy 21: Pittsburgh/ Allegheny Economic Development Strategy to begin the 21st Century. A Proposal to the Commonwealth of Pennsylvania*, June 1985, 1.

33. Jonathan Dahl, "Travel is Off, Airlines Ailing, but Airports Just Keep Expanding," *Wall Street Journal*, September 26, 1991. Significant new airports, or major expansion projects for existing ones, cited by Dahl include (besides Pittsburgh) Denver, Memphis, Atlanta, and Newark. Except for a small 3 percent increase in traffic at Denver, air travel had slumped at all the other cities in 1991 (–6 percent in Pittsburgh).

Bill O'Driscoll, "Keeping It Up," *In Pittsburgh*, April 29–May 5, 1991, 8–9, 24, examines the prospects for USAir. See also Wes Cotter, "Cost Cuts Keep USAir Flying, But Airline's Fate Still Cloudy," *Pittsburgh Business Times*, October 21, 1991, 15–17; Steve Creedy and Jim McKay, "Airline Seeking Labor Savings, Sees Big Loss," *Pittsburgh Post-Gazette*, March 8, 1994; Tom Belden, "USAir Employees Brace for Painful Cuts," *Philadelphia Inquirer*, May 15, 1994; and Belden, "Timing Is Bad for an Airline in a Spin," *Philadephia Inquirer*, September 10, 1994.

The partnership with British Airways, first announced in July 1992, briefly improved the long-term prospects for USAir. Nonetheless, ticket price wars and other financial drains led USAir to eliminate 2,500 full-time jobs in the fall of 1993, and schedule a reduction of operating costs totaling $200 million (Jim McKay, "USAir to Cut 2,500 Jobs," *Pittsburgh Post-Gazette*, October 1, 1993). The financial condition of USAir continued to deteriorate through 1994.

34. Michael Marriott, "Pittsburgh Airport of Future Being Built," *New York Times*, November 12, 1991; Tommy Ehrbar, "Tomorrow Takes Off," *Pitt Magazine* 5 (December 1990), 15.

35. Ehrbar, "Tomorrow Takes Off," 15.

36. Chriss Swaney, "Increased Activity Near Pittsburgh Airport," *New York Times*, March 27, 1992. Julia Wilson, "Airport-Area Developers Await Financing, Tenants Amid Market Turbulence," *Allegheny Business News*, December 23, 1991, 13, 16.

37. Ehrbar, "Tomorrow Takes Off," 15.

38. Lee Wolverton, "Grounded," *Pittsburgh*, October 1994, 60.

39. *Strategy 21*, 3A–K. The 1990 version of Strategy 21, requesting more than $400 million from the state of Pennsylvania, also had little relevance to the Mon Valley. It requested the largest sums for an expansion of the David Lawrence Convention Center in Pittsburgh and construction of phase 1 of a busway linking downtown Pittsburgh and the new airport.

Other transportation funding requests included "intermodal" transportation facilities on the North Side and the edge of the central business district; extension of the Martin Luther King East Busway to Turtle Creek; and construction by the city of Pittsburgh of a heliport to serve the Pittsburgh Technology Center.

Job promotion, trade and business facility funding requests, besides the Convention Center, included improving the Leetsdale Industrial Park, creating a world trade center in Pittsburgh and a Pitt International Center in Oakland.

There was a significant emphasis on recreational and cultural funding: $8.2 million for a Steel Industry Heritage Park; $5.8 million for the Carnegie Institute's Andy Warhol Museum on Pittsburgh's North Side; $7 for the Historical Society of Western Pennsylvania's proposed Regional History Center; $6 million for ribbon parks along the north bank of the Allegheny River; $6 million for improving Point State Park; $5 million toward river park and commercial development in the Natrona, Brackenridge, and Tarentum area. Particularly interesting was the proposal for a regional recreational authority. Tim Vercellotti and Jon Schmitz, "403 Million Sought from State for City, County Development," *Pittsburgh Press*, November 2, 1990; John Schmitz and Tim Vercellotti, "Transportation, Recreation, Tourism Goals Outlined in $1 Billion Strategy 21 Update," *Pittsburgh Press*, November 4, 1990.

Still another update in 1992 proposed a modest $47.3 million in state funding (a $3 billion budget deficit discovered immediately after the 1990 elections had led to the largest tax increase in Pennsylvania history). This version of Strategy 21 was exceptionally oriented toward cultural development: $17.75 million for the Pittsburgh Cultural Trust for an office, theater, movie theater, garage, and plaza project; $6 million for the Warhol Museum; $7 million for the Pittsburgh Regional History Center; and $5.5 million for conversion of a failed downtown mall, the Bank Center, into a library for Point Park College and the Carnegie.

Other funding requests included $7 million for the Convention Center expansion; $3 million toward North Side Federal Street rehabilitation; $2.1 million for the RIDC's Keystone Commons East Pittsburgh industrial park; and

$3.5 million for the industrial parks in Duquesne and McKeesport (Greensburg *Tribune-Review*, June 5, 1992).

40. Carnegie Mellon University, School of Urban and Public Affairs, *Airport Area Economic Development: Recommendations for the Pittsburgh Region. A Study of the Economic Development Implications of an Expanding Airport on a Regional Economy*, Prepared for the Economic Development Department of Duquesne Light Company, April 1986, 47; Jack Wagner, "Tunneling Toward Success," *Pittsburgh Post-Gazette*, January 1, 1992.

41. The Pittsburgh Technology Center was the most substantial of a group of funding proposals for university-based advanced technology projects. The others, and the amounts budgeted by the state as of 1988, were: the University of Pittsburgh Applied Research Center, U-PARC ($5 million); CMU Software Engineering Institute ($4.5 million); Pittsburgh Supercomputing Center ($6 million).

42. Cynthia Piechowiak and Ellen M. Perlmutter, "The Power Brokers," *Pittsburgh Press*, January 31, 1988. According to Mayor Richard Caliguiri, the kind of alliance between the city, RIDC, and universities embodied in the Technology Center had not existed in Renaissance I.

43. Urban Redevelopment Authority of Pittsburgh, *Pittsburgh Technology Center* (brochure, n.d.), 2; URA of Pittsburgh, *1988 Annual Report*, 6; URA of Pittsburgh, *1987 Annual Report*, 8.

44. Bob Dvorchak, "Reviving Steel City with a New Image," *Philadelphia Inquirer*, September 14, 1986; Debra Meyer, "Strategy 21 Advances with Funds for Pitt's Biotechnology Center," *University Times*, April 30, 1987, 2; John D. Oravecz, "Casey Vows to Help City Building Future in High Tech," *Pittsburgh Press*, February 6, 1987.

45. URA of Pittsburgh, *1986 Annual Report*, 7. The URA claimed in 1986 that the Technology Center would generate $70 million in private investment and 6,000 jobs by 1995. Two years later, however, the URA anticipated $260 million in private investment, 11,000 direct and spinoff jobs, and more than $3 million in tax revenues for Pittsburgh (URA of Pittsburgh, *1988 Annual Report*, 6). As of 1991, the agency projected site preparation commensurate with 1.4 million square feet of private development.

46. In 1987 the University of Pittsburgh envisioned, besides its own building, "three commercially financed buildings for lease to engineering, fabrication and product development companies." CMU, in 1988, "unveiled a concept based on the Boolean cube, a model for computer design in the field of artificial intelligence . . . as many as 18 seven-story segments could join together in a structure of shapes and hues that change with the perspective of the viewer" (its architect would be the eminent Peter Eisenman). Another CMU structure was to be marketed by Oxford Development Company to prospective tenants. The recession, the university's inability to keep costs within the $17 million in state

funds, and the withdrawal of Oxford Development Company, which claimed it could not afford to build the Boolean cube design because of its unconventional dimensions, reduced CMU's ambition to a single building, scheduled for groundbreaking in 1992. Meyer, "Strategy 21 Advances," 2; URA of Pittsburgh, *1988 Annual Report*, 6; Patricia Lowry, "CMU Switches Tech Site Architect," *Pittsburgh Press*, February 8, 1990; Joyce Gannon, "CMU Scales Back Plans for High-Tech Park," *Pittsburgh Post-Gazette*, February 9, 1990; MacKenzie Carpenter, "New Buildings, Undergraduate Program Stressed," *Pittsburgh Post-Gazette*, August 30, 1991.

47. Tom Barnes, "Ground and Water Tests Delay Pitt's Biotechnology Center," *Pittsburgh Post-Gazette*, November 10, 1989; Patricia M. Lowry and Ellen M. Perlmutter, "Cyanide-tainted Soil Latest Delay in Saga of City's High-Tech Center," *Pittsburgh Press*, February 19, 1990; Jon Schmitz and Mary Niederberger, "Pacts Let for First Building at Troubled Oakland Center," *Pittsburgh Press*, November 27, 1990; Earl Kohnfelder, "First Technology Center Building Taking Shape," *Pittsburgh Press*, July 15, 1991; URA of Pittsburgh, *1990 Annual Report*, 5. Following DER development clearance in August 1990, the URA, CMU, and Pitt agreed to establish an independent organization to market the Technology Center, the Pennsylvania Department of General Services renewed its commitment for the Pitt building, and CMU proceeded with its design process.

According to Evan Stoddard, the URA's former director of economic development, development is feasible over the section of inert cyanide, but neither lending agencies nor companies would touch it for fear of potential liability for cleanup or hazards. The URA plans to use the site for a tennis court and jogging path. Tom Barnes, "CMU Research Building to Take Off," *Pittsburgh Post-Gazette*, January 29, 1992; "Universities Give New Life to Old J&L Mill Site," *Greater Pittsburgh Newspaper*, July 9, 1992.

48. URA of Pittsburgh, *Urban Redevelopment Works in Pittsburgh*, Spring 1993, 1; Tom Barnes, "High-Tech Research Center Planning," *Pittsburgh Post-Gazette*, March 4, 1993; Ron DaParma, "Slow-Going Technology Park Shaping Up," *Tribune-Review*, July 17, 1994. CMU's Research Institute and the Union Switch & Signal engineering center and garage were under construction in 1994 and expected to open by early 1995. Approximately 1,000 persons would then be employed at the PTC.

49. URA of Pittsburgh, *Pittsburgh Technology Center*, 2.

50. *Strategy 21*, 2, 2c; URA of Pittsburgh, *1989 Annual Report*, 8.

51. Ibid., 9; *Urban Redevelopment Works in Pittsburgh*, Winter 1989, 5. The contaminants, polychlorinated biphenyls (PCBs), were encapsuled, placed in containers, and buried in a section that could be used for open space.

52. URA of Pittsburgh, *1990 Annual Report*, 6; URA of Pittsburgh, *1991 Annual Report*, 6–7; *Urban Redevelopment Works in Pittsburgh*, Fall 1991, 2;

Urban Redevelopment Works in Pittsburgh, Spring 1992, 2. The URA also began demolition in 1991 of a last group of vacant buildings, anticipating that the site will be used for housing. In October 1993, the URA celebrated the opening of the park and tennis courts, supplemented by a hiking trail and river overlook at the tip of the island. All the development was in the upper end. The middle and lower sections were vacant except for a marina and boat storage building near the Thirty-first Street Bridge.

Plans for Washington's Landing included housing and a town center–like commercial section in the lower portion. In the summer of 1994, housing plans were announced—a $17 million 90–100 townhouse project on a seven-acre section. Prices will run from $140,000 to $211,000. Tom Barnes, "Washington's Landing: The Smell of Success," *Pittsburgh Post-Gazette,* October 5, 1993; Tom Barnes, "Island Townshouses Next Year," *Pittsburgh Post-Gazette ,* July 15, 1994); Joyce Gannon, "A Smooth Landing," *Pittsburgh Post-Gazette,* Sunday Real Estate Section, July 24, 1994.

53. Strategy 21 proposed a three-part Allegheny Redevelopment program: Three Rivers Stadium area featuring a Science Center, Herr's Island, and the Strip District.

54. URA of Pittsburgh, *Pittsburgh 79,* 20.

55. URA of Pittsburgh, *1986 Annual Report,* 8–9, 11.

Chapter 4. A Second Renaissance

1. Government employment in the decade remained stable, increasing from 30,748 in 1982 to 31,517 in 1992. However, it was the third largest employer, exceeded only by hospitals and higher education.

Although Pittsburgh metropolitan area unemployment, at 6.3 percent for 1992, compared favorably with the state (6.8 percent) and nation (7.4 percent), the number of jobs in the city decreased by 9,196 between 1982 and 1992 (from 327,600 to 318,404). This trend was expected to continue into 1993, with a projected additional loss of 3,000–4,000 jobs. City of Pittsburgh, Department of Finance, *Employment Diversification in the City of Pittsburgh, 1982 to 1992,* 1992, 5–8. This report covers employers of fifty or more in Pittsburgh, constituting more than three-quarters of all jobs.

2. Cultural development in the Lower North Side was paralleled by commerical revitalization. Alcoa announced plans in April 1994 to build a new $20 million, five-story corporate headquarters along the Allegheny River between the Seventh and Ninth Street Bridges. About the same time, SMS Engineering moved into its new $49 million, five-story headquarters across from the future Alcoa building along Isabella Street. These structures joined the decade-old One and Two Northshore Center behind Allegheny Landing. And Four North Shore Center, a renovated building next to the Warhol Museum, was almost fully occupied. Ron DaParma, "Development Shores Up City's North Side," *Tribune-*

Review, April 24, 1994; Joyce Gannon, "Downtown Without Being Downtown," *Pittsburgh Post-Gazette*, Sunday Real Estate Section, May 8, 1994.

3. The Society for Contemporary Crafts had originally been located in the Allegheny River town of Verona, where it was known as The Store.

4. Vince Rause, *New York Times Magazine*, November 26, 1989, 46, 56; Linda Quinlan, "Pittsburgh's Promise: Steel City's Rebirth Not All Smoke and Mirrors," *Wolfe Magazine*, August 2, 1989, 2B; Peter Miller, "Pittsburgh: Stronger Than Steel," *National Geographic* 180 (December 1991), 138. Despite the frequent acclaim for Pittsburgh's transformation, city promotion and public relations administrators(notably the Greater Pittsburgh Convention and Visitors Bureau) still encountered anachronistic perceptions of Pittsburgh as a smoky steel city. Other concerns included the inadequacies of the Convention Center and the insufficiency of hotel space for large conventions (at the same time, however, some existing hotels were struggling with occupancy rate of 50 percent or less). A Pittsburgh Film office, established in 1990, has been successful in bring film production and its economic and image-building benefits to the city, but has not received the steady funding it merited from city or county. See Tom Barnes, "$400,000 Earmarked to Attract Tourists," *Pittsburgh Post-Gazette*, October 2, 1991; "The Cost of Selling Pittsburgh," editorial, *Pittsburgh Post-Gazette*, October 3, 1991; "Convention Problem," *Pittsburgh Press*, May 14, 1992; and the following articles in a special section on "Hotels, Resorts & Conventions" in the *Pittsburgh Business Times*, May 20, 1991: Karen Zapf, "Room for Improvement," 1, 14–15; William Opalka, "Paul Kelly [Vista Hotel general manager] Checks In," 16; Mary K. Poppenberg, "City's Office of Promotion: Trying to Change Image," 19; Joe McGrath, "Market Forces Shape Strategy to Draw Conventions," 21. McGrath is president of the Convention and Visitors Bureau. Funding for promotion efforts increased following state approval of an increase in the hotel room tax from 3 to 5 percent in 1990. For the film office, see Barbara Vancheri, "Resourceful Curran Sets the Scene for Films in Pittsburgh," *Pittsburgh Post-Gazette*, January 31, 1994; Vancheri, "Film Office Chief Robert Curran Headed to MGM," *Pittsburgh Post-Gazette*, March 22, 1994; "Pittsburgh's Loss," editorial, *Tribune-Review*, March 23, 1994.

A historical perspective on Pittsburgh's image is provided in Anthony Penna, "Changing Images of Twentieth century Pittsburgh," *Pennsylvania History* 43 (1976), 49–63. An intriguing event described by Penna was Pittsburgh Forward, a Chamber of Commerce project launched in January 1926. Lasting seven weeks (and repeated in 1927), it was designed to kindle support for the city plans devised by the Citizens Committee on City Plan. It involved the display of Pittsburgh-made products in downtown stores.

5. Ferdinand Protzman, "Hard Times in the Ruhr," *New York Times*, May 2, 1993. A city of 450,000 dating back to the Middle Ages, Duisburg followed the Pittsburgh model of economic transition through advanced technology, research, and an expanding service sector.

6. Flaherty's administration is discussed in Shelby Stewman and Joel A. Tarr, "Four Decades of Public-Private Partnerships in Pittsburgh," in *Public-Private Partnerships in American Cities: Seven Case Studies*, ed. R. Scott Fosler and Renee A. Berger (Lexington, Mass: D.C. Heath, 1982), 59–127; Shelby Stewman and Joel A. Tarr, "Public-Private Partnerships in Pittsburgh:An Approach to Governance," in *Pittsburgh-Sheffield: Sister Cities*, ed. Tarr (Pittsburgh: Carnegie Mellon University, 1986), 141–81 (an abbreviated version of the previous article); and Michael P. Weber, "Pittsburgh: Rebuilding a City: The Pittsburgh Model," in *Snowbelt Cities: Metropolitan Politics in the Northeast and Midwest Since World War II*, ed. Richard M. Bernard (Bloomington: Indiana University Press, 1990), 227–46; Brian J. L. Berry et al., "The Nation's Most Livable City: Pittsburgh's Transformation," in *The Future of Winter Cities*, ed. Gary Gappert, vol. 31 of *Urban Affairs Annual Reviews* (1987), 173–95.

7. Andrew Sheehan and Steve Massey, "The Rewards of Frugality," *Pittsburgh Post-Gazette*, December 21, 1990.

8. Quoted in Stefan Lorant, *Pittsburgh: The Story of an American City* (Lenox, Mass.: Author's Edition, October 1988), 526, 528.

9. Ben A. Franklin, "Pittsburgh 'Renaissance' Meets Modern Resistance," *New York Times*, June 13, 1980.

10. Lorant, *Pittsburgh*, 452.

11. Peter Flaherty, interview with Morton Coleman, August 13, 1991; letter from Flaherty to Morton Coleman, August 21, 1991, in Morton Coleman, "Skybus: A Case Study of the Impact of Politics on Industrial Targeting Strategy" (draft). Coleman concludes in this informative analysis that "the mass transit debate . . . signaled a decline in the power of both segments of the Pittsburgh public/private partnership that had provided economic development leadership in the decades following World War II" (24).

12. Residential and commercial development in the North Hills of Allegheny County contributed substantially to a county revenue surplus for 1993, and to a proposal by County Controller Frank Lucchino to devote the surplus to spending programs, including $12 million more for human services. This prompted the local business newspaper to complain of the old attitude that government should keep spending "until the money is gone" (except for economic development, budgeted at a miserly 0.27 percent of county expenditures). "Don't Spend It All," *Pittsburgh Business Times*, November 30–December 6, 1992.

13. Flaherty had wanted the convention center located on the South Side.

14. In contrast to Pittsburgh, Minneapolis has successfully combined hotel facilities and convention center. Toward the end of 1992, the Minneapolis Hilton and Towers opened with 816 rooms—an increase of 20 percent in downtown hotel space. The new facility is three blocks from the convention center. See David Wallace, "New Hotel in Downtown Minneapolis," *New York Times*,

November 11, 1992. Closer to Pittsburgh, Cleveland can provide four times the 3,000 hotel rooms available in downtown Pittsburgh; the Cleveland Convention Center and Auditorium (317,000 square feet) and International Exposition Center (1.8 million square feet) far exceed the 132,000 square feet of the David L. Lawrence Convention Center ("Convention Problem," *Pittsburgh Press*, May 14, 1992). And Pittsburgh officials envied Philadelphia's 1993 Pennsylvania Convention Center ($523 million, 440,000 square feet). Frank Reeves, "New Philadelphia Convention Center Is Rich in Promise," *Pittsburgh Post-Gazette*, September 13, 1993.

One might reasonably argue that a city of Pittsburgh's population (370,000) and compact central business district could not reasonably compete for convention traffic with larger and more populous cities like Cleveland, Chicago, New York, Atlanta. Still, it is too small for Pittsburgh's potential as a convention city. In 1990, Pittsburgh and Allegheny County requested $105 million from the state to enlarge the convention center, but Governor Casey vetoed the proposal. By late 1993, convention center improvement had been reduced to a request for $75,000 from the state Department of Community Affairs for study expansion possibilities. Tom Barnes, "Bond Issue May Update Arena, Convention Center," *Pittsburgh Post-Gazette*, July 18, 1991; Barnes, "Taking a Convention Approach to Growth," *Pittsburgh Post-Gazette*, September 13, 1993. According to Joseph McGrath, president and executive director of the Greater Pittsburgh Convention and Visitors Bureau, Pittsburgh had lost nineteen potential bookings and as much as $100 million in revenues in 1992 because of the Convention Center's limitations. Rich Cholodofsky, "Officials Weigh New or Expanded Convention Center," *Tribune-Review*, October 15, 1993; Ron DaParma,"Undersized Center Costs City Convention Bookings," *Tribune-Review*, January 11, 1994.

For a critical evaluation of convention center economics (outside of cities rich in tourists, hotels, and amenities) see Lawrence Tabak, "Wild About Convention Centers," *Atlantic Monthly* 273 (April 1994), 28, 30, 33–34.

15. Caliguiri (b. 1931) had cultivated a strong base of neighborhood support in thirteen years with the city parks department. Named an assistant secretary in Mayor Barr's office in 1968, he was appointed parks director the next year. When Flaherty assumed office in 1970, Caliguiri was dismissed but quickly returned to city government as assistant public works director. He took over a vacant council seat in 1970. Caliguiri challenged Flaherty in the Democratic primary for mayor in 1973, but lost. Elected council president in 1977, he became mayor upon Flaherty's departure for Washington in April. Although the party machine favored County Commissioner Tom Foerster for the next full term for mayor, Caliguiri, who did not run in the primary, ran successfully as an independent. He was reelected in 1981 and 1985. See Rich Gigler, "Caliguiri Career a Blend of Old, New Politics," *Pittsburgh Press*, May 6, 1988; Mary Pat Flaherty, "Caliguiri's Drive Took Him to the Top," ibid.

Caliguiri's use of parks and recreation to build a political power base is reminiscent of Robert Moses's earlier career in New York. Another similarity is the penchant for large-scale physical development, though Moses could not have cared less about the welfare of New York's neighborhoods.

16. Lorant, *Pittsburgh*, 616, 619. Caliguiri first referred to Renaissance II in his inaugural address in 1978. He cited the goals of neighborhood redevelopment and downtown street improvements. But the agenda quickly expanded to encompass the renewed public-private partnerships and major downtown office expansion. Herb Stein, "What's Going on Downtown?" *Pittsburgh*, November 1980, 42.

17. Caliguiri had, while a member of the council in 1972, sponsored legislation on behalf of a home-rule charter. Jon Schmitz, "Charter Makes Mayor Real Power in the City," *Pittsburgh Press*, May 6, 1988.

18. John P. Robin, personal interview, June 2, 1993

19. Stewman and Tarr, *Public-Private Partnerships in American Cities*, 94.

20. PNC Financial Corp purchased the thirty-four-story Two Oliver Plaza in January 1993.

21. Stewman and Tarr, *Four Decades of Public-Private Partnerships in Pittsburgh*, includes a series of informative tables which list (1) various types of Pittsburgh partnerships (environment, organizational, social, managerial, and brick-and-mortar); (2) individual projects (smoke control, flood control, office complexes in Renaissance I and II, up to the date of publication); (3) participants in the partnerships divided according to initiator and implementer.

22. One Mellon Bank Center, imposing only in its bulk and height, was originally to be the Dravo Building, built by U S. Steel as part of a Grant Street East Complex.

23. Quoted in Lorant, *Pittsburgh*, 562.

24. Bill O'Driscoll, "Will Success Spoil the Strip District," *In Pittsburgh*, September 17–23, 1991, was especially helpful in the preparation of this paragraph. See also,Theresa Klecker, "Developers Eye Strip District as Sole Downtown Extension," *Pittsburgh Business Times*, June 10–16, 1991, 18–19. According to Raymond R. Christman, president of Technology Development and Education Corporation and executive director of the URA during the Caliguiri administration, the public subsidy requested, $35–40 million, would have threatened support of the Carnegie Science Center and Pittsburgh Technology Center. In addition, a Strip festival market would not only have competed with Station Square, but it would have been a poor investment because "the bloom was coming off the rose with festival marketplaces nationwide. In Toledo, Richmond, Tampa, and other cities, this type of retail development was beginning to fail badly." Raymond R. Christman, letter to the editor, *Pittsburgh Press*, August 31, 1991. Toledo's harborside development "Portside" was "to come

alive with shops, restaurants, amusements. . . . But today, tourists looking for something to do cup their hands to peer into Portside's dusty windows. It's all locked up." Jack Markowitz, "A Tale of Two Cities, Two Newspapers," *Tribune-Review*, November 29, 1992.

25. WETCO (Waterways Eatery and and Travel Corporation) was the creation of Tom Jayson, restaurateur (Dingbats) and nightspot entrepreneur (Chauncy's in Station Square and the 2001 disco chain of the 1970s). Associated with him in the Strip project was Ron Gold, an investor in Cleveland's riverside renaissance known as the Flats. Phase I of "Riverside—Down by the Strip" will spread over 12.5 acres leased from Buncher and will cost an estimated $50 million. The entire project will encompass thirty-nine acres if it goes as planned. If so, the WETCO project will encompass nightclubs, restaurants, banquet facilities, sports bar, concert hall, hotel, spa, residential village, and theater. See Lydia Strohl, "Tom Jayson Defies History and Odds with Down by the Riverside Venture," *Pittsburgh Business Times*, November 18–24, 1991; O'Driscoll, "Will Success Spoil the Strip District," 8; Theresa Klecker, "Developers Eye Strip District as Sole Downtown Extension,"*Pittsburgh Business Times*, June 10–16, 1991; Sam Spatter, "Strip Tease," *Pittsburgh Press*, June 24, 1991; Andrew Sheehan, "Off-Track Betting Parlor Planned in Strip," *Pittsburgh Post-Gazette*, June 27, 1991; Heather McFeeley, "Floating Boardwalk, A First for Pittsburgh," *Allegheny Business News*, June 26–July 9, 1991; Tom Barnes, "Strip in Jumping," *Pittsburgh Post-Gazette*, September 21, 1991; Diana Nelson Jones, "Strip Ponders a New Role," *Pittsburgh Post-Gazette*, July 24, 1991.

In the spring of 1993, a floating concert stage was added to the barge. The addition of 75 boat slips brought the total to 125. The Boardwalk has become a favorite parking spot for boaters. "Surging Rivers," editorial, *Pittsburgh Post-Gazette*, May 28, 1993; Bill Steigerwald, "On the Waterfront," *Pittsburgh Post-Gazette*, July 18, 1993. In December 1993, Jayson announced plans for an entertainment mall consisting of, at the outset, of thirteen nightspots and restaurants. Eric Heyl, "Strip District Will Get Mall Complex," *Tribune-Review*, December 7, 1993; Mark Houser, "Development to Alter Look of Strip," *Tribune-Review*, March 20, 1994.

26. According to O'Driscoll, "Will Success Spoil the Strip District," Ray Christman is pessimistic about the possibility of maintaining a balance of uses in the Strip: " 'The area will go one way or the other,' " he says. " 'The new development will either fail or take over' " (8).

27. The Strip, since the early 1980s, has had its version of the undead—a prospective development involving residential apartments and historic preservation. Bounded by the Allegheny River, Twenty-third, Twenth-fourth, and Railroad Streets are the three nineteenth-century Armstrong Cork Company buildings. Acquired by the York Hannover Company of Toronto in 1982, they were to be converted into a $48 million, 324-unit apartment complex, Armstrong Square, with marina, shops, restaurant, and rents ranging from $550 to

$1,600 a month. The city agreed to contribute a riverfront park, street improvements, and a parking lot. York Hannover, however, was unable to finance the project. It filed a suit against HUD in January 1992, charging that the agency had reneged on a 1989 commitment to provide a $24.5 million loan guarantee; instead, it had reduced the guarantee to $17.2 million (in the belief the proposed rentals were too high) and thus thwarted the possibility of acquiring private financing. The company lost the case, despite its claim that the rentals were comparable to the successful Pennsylvanian, formerly Union Station, only ten blocks away. Opened in 1988, the Pennsylvanian consisted of 242 units and represented an outstanding object lesson in the practicality of historic preservation.

The mortgage holders foreclosed on the property in the spring of 1992 when York Hannover defaulted on its payments (it had fallen behind in property taxes as well). The investors turned to Boston Bay Capital, a historic preservation specialist, as a possible developer. A tentative agreement was reached with its affiliate, Preservation Investments, Inc., in November 1992. York Hannover left the scene with nothing to show for the $10 million it had invested. See Tom Barnes, "Outlook Brightens for Apartments in Strip," *Pittsburgh Post-Gazette*, November 18, 1991; Barnes, "Firm Files Suit Against Hud," *Pittsburgh Post-Gazette*, January 16, 1992; Bill O'Driscoll, "Armstrong Square Developer in Default," *In Pittsburgh*, September 3–9, 1992, and "Investors Regain Control of Armstrong Square," *In Pittsburgh*, November 12–18, 1992; Ron DaParma, "Strong-Arm Tactics May be Needed to Salvage Armstrong Square," *Tribune-Review*, September 13, 1992; "Developer Negotiates for Strip District Site, "*Allegheny Bulletin*, September 29, 1992; "New Investor May Take Over Pittsburgh Complex," *Tribune-Review*, November 20, 1992; Suzanne Elliott, "New Developer Floats Foundering Armstrong Cork Site," *Pittsburgh Business Times*, November 30–December 6, 1992, 4. As of late 1993, the property remained in limbo. It had reverted back to its owners who owed the city over $200,000 in back taxes.

28. Raymond Reaves, director of the Allegheny County Planning Department, maintains that the Flaherty administration contributed significantly to the subway and East Valley Expressway (Raymond Reaves to author, written commentary).

29. "Message from the Mayor," City of Pittsburgh, *1990–1995, Six-Year Development Program (Draft)*, n.p.; "Message from the Mayor," City of Pittsburgh, *1991–1996, Six-Year Development Program (Draft)*, n.p.

30. City of Pittsburgh, *Six-Year Development Program, 1992–1997*, 58.

31. The downtown daily working and transient population in the early 1990s was 140,000 and 80,000, respectively.

32. City of Pittsburgh, *Six-Year Development Program, 1992–1997*, 58.

33. Occupying an imposing 790,000-square-foot nineteenth-century structure located in the center of the Golden Triangle at Smithfield Street and Sixth Avenue, Gimbels department store closed in 1986 and remained vacant for six years. It was finally purchased in November 1992 by Richard Penzer, a New York realtor-investor. It reopened in 1994 with a Burlington Coat Factory store and a Barnes and Nobles bookstore; Penzer hopes to rent the fifth to fifteenth floors for office use. Meanwhile, the University of Pittsburgh Medical Center opened a satellite facility there in September 1994.

In April 1993 Penzer acquired Warner Centre, a downtown retail and office complex; by that time he owned almost 40 percent of second-tier space in the Golden Triangle. Joyce Gannon, "New Gimbels Owner Thinks Big," *Pittsburgh Post-Gazette*, January 24, 1993; Jay Iwanowski and Suzanne Elliott, "Gimbels Building Retail Plan Testing Bargain-Hunting Demand Downtown," *Pittsburgh Business Times*, February 1–7, 1993, 10; Joyce Gannon, "N.Y. Developer Penzer Acquires Warner Center," *Pittsburgh Post-Gazette*, April 17, 1993; Suzanne Elliot, "King of B Space," *Pittsburgh Business Times*, May 17–23, 1993; Joyce Gannon,"Return of a Landmark," *Pittsburgh Post-Gazette*, February 27, 1994; Mark Houser,"Gimbels' Reopening Energizes Downtown Development Efforts," *Tribune-Review*, March 13, 1994; Joyce Gannon,"Week-Old Burlington Store Already Considering Expansion," *Pittsburgh Post-Gazette*, March 25, 1994.

A recent coup for the downtown was the announcement by the May Company of St. Louis (owner of Kaufmann's) in October 1992 that it would bring 100 jobs to the venerable department store on Smithfield Street. The store will be the headquarters of a new division involving forty stores in four states. See Ron DaParma, "Pittsburgh to be Hub of 40-Store Kaufmann's Chain," *Tribune-Review*, October 17, 1992.

In 1994, the Federated Department Stores acquired the Joseph Horne Company, changing the name to Lazarus. The new owner plans to abandon the existing store and build a new, smaller one closer to the vicinity of Grant and Smithfield. Joyce Gannon, "Downtown Flagship Store's Fate Under Study," *Pittsburgh Post-Gazette*, April 30, 1994; Cristina Rouvalis, "Federated Buys Local Institution, Changes Vowed to Upgrade Stores," ibid.; Georgia Sauer and Joyce Gannon, "Lazarus to Move Downtown Store," *Pittsburgh Post-Gazette*, October 27, 1994; Joyce Gannon, "Lazarus Relocation Could Alter Shopping Patterns," *Pittsburgh Post-Gazette*, September 28, 1994.

34. Jim Davidson, "Postcard Facade: As Retailers Leave, What Is Golden Triangle's Future?" *Pittsburgh Press*, July 27, 1992; Jim DeAngelis, *Who Shops Downtown and Why*, Overall Findings from the 1988 City of Pittsburgh Holiday Survey of Allegheny County Residents, Commissioner by the Department of City Planning, University of Pittsburgh, Center for Social and Urban Research, August 3, 1989; Tom Barnes, "Cohen Urges Action to Cure 'Ailing' Down-

town," *Pittsburgh Post-Gazette*, January 29, 1992. The article refers to Dan Cohen, a City Council member.

A new Pittsburgh Downtown Partnership was organized in 1994 as a CBD promotion and improvement agency. Its director, Errol Frailey, had managed a similar organization in Louisville, Kentucky—Louisville Central Area. John M. R. Bull, "Pro-Downtown Group Gets Name, Director," *Pittsburgh Post-Gazette*, May 3, 1994;

Jon Schmitz, "Business Booster Has Work Cut Out," *Pittsburgh Post-Gazette*, May 9, 1994.

35. City of Pittsburgh, *Six-Year Development Program, 1990–1995*, 175, 42.

36. The Department of City Planning operates under a seven-member commission appointed by the mayor. Its obligation to prepare a master plan is discharged in part through annual publication of the city's Six-Year Development Program. The department operates through four divisions: Comprehensive Planning, Development, and Research; Community Planning and Budgeting; Development and Administration; Land Use Control. Functional planning areas include economic development, housing, environment, transportation, zoning (administered through a zoning administrator), neighborhoods, capital investment programming.

To some extent, the Department of City Planning's activities in economic development and neighborhood revitalization parallel those of the URA. It proposed, for example, the site for the Carnegie Science Center, and approved the project development plan in 1988 (urban renewal projects must be certified by the planning department). It prepared land use proposals for another Strategy 21 project, Washington's Landing, and worked with the URA and RIDC developing the Pittsburgh Technology Center. The department released in 1989 a master plan for riverfront development. It coordinated the environmental reviews necessary for approval of $17 million in Urban Development Action Grants in support of the CNG Tower and Benedum Center.

In the realm of neighborhood revitalization, City Planning has administered the federal Community Development Block Grant since its inception in 1974. This program has provided most of the financial support for the city's neighborhood revitalization efforts. It operates jointly with the URA the city's program for neighborhood business district revitalization. The director during the entire Caliguiri administration (like Robin in the URA) was Robert H. Lurcott, who moved to the Pittsburgh Trust for Cultural Resources in 1989. He was succeeded by Jane A. Downing. City of Pittsburgh, Department of City Planning, *Planning '88: A Progress Report* and *1989 Annual Report*.

37. Urban Redevelopment Authority of Pittsburgh, *1986 Annual Report*, 5.

38. Ibid., 2.

39. URA of Pittsburgh, *The Changing City*, June 1969, 8. The effort to create a major arts or cultural center in the Lower Hill in the 1960s is discussed

in William J. Mallett, "The Lower Hill Renewal and Pittsburgh's Cultural District," *Pittsburgh History* 75 (Winter 1992–93), 172–90.

40. G. Evan Stoddard, personal interview, October 18, 1991.

41. URA of Pittsburgh, *The Changing City*, June 1969, 3, 6. The URA claimed that 4,500 new dwelling units were completed or in progress in renewal areas by the spring of 1970; of these, 2,400 would be occupied by those of low or moderate incomes. Of the additional 2,600 units planned in 1970, 90 percent would be assigned to lower-income population.

42. John P. Robin, personal interview, June 2, 1993.

43. Ben A. Franklin, "Pittsburgh 'Renaissance' Meets Modern Resistance," *New York Times*, June 13, 1980; Ellen Perlmutter, "Jack Robin: Our Future Is His Legacy," *Pittsburgh Press*, Sunday Magazine, April 7, 1985; Michael P. Weber, *Don't Call Me Boss: David L. Lawrence, Pittsburgh's Renaissance Mayor* (Pittsburgh: University of Pittsburgh Press, 1988), 193, 231, 233–34.

44. John P. Robin, interview, June 2, 1993.

45. Robin held a wide range of other positions including: vice-chairman, Allegheny County Planning Commission; director of Port Authority Transit of Allegheny County; member of the Mayor's Oakland Task Force and the Mayor's Development Council.

46. *The Pittsburgh Renaissance Project: The Stanton Balfour Oral History Collection, Final Report*, Submitted by the Graduate School of Public and International Affairs, University of Pittsburgh, to the Buhl Foundation, September 1974, 23, 65; John P. Robin, *Urban Redevelopment In Pittsburgh: Retrospective, Prospective*, Phi Beta Kappa Lecture, University of Pittsburgh, October 19, 1977.

47. Robin, *Urban Redevelopment in Pittsburgh*.

48. Ibid. Robin believed that Flaherty's attitudes toward development and the public-private partnership were changing by the time he left for Washington in 1977. He pointed to the mayor's nomination of Robert Dickey III, chairman of Dravo and the Allegheny Conference, to chair the Auditorium Authority and "energize" the Convention Center project; to the appointment of consultants to explore the prospects for North Shore redevelopment; and to Flaherty's support of the East Busway and the replacement of skybus by rapid rail transit to the South Hills.

Although Robin objected to what he considered illegitimate criticisms of Renaissance I (such as the "Marxist myth" that it was all conceived in the interests of finance capitalism), he was not an uncritical apologist. He admitted that more structures or landmarks should been kept "to give us a better sense of urban continuity"; that the architecture of Gateway Center I, II, III was "dreadful"; that the Lower Hill project never achieved the vision of a "New

Acropolis"; that Allegheny Center was an isolated enclave; and that the East Liberty mall needed design changes.

49. Pennsylvania Economy League, Western Division, *Downtown Development in Renaissance II: Cost Benefit Study*, prepared for the URA of Pittsburgh, April 1988, chaps. 1–2.

50. Ibid., chap. 2:4, 23–24. Agreements between PPG, the city, and URA in 1979 provided for URA site acquisition, relocation of businesses, street vacating and preparation of the site for development. However, court action prevented URA acquisition of the land, and it was purchased by PPG on the open market. PPG was a key precipitant of the downtown component of Renaissance II; it helped alert the city to the prospect of losing companies for lack of new office space.

Fifth Avenue Place was an entirely private undertaking, not involving the URA. The same was true of One Oxford Centre. The land had been purchased by Allegheny County in 1969 for prospective use as a supplement to the County Court House and City-County Building. When this plan was abandoned, the property was sold to Oxford Development Company in 1979.

Tax abatement for commercial property was instituted by Pittsburgh in 1980 (three-year exemption on 100 percent of all assessment increases attributable to cost of improvements and construction), and revised in 1985 (five-year abatements capped annually at $50,000). The Economy League maintained that the tax abatements were of marginal significance because they only concerned the city of Pittsburgh, not the county or school district.

51. Among the many other examples of URA initiative or coordination of development was the Water Works Mall expansion. The URA represented the city in negotiations for this project, located along Freeport Road in the northeast corner. Phase I had generated 2,500–3,000 jobs. The planned expansion of 450,000 square feet would nearly double its size.

52. G. Evan Stoddard, "A Generation of Change in Pittsburgh's Economy," mimeo, 1991, 9–10. Stoddard had previously been involved in economic development in the Department of City Planning and Department of Economic Development. He joined the URA in 1982.

53. Ibid., 10.

54. Joseph Plummer, "Who's in Charge in Pittsburgh?" *Pittsburgh Post-Gazette*, October 22, 1986; Virginia Linn, "Critics Fault Allegheny Conference," *Pittsburgh Post -Gazette*, February 24, 1988.

55. Joseph Plummer, "An Agenda for the Conference," *Pittsburgh Post-Gazette*, November 12, 1986; Cynthia Piechowiak and Ellen M. Perlmutter, "Region's Fast Change Challenges Old-Boy Network," *Pittsburgh Press*, November 15, 1987; Editorial: "Third-Year Themes," *Pittsburgh Post-Gazette*, November 18, 1987; Ellen M. Perlmutter, "Will There Be a Renaissance III," *Pittsburgh Press*, Sunday Magazine, September 1, 1991.

56. Robert Pease maintains that the power of the Allegheny Conference was exaggerated; it was not all-powerful, and expectations were often unrealistic (personal interview, July 8, 1993).

57. Seventeen of the twenty-one were chairmen or the CEO of corporations, two headed advanced technology companies, and two were university presidents. Roger S. Ahlbrandt and Morton Coleman, *The Role of the Corporation in Community Economic Development as Viewed by 21 Corporate Executives*, University of Pittsburgh Center for Social and Urban Research, January 5, 1987.

58. Ibid., 25, 28, 27.

59. Ibid., 26; Piechowiak and Perlmutter, "Region's Fast Change Challenges Old-Boy Network."

60. "The Conference's Future," editorial, *Pittsburgh Post-Gazette*, December 3, 1990.

61. Ahlbrandt and Coleman, *The Role of the Corporation in Community Economic Development*, 56, 42.

62. A similar perception of decline from a golden age has occurred in Hartford, Conn. "A decade ago . . . Hartford was still dominated by a group of corporate executives known as the Bishops. . . . [They] moved mountains here . . . led mostly by Aetna." Aetna's recent disinclination to save the Hartford Whalers hockey team symbolized a new era of corporate retrenchment in civic development. Kirk Johnson, "Corporate Elite a Fading Force in Cities' Lives," *New York Times*, September 6, 1992.

63. Timothy K. Barnekov and Daniel Rich, "Privatism and Urban Development: An Analysis of the Organized Influence of Local Business Elites," *Urban Affairs Quarterly* 12 (June 1977), 442. The authors describe business-controlled development committees as elite institutions that differ from chambers of commerce or downtown associations and that embody an "ethos of privatism" not necessarily in the public interest. However, Robert W. MacGregor, "Privatism and Urban Development: A Response," ibid., 461–74, offers a counterargument.

64. Kristin A. Goss, "Cleveland Tomorrow: Company Chiefs Effect a Renaissance," *The Chronicle of Philanthropy* 3 (January 15, 1991), 17–19.

65. Barbara Ferman, "Democracy Under Fire: The Politics of Economic Restructuring in Pittsburgh and Chicago," presented at the annual meeting of the American Political Science Association, 1989; Robert H. Salisbury, "Urban Politics: The New Convergence of Power," *Journal of Politics* 26 (November 1964), 775–97. The extensive literature on the subject of public-private coalitions includes R. Scott Fosler and Renee A. Berger, eds., *Public-Private Partnership in American Cities: Seven Case Studies* (Toronto: Lexington Books, D.C. Heath, 1982), which deals with Pittsburgh, Baltimore, Chicago, Twin Cities, Dallas, Atlanta, and Portland; Donald M. Fraser and Janet M. Hively, "Minneapolis: The City That Works," in *The Future of Winter Cities*, ed. Gary Gap-

pert, vol. 31 of *Urban Affairs Annual Reviews*, Max O. Stephenson, Jr., "Whither the Public-Private Partnership: A Critical Overview," *Urban Affairs Quarterly* 27 (September 1991), 109–27. Stephenson questions whether the public-private partnerships centered on downtown development can be "reconciled with profound societal concerns for both equity and political representation" (112). A vigorous defense of downtown renewal policy—the creation of an office-based economy—as necessary and desirable is found in Bernard J. Frieden, "The Downtown Job Puzzle," *The Public Interest*, Fall 1989, 71–86; and Bernard J. Frieden and Lynne B. Sagalyn, *Downtown, Inc.: How America Rebuilds Cities* (Cambridge, Mass.: MIT Press, 1989). An alternative model of so-called progressive local government in such communities as Santa Monica, Santa Crux, Burlington, and Berkeley is examined in Pierre Clavel, *The Progressive City: Planning and Participation, 1969-1984* (New Brunswick, N.J.: Rutgers University Press, 1986): "These governments have tended to encourage participation and were willing to experiment with property rights in the interest of the majority of the population; they sometimes engaged in dramatic confrontations with long established powers" (xii).

Also relevant are Richard M. Bernard, ed., *Snowbelt Cities: Metropolitan Politics in the Northeast and Midwest Since World War II* (Bloomington: Indiana University Press, 1990); and Gregory D. Squires, ed., *Unequal Partnerships: The Political Economy of Urban Redevelopment in Postwar America* (New Brunswick, N.J.: Rutgers University Press, 1989).

66. Park Martin, interviewed on November 17, 1971, quoted in *The Pittsburgh Renaissance Project: The Stanton Balfour Oral History Collection, Final Report*, submitted by the Graduate School of Public and International Affairs, University of Pittsburgh, to the Buhl Foundation, September 1974, 26.

67. Ibid., 35, 39.

68. Raymond Reaves, director of the Allegheny County Planning Department, maintains that Flaherty was not so much indifferent to downtown as unwilling to defer to the corporate elite in policy formulation (written commentary to author).

69. Allegheny Conference on Community Development, *Report, 1981*, 5. Extending from Fort Pitt Boulevard to the vicinity of Liberty Center, Grant Street was spanned by significant municipal buildings (Allegheny County Court House, City-County Building) and private landmarks (Frick Building, Grant Building, Union Trust Building, William Penn Hotel, USX Tower). The report comments that at the time of the 1978 study, Grant Street was a "chaos of trolley tracks and wires, traffic signs and signals, decaying concrete and disunified paving styles."

70. The ACCD, particularly through the efforts of David M. Roderick of USX and Douglas Danforth of Westinghouse, worked with Mayor Caliguiri to prevent the Pirates baseball team from being sold to outsiders in 1985–1986.

This was a significant example of the restored partnership applied to protecting a Pittsburgh competitive asset. It also demonstrated Caliguiri's ability to overcome significant odds on behalf of an objective he considered vital to the city's interests. The Pirates had suffered from poor attendance, mediocre performance on the field, drug scandals, and an apparent inability to compete with the Steelers football team in the affections of local sports fans. Originally, the city was to contribute about $25 million to a consortium of individuals and corporations who would buy the franchise from the Galbreath family. But this scheme failed, and the city instead sold bonds to fund its share. The Pirates were put up for sale again in 1994. The city had a six-month option to fund a buyer who would keep the franchise in Pittsburgh.

Another example of the restored partnership and Caliguiri's commitment to enhancing the city's appeal was reconstruction of the zoo launched in 1980; it involved a collaboration between his office and the corporate community—the Allegheny Conference in particular. Jon Schmitz and Mary Niederberger, "Disease Ends Life of City's Rebuilder," *Pittsburgh Press*, May 6, 1988.

71. Robert Pease to author,Interview, July 8, 1993. The social programs were supported by private money.

72. Examples of the organizations assisted included Operation Dig (minority construction training); Youth City (drug abuse and other social problems); Bidwell Cultural and Training Center; Operation Better Block (Homewood-Brushton community improvement); Women in the Urban Crisis (improvements in inner city life); The Misters, Inc. (economic advancement of black population through self-help). Allegheny Conference on Community Development, *1973 Report*, 15.

73. This was part of a Ford-financed $6 million, fifty-city experiment.

74. Allegheny Conference on Community Development, *1981 Report*, 11. The new direction included ACCD participation on Oakland and North Side planning committees. In Oakland, a ACCD staff member headed the mayor's local task force which "brings together all segments of the community and helps to resolve conflict on key community issues" (ibid.).

75. *Portrait of the Past. Choices for the Future. A Report from the Allegheny Conference on Community Development* (1990), 2.

76. A graduate of Carnegie Mellon's School of Urban and Public Affairs, Stafford was president of Farr Communications, Inc., owner of radio station WESA in Charleroi. He was also chairman of Laurel Vista, Inc., a Somerset County potato farm. Director of research for Richard Thornburgh during his gubernatorial campaign, he had joined the governor's staff as secretary for legislative affairs (1979–1983). He then became director of corporate finance for an investment banking firm, but rejoined the Thornburgh administration (1985–1986) as chief policy adviser. Stafford's experience in the machinery of state government was undoubtedly instrumental in his selection as executive

director because a regional agenda necessitates extensive negotiations with Harrisburg.

77. Allegheny Conference on Community Development, *1973 Report*, 6.

78. In 1981 the ACCD had also initiated an Intergovernmental Cooperation Study, with an advisory committee that included Mayor Caliguiri and County Commissioner Thomas Foerster. Directed by William Dodge, its objective was to "recommend practical means of encouraging municipalities to work together to provide public services, purchase equipment and carry out other government functions more efficiently than each could alone" (Allegheny Conference on Community Development, *1981 Report*, 11).

79. Allegheny Conference on Community Development, *1984 Report*, 6.

80. Vincent A. Sarni, "Choices for the Future," November 25, 1991, 3–5.

81. *A Regional Leadership Alliance for Western Pennsylvania (The Affiliation of the Allegheny Conference on Community Development and the Pennsylvania Economy League/Western Division)*. This brochure points out that Western Pennsylvania claims over 1,100 municipalities, 230 school districts, 1,000 special government districts, and countless civic organizations.

82. *Progress and Prospects: A Report on the Agenda of the Allegheny Conference on Community Development*, November 23, 1992; Southwestern Pennsylvania Growth Alliance, *Regional Federal Agenda, 1993*. This report deals with reuse of old industrial sites, ISTEA, national competitiveness and advanced manufacturing technology, barge fuel tax, water and sewage treatment, and federal mandates.

83. Richard Stafford, "Thinking and Acting as a Region: The Strategic Agenda of the Allegheny Conference on Community Development," presented at the University of Pittsburgh, Graduate School of Public and International Affairs, November 30, 1992.

84. Andrew Sheehan, "Flap Builds Over Aviary," *Pittsburgh Post-Gazette*, September 19, 1991; Christine Vorce and Douglas Heuck, "N. Side Groups Willing to Take Aviary Under Wing to Prevent Closing," *Pittsburgh Press*, September 21, 1991; Tom Barnes, "Aviary Making First Fiscal Flight," *Pittsburgh Post-Gazette*, January 24, 1993; Sally Kalson, "For the Birds," *Pittsburgh Post-Gazette*, Magazine, May 9, 1993, 8–11; Sue Gottlieb, "Phipps Conservatory Plants Seeds for Privatization," *Oakland* 6 (December 1992), 1, 11; Andrew Sheehan, "Public-Private Partnership Seen as Future for Phipps," *Pittsburgh Post-Gazette*, September 25, 1991; Ellen M. Perlmutter, "Phipps Has Growing Pains," *Pittsburgh Post-Gazette*, February 15, 1993; Tod Gutnick, "Pittsburgh Will Privatize Phipps Conservatory," *Tribune-Review*, May 8, 1993; Andrew Sheehan, "Zoo May Go Private or Rely More on Gifts," *Pittsburgh Post-Gazette*, September 26, 1991; Gary Rotstein, "Supporters Say Zoo Better Off Without City," *Pittsburgh Post-Gazette*, August 8, 1993; Tom Barnes, "Public-Private Zoo Called For," *Pittsburgh Post-Gazette*, August 21, 1993; John M. R. Bull, "Coun-

cil OKs CMU Running Golf Course," *Pittsburgh Post Gazette*, April 1, 1993; Bill O'Driscoll, "The Privatization of Pittsburgh: How Far Should We Go?" *In Pittsburgh*, December 3–9, 1993, 10–11, 14, examines the progress of privatization in other spheres of city government. Also, "Pittsburgh: Downsizing in Difficult Times," interview with James Turner, chief administrative officer, City of Pittsburgh, University of Pittsburgh, Institute of Politics, *Report*, Winter 1983, 5.

85. Jeff Domenick, "Regional Tax Plan Rejected," *Tribune Review*, November 24, 1992. With one exception, the sales tax measure was opposed by all the Allegheny County suburban legislators in 1992. Only half of Pittsburgh's six representatives favored it. In addition, Governor Robert Casey had threatened to veto any such tax bill.

Several cultural institutions were specified for funding in the successful December 1993 measure. These included the Carnegie Library, Carnegie Museum, Pittsburgh Zoo, Phipps Conservatory, Three Rivers Stadium, the National Aviary, city and county parks. The distribution will be managed by a seven-member board.

Chapter 5. Pittsburgh Neighborhoods: A System of Subsidized Empowerment

1. Gary Rotstein, "East Liberty to Undo Last Vestiges of Mall," *Pittsburgh Post-Gazette*, February 25, 1993. As portrayed by Patricia Lowry, former art and architectural critic of the defunct *Pittsburgh Press*, the pedestrian mall was not the only flaw in East Liberty renewal plan:

> About $100 million in public and private funds was spent creating a pedestrian shopping mall edged with low-income housing. Streets were realigned to form Penn Circle, which became a noose that all but strangled the business district. By the mid-'70s, as more and more businesses closed, almost everyone admitted it had been a mistake of gargantuan proportions. More than 2,500 families had been displaced from older homes, and the three high-rise apartments that were built changed forever the village character of East Liberty.

Pittsburgh neighborhoods, like the mill town communities, were hemorrhaging population long before the downfall of the industrial economy. From a population peak of 676,806 in 1950, Pittsburgh dropped to 604,332 by 1960, 520,117 by 1970, 423,959 in 1980, and 369,879 in 1990. "When Planning Runs Amok," *Pittsburgh Post-Gazette*, Sunday Magazine, March 28, 1993, 16.

2. According to the Planning Department's Social Planning Advisory Committee in 1964, the project had been initiated by merchants and other "leading citizens" of the area, and the plan had been developed in consultation with them. The opportunity for broader citizen involvement occurred after Kingsley Association, the Health and Welfare Association and ACTION-Housing helped organize the East Liberty Citizens' Renewal Council. But while the advisory

committee described the East Liberty plan as unique in creating a new awareness of the need for citizen participation, it also asserts that the basic planning decisions were all made prior to the involvement of most citizens. See Pittsburgh Department of City Planning, Community Renewal Program, *Citizen Participation Report: Relationship to Urban Renewal and Planning,* 1964, 7–8.

3. James V. Cunningham, *The Resurgent Neighborhood* (Notre Dame, Ind.: Fides Publishers, 1965), 139.

4. Morton Coleman, "Interest Intermediation and Local Urban Development," Ph.D. diss., University of Pittsburgh, 1983), 138–39; James Cunningham to author, April 21, 1993; Morton Coleman, written communication, April 19, 1993.

5. David P. Epperson, director of the Mayor's Committee on Human Resources (1967–1969), describes Coleman as the key participant in the formulation of the antipoverty program (personal interview, September 17, 1993).

6. Coleman, "Interest Intermediation and Local Urban Development," 139. According to Coleman, aspects of the antipoverty program influenced by Urban Extension included creating neighborhood citizen boards; appointing a coordinating agency for each neighborhood; a comprehensive approach to neighborhood improvement; hiring neighborhood residents for services; preparing a neighborhood plan. National programs that influenced the character of antipoverty and community action were the Ford Foundation's Gray Areas Program and the President's Committee on Juvenile Delinquency (written commentary, April 19, 1993).

7. Sam Spatter, "2 Advocates of Better Housing Are Outlived by Efforts," *Pittsburgh Press,* June 24, 1991.

8. James V. Cunningham, *Urban Leadership in the Sixties,* Brandeis University, Lemberg Center for the Study of Violence, 1970, 57, 58.

9. James V. Cunningham, personal interview, May 23, 1990. Arriving in Pittsburgh in 1943, Schwartz worked for the Irene Kaufmann Settlement until 1947, then for the United Jewish Federation from 1948 to 1957, when he joined the Social Work faculty at the University of Pittsburgh.

10. See Roger S. Ahlbrandt and James V. Cunningham, *Pittsburgh Residents Assess Their Neighborhoods,* University of Pittsburgh, School of Social Work and University Center for Social and Urban Research, December 1980; also Ahlbrandt, *Neighborhoods, People, and Community* (New York: Plenum Press, 1984), based on a survey of nearly 6,000 Pittsburgh residents.

11. On the Pittsburgh Neighborhood Atlas, see James V. Cunningham, Roger S. Ahlbrandt, Rose Newell, and Robert Hendrickson, "The Pittsburgh Atlas Program: Test Project for Neighborhoods," *National Civic Review* 65 (June 1976), 284–89; Roger S. Ahlbrandt and James V. Cunningham, "Pitt Helps City Move Toward Neighborhood Government," *Pitt,* August 1976, 15–18;

Roger S. Ahlbrandt, Margaret K. Charny, James V. Cunningham, "Citizen Perceptions of Their Neighborhoods," *Journal of Housing,* July 1977, 338–41; "New Atlas to Serve as Guide to Pittsburgh Neighborhoods," *University Times,* March 31, 1977, 10; Roger S. Ahlbrandt, Jr., and James V. Cunningham, "Neighborhood Information, Citizen Education and Citizen Participation," presented at the annual meeting of the American Political Science Association, September 1977. Other joint publications of Ahlbrandt and Cunningham dealing with neighborhood life and organization include: "The Ungreening of Neighborhood Planning," *South Atlantic Urban Studies* 4 (1979), 6–22; *A New Public Policy for Neighborhood Preservation* (New York: Praeger, 1979); and *Pittsburgh Residents Assess Their Neighborhoods.* Another source of information about neighborhoods was the City Planning Department's regularly published Neighborhood Profiles.

12. The Charter Commission authorization proposal was introduced by Councilman RichardCaliguiri. The commission held more than 200 hours of meetings and hearings between November 1972 and September 1973. It held fourteen public hearings in October and November 1973, following introduction of the discussion draft. The commission was prohibited from dealing with a range of issues: city employee working conditions and benefit programs, taxes and assessments, eminent domain, public education, and election laws.

13. James V. Cunningham," Findings and Flaws—What the Pittsburgh Home Rule Effort Is All About," presented to the Board of the South Oakland Citizens' Council, November 16, 1973.

14. James V. Cunningham, written commentary, April 21, 1993.

15. Letter from Robert Pease to Charter Commission, November 27, 1993, in Charter Commission Records Portfolio. A similar vein of criticism was that the "relationships between district representation, neighborhood service and boards, and the ombudsman and citizen hearing mechanisms have not been very well thought out and linked" (letter from Walt Plosila to Charter Commission, October 9, 1973, ibid.). The Charter Commission is discussed in James V. Cunningham, "Drafting the Pittsburgh Charter: How Citizens Participated," *National Civic Review,* September 1974, 410–15.

16. James V. Cunningham and Milton Kotler, *Building Neighborhood Organizations: A Guidebook Sponsored by the National Association of Neighborhoods* (Notre Dame, Ind.: University of Notre Dame Press, 1983), 2.

17. James V. Cunningham," Realtors, Race and Low-Cost Housing," *America,* March 11, 1950, 661–63.

18. James V. Cunningham, "Citizen Participation in Public Affairs," *Public Administration Review* 32 (October 1972), 599; Cunningham, "Assessing the Urban Partnership: Do Community Forces Fit?" *National Civic Review,* November 1981, 523.

19. Tom Barnes, "Zoning Change Creates Worries," *Pittsburgh Post-Gazette*, June 21, 1993. On the federal government and its powers, see Robert Higgs, *Crisis and Leviathan* (New York: Oxford University Press, 1987). Others are equally concerned with the suffocating glut of state and local legislation restricting individual freedom. Clint Bolick, *Grassroots Tyranny: The Limits of Federalism* (Washington, D.C.: Cato Institute, 1993), argues that "the examples of grassroots tyranny set forth in this book illustrate the pervasiveness of local government in regulating almost every aspect of personal behavior. . . . Indeed, local government in its various forms is today probably more destructive of individual liberty than even the national government" (8–9). Bolick emphasizes the extent to which local governance is now the province of "appointed bureaucrats with enormous powers and little accountability to the public" (5). See also Thomas J. Anton, *American Federalism and Public Policy* (New York: Random House, 1989).

While state and local laws and regulations do indeed multiply and engulf the individual like an army of red ants, it should be noted that local and state bureaucrats often are enforcing federal mandates, like good soldiers.

Frederic Howe, an early twentieth-century reformer who confronted some of these issues, concluded that the only alternative to leviathan government and the bureaucratically driven welfare state, local or national, was cooperative democracy. See Roy Lubove, "Frederic C. Howe and the Quest for Community in America," *Historian* 39 (February 1977), 270–91.

20. Southwestern Pennsylvania Growth Alliance, *Regional Federal Agenda, Agenda, 1993*, 17–19. One of the more ridiculous expressions of federal micromanagement is found in bridge design requirements. Federal highway standards require that bridges using federal funds for repair must have a minimum width of twenty-four feet and conform to military loading requirements—as for interstate bridges. Yet, not only are county bridges usually of a narrower width, but their widening often conflicts with wetlands or historic preservation requirements and goals. And such bridges, of course, carry only local traffic and hardly merit interstate loading requirements.

21. Cunningham and Kotler, *Building Neighborhood Organizations*, 54–55, 67. Cunningham attributes the creation of the SAC to Bob Connolly, a community organizer trained at the University of Pittsburgh and Saul Alinsky's Industrial Areas Foundation. After he left, the SAC contracted for staff service with a Connolly-organized Pittsburgh Industrial Areas Foundation affiliate. The abrasive tactics and control of the organization by a small clique alienated moderates, who revolted in 1977 and broke the Alinsky connection. It lives on as an organization of volunteers "who have an interest in maintaining and improving the quality of life of the neighborhood." See Ruth Hawk, "Shadyside Coalition Helps Shape Future," *Tribune-Review*, April 20, 1993.

22. James V. Cunningham, "Resident Participation: The Struggle of the American Urbident for Freedom and Power," prepared for the Ford Foundation,

August 1967, 220. Remarking on the early appearance of the "community corporation," Cunningham seemed less concerned with its potential than with the prospect that it might divert the more "aggressive" citizens from the "significant issues and from the main goal of a share in urban power" (223–24).

23. Meyer Schwartz," Point-Counterpoint in Urban Organizing," presented at the Urban Organizing Conference, University of Pittsburgh, School of Social Work, November 14, 1967, 18, 9, 20. Schwartz believes that this presentation made him persona non grata with the university administration. He relates (letter to the author, May 7, 1993) that he was summoned to the University Public Relations Office several weeks later and shown a copy of a memorandum from the chancellor advising that Schwartz was to be kept invisible while top administers responded, if necessary, to the issues he raised. When Schwartz asked if he was to be "put on the shelf," he was given a noncommittal smile. Indeed, the dean of the School of Social Work, William H. McCullough, received a memorandum from a high-level administrator requesting that Schwartz not represent the university at public functions. Schwartz left the University in 1971 to become dean of the Simmons College School of Social Work. More than anything else, the episode reveals the tensions that permeated the 1960s.

24. Ibid., 27–28.

25. Robert Fisher, *Let the People Decide: Neighborhood Organizing in America* (Boston: Twayne, 1984), 162, 165.

26. Daniel Boorstin, *Hidden History* (New York: Harper and Row, 1987), 204.

27. Peter Drucker writes: "Forty years ago, when I first began to work with nonprofit institutions, they were generally seen as marginal to an American society dominated by government and big business respectively.... We then believed that they could and should discharge all major social tasks.... Today, we know that nonprofit institutions are central to American society and are indeed its most distinguishing features" (*Managing the Nonprofit Organization: Principles and Practices* [New York: Harper Collins, 1990], xiii).

Teresa Odendahl, *Charity Begins at Home: Generosity and Self-Interest Among the Philanthropic Elite* (New York: Basic Books, 1990) complains, "Elite American philanthropy serves the interests of the rich to a greater extent than it does the interests of the poor, disadvantaged, or disabled." It is, however, difficult to take seriously a critique rooted in such ridiculous propositions as: "A system of private charity is not in the interests of the disadvantaged. The material benefits and the extent of control over their own destinies that are provided them by philanthropy are considerably less than in the Social Democratic countries of Western Europe, the Communist East European states, and even some 'developing' nations" (3, 11). In the same vein, we also learn that "the trend in much of the world has been for the State to determine which institutions and services are necessary for its citizens to enjoy a certain quality of life" (13). Such paroxysms of joy over state coercion might be difficult to encounter outside the academic world.

For evaluations of philanthropy and nonprofits in American society, see Alan Pifer, "Philanthropy, Voluntarism, and Changing Times," *Daedalus* 116 (Winter 1987), 119–31; and Susan A. Ostrander and Stuart Lanton, eds., *Shifting the Debate: Public/Private Sector Relations in the Modern Welfare State* (New Brunswick, N.J.: Transaction Books, 1987).

James C. Crimmins and Mary Kreil, *Enterprise in the Nonprofit Sector* (Washington, D.C.: Partners for Livable Places, 1983) deals with a subject of increasing concern to businesses which must compete with tax-exempt nonprofits encroaching on what they consider to be their market. See also James Cook, "Businessmen with Halos," *Forbes*, November 26, 1990, 100–14; Alison Leigh Cowan, "With Catalogues and Cookies, Nonprofit Groups Seek Profits," *New York Times*, June 17, 1990, sec. E; Seth H. Lubove, "Firms Spur Efforts to Restrict Government, Non-profit Rivals," *Wall Street Journal*, June 9, 1986.

The Philadelphia Inquirer published a series on nonprofits: Gilbert M. Gaul and Neill A. Gorowski, "Warehouses of Wealth: The Tax-Free Economy," April 18–24, 1993, which explored nonprofit commercialization and the consequences of their tax-free status. The article titles suggest their scope: "Nonprofits: America's Growth Industry," "The Rise of Medical Empires," "A Tax Break Colleges Can Bank on," "The IRS, An Enforcer That Can't Keep Up," "In High-Level Jobs at Nonprofits, Charity Really Pays," "For Nonprofits Only: A Cheap Pool of Money," "Foundations Build a Giant Nest Egg."

28. W. Dennis Keating, Keith P. Rasey, Norman Krumholz, "Community Development Corporations in the United States: Their Role in Housing and Urban Redevelopment," in *Government and Housing: Developments in Seven Countries*, ed. Willem van Vliet and Jan van Weesep (Newbury Park, Calif.: Sage, 1990), 209; Avis C. Vidal and Bob Komives, "Community Development Corporations: A National Perspective," *National Civic Review* 78 (May–June 1989), 168; Committee for Economic Development, Research and Policy Committee, *Public-Private Partnership: An Opportunity for Urban Communities* (New York: CED, February 1982), 54; Neal R. Pierce and Carol F. Steinbach, *Corrective Capitalism: The Rise of America's Community Development Corporations* (New York: Ford Foundation, July 1987). Beneficiaries of the Ford Foundation social investments included (besides ten minority-based CDCs as of 1982), public TV, low-income housing, and land preservation.

29. Leading proponents of the Local Initiatives Support Corporation (LISC) included Mitchell Sviridoff, then Ford Foundation vice-president for national affairs, and Franklin A. Thomas, director of the Bedford-Stuyvesant Restoration Corporation, later president of the Ford Foundation. See Anne Lowrey Bailey," Building a Bridge from Big Dollars to Inner Cities," *Chronicle of Philanthropy*, November 2, 1992, 6–7.

Sviridoff reaffirmed the CDC strategy of neighborhood revitalization in,"The Seeds of Urban Revival," *The Public Interest*, Winter 1994, 82–103. He describes the CDC as a distinctive force which combines entrepreneurial, management, political and organization skills, and provides the basis for an "ordered civil environment," or "community esprit."

Less enthusiastic, more skeptical about the value of the CDC is Nicholas Lemann. He claims that low-income neighborhood economic development is a chimera and that the model of mobility is for the upwardly mobile to get jobs outside the neighborhood and move out to better areas. He favors a service-oriented rather than a place-oriented attack on poverty. Lemann, "The Myth of Community Development," *New York Times Sunday Magazine*, January 9, 1994, 26–31, 50, 54, 60.

Ed Schwartz, "Reviving Community Development," *American Prospect*, Fall 1994, 82–87, contests Lemann's negative evaluation of community development. He argues that lack of coordination among housing, economic, and service programs, and among government and private agencies has hampered the effectiveness of neighborhood-based development. He expects the Clinton administration's Enterprise and Empowerment Zone program will encourage such coordination.

30. The Enterprise Foundation, *Annual Report, 1990*, 1, 3. By 1990, the EF had raised a total of $270 million for nonprofit, low-income housing; more than 750 corporations, foundations, or individuals had contributed. See also Elizabeth Greene, "Enterprise Foundation Seeks to Reconstruct America," *Chronicle of Philanthropy*, April 23, 1991, 7–8. An EF affiliate, the Enterprise Social Investment Corporation, had raised $200 million from corporate investors based on the 1986 low-income housing tax credit legislation for rental housing. ESIC also acted as a developer for low-income housing in Maryland. Another affiliate, the Enterprise Loan Fund, raised funds at below-market rates for recycling to nonprofit developers and low-income homeowners in Maryland. There is also the Enterprise Development Company, which builds mixed-use projects such as festival marketplaces. EF operating divisions included Program Services (technical assistance on housing development and management); Rehabilitation Work Group (training in low-cost construction techniques); Community Services (assists neighborhood groups in coordinating EF-assisted housing with social services); Policy Staff (lobbying government agencies on behalf of low-income housing programs).

31. Robert A. Rankin, "Helping the Residents Rebuild a Community," *Philadelphia Inquirer*, May 24, 1992; Felicity Barringer, "Shift for Urban Renewal: Nurture the Grass Roots," *New York Times*, November 29, 1992.

32. Kristin A. Goss, "A Big Push the Revive Inner Cities," *Chronicle of Philanthropy*, March 12, 1991, 1, 16. Donors included the Prudential Insurance Company and a group of foundations: Rockefeller Foundation; William and

Flora Hewlett Foundation; Knight Foundation; Pew Charitable Trust; John D. and Catherine T. MacArthur Foundation; Surdna Foundation.

33. Richard Swartz, written commentary, July 1993.

34. Robert L. Woodson, "Transform Inner Cities from the Grass Roots Up," *Wall Street Journal,* June 3, 1992. Similar sentiments were expressed by Peter Garcia, president, Chicanos Por La Causa, Inc., Phoenix: "Community development isn't about building buildings. It's about building people so that they can build their own communities," *LISC Link* 3 (Summer 1992), 11.

35. Paul S. Grogan," Miami Can Teach L.A.," *New York Times,* May 13, 1992. Otis Pitts, a retired policeman, provided the local leadership in the creation and development of Tacolcy.

36. Martin Gottlieb, "In a 90s War on Poverty, Who Hands Out Money?" *New York Times,* June 20, 1993. The second quotation is from Susan E. Shepard, commissioner of New York City's Department of Investigation. Also quoted is Michael Gecan, board member of the Saul Alinsky–inspired Industrial Areas Foundation. He contends that no community group can obtain government funding without ending up on a leash. To do so is to be "virtually doomed." This view supposes that any relation between a community group and government is necessarily adversarial or disadvantagous to the local group. And the IAF confrontational strategy does not comprehend that government needs the CDCs as much as the other way around in cities like Pittsburgh.

37. National Congress for Community Economic Development, *Changing the Odds: The Achievements of Community-Based Development Corporations* (Washington, D.C., December 1991), 2, 6–7. The survey data were based on 1,160 responses. Another survey by the Council for Community-Based Development in 1989 found that 307 corporations and foundations provided $90.1 million in grants for community-based development. Independent foundations were described as the most active supporters; 165 contributed $65 million, or 72 percent of the total. Corporation grants totaled $15.8 million (18 percent). Council for Community-Based Development, *Expanding Horizons II: A Research Report on Corporate and Foundation Grant Support of Community Based Development* (Washington, D.C., 1991), 3, 8.

38. The Ford Foundation contributed $4.75 million to the start-up funds. The six corporations, which provided the other half, were Aetna Life and Casualty, Prudential Life, International Harvester, Levi Strauss, Atlantic Richfield, Continental Illinois Bank.

39. Local Initiatives Support Corporation, *A Two-Year Report,* September 1, 1984, 7. Mitchell Sviridoff, president of LISC in 1982, formerly vice-president for national affairs, Ford Foundation, observed that LISC was created to help answer five questions: Could a national intermediary with limited objectives induce corporations to invest in community development despite unsatisfactory earlier experience? Could such investment leverage additional sums for

other sources? Could philanthropic funding be induced to shift from traditional outlets to "more business-like emphasis on investment?" Could community development investment generate sufficient income to reduce dependency on government and private philanthropy? Finally, what difference would it make if the questions were answered in the affirmative? Sviridoff, "Neighborhood Revitalization: The Role of LISC," *Community Action* 1 (1982), 5–8.

40. Local Initiatives Support Corporation, *A Two-Year Report*, September 1, 1984, 3, 7.

41. Local Initiatives Support Corporation, *Annual Report, 1988*, 13. Also in 1987, LISC established a Local Initiatives Managed Assets Corporation. This was designed to create a secondary market for community development loans. In fall 1991, LISC launched an equity fund to channel corporate and other investor money into a Retail Initiative, Inc. The fund will provide nonprofit community developers (perhaps in partnership with for-profit partners) with start-up financing and loans up to 30 percent of development costs. A precedent was Newark where the New Community Corporation joined with Pathmark Foods to build a shopping center. See Maggie Garb, "LISC Gives a Lift to Urban Supermarkets," *New York Times*, November 8, 1992.

42. Local Initiatives Support Corporation, *Annual Report, 1990*, inside front cover.

43. The twenty-four Areas of Concentration in 1990 were: Boston; California (Bay Area, Los Angeles, San Diego); Chicago; Cleveland; Detroit; Hartford/New Haven; Houston; Indianapolis; Northwest Indiana (Gary and metropolitan area); Kalamazoo; Kansas City; Miami; Michigan (multicity); Monongahela Valley; New York City; Newark; Palm Beach County; Philadelphia; Rhode Island; Richmond; Seattle/Tacoma; St. Paul; Toledo; Washington, D.C. There were also eight affiliate communities where the LISC contributed funds to an agency for recycling to CDCs.

44. Local Initiatives Support Corporation, *Annual Report, 1989*, statement by LISC president Paul S. Grogan.

45. Ibid., 12.

46. Ibid. LISC's first decade "demonstrated that community redevelopment rests on the twin pillars of real estate and social investment" (19).

47. Raymond Reaves, director of the Allegheny County Planning Department, believes that "the problems throughout the neighborhoods are social, not physical or related to the availability of capital. Therefore, the physical manifestations, such as housing and commercial development, do not deal with the basic problem" (written commentary, September 9, 1993). Even more basic, perhaps, is the fact that the combined efforts of the federal, state and local governments, foundations, social service agencies, or criminal justice system cannot seem to make a dent in the social pathologies. It would be pointless to

burden CDCs with utopian expectations,and then blame them for not living up to the impossible.

48. Committee for Economic Development, *Public-Private Partnership*, 49.

49. Roger S. Ahlbrandt, Jr., and Paul C. Brophy, *Neighborhood Revitalization: Theory and Practice* (Lexington, Mass.: Lexington Books, D.C. Heath, 1975), 86–87; and, by the same authors, "Neighborhood Housing Services: A Unique Formula Proves Itself in Turning Around Declining Neighborhood," in *Housing Rehabilitation: Economic, Social, and Policy Perspectives,* ed. David Listokin (New Brunswick, N.J.: Center for Urban Research, 1983), 293–303. Also by Ahlbrandt, *Flexible Code Enforcement: A Key Ingredient in Neighborhood Preservation Programming* (Washington, D.C.: National Association of Housing and Redevelopment Officials, August 1976), which stresses the desirability of the NHS concept of code enforcement programs characterized by citizen involvement, flexibility, a service rather than punitive orientation, and concentration in small areas. He contrasts this with the punitive emphasis in the 1965 federally aided code enforcement program, FACE.

50. Department of City Planning, *Citizen Participation Report,* 3. The Social Planning Advisory Committee's report was prepared by Morton Coleman, with Social Planners Norman Taylor and Bert Shulimson. James Cunningham was on the committee.

51. Ibid., 27–28. The Community Organizations of Pittsburgh was established by twenty-two neighborhood organizations on September 18, 1963, at the North Side's Manchester Neighborhood House. Affiliated groups rose to twenty-seven by October: Allegheny West Neighborhood Council; Beechview Community Council; Beltzhoover Men's Fellowship; Brighton Community Club; Central North Side Neighborhood Council; Chadwick Civic League; Citizens Committee for Hill District Renewal; East Liberty Chamber of Commerce; East Liberty Community Renewal Council; Hazelwood-Glenwood Urban Extension Council; Hill District Homeowners' and Tenants' Association; Homewood-Brushton Renewal Council; Homewood Community Improvement Association. Kingsley Neighborhood Council; Manchester Neighborhood Council; Morewood-Shadyside Civic Association; Neighborhood Centers Association; North Side Chamber of Commerce; North Side Civic Promotion Council; North View Heights Residents' Council; Oakland Chamber of Commerce Perry Hilltop Action Council; Sheraden Citizens' Improvement Council; South Pittsburgh Development Council; Spring Hill–City View Representation Committee; Squirrel Hill Merchants' Council; West End Board of Trade.

52. Billie Bramhall, "Planners Advocate for Community Within Planning Department," *Planner's Notebook* 4 (June 1974), 1–8. Robert H. Lurcott and Jane A. Downing, "A Public/Private Support System for Community Based Organizations Involved in Economic Development in Pittsburgh," Department of City Planning, Pittsburgh, occasional paper no. 4, June 1987, 3. See also

Roger S. Ahlbrandt, "Public-Private Partnerships for Neighborhood Renewal," *American Academy of Political and Social Science, Annals* 488 (November 1986), 125; Alberta M. Sbragia, "Pittsburgh's 'Third Way': The Nonprofit Sector as a Key to Urban Regeneration," in *Leadership in Urban Regeneration: Cities in North America and Europe*, ed. Dennis Judd and Michael Parkinson, *Urban Affairs Annual Reviews* 37 (1990); Sbragia, "Pittsburgh: A Tale of Two Cities," unpublished manuscript, Department of Political Science, University of Pittsburgh, 17–18; Louise Jezierski, "Neighborhoods and Public-Private Partnerships in Pittsburgh," *Urban Affairs Quarterly* 26 (December 1990), 233.

53. James V. Cunningham, written commentary, April 21, 1993.

54. The city defined a capital improvement as one that extended a facility's life by twenty-five years or a major improvement costing over $10,000. If Community Development Block Grants were used, they had to benefit low- and moderate-income populations, eliminate blight or slums, or respond to urgent needs. Decisions about neighborhood investment, improvements, or budgeting were influenced by the Planning Department's six-part topology. As of around 1990, the criteria and neighborhoods were as follows (based on the 1980 census):

1. Stable and prosperous neighborhoods, with high real estate values and strong local organizations: Banksville, Chartiers City, Regent Square, Greenfield, Highland Park, Swisshelm Park, Overbrook, Brighton Heights, Lincoln Place, Mount Washington, Elliott, Squirrel Hill, Duquesne Heights, Point Breeze, Stanton Heights, New Homestead, Windgap, Oakwoood, Sheraden, Crafton Heights, East Carnegie, Ridgemont, Shadyside, North Oakland, Westwood, Bon Air, Brookline, Morningside, Summer HIll Beechview, Carrick.

2. Three North Side neighborhoods of architectural significance that suffered deterioration in the 1950s and 1960s, but revived over the next two decades through rehabilitation tied to historic preservation: Allegheny West, Central North Side, Manchester.

3. Moderate-income areas with extensive home ownership and slowly increasing property values: Allegheny Center, Troy Hill, Allentown, Marshall-Shadeland, Mount Oliver, Spring Garden, Spring Hill–City View, South Side Slopes, Upper Hill, Upper Lawrenceville, Observatory Hill, Knoxville, Arlington, Hays, Bloomfield, Polish Hill, Lower Oakland.

4. Moderate-income areas with fewer homes owned by tenants, signs of deterioration, a weak housing market and some speculation: Central Lawrenceville, Lincoln-Lemington, Belmar, Lower Lawrenceville, Homewood North, California-Kirkbride, Central Oakland, South Side Flats, Friendship Perry, East Liberty, Beltzhoover, Hazelwood, Esplen, Crawford-Roberts, East Hills, Hilltop, East Allegheny, Fineview, Garfield, West End.

5. The city's poorest neighborhoods, showing substantial deterioration, vacancies, and a weak housing market: the Middle Hill, Homewood West, West Oakland, Homewood South, the Bluff, Larimer.

6. Public housing neighborhoods, where more than 10 percent of city population lived in eight Housing Authority communities, and fifteen high-rises for the elderly): Arlington Heights, St. Clair Village, Broadhead Manor, Terrace Village, Allegheny Dwellings, Northview Heights, Glen Hazel, Bedford Dwellings.

From City of Pittsburgh, *Six-Year Development Program, 1992–1997, Development Policies*, 8, 53–54. See also Sue Gottlieb, "Planning for the City's Future: The Capital Budget," *Oakland* 7 (January 1993), 1, 8; Dayna Di-Rienzo," Understanding the City's Long Range Land Use Plan," *Oakland* 8 (May 1993), 1, 20. Carolyn Teich Adams, *The Politics of Capital Investment: The Case of Philadelphia* (Albany: State University of New York Press, 1988) maintains that investment in neighborhood facilities in Philadelphia is greatly influenced by the structure of capital markets.

55. Morton Coleman, written commentary, April 23, 1993.

56. Mike Brourman, "Ethnic Poor of City Organize to End Neglect," *Pittsburgh Post-Gazette*, September 15, 1969. Paradoxically, white neighborhoods complained of being neglected by the poverty program, but they also resisted overtures to be included in (and thus identified with) the program. When federal funding was drastically reduced in 1969 (from $13 to $6 million), it further limited any possibility of expanding beyond the eight poverty neighborhoods (David P. Epperson, personal interview, September 17, 1993).

57. Richard Swartz, written commentary, July 1993.

58. Community Technical Assistance Center, *5 Year Report, 1981–1986*, 20. The workshops were held in May and June at the William Penn Hotel and at Bethany College in West Virginia.

59. David Brewton, personal interview, August 18, 1993.

60. "Shaping Our Future: A Community Vision for Pittsburgh Regional Development," a report of the Working Group on Community Development, Winter 1988, 3, 11–12.

61. James V. Cunningham, "Power, Participation, and Local Government: The Communal Struggle for Parity," *Journal of Urban Affairs* 5 (1983), 265–66. The Pittsburgh City Council was inspired by these events to enact a plant-closing notification bill, but it was vetoed by Mayor Caliguiri, and SNAC petered out. The plant subsequently became a successful cracker and cookie producer with much improved labor relations. Jim McKay, "Nabisco Plant Transformed from Problem Child to Star," *Pittsburgh Post-Gazette*, April 4, 1991.

62. SVA's role is examined in Dale Hathaway, *Can Workers Have a Voice? The Politics of Deindustrialization in Pittsburgh* (University Park: Pennsylvania State University Press, 1993).

63. Michael deCourcy Hinds, "In Pittsburgh, Rising Hopes for an Unusual Bakery Owned by Its Workers," *New York Times*, January 27, 1992.

64. Urban Redevelopment Authority of Pittsburgh, Center for Business Assistance," City to Take Pride in New Bakery Start-Up," *Economic Development Pittsburgh* (Third Quarter, 1991), 1.

65. The City Pride saga is discussed in Margie Romero, "Making Bread From Scratch," *In Pittsburgh*, November 13–19, 1991, 16–17; Ray Marano, "City Pride Baking Co.: Gritty Details of a Micro-Deal," *Pittsburgh Business Times*, November 4, 1991, 5; Chris Swaney, "In Pittsburgh, Baking Company is Reborn," *New York Times*, real estate section, December 29, 1991; "Bakery Workers Help Save Jobs in Pittsburgh," Federation for Industrial Retention and Renewal, *News* 4 (Spring 1992), 1, 10; Patricia A. Moore, "The Proof Is in the Pride," *Pittsburgh City Paper* November 25–December 1, 1992, 8–9; Rich Cholodofsky, "Carlow May Buy City Pride Bakery," *Tribune-Review*, March 12, 1993; Tim Ziaukas, "Adventure Capitalist [Michael Carlow]," *Pittsburgh*, June 1993, 21–25. William S. Kowinski, "The Tale of City Pride: People Who Wouldn't Give Up," *Smithsonian* 24 (October 1993), 118–22 + , provides what might be termed the "human interest," noneconomic, noncritical perspective; Wes Cotter, "Carlow Guarantees City Pride Bakery Will Not Be Closed," *Pittsburgh Business Times*, October 11–17, 1993, 1, 49; Len Boselovic, "City Pride's Demise: Trouble from the Start," *Pittsburgh Post-Gazette*, March 8, 1994.

According to Charles McCollester, the Steel Valley Authority had devised a business plan, but it was ignored. Besides undercapitalization, unsatisfactory equipment purchases, and poor marketing strategy, City Pride suffered from a failure of management. Dan Curtis, McCollester maintains, was a good promoter and visionary, but not a manager. Although the SVA urged he be replaced, bankers and venture capitalists insisted on his retention. Charles McCollester, personal interview, December 8, 1993; McCollester, "Let City Pride Bakery Give Pittsburgh Its Daily Bread," *Pittsburgh Post-Gazette*, March 15, 1994.

66. Administered by the Planning Department (Division of Community Development and Administration), CDBG funds were almost entirely devoted to neighborhood development. Pittsburgh distributed $284.4 million from 1974 to 1988 and devoted almost 60 percent to grants and loans for housing rehabilitation. The next largest segment went for the support of small and medium-sized neighborhood businesses, job creation, neighborhood infrastructure. CBDG also funded nonprofit organizations serving low-income population ($1.6 million in 1988 to forty-two agencies). City of Pittsburgh, Department of City Planning, *Planning '88: A Progress Report*, 9.

67. While involved in the negotiations for a technical assistance center, Feehan was pursuing a dual master's degree in social work and public administration at the University of Pittsburgh (where he was a student of Cunningham) and participating in the development of the Allegheny Conference's com-

munity education program. Health and Welfare Planning Association, *Newsletter*, March 1981, 2. CTAC was administered through the HWPA for the first six months. Also involved in the creation of CTAC was Tom Murphy, a North Side neighborhood leader prior to his election to the state legislature.

68. Memorandum from David M. Feehan to David Bergholz, January 9, 1980; Memorandum from David Bergholz to Tom Cox, January 10, 1980; "Community Technical Assistance Center Proposal: "Additional Information for Members of the Council, City of Pittsburgh," n.d.; James V. Cunningham, personal interview, August 12, 1993. I am indebted to Robin Jones (then president of the Pittsburgh Neighborhood Alliance and a participant in the negotiations for a technical assistance center) for these and other documents relating to the creation of CTAC. Also, Dayna DiRienzo, "Building Stronger Neighborhoods: Community Groups Find Resource Bonanza at CTAC," *Oakland,* January 1994, 4.

69. *Evaluations of the Community Technical Assistance Center and the Community Design Center of Pittsburgh,* prepared for the Pittsburgh Partnership for Neighborhood Development, by Urban Partners, September 1991, 2–22. As of 1989, the Pittsburgh Partnership contributed to the support of CTAC as well as the Design Center.

70. Interview with Robin Jones, June 1993; Lurcott and Downing, *Public/ Private Support System for Community Based Organizations,* 4. The latter also point out that "in 1981, neighborhood organizations helped to develop the goals and objectives for a housing-focused revitalization program that included an urban development action grant for six neighborhoods on Pittsburgh's North Side" (5).

71. Richard Swartz, personal interview, July 8, 1993.

72. According to the Pittsburgh History & Landmarks Foundation, the Architects' Workshop–Community Design Center originated "when Landmarks asked the Pittsburgh AIA to provide some free design services to Carson Street building owners as part of our Birmingham Restoration program. The Pittsburgh chapter did so, and then made this service permanent as the Architects' Workshop." "Community Design Center of Pittsburgh," *PHLF News* 131 (September 1993), 4.

73. Pittsburgh Partnership for Neighborhood Development, *Progress Report, 1990,* 23–24. The center had become ineffectual by 1987 and was completely reorganized. The new director constituted the entire staff, and it no longer provided direct design services. *Evaluations of the Community Technical Assistance Center and the Community Design Center of Pittsburgh,* 3-2–3-7.

74. *Neighborhoods for Living Center News,* December 1991, 1. NeighborFair is supported by contracts with the city, URA, and private organizations, as well as corporate and charitable contributions.

75. The PPND board of directors as of March 1993 included representatives of Mellon Bank, Integra Bank, Heinz Endowments, Pittsburgh Foundation, Department of City Planning, Penn's Southwest Association, Dollar Bank, University of Pittsburgh, Carnegie Mellon University, Magee Women's Hospital, Community College of Allegheny County, Pittsburgh National Bank, URA.

76. Seven Pittsburgh foundations each distributed grants totaling $11 million or more in 1992: Richard King Mellon Foundation, Howard Heinz Endowment, Vira Heinz Endowment, Alcoa Foundation, McCune Foundation, Rockwell International Corp. Trust, Sara Scaife Foundation. Eighteen more local foundations distributed grants ranging from $857,000 to $8,744,000. The Howard Heinz and Vira Heinz Endowments, and Pittsburgh Foundation, were administered by the same executive director (Alfred Wishart) until recently and distributed nearly $43 million in 1992. The Pittsburgh Foundation now operates independently. (Some foundations contributed directly to CDCs— McCune Foundation to the Bloomfield-Garfield Corporation, and Pittsburgh Foundation to Homewood-Brushton Revitalization and Development Corporation).

The information in this section is drawn from "25 Largest Pittsburgh-Area Foundations, Ranked by 1992 Grant Payout," *Pittsburgh Business Times*, May 3–9, 1993, 21. The entire list, in descending order of grant amount for 1992, is (in rounded figures): Richard King MellonFoundation, $44,991,000; Howard Heinz Endowment, $22,047,000; Vira I. Heinz Endowment, $13,500,000; Alcoa Foundation, $12,091,000; McCune Foundation, $11,600,000; Rockwell International Corporation Trust, $11,400,000; Sarah Scaife Foundation, $11,081,000; Mellon Bank Foundation, $8,744,000; Allegheny Foundation, $7,673,000; Pittsburgh Foundation, $7,379,000; H.J. Heinz Co. Foundation, $7,003,180; Claude Worthington Benedum Foundation, $6,836,000; Westinghouse Foundation, $6,749,000; Scaife Family Foundation, $6,607,000; USX Foundation, $6,178,000; PPG Industries Foundation, $3,916,000; Jewish Healthcare Foundation of Pittsburgh, $3,400,000; Carthage Foundation, $3,241,000; Consolidated Natural Gas Company Foundation, $3,083; Hillman Foundation, $2,932,000; PNC Bank Foundation, $2,181,000; Buhl Foundation, $2,042,000; Mary Hillman Jennings Foundation, $1,454,000; Hunt Foundation and Roy A. Hunt Foundation, $1,253,000; Laurel Foundation, $857,000.

77. Jane Downing, personal interview, July 1, 1993.

78. Henry Beukema, personal interview, June 23, 1993; Jon Schmitz and Ellen M. Perlmutter, " 'Lucky Five' Neighbor Groups Top Fund Race," *Pittsburgh Press*, December 1, 1985.

79. Pittsburgh Partnership for Neighborhood Development, *Annual Report, 1989–1990*, 3.

80. PPND technical support included funding of the Community Design Center and Community Technical Assistance Center. It also supported "training and information exchange programs," as illustrated by a grant to bring Bertha Gilkey, a tenant management expert, to Pittsburgh on behalf of the Northside Tenants' Reorganization, and the award of two internships a year for CDC staff to attend the Development Training Institute in Baltimore. Pittsburgh Partnership for Neighborhood Development, *Progress Report, 1990,* 3, 5.

81. Local contributors included Dravo Corporation, Howard Heinz Endowment, Hillman Foundation, Richard King Mellon Foundation, the POISE Foundation, the Pittsburgh Foundation, the Pittsburgh Leadership Foundation (Allegheny Conference on Community Development, *1981 Report,* 11). Community or neighborhood redevelopment first "emerged as an area of Conference concern" around 1980 when staff members participated in planning activities in Oakland and the North Side (ibid.).

82. Pittsburgh was an LISC area of concentration through 1989. Subsequently, the Mon Valley Initiative became the regional area of concentration. In the early 1980s, Manchester Citizens' Corporation received funding for the rehabilitation of seventy-five units of multifamily housing for resale as condominiums. Money went to the North Side Civic Development Council for pre-development capital and bridge financing in connection with the acquisition and remodeling of a 65,200-square-foot former UPS warehouse for light industrial use. Several loans went to the Oakland Planning and Development Corporation to establish a real estate office to combat speculation; to rehabilite fifteen units of housing for the elderly; to construct fifty-six condominium units for sale to low-to-moderate-income families. And the Perry Hilltop Citizens' Council received funding to reopen a neighborhood real estate office to combat racial steering. Local Initiatives Support Corporation, *A Two Year Report, September 1, 1984,* 34; ACCD, *1983 Report,* 12.

83. PPND, *Annual Report, 1989–1990,* 3; PPND, *Progress Report, 1990,* 3, 4. The partnership also established a Pittsburgh Equity Fund in 1990 in collaboration with James Rouse's Enterprise Social Investment Corporation. Like the other such equity funds, it offered corporations an opportunity for tax credits for investing in low-income housing based on the 1986 tax legislation.

84. Richard Swartz, personal interview, July 8, 1983; Jane Downing, personal interview, July 1, 1993; Robin Jones, personal interview, June 23, 1993.

85. PPND, *Annual Report, 1989–90,* 2; PPND, *Progress Report, 1990,* 1–2.

86. Sandra Phillips, personal interview, August 12, 1993.

87. The MCC encountered difficulties in the mid-1980s. A combination of a $215,000 deficit and internal conflicts led for a period to funding withdrawals and a suspension of development projects. Ellen M. Perlmutter, "Deficit, Feuding, Lost Funds Plague Manchester Group," *Pittsburgh Press,* December 15, 1985.

88. Schmitz and Perlmutter, " 'Lucky 5' Neighborhood Groups Top Fund Race."

89. The Westside Community Development Corporation is a recent addition to the partnership.

90. Henry Beukema, personal interview, June 23, 1993.

91. Jane Downing, personal interview, July 1, 1993.

92. Richard Swartz, written commentary, July 1993.

93. The Neighborhood Fund originated when City Planning proposed that the Community Technical Assistance Center administer a $100,000 fund for neighborhood groups. Since this was not legally possible, a subcommittee headed by Robin Jones devised the Neighborhood Fund (Robin Jones, personal interview, June 22, 1993).

94. Robin R. Jones, "The CDC Experience of Pittsburgh," presented to the annual meeting of the ACSP, Portland, Oregon, October 1989, 5, 6; City of Pittsburgh, Department of City Planning, *1989 Annual Report*, 19. Subsequently, the Neighborhood Fund, Inc., was dissolved, becoming the Neighborhood Fund; both it and the CBO Fund were administered by an Advisory Committee on Community Based Organizations (Jones, "The CDC Experience," 21).

95. Organizations receiving CBO funds (ranging from $8,000 to $33,125) in 1992 included: Beltzhoover Neighborhood Council; Central Northside Neighborhood Council; East Liberty Concerned Citizens; Eastside Alliance; Fineview Citizens' Council; Friendship Development Corporation; Lawrenceville Citizens' Council; Lawrenceville Development Corporation; Mount Washington CDC; Neighborhood Housing Services; Northside Development Council-Conference; Northside Tenants' Reorganization; Perry Hilltop Citizens' Council; Polish Hill Civic Assosication; SPERT (South Pittsburgh Economic Revitalization Team); Spring Garden; West End–Elliott Joint Council Project; Westside CDC.

96. Organizations assisted under this program in 1992 included: Bedford Dwellings; Broadhead Manor Residents' Council; Federal American Council; Garfield Row House; People on the Move; Street Clair Citizens' Council; Westgate Village Residents' Council.

97. NEDIF funding in 1992–1993 went to the Lawrenceville Citizens' Council, Lawrenceville Development Corporation, and West End Elliott Joint Council.

98. Allegheny West Civic Council, Bloomfield-Garfield Corporation, Breachmenders, Inc., Calbride Place Citizens' Council, Central Northside Neighborhood Council, Charles Street Area Council, East Allegheny Community Council, East Liberty Development, Inc., Eastside Alliance, Fineview Citizens' Council, Friendship Development Associates, Garfield Jubilee Asso-

ciation, Glen Hazel Citizens' Corporation, Hill Community Development Corporation, Hill District Ministries, Inc., Homewood-Brushton Revitalization and Development Corporation, Lawrenceville Citizens' Council, Lincoln-Larimer-Lemington-Belmar Citizens' Revitalization and Development Corporation, Lincoln Park Community Center, Inc., Manchester Citizens' Corporation, Mount Washington Community Development Corporation, Northside Civic Development Council, Northside Leadership Conference, Northside Tenants' Reorganization, Oakland Planning and Development Corporation, Observatory Hill, Inc., South Side Local Development Company, Spring Garden Neighborhood Council, Steel Valley Authority, Troy Hill Citizens.

99. PCRG, *Summary of Neighborhood Lending, 1991, in the City of Pittsburgh*, 3. The Preservation Fund of Pittsburgh's History & Landmarks Foundation (PH&LF) financed this publication.

100. Quoted in Thomas Olson, "Bank Watchdog in Race for City Council," *Pittsburgh Business Times*, April 19–25, 14.

101. Stanley Lowe and Jennifer L. Blake, *Using the Community Reinvestment Act in Low-Income Historic Neighborhoods*, National Trust for Historic Preservation, information series no. 56, 1992, 6.

102. Ibid., 11.

103. Ellen M. Perlmutter, "Three Banks Lead Pack in Race for City Funds," *Pittsburgh Press*, November 20, 1989.

104. "The Dollar Bank Dilemma," editorial, *Pittsburgh Post-Gazette*, January 7, 1991; Ellen M. Perlmutter, "Dollar Bank Meets Critics of Lending Record," *Pittsburgh Press*, January 26, 1991. Dollar agreed to establish a housing program that would facilitate purchase of vacant houses in selected city neighborhoods. This was similar to an arrangement worked out with Pittsburgh National Bank eighteen months earlier. The PCRG had prepared a statement of protest to be sent to Dollar's regulatory agency, with copies to congressmen and a letter to the mayor requesting withdrawal of city funds. The action was influential in persuading Dollar Bank to negotiate with the CDRG.

105. Steve Massey, "Community Group Targets Thrifts," *Pittsburgh Post-Gazette*, April 7, 1993.

106. Perlmutter, "Three Banks Lead Pack."

107. Jon Schmitz, "City Mum on Ratings for Local Bank Loans," *Pittsburgh Press*, March 6, 1991; Eleanor Chute, "City Banks Tripled Total Cash Loaned in Neighborhoods," *Pittsburgh Press*, March 11, 1992. A succinct (and favorable) account of the PCRG is John T. Metzger, "The Community Reinvestment Act and Neighborhood Revitalization in Pittsburgh," in *From Redlining to Reinvestment: Community Responses to Urban Development*, ed. Gregory D. Squires (Philadelphia: Temple University Press, 1992), 73–108.

108. PCRG received $116,500 for its services to five lenders in FY1990. Lowe and Blake, *Using the Community Reinvestment Act,* 7. For examples of efforts in other cities to increase lending to low-income or minority populations for housing or business development, see Leslie Wayne," New Hope in Inner Cities: Banks Offering Mortgages," *New York Times,* March 14, 1992 (on Philadelphia's ACORN group); Michael Quint, "A Bank Shows It Can Profit and Follow a Social Agenda," *New York Times,* May 24, 1992 (on the South Shore Bank, Chicago); Paulette Thomas, "Small Businesses, Key to Urban Recovery, Are Starved for Capital," *Wall Street Journal,* June 11, 1992; Fred R. Bleakley, "How Groups Pressured One Bank to Promise More Inner-City Loans," *Wall Street Journal,* September 22, 1992 (on the Bank of Syracuse and the Syracuse Community Reinvestment Coalition); Udayan Gupta, "Community-Loan Funds Bridge Inner-City Capital Gap," *Wall Street Journal,* January 13, 1993 (on the Delaware Valley Community Reinvestment Fund, Seattle Cascadia Revolving Fund).

109. Critics argue that the CRA "has become a tool with which minority activists put pressure on banks to make imprudent loans in bad neighborhoods" and that banks are expected to pursue contradictory goals: simultaneously tighten loan requirements and expand credit to inner-city residents. Samuel L. Taylor, "A Case of Manufactured Racism," letter to the editor, *Wall Street Journal,* May 7, 1992; Jay G. Baris, "Inner-City Banking's Catch-22," *New York Times,* August 2, 1992; Tim W. Ferguson, "The Next Lender Litigation Wave: Mortgage Bias," *Wall Street Journal,* May 25, 1993. Another criticism is that statistics on loan rejection rates are manipulated to make it seem that differential group outcomes lack any explanation other than bias. "Racism in Loans 'Built In,'" *Pittsburgh Press,* October 27, 1991.

110. Peter Passell, "Redlining Under Attack," *New York Times,* August 31, 1994.

111. Jonathan R. Macey, "Banking by Quota," *Wall Street Journal,* September 7, 1994.

Chapter 6. Community Development Corporations

1. Urban Redevelopment Authority of Pittsburgh (URA), *1990 Annual Report,* 11; *Urban Redevelopment Works in Pittsburgh,* Spring/Summer 1989), 3; "Saving Houses," *Pittsburgh Press,* June 30, 1991. Before mid-1989, the program had been limited to developers; it was extended to all city neighborhoods in 1991—an expansion made possible by the addition of four banks—Dollar, Integra, Union National, and Mellon—to Pittsburgh National Banks as lending sources. In certain target neighborhoods borrowers could receive zero interest financing for 25 percent of the combined mortgage and rehabilitation (no payment required until the house was sold).

Friendship, an East End neighborhood with a population of 1,329 in 1990, illustrated the potentials of the HRP. Most of the homes involved, besides being rundown, were converted from rental to owner-occupied, thus encouraging hope that "our neighborhood is alive and well" ("Urban-Loan Programs Spruce Up Handyman Specials," *Allegheny Bulletin*, November 11, 1992).

2. Richard Swartz to author, written commentary, July 1993.

3. URA, Department of Housing, *Overview 1990*, 9. The investment disincentives for low-income rental housing included extended depreciation schedules and additional limitations on tax credits and passive loses.

4. Ibid., 9, 10. Of the 55 developments, 21 were single-family homeownership (226 units), and 34 multifamily rental (669 units). Total development costs exceeded $41 million.

5. URA housing program information and cumulative statistics can be found in Department of Housing, *Overview, 1990*. See also the URA's *Annual Reports*, and *Urban Development Works in Pittsburgh* bulletins. A summary and economic evaluation of the housing programs appears in Pennsylvania Economy League, *The Urban Redevelopment Authority of Pittsburgh; Housing and Economic Development Programs in the city of Pittsburgh's Neighborhoods* (Pittsburgh, December 1989). Several of the more important programs are summarized in *Oakland* 8 (June 1993), 1, 12 (published by the Oakland Planning and Development Corp.) The URA also publishes numerous brochures explaining the housing assistance options. For example, "Pittsburgh Home Ownership Program: Low-Interest Mortgages Featuring Grants for Income-Eligible Borrowers"; "Housing Recovery Program"; "Pittsburgh Home Improvement Loan Program: Low-Interest Loans for Home Repair"; "The Pittsburgh Home Rehabilitation Program"; "Low Interest Financing Programs for Residential Rental Properties" (multifamily revenue bond program, rental housing and improvement program).

6. Besides the Pittsburgh Homeownership Program, and the already mentioned Housing Recovery Program, the URA offered the following programs designed to expand the affordable single-family housing supply:

a. Neighborhood Housing Program. Begun in 1974, it provided second mortgage loans to commercial and nonprofit developers (where construction costs exceeded market value, creating an appraisal gap, or to make an affordable monthly payment possible. By the end of 1990, the URA had provided $7. 4 million in second mortgage financing for 340 units.

b. Equity Participation Program. Started in 1979, it provides below-market first and second mortgage financing to developers up to 50 percent of development cost to help lower-income families become homeowners. By the end of 1990, it had generated 940 housing units at a subsidy of more than $10.9 million.

    c. Pittsburgh Construction Loan Fund. Established in 1987, this is a revolving loan fund offering low-interest construction financing to developers for new-sale housing or extensive rehabilitation. Like the Equity Participation Program, it made financing available for lower-cost housing in neighborhoods where construction capital was difficult to obtain.

    d. There were also two minor programs. By the end of 1990, fourteen Site Assistance loans ($1,109,834) encompassed eighty-three housing units and the Community Development Investment Fund had supplied four loans ($510,674) for fifty-one housing units.

7. Other multifamily housing programs in 1990 included:

    a. Rental Rehabilitation Program. Created in 1984, it funded commercial and nonprofit developers for rental housing rehabilitation in specified neighborhoods. The interest subsidy, as low as zero percent interest, depended on constructions costs and the number of housing units. Loans could range up to $8,750 per unit. By the end of 1990, RRP had financed the rehabilitation of 456 rental units at a cost of more than $3.5 million.

    b. Multifamily Revenue Bond Program: Established in 1982, the MRBP issued revenue bonds to permit first mortgage financing for rental housing construction or rehabilitation. By the end of 1990 the program had financed, through tax-exempt revenue bonds totaling $42 million, 430 rental units for lower-income households.

    c. Four other smaller programs had existed in this category. The Section 312 Multifamily Program provided below-market rate loans to developers. It had supplied twenty-two loans ($4,565,100), producing 199 units of rehabilitated multifamily housing through 1987. The Single Room Occupancy Grant Program had provided four loans ($1,465,294) for 401 units. Three Site Assistance loans ($113,116) covered three units. And five Community Development Investment Fund loans ($173,728) produced nineteen units of multifamily housing by 1990. This was the only one that still operated in 1990.

8. The two most important single-family URA rehabilitation programs were the Home Improvement Loan Program (regular and subsidized), and the Pittsburgh Home Rehabilitation Program. The former, launched in 1978, provided low-interest financing totaling $78.9 million toward the rehabilitation of 13,358 units by the end of 1990. The Pittsburgh Home Rehabilitation Program, established in 1975, offered zero percent interest loans to the lowest income homeowners (up to $15,200 for one person to $28,700 for a family of eight). It had, by the end of 1990, financed 5,478 units at a cost of $48.2 million.

The final category of housing assistance encompassed two weatherization programs. The more important, numerically, was the Weatherizing Homes in Pittsburgh Program. Instituted in 1977, and funded by the Pennsylvania Department of Community Affairs, it encouraged energy saving through payments to homeowners and renters for storm window installation, insulation, and similar conservation efforts. It had financed the weatherization of 11,911 units at a cost of $11,468,393 by the end of 1990. The second program, Rent Brake, was established in 1980 and administered by ACTION-Housing. It provided grants to landlords for energy conservation (80 percent per rental unit up to a limit of $2,000); landlords, in return, agreed to rent controls for up to two years. At a cost of $3,995,187, Rent Brake (which no longer exists) helped weatherize 2,073 units.

9. Pennsylvania Economy League, *The Urban Redevelopment Authority of Pittsburgh*, 8, 36. The league found that the URA loan programs, even though oriented to social objectives, were "reasonably successful" as of 1989 if measured by conventional investment criteria. The two no-interest programs for the lowest-income homeowners—Homeowner's Emergency Loan Program and Pittsburgh Home Rehabilitation Program—showed a high ninety-day delinquency rate of 15.61 percent.

A new housing subsidy program was launched in September 1993. This was the Pittsburgh Vacant Housing Program. A $2.4 grant to the URA through the HUD Hope 3 fund will be used to rehabilitate up to 200 vacant homes (in collaboration with ACTION-Housing and two dozen community groups). The houses will sell for as little as half the renovation cost. The community groups will seek out potential purchasers and work with them on financing and credit counseling. Gary Rotstein, "Homes Get New Lease on Life," *Pittsburgh Post-Gazette*, September 29, 1993; Ron DaParma, "Marketing of Renovated Vacant Homes to Begin," *Tribune-Review*, September 29, 1993.

Still another low-income housing effort begun in 1993 was the national Campaign for Home Ownership initiated by NeighborWorks. Its goal is to assist 10,000 families to borrow up to $650 million within five years in twenty cities. In Pittsburgh, the Neighborhood Housing Services is the participating agency. NHS will work with local banks (Dollar, Integra, Mellon) to provide financing and provide credit and homeownership counseling. The agency anticipates increasing homeownership in Pittsburgh by 150 to 200 units a year through the program. Harry Stoffer, "Help Buying a Home," *Pittsburgh Post-Gazette*, June 12, 1993.

10. Following revelations by the *Pittsburgh Post-Gazette* in the summer of 1993 that the city of Pittsburgh was the leading slumlord, the URA instituted Hope 3. The newspaper investigations revealed that city owned thousands of units of property confiscated for tax defaults, mostly vacant lots but also 93 dilapidated dwellings occupied by rent-paying tenants. Another 129 buildings had been condemned but still stood. Others in the total of 1,381 dwellings that

the city controlled were not officially occupied, but many probably were by drug users or squatters.

The City Council transferred 192 buildings to the URA, which will contribute up to $75,000 per house for rehabilitation in the form of grants and loans to purchasers. Eligibility and URA contribution will vary according to family size and income ($12,000 to $29,000). The program was financed by $2.4 million in federal home improvement funds. See "Intolerable" (editorial) and John M. R. Bull, "Council Proposes a Summit Meeting," *Pittsburgh Post-Gazette*, August 1, 1993; Bull, "City to Fix Up, Sell Houses," *Pittsburgh Post-Gazette*, August 12, 1993.

11. Pennsylvania Economy League, *The Urban Redevelopment Authority of Pittsburgh*, 2. Superficially, the URA loan repayment experience fell short of conventional lending expectations: "Seven percent of the loans have been written off and another eight percent are delinquent or doubtful. The repayment experience has been particularly poor in the programs designed to assist minorities and women." Yet the URA was not a conventional lending agency. It had social as well as purely economic criteria: "The mission of the URA's Department of Economic Development is to retain key businesses, support businesses owned by minorities and women, and to encourage development in low- and moderate-income neighborhoods." By this measure, it was obliged to make riskier loans than would be acceptable for a private lender. And in the case of loans to women and minorities, they went to small businesses, often start-ups, located in less affluent neighborhoods—comparatively high-risk borrowers under any circumstances who would not otherwise have received funding and at least an opportunity to succeed (10, 13–14).

12. This was previously known as the Pittsburgh Business Assistance Revolving Loan Fund.

13. A Small and Minority Contractors' Assistance Program, a revolving fund, had been established in 1978. It provided loans ranging from $5,000 to $20,000.

14. The NEDIF, formerly the Neighborhood Job Development Program, provided thirteen loans totaling $703,410 in 1990. Cumulative activity, 1986–1990, was fifty-seven loans totaling $2.8 million and leveraging $6.4 million in private investment.

15. There were 280 Street Face projects, from its inception in January 1986 to 1990; $2 million in public matching grants leveraged $4.8 million in private expenditures.

16. In 1990, the CDIF supplied thirteen grants totaling $655,581; this leveraged private investment of $3.3 million.

17. Richard Swartz to author, written commentary, July 1993.

18. Urban Redevelopment Authority of Pittsburgh, *1992 Report*, 24–25. Along with the Working Group, the following CBOs participated in the creation

of EFFORTS: Pittsburgh Community Reinvestment Group, Minority Enterprise Corporation, Greater Pittsburgh Commission for Women, National Association for Women Business Owners. In its first year, the program provided nine loans totaling $218,000.

19. URA, *1986 Annual Report,* 23; URA, *1990 Annual Report,* 25. Prior to 1988, Lawrenceville was classified as a Planning Zone; it achieved full status as an Enterprize Zone that year.

20. Enterprise Zone status also provided funding advantages to the designed CDC. In the case of Lawrenceville, for example: "The enterprise zone designation has allowed LDC to conduct the business outreach program, act as a network to the URA and State of Pennsylvania, develop an inventory of property on a database program, prepare a color-coded 'map' of Lawrenceville, hire a full time staff member, supplement an ongoing job development and job placement program, and assist the LBA with their strategy to revitalize Butler Street" (Lawrenceville Development Corp., *Annual Report, 1991,* 5).

21. Roy Lubove, "Pittsburgh's Allegheny Cemetery and the Victorian Garden of the Dead," *Pittsburgh History* 75 (Fall 1992), 148–56. This is an essay review based on the lavishly illustrated volume by Walter Kidney, *Allegheny Cemetery: A Romantic Landscape in Pittsburgh* (PH&LF, 1990).

22. Population data (in rounded figures) is drawn from Pittsburgh Department of City Planning, *1990 Census of Population and Housing Reports. Report No. 1: Pittsburgh Population by Neighborhood, 1940 to 1990.* The percentage of minority population in Lower Lawrenceville increased from 7.7 percent in 1950 to 14.7 percent in 1990 (although the absolute number decreased from 600 to 390). Comparable figures for minority population were 0.7 and 2.8 percent in Central Lawrenceville, and 0.6 and 2.0 in Upper Lawrenceville.

23. Tim Ziaukas, "From Loups to Lups: After Two Hundred Years, Lawrence-Lawrenceville Gets Hip," *Pittsburgh,* May 1991, 38–42, 58.

24. Urban Redevelopment Authority of Pittsburgh, *1989 Annual Report,* 24; URA, *Lawrenceville Industrial Park* (brochure, n.d.). The Doughboy, a bronze statue by New York sculptor Allen Newman, took its place at the triangle formed by the intersection of Penn and Butler in 1921. The sponsor, the Lawrenceville Board of Trade, raised the necessary $10,000. Marilyn Evert and Vernon Gay, *Discovering Pittsburgh's Sculpture* (Pittsburgh: University of Pittsburgh Press, 1983).

25. The three-bedroom townhouse units will sell for $77,800 to buyers with maximum incomes of $40,600. They will be assisted by URA-deferred second mortgages. URA financing of $1.7 million was supplemented by funds from the Pittsburgh Partnership, PNC Bank and Enterprise Zone. Joyce Gannon, "Sprucing Up the Neighborhood," *Pittsburgh Post-Gazette,* July 31, 1993.

26. The Pennsylvania National Bank Building is now occupied by an architectural firm, and three community groups: LDC, Lawrenceville Citizens'

Council, and the Community Employment Project (*Bulletin* 18 [June 1993], 6).

27. Lawrenceville Development Corporation, *Annual Report, 1991*, 1–2.

28. Jane Downing to author, Interview, July 1, 1993.

29. Richard Swartz to author, written statement, July 1993.

30. Roy Lubove, *Twentieth Century Pittsburgh: Government, Business and Environmental Change* (New York: Wiley, 1969), 27–28; David W. Lonich, "Metropolitanism and the Genesis of Municipal Anxiety in Allegheny County," *Pittsburgh History* 76 (Summer 1993), 79–87.

31. Larry Evans, "Adventures in Stolen City," *In Pittsburgh*, July 25–31, 1990, 21. The comment was by Randy Zotter, a realtor. Indeed, Zotter's grievances included the City of Pittsburgh's devious annexation of Allegheny City: "So I think secession is not out of the question. . . . After all, we *were* stolen."

32. Mary Kane, "Northsiders Fed Up with Homeless Shelters," *Pittsburgh Press*, February 18, 1991; Tom Barnes, "Sprucing Up: North Siders Tackle Neighborhood Blight," *Pittsburgh Post-Gazette*, October 7, 1991.

33. David M. DeBarr, letter to editor, *Pittsburgh Press*, November 19, 1990. DeBarr remembers "as a young child, slowly losing friends and neighbors and having vacant lots appear where their homes once stood. . . . The businesses went too . . . the little stores that would let you bring back the money later if you were a little short . . . the school where all of the teachers knew your name."

34. Richard Swartz to author, written commentary, July 1993. After leaving Pittsburgh, Cox worked for Neighborhood Progress, Inc., in Cleveland. He returned to Pittsburgh to serve as Mayor Tom Murphy's deputy mayor.

35. URA, *Urban Redevelopment Works in Pittsburgh*, Spring 1987, 1. The Brewery had closed in the 1940s.

36. The development group for Riverside Commons included the East Allegheny Development Council. Kendra Berteotti, "Riverside Commons Targets Women, Minorities," *Pittsburgh Business Times*, November 19–25, 1990; Eleanor Chute, "North Side Commercial Venture Appears to be Making Comeback," *Pittsburgh Press*, December 23, 1991; Karen Zapf, "Riverside Commons Secures a Tenant, Two More on Line," *Pittsburgh Business Times*, April 27–May 3, 1992; Margie Romero, "Letdown?" *In Pittsburgh*, May 13–19, 1992, 8, 11; Betsy Benson, "Riverside Commons Incubator Hatching Tenants," *Pittsburgh Business Times*, May 10–16, 1993, 19; URA, *1990 Annual Report*, 25; URA, *1991 Annual Report*, 10.

The North Side suffered an economic setback in winter 1992 when Sears closed its Allegheny Center Mall store, the mall's anchor business. Its demise was precipitated by the 1989 opening of the Sears suburban facility at Ross Park Mall to the north. The frustration of North Side community leaders was expressed by Marjorie Pierce, president of the Fineview Citizens' Council: "We are working so hard to build up the North Side. . . . It seems like every time we gain something, something else is taken away from us." Earl Bohn, "Sears Says It Will Close Its Allegheny Center Site," *Pittsburgh Post-Gazette*, January 3, 1992. However, though less appealing than a retail store or art museum, Integra Financial Corp. soon took over the space vacated by Sears.

37. John C. Brown, Jr., letter to the editor, *Pittsburgh Post-Gazette*, June 24, 1993. The structures cited by Brown included Penn-Highland, Regent Theatre, East Liberty Station Shopping Center, a former Coca-Cola bottling plant on Centre Avenue (which became Centre Commons, an office building).

38. The minority population increased from 12.6 percent in 1950 to 60.8 percent in 1990.

39. Franklin Toker, *Pittsburgh: An Urban Portrait* (University Park: Pennsylvania State University Press), 211–12.

40. "Dave Bergholz Talks About East Liberty," *The Voice*, July 4, 1984, 8.

41. URA, *1987 Annual Report*, 22.

42. Margie Romero, "ELDI Turns to Community to Aid Regent Theatre Renovation," *In Pittsburgh*, April 29–May 5, 1992; Gary Rotstein, "East Liberty Theater is Gaining Support," *Pittsburgh Post-Gazette*, May 4, 1993; "Regent Theatre Completes $1 Million Capital Campaign," *Bulletin* 18 (June 1993); ELDI, *The Regent Returns: A Capital Campaign*. A grant from the Vira I. Heinz Endowment enabled the campaign to reach its $1 million goal. ELDC planned construction for fall 1993 and opening for fall 1994.

43. Marlo Verrilla, "Old Streets Made New: Shopping Districts Update Streets, Retail Shops," *Pittsburgh Business Times*, November 19, 1990, Enterprise supplement, 1s, 16s.

44. Tom Barnes, "Use of E. Liberty High-Rise focus of Feud," *Pittsburgh Post-Gazette*, January 1, 1992; Jim Wilhelm, "East Liberty Office Building Pushed As Apartments for Elderly," *Pittsburgh Press*, February 7, 1992; Tom Barnes, "Council Vote Backs Senior High-Rise Plan," *Pittsburgh Post-Gazette*, February 20, 1992. Court challenges by business interests, who insisted the building could be used for offices which would provide customers for local merchants, delayed development. Although the state court of appeals approved the project in September 1993, further appeal was possible and therefore bank financing was not forthcoming. Tom Barnes, "Housing Plan Crawls at Highland Building," *Pittsburgh Post-Gazette*, October 4, 1993.

45. Letter from Karen La France to author, December 22, 1993.

46. "Return to the Garden," *The East Liberty Quarterly*, Fall 1986, 2; Margie Romero, "East Liberty Renaissance . . . Again," *In Pittsburgh*, March 30–April 5, 1988, 22, 23.

47. Walter Kidney, "Motor Square Garden: An Architectural Perspective," ibid., 23.

48. "Club Plans Move to Historic Motor Square Garden," *AAA Motorist* 38 (July/August 1991), 1, 3.

49. East Liberty, like the North Side earlier, was faced with the closing of a Sears retail store in March 1993. Now boarded up (but acquired by the city in late 1994), it is a large-scale eyesore. The site extended over six acres; the building provided 132,000 square feet of space.

50. ELDI, *25 Things You Can Do to Improve Your Community*. Also Joyce Gannon, "Residents Say Stigma Undeserved: Historic Row House Area In East Liberty Struggles Amid Perception of Crime," *Pittsburgh Post-Gazette*, October, 9, 1993; Gary Rotstein, "Safety a Factor in East Liberty Renewal," *Pittsburgh Post-Gazette*, October 11, 1993; Gary Rotstein, "A New Image for East Liberty," *Pittsburgh Post-Gazette*, July 18, 1994.

51. West End–Elliott Joint Project, Inc., *Urban Design Plan. West End Valley, Pittsburgh, Pa.*, John C. Laatsch and Associates, March 31, 1987, 47.

52. Ginny Frizzi, "Program Builds Community Business," *Allegheny Business News*, January 1991, 16.

53. Richard Swartz to author, written commentary, July 1993. Patrick Media was later bought out by Martin Media.

54. Reverend Henry, a former naval officer, held a B.S. in mechanical engineering from the University of Virginia and an M.Ed. from Duquesne University. Ordained in 1955, he became pastor of Saint Lawrence O'Toole Parish in 1969 (*Bloomfield-Garfield Bulletin* 1 [November 1976], 1).

55. Swartz had joined Housing Opportunities, Inc., in 1979 as program coordinator. Along with graduate work in public administration and social work at the University of Pittsburgh, he was a graduate of the one-year program in community and economic development at the Development Training Institute, Baltimore. Housing Opportunities, Inc., was established in 1975. It is best known now for its Housing Opportunities Earned Home Ownership Program, which provides low-income potential homeowners with mortgages at low interest and with low down payments. In the fiscal year ending June 30, 1993, it had helped over 800 Allegheny County families to buy homes (or saved them from foreclosure). See Thomas Olson, "Housing Opportunities' Low-Income Program Studied," *Pittsburgh Business Times*, May 31–June 6, 1993, 5; "Agency Puts $5 Million in Housing," *Pittsburgh Post-Gazette*, June 30, 1993; Steve Massey, "Helping First Time Buyers," *Pittsburgh Post-Gazette*, August 28, 1993; Ron DaParma, "More Buyers Given Housing Opportunities," *Tribune-Review*, June 26, 1994.

56. Richard Swartz to author, written commentary, July 1993.

57. "BGC Recounts Victories, Looks to Future," *Bloomfield Garfield Bulletin* 2 (May 1977), 1; "BGC Records Strength, Sets '78-'79 Goal, "*Bloomfield-Garfield Bulletin* 3 (Summer 1978), 1.

58. Kelly B. Casey, "Garfield Battles Hookers," *Tribune-Review*, August 29, 1993; " 'They Come Every Day . . . They'll Probably Be Back Tomorrow,' " *Pittsburgh Post-Gazette*, October 1, 1993 ("they" refers to drive-by shooters); Cindi Lash, "Garfield Mother Shot to Death," *Pittsburgh Post-Gazette*, March 24, 1994; Mike Belko, "Caught in the Crossfire," *Pittsburgh Post-Gazette*, March 25, 1994.

59. Rick Swartz, "BGC Meets with Mayor's Office Over Friendship Area Future," *Bloomfield-Garfield Bulletin* 10 (Winter 1986), 1, 3.

60. Tom Barnes, "Preservers of Neighborhoods: Activists' Work Keeps City Districts Alive," *Pittsburgh Post-Gazette*, January 15, 1990. Cited by Barnes as counterparts to Agnes Brose were Harriet Henson, director since 1984 of the Northside Tenants' Reorganization, and Michele T. Balcer, head of the Arlington Civic Council since 1986.

61. Richard Swartz to author, written commentary, July 1993.

62. Melinda Holben, "Tending the Grassroots," *Pitt Magazine* 5 (December 1990), 40–41. The family health center, located on Penn Avenue, originated in a BGC proposal in 1986. The center receives staff support from the Urban League.

63. Richard Swartz to author, written commentary, July 1993.

64. In the summer of 1993, BGC and the Friendship Preservation Group declared war against a 7-Eleven store located on the corner of South Pacific and Friendship Avenues. The concern was over beer sales by the 7-Eleven (which has held a "deli-type" liquor license since 1983 allowing for both bar and over-the-counter beer sales). The neighborhood groups complained that the late-night beer sales "resulted in illegal parking, public drunkenness, noise and trespassing on neighboring residential property," not to mention public urination. The store owner responded with a SLAPP legal action (Strategic Lawsuits Against Public Participation), which was later withdrawn. The BGC, Friendship Preservation Group, and others continued to plague the 7-Eleven throughout the fall and winter of 1993. The store agreed to remove sidewalk phones used by drug dealers and to assign a employee to remove litter within a one-block radius every day. The residents, however, demanded an end to beer sales and curtailment of store hours. John Campanelli, "SLAPPed Neighborhood Groups Refuse to Turn Cheek," *In Pittsburgh*, October 21–27, 1993, 6; Matthew P. Smith, "Sit-in At Store Brings Results," *Pittsburgh Post-Gazette*, November 11, 1993; Michael Romanello, "Neighbors Take Sides in Battle Over Friendship 7-Eleven Beer Sales," *East Side Observer*, December 1993, 1, 20.

65. "A Neighborhood Place," editorial, *Pittsburgh Post-Gazette*, December 10, 1990; "Kayla's Place," NeighborFair Pittsburgh, Inc., *News*, June 1993, 4; George Klimis, "Restaurant Boosts Garfield's Image," *Tribune-Review*, January 31, 1994; Yvette Aldrich, "Restaurant a Sign of Revival," *Pittsburgh Post-Gazette*, June 20, 1994.

Experienced in the food service business and a Garfield resident, Johnson worked with Swartz and the Minority Enterprise Corporation on plans for the prospective restaurant. It opened in March 1993. The entire project, according to Swartz, signaled "to the neighborhood that there are people willing to invest time and money in Garfield, and Kayla's Place stands as a testament to the vitality of the community."

In April 1993, Jack Hutchings opened an art gallery—Garfield Artworks—at 4931 Penn Avenue, next to Kayla's. His aspiration to nurture an artist's colony in Garfield was strongly supported by Rick Swartz, who viewed it as compatible with the BGC strategy to revitalize the business district. Also opened recently on Penn Avenue is the Upstairs Theater. Vacant three- and four-story structures on Penn Avenue are inexpensive, ideal for a Soho-like renaissance. But, as Swartz recognizes, it will be necessary to overcome concerns about personal safety in the neighborhood. Mike Seate, "In Tough City Neighborhood, A Gallery Hangs on," *Tribune-Review,* Allegheny Scene, September 25, 1994.

66. BGC received a grant in 1993 from the Pittsburgh Partnership to hire an intern to work with the Friendship, Bloomfield, and Garfield neighborhoods, as well as a new Penn Avenue Business Association, to "change a lingering perception of the street, building a stronger business district, and recharge the spirit of Penn Avenue." Greg Heisler, "Penn Avenue Business Association: It's Just Good Business," *Bulletin,* June 1993, 2.

67. Pittsburgh Partnership for Neighborhood Development, *Progress Report, 1900,* 10.

68. Richard Swartz to author, written commentary, July 1993. Of the thirty-six units in Laurentian Hall, one was used for the resident manager. One proposed BGC housing project brought into the open a long simmering feud with the Bloomfield Citizens' Council. A twelve-unit apartment at 235–237 Millvale Avenue had been severely damaged by fire in June 1993. BGC acquired the property and planned a development of twelve apartment units or eight condominiums. Court action by Bloomfield Citizens' Council and Friendship Park North was filed in the hopes of blocking use of public funds. The opponents of the BCG plans wanted no high-density redevelopment of the site, especially if it would involve Section 8 rental housing. After months of heated confrontation, BGC in December proposed a side-by-side duplex—owner-occupied units above and rental units on the first floor. The Friendship Park organization withdrew its court challenge and agreed to the plan,though it would have preferred simply two homes, no rentals. Gary Rotstein, "In Bloomfield, a Feud That Won't Die," *Pittsburgh Post-Gazette,* December 27, 1993.

69. Richard Swartz personal interview, July 2, 1993.

70. Roy Lubove, "I. N. Phelps Stokes: Tenement Architect, Economist, Planner," *Journal of the Society of Architectural Historians* 23 (May 1964), 75–87.

71. *Jubilee Journal,* Spring 1992; ibid., Spring 1993.

Chapter 7. Community Development Corporations, II

1. Diana Nelson Jones, "Partners in Putting New Face on Neighborhood," *Pittsburgh Post-Gazette,* April 30, 1990; Breachmenders (Brochure, n.d.). The name of Breachmenders comes from Isaiah 58:6, 10, 12:

> Loosen the bonds of wickedness,
> Undo the heavy burden,
> and let the oppressed go free . . .
> Then you shall be called,
> Restorers of streets to dwell in, and
> Menders of the Breach.

2. Robin Jones, personal interview, August 26, 1993.

3. Joyce Gannon, "Caring for the Community," *Pittsburgh Post-Gazette,* May 15, 1993; David Brewton, remarks at annual meeting, ACTION-Housing, Inc., June 21, 1993.

4. Breachmenders, brochure, n.d.

5. David Brewton, personal interview, August 18, 1993.

6. Letter from David Brewton and Caroline Boyce to Sandra Phillips (PPND), December 1, 1992. Dayna DiRienzo, "Job Links Grads Find Permanent Work Through Temporary Jobs at UPMC," *Oakland* 8 (October 1993), 11; DiRienzo, "Job Links Enters Fourth Year of Service to Oakland," November 1993.

7. Jones, "Partners in Putting New Face on Neighborhood."

8. "Neighborhood Success Story: CCAP," *NeighborFair Pittsburgh Inc,* July 1993, 4.

9. "More Housing Renovation Underway in West Oakland," *Oakland* 4 (June 1991), 3; Joyce Gannon, "Caring for the Community," *Pittsburgh Post-Gazette,* May 15, 1993; Community Loan Fund of Western Pennsylvania, *Investing with a Social Dividend,* n.d.

10. In the decade following 1983, Breachmenders rehabilitated eleven houses for sale and built one more. In addition, it rehabilitated fifty-eight rental units. Breachmenders completed renovation of a four-story, thirty-unit apartment house at 141 Robinson Street in spring 1994. Section 8 subsidies will be provided for low-income tenants.

11. *Breachmenders Summer Youth Trainees,* August 31, 1994; Scarlet Morgan,"Breachmenders Response to the Rising Tide of Gang Violence," *Breachmenders Bulletin,* March 1994, 1–2.

12. OPDC was founded by Peoples Oakland and Community Human Services. See Sue Gottlieb, "Cooperative Community-Oriented Planning and Development are Goals of OPDC," *Oakland* 8 (September 1993), 5. Community Human Services operates in South Oakland, and is a grass-roots advocacy and

service organization. Also active in that neighborhood is the South Oakland Citizens' Council, established in 1965, which maintains an Oakland Social Services Program consisting of a Family Service Unit and Community Activity Center. Among its activities is a Food Pantry, Dollar Energy Fund Agent, and legal counseling (in cooperation with Neighborhood Legal Services).

13. People's Oakland was formed in opposition to the renewal plans that led to the bulldozing of Forbes Field in the early 1970s. It eventually focused its program on mental health services. Cliff Ham, "Forbes Field was a Local Landmark," *Oakland* 8 (October 1993), 5.

14. Steven Ochs, "Different Directions," *In Pittsburgh*, August 7–13, 1991, 5–6.

15. Caroline Boyce, personal interview, October 12, 1993.

16. Courtney S. Walston, "Oakland: Moving into the 1990s," *University Times*, July 20, 1989, 3–6.

17. Central Oakland population in 1950 and 1990: 8,450/5,640; North, 8,060/10,360; South, 7,840/3,360; West, 7,900/1,900. Minority population in 1950 and 1990: Central, 0.5/21.8 percent; North, 1.2/16.1 percent; South, 4.6/39.2 percent; West, 23.6/72.7 percent.

18. In the fall of 1993, two-bedroom units at Holmes Court "garden condominiums" ranged from $28,700 to $59,500. URA financing was available for units involving income limitations.

19. OPDC also renovated Pacelli House, a Victorian structure on Dawson Street, which was turned into six low-income rental units, managed by OPDC.

20. For OPDC development activities, see "About OPDC," *Oakland* 1 (June 1988), 1–2, 8; OPDC, *Ten Year Report, 1980–1990*, May 1990; Pittsburgh Partnership for Neighborhood Development, *Progress Report, 1990*, 17–18.

21. OPDC, *Ten Year Report, 1980–1990*, 2.

22. Caroline Boyce to author, Interview, October 12, 1993.

23. Mike Donovan, "Keeping the Giant in Oakland Makes Life Simple," *Neighbors*, October 15, 1993, 10. Among other things, OPDC helped package URA and PNC Bank loans on behalf of the new franchisee. Caroline Boyce, personal interview, October 15, 1993.

24. Caroline Boyce left OPDC in 1994 to become director of Preservation Pennsylvania.

25. The minority population of the South Side Flats in 1950 and 1990 was 2.0/3.4 percent; for the South Side slopes it was 1.0/2.2 percent.

26. Mary Pat Flaherty, " 'We Have a Way to Go,' " *Pittsburgh Press*, January 16, 1983.

27. Walter C. Kidney, *A Past Still Alive* (Pittsburgh History & Landmarks Foundation, 1989), 123.

28. Pittsburgh History & Landmarks Foundation, *Birmingham: An Area with a Past That Has a Future*, The Stones of Pittsburgh, no. 7, n.d. (circa 1970), 13. Landmarks also claimed that the revitalization program, in cooperation with the South Side Chamber of Commerce and Department of City Planning, would provide a variety of improvements: street lighting, a riverfront park (built in the 1980s), a revitalized Bedford Square Market area and (of dubious desirability) a Carson Street Mall and an expressway.

29. Margie Carlin, "A Walk on the South Side," *Pittsburgh Press*, Roto, June 23, 1974. Landmarks' role in South Side restoration in the 1960s and 1970s is briefly discussed in "The South Side: Securing its Progress," *PH&LF News* 132 (December 1993), 4–5.

30. Flaherty, "We Have a Way to Go."

31. "To Restore," *Closer Look* 2 (n.d.), 2.

32. Member organizations of the Planning Forum, besides SSLDC, include the South Side Antiques, Arts, and Crafts Association (SACA), Brashear Association, Friends of the South Side Branch Library, South Side Antiques, South Side Chamber of Commerce, South Side Community Council, and representatives from religious, educational, and social service organizations. SACA, it should be noted, does not simply represent artists or art-related businesses. It actively recruits "designers, architects, photographers, film makers, book dealers, musicians, actors, art gallery owners, and others involved in the arts, all of which contribute to the cultural life of the South Side." South Side Planning Forum, *The South Side Neighborhood Plan: Modification No. 1*, October 1992, 11. The South Side plan is updated every two years.

33. Caroline Boyce, personal interview, October 12, 1993.

34. South Side Local Development Company (SSLDC), *"The South Side Works," A Community-Based Planning Evaluation: LTV Steel's South Side Mill Site, Pittsburgh, Pennsylvania*, April 15, 1992, 15.

35. Ellen M. Perlmutter, "Residents Protest Project Proposals," *Pittsburgh Press*, June 26, 1991; Rebecca Flora, "Urban Developers Shouldn't Ignore the Benefits of Rehab," *Pittsburgh Business Times*, November 18–24, 1991, 29; "South Side Legal Battle," editorial, *Pittsburgh Press*, February 10, 1992; Joyce Gannon, "Local Real Estate Catches His Eye," *Pittsburgh Post-Gazette*, March 5, 1993; Suzanne Elliott, "Second Chance," *Pittsburgh Business Times*, May 31–June 6, 1993. Grant's legal grievance was based on the claim that the historic designation nomination came barely days before he was scheduled to close on the deal and that he lost $500,000.

36. The Mackintosh-Hemphill Foundry buildings were purchased in 1993 by developer Thomas R. Tripoli, who plans to recycle them into a thirty-five-room hotel and brew pub. Presumably, the external architectural integrity of the structures will be retained. Gary Rotstein, "Motel, Dining, History in Plans," *Pittsburgh Post-Gazette*, September 9, 1994.

37. In keeping with the Catholic diocese's reorganization plans, Saint John the Evangelist Church, South Fourteenth Street, was demolished in the summer of 1993. The fate of Saint Michael's Church is uncertain.

38. Suzanne Elliott, "South Side Retail Business Corridor May Gain City's Historic Designation," *Pittsburgh Business Times*, January 11–17, 1993, 2; SSLDC, *Developments*, Fall 1992.

39. Author's notes, Historic Review Commission, public hearing, March 5, 1993.

40. Tom Barnes, "South Side Group Tries to Stop Sale of Mon Land," *Pittsburgh Post-Gazette*, May 14, 1992.

41. The Board of Education withdrew its offer and the land remained unsold as of summer 1993.

42. SSLDC, *"The South Side Works"*, letter of transmittal from Rebecca Flora to Hugh Brannon, president of the South Side Planning Forum, and Harry A. Henshaw, director of real estate, LTV Company, 28.

43. Ibid., 23, 13, 30.

44. The South Side Planning Forum, as mentioned, had adopted the South Side Neighborhood Plan in 1990. A Riverfront Plan had also been approved by the Planning Forum in April 1992. Including the LTV-site proposal, the Planning Forum thus adopted three plans in 1992.

45. Rebecca Flora, "Community Development is Maintaining a Sense of Community," South Side Local Development Company, *1992 Annual Report*, 1. SSLDC has recently ventured into housing development. It completed in July 1991 the five units of Phase I of Edwards Court, located in the South Side flats at Thirteenth and Breed Streets. These, and the five units of Phase II, will be priced for middle-income buyers. And in 1933 SSLDC planned to rehabilitate and sell two abandoned, vandalized townhouses at South Eleventh and Bingham Streets; in addition, the adjoining two-story brick house would be renovated. SSLDC is also working with a developer who hopes to transform a ninety-five-year-old red brick former Catholic school on South Fifteenth Street into loft-condominiums. A second former Catholic school on Pius Street is also being converted into condo units. Urban Redevelopment Authority of Pittsburgh, *Urban Redevelopment Works in Pittsburgh*, Fall 1991, 3; Joyce Gannon, "Urban Retreats," *Pittsburgh Post-Gazette*, June 1993; South Side Local Development Company, *Developments*, Spring 1993, 1–2; Joyce Gannon, "Schooled in Condo Living: Former South Side Catholic School Converted into Condominiums," *Pittsburgh Post-Gazette*, July 10, 1994.

In the summer of 1993, SSLDC was also studying the possibility of a 300-unit housing development between Sixteenth and Nineteenth Streets on 8.3 acres parallel to the Monongahela River. The project was launched in 1994 (with substantial URA funding and land acquisition—three sites costing almost $3 million). The initial phase is the twenty-six-unit Fox Way Commons, bounded by South Seventeenth and Eighteenth Streets, Fox Way, and Wharton Street. The original plan, calling for 118 owner-occupied townhouse units and 188 rental units, was changed in the summer of 1994 in response to community preferences for homes rather than rental property. The revised plan provided for 160 for-sale units and 124 rentals (48 of which would be for the elderly). Ron DaParma, "Project Could be Forerunner of Complex," *Tribune Review,* July 29, 1993; Rebecca Flora, personal interview, August 5, 1993; Gary Rotstein, "Down by the Riverside: Housing Plan Takes Advantage of South Side's Riverfrong Assets," *Pittsburgh Post-Gazette,* January 31, 1994; Tom Barnes, "City Buys Sites on South Side," *Pittsburgh Post-Gazette,* February 22, 1994; Gary Rotstein,"Resident Input Boosts Number of For-Sale Units in S. Side Plan," *Pittsburgh Post-Gazette,* May 31, 1994; "SSLDC Moves Ahead with Fox Way Commons Development," South Side Local Development Company, *Developments,* Winter 1994, 1; "South Side Plans Riverfront Housing," URA Pittsburgh, *Urban Development Works in Pittsburgh,* Spring 1994, 5.

Other recent activities—commercial, cultural, recreational—include the negotiations leading to a URA loan toward the reopening of the Neville Ice Rink on Twenty-first Street; helping to adapt the Gimbels warehouse for reuse; and, as of 1989, managing the South Side Summer Street Spectacular, a festival that helps to fund neighborhood groups. Beth Pollock, "South Side Development Focus now on Housing," *Pittsburgh Business Times,* January 7–13, 1991; Pittsburgh Partnership for Neighborhood Development, *Progress Report, 1990,* 22.

46. The Murphy administration's rationale for its arrangement with Hospitality Franchise Systems (HFS), negotiated secretly with no consultation with neighborhood interests, is that the city, facing a $27 million deficit, had no money and that it had to act quickly to prevent LTV from selling the land to someone else—leaving the city with no leverage at all. The arrangement also provides that HFS pay for a master development plan. If neighborhood opposition or other obstacles prevent gambling on the site, HFS can withdraw, but the city will have two years to acquire another purchaser.

47. Dan Donovan, "Westgate Strives for New Image," *Pittsburgh Press,* September 23, 1991.

48. Westside Community Development Corporation, "Financing Proposal for the Westside Laundromat," February 1991 (to the Pittsburgh Partnership for Neighborhood Development).

49. Jon Schmitz, "4 Inner-City Rite Aids Slated," *Pittsburgh Post-Gazette,* June 25, 1993.

50. Tom Barnes, "Westgate Village Pins Hopes on Project," *Pittsburgh Post-Gazette,* March 11, 1991; "Making the Projects Livable," editorial, *Pittsburgh Post-Gazette,* March 12, 1991.

51. Gary Rotstein, "Selling Hope in a Tough Market," *Pittsburgh Post-Gazette*, February 13, 1993; Rotstein, "Westside Board Suspends President," *Pittsburgh Post-Gazette*, March 3, 1993.

52. The problem centered in the Manchester Development Corporation, established in 1983 as a for-profit subsidiary of the Manchester Citizens' Corporation. The problems included a failure to keep separate records for the two operations, a $215,000 deficit, missing funds, and internal animosities (Ellen M. Perlmutter, "Deficit, Feuding, Lost Funds Plague Manchester Group," *Pittsburgh Press*, December 15, 1985).

53. Jane Downing, personal interview, July 1, 1993.

54. Meg Cheever, "Conversation" (Mulugetta Birru), *Pittsburgh*, August 1992, 112, 63, 111.

55. URA, *1990 Annual Report*, 23; HBRDC, *New Informer*, March 15, 1991, 4.

56. Ellen M. Perlmutter, "Market Holiday," *Pittsburgh Press*, February 23, 1991; David Guo, "An Able Hand in Homewood-Brushton," *Pittsburgh Post-Gazette*, May 14, 1991; Lynda Guydon Taylor, "Farmers Market Opens," *Pittsburgh Post-Gazette*, May 25, 1991; Alex Kotlowitz, "Community Groups Quietly Make Strikes in Inner-City Housing," *Wall Street Journal*, September 17, 1991; "Homewood Mall Wins $350,000 in City Funds," *Pittsburgh Business Times*, June 22–28, 1992.

57. Heather McFeeley, "Homewood-Brushton," *Allegheny Business News*, March 13, 1991, 20.

58. The URA provided $100,000 in August 1993 toward the $750,000 first phase of the Coliseum project. It contributed an equal sum toward renovation of a Frankstown Avenue building—a collaborative project between the HBRDC and the Black Contractors' Association for twenty-five units of incubator space for minority construction firms. Tom Barnes, "Homewood Gets City Aid for Coliseum, Office," *Pittsburgh Post-Gazette*, August 13, 1993.

59. Gary Rotstein, "Homewood Shops Hope Good Times Ahead," *Pittsburgh Post-Gazette*, July 6, 1993. Rotstein points out that merchants in 1992 had to finance increased security and cut hours at the same time that sales fell.

60. Kidney, *A Past Still Alive*, 122.

61. Supplementing the MCC in efforts to renew Manchester was the Bidwell Education, Music, and Recreation Center. The center operates an after-school, settlementlike program for youth. Another significant community resource is the Manchester Craftsmen' Guild, created and directed by William E. Strickland, Jr. Strickland also manages the Bridwell Training Center, a vocational school located in the Craftsmen's Guild. See Abby Mendelson, "Manchester Revisited: A Peaceful Revolution Works to Save a Neighborhood," *Pittsburgh*, March 1989, 27–28; Candy C. Williams, "Strickland's Mission: Develop Self-

Worth Through Self-Expression," *Tribune Review*, Sunday Focus, April 17, 1994.

62. Pittsburgh Partnership for Community Development, *Progress Report, 1990*, 20–21. Tragically, a good deal of the documentary record of Manchester since the 1950s, and the MCC, was lost in a fire in February 1993 at its offices on Nixon Street.

63. Laurence Glasco, "A Double Burden: The Black Experience in Pittsburgh," in *City at the Point: Essays in the Social History of Pittsburgh*, ed. Samuel P. Hays (Pittsburgh: University of Pittsburgh Press, 1989), 75–76.

64. The Irene Kaufmann Settlement was established in 1909 at the present site of the Hill House Center. When the former departed in 1957, it was replaced by the Anna B. Heldman Center. A Health and Welfare Association study on the Hill District in 1962 recommended establishing a new social agency to deal with the area's problems. This led, in 1964, to the merger of the Heldman Center, Hill City Youth Municipality, and Soho Community House. The current facility for the Hill House Center opened in 1972.

In 1969, the Hill House Association organized the Hill House Housing Development Corporation to take advantage of the HUD section 236 program. This enabled local nonprofit organizations to establish housing development corporations that could receive 100 percent financing for housing plan development. Each approved project resulted in the creation of a separate corporation. *The Hill House Association*, n.d., 2, 9; Shari Kubitz, "Hill House at 25," *Pittsburgh Post-Gazette*, October 16, 1989. The Hill House Center is one of four buildings within six blocks that constitute the association.

65. Earl Kohnfelder, "Uptown Residents Taking to Streets to Drive Out Prostitutes," *Pittsburgh Press*, May 13, 1991; M. Galicchio, "Controversial State Liquor Store to Close," *Tribune-Review*, December 23, 1992; Gary Rotstein, "Nothing Makes It Go Away," *Pittsburgh Post-Gazette*, July 11, 1994; Kelly B. Casey, "Uptown Residents Seething Over Sex for Sale," *Tribune-Review*, August 7, 1994.

66. Tom Barnes, "Council Votes to Raze Stanton Heights Mall," *Pittsburgh Post-Gazette*, June 30, 1993; "Crumbling Strip to Be Demolished," *Tribune-Review*, June 24, 1993; Tom Barnes, " 'Crack House' Shut Down," *Pittsburgh Post-Gazette*, June 30, 1993.

The Garfield-Jubilee Association had planned to develop a shopping center on the Stanton Heights site (the URA had already allocated funds to buy the property) when it learned in December 1993 that the property had been sold to a Jehovah's Witnesses congregation for a Kingdom Hall. However, the congregation agreed in April 1994 to sell two-thirds of the 3.7-acre site to the URA. With URA assistance, the Garfield Jubilee Association will build three stores, including a supermarket and drugstore. Tom Barnes, "Land Sale Deflates Center's Backers," *Pittsburgh Post-Gazette*, December 25, 1993; Gary Rotstein,

"Stanton Plaza Plan Revived with Church," *Pittsburgh Post-Gazette*, April 15, 1994.

67. URA, *1991 Annual Report*, 19.

68. Marylynne Pitz, "10-Year Effort Bears Fruit," *Pittsburgh Post-Gazette*, August 9, 1991.

69. Robert Pease to author, written commentary.

70. Vince Rause, "Welcome Back to the Hill," *Pittsburgh*, March 1992, 32.

71. Ibid., 33.

72. By the late summer of 1994, all 203 rental units were occupied. Rents ranged from $284 a month for a one-bedroom unit to $795 a month for a three-bedroom unit; and twenty-five of the twenty-seven sale units had been sold. Eligibility requirements for the 101 "affordable " rental units included income for $13,400 to $15,420 for individuals, and $19,020 to $22,020 for a family of four. Suzanne Elliott, "Crawford Square Builds Homes in Hill," *Pittsburgh Business Times*, August 16–22, 1993, 5; "Hill District," *Pittsburgh Post-Gazette*, September 10, 1993; Ron DaParma, "URA Funds Projects in 3 Neighborhoods," *Tribune-Review*, September 11, 1993; Gary Rotstein and Tom Barnes, "Rebuilding the Hill: Brightened Outlook for a Blighted Area," Part I, *Pittsburgh Post-Gazette*, December 12, 1993; Rotstein and Barnes, "Rebuilding the Hill: Next Step, Shopping Center to be Developed," *Pittsburgh Post-Gazette*, December 13, 1993.

In the winter of 1994, tenants in the rental units complained about unsatisfactory heating, snow clearance, and unresponsive management. Homeowners, organized in a Crawford Square Homeowners Association, complained later in the year that facilities on the blueprints (rear door, rear deck) were deleted, that promised tennis courts were never built, that air conditioning did not work, that landscaping was not done. Although the URA maintains that any large development will have such problems at the outset, McCormack Baron was replaced as developer for the next phase of thirty sale units. Tom Barnes, "Phase 2 of Crawford Square Will Involve New House Builder," *Pittsburgh Post-Gazette*, August 26, 1994; Barnes, "Criticism at Crawford Square," *Pittsburgh Post-Gazette*, September 12, 1994.

73. Matthew P. Smith, "Filling a Need on Hill," *Pittsburgh Post-Gazette*, April 11, 1993; URA, *1991 Annual Report*, 19; URA, Department of Housing, *Overview 1990*, 18. Western Restoration Center will consist of the Western Manor (thirty-one units); Center City Apartments (thirty-nine units) and a community health center; Riverview Terrace (forty-seven units) for the frail elderly along with supportive services.

74. URA, *1990 Annual Report*, 13.

75. Daniel Bates, "Hill District Struggling to Redevelop Commercial District Despite Obstacles," *Pittsburgh Business Times*, February 24, 1992, 11, 12.

Two independent developers have also expressed interested in using the New Granada as the anchor for redeveloping the entire block bounded by Wylie and Centre Avenues, Erin Avenue, and Devilliers Street. Tom Barnes, "Arts Revival for Hill"? *Pittsburgh Post-Gazette*, September 6, 1993.

Another Hill project is the effort to resurrect the Phoenix Hill Shopping Center on Centre Avenue not far from Crawford Square. Opened in 1975 on URA-owned property, it was acquired by new owners at a sheriff's sale in 1983. They went bankrupt in the summer of 1990. The property was purchased in the fall of 1991 by the Allegheny Union Baptist Association, a group of 152 Western Pennsylvania Baptist churches who hope to restore a supermarket and small retail facilities to the neighborhood.

76. Polish Hill is a tight-knit ethnic community. Its spectacular Italian Baroque Immaculate Heart of Mary Church was built in 1905–1906. Two domed towers frame a classical portico. Behind these towers is a dominant central dome ninety-eight feet high. The terrain of Polish Hill is remarkably steep and windy, even for Pittsburgh. The neighborhood lies above the Strip, where it pushes into Lawrenceville. The 1990 population is 1,610, down from nearly 4,900 in 1950. Old-time residents still remember when " 'if you did something wrong, you were in fear. Because before your dad walked up from work, he already knew what you did. Your neighbor could scold you; you respected your elders' " This was recalled by Ann Davis, age seventy-four. Mary Ann Thomas, "Polish Hill Embraces Center," *Pittsburgh Press*, November 20, 1990. See also Clarke Thomas, "Happy on the Hill," *Pittsburgh Post-Gazette*, January 22, 1992.

77. The site had been vacant for two years as a result of a 1990 fire that destroyed the existing four houses. The four units represented phase two of the EACC's Avery Homes project. Phase 1, completed in 1989, involved the restoration of four houses across the street. Financing for the new units was provided by the URA, Pittsburgh Partnership, Pittsburgh History & Landmarks Foundation, PNC Bank, PNC Foundation. "4 North Side Rowhouses Replace Razed Homes," *Pittsburgh Post-Gazette*, July 31, 1993; "East Allegheny," NeighborFair Pittsburgh Inc., *News*, September 1993, 2.

78. URA, *1989 Annual Report*, 26–27. Figures for total CBO housing and commercial development from the formation of the Pittsburgh Partnership in 1983 to June 1, 1993, are as follows:

    1. Community-based housing (total: 1,151 units: 548 sale, 603 rental).

        a. *Completed projects:* PPND affiliates: 572 units (363 sale, 209 rental). The largest production was by Oakland Planning and Development, 240 units, followed by Bloomfield-Garfield Corporation, 89 units. Independents (project financing by PPND, but not operating expenses): 43 units (19 sale, 24 rental). Total: 615 (382 sale, 233 rental).

        b. *Under construction:* PPND affiliates: 39 units (4 sale, 35 rental) Independents: 64 units (7 sale, 57 rental). Total: 103 units (11 sale, 92 rental).

c. *In predevelopment:* PPND Affiliates: 310 units (96 sale, 214 rental). Independents: 123 units (59 sale, 64 rental). Total: 433 units (155 sale, 278 rental).

2. Commercial Development (total: 733,101 square feet).

a. *Completed projects:* PPND affiliates: 576,001 square feet. Independents: 10,000 square feet. Total: 586,001 square feet.

b. *Under construction:* PPND affiliates: 16,000 square feet. (HBRDC). Total: 16,000 square feet.

c. *Predevelopment:* PPND Affiliates: 114,400 square feet. Independents: 16,700 square feet. Total: 131,100 square feet. Pittsburgh Partnership for Neighborhood Development, *Investment Highlights,* July 1993.

Chapter 8. Community Development in Allegheny County

1. Allegheny Conference on Community Development (ACCD), *1984 Report,* 14; ACCD, *1987 Annual Report,* 12; ACCD, *1988 Annual Report,* 7; LISC, "Monongahela Valley LISC," 1993; "Joint Statement: A New Partnership in the Mon Valley," 1988.

2. Eichler, who received a master's degree from the School of Social Work, had worked with Morton Coleman, who recommended him for a position at the Allegheny Conference. Although originally hired by Pease as a staff member of the conference, he was later employed by LISC as program manager and housed at the conference. Robert Pease, personal interview, July 8, 1993, and written commentary, September 10, 1993; Morton Coleman, personal interview, July 26, 1993; see also Ross Gittell, "The Role of Community Organization in Economic Development: Lessons from the Monongahela Valley," *National Civic Review* 78 (May–June 1989), 192–95; Gittel, *Renewing Cities* (Princeton: Princeton University Press, 1992), 149–56.

3. This section is based on remarks by Michael Eichler at the Mon Valley Initiative's fifth annual dinner meeting, October 22, 1993.

4. Jo DeBolt to author, written commentary, August 1993. Bergholz was assistant director of the Allegheny Conference. Beukema was program officer at the Howard Heinz Endowment.

5. Jo DeBolt to author, written commentary, November 1993.

6. The MVDT consisted of the following: *Development specialists* Jo Harper [DeBolt], director of development; Silvio Baretta, development specialist; Karl Schlachter, housing specialist; *Community organizers* Pat McElligott, director of organizing and community organizer in Monessen and Charleroi; Ray Garofola, community organizer in Monongahela, Glassport, Swissvale, Homestead, and Rankin; Pauline Cooper, community organizer in Braddock, McKeesport, Clairton, Turtle Creek, and Duquesne; Marianne Rodacy, community organizer in

Elizabeth. Beginning in 1991, LISC and Eichler launched MVDT-like projects in Little Rock, New Orleans, and Palm Beach County, Florida.

7. Allegheny Conference on Community Development, *1988 Annual Report*, 6–7.

8. Populations represented by the four CDCs in 1990 were: Duquesne Business Advisory Corporation (1979), 8,500; Homestead Economic Revitalization Corporation (1978), encompassing Homestead, 4,180, Munhall, 13,000, and West Homestead, 2,500; McKeesport Development Corporation (1984), 26,000; Wilmerding Community Improvement Advisory Committee, 2,200. All communities are in Allegheny County.

9. Populations represented by the nine CDCs in 1990 were: Greater Charleroi Community Development Corporation (Washington County), encompassing Charleroi, 5,000, and North Charleroi, 1,560; Community Economic Development Corporation of Clairton, 9,600; Elizabeth Area Development Corporation, encompassing Elizabeth Borough, 1,595, Elizabeth Township, 14,700, and Forward Township, 3,870; Glassport Development Corporation, 5,580; Monessen Community Development Corporation (Westmoreland County), 9,800; Monongahela Area Revitalization Corporation (Washington County), encompassing Monongahela City, 4,900, and New Eagle, 2,170; Rankin Community Development Corporation, 2,500; Swissvale Economic Development Corporation, 10,600; and Turtle Creek Development Corporation, 6,550.

10. Allegheny Conference on Community Development, *1988 Annual Report*, 9. The Tindall Building had been fire-damaged. In 1994 the Homestead Area Economic Revitalization Corporation initiated efforts to upgrade a half-mile section of East Eighth Avenue, the main business artery running through Homestead, Munhall, and West Homestead. This will be coordinated with street facade upgrading by store owners. Todd Gutnick, "Homestead Area Plans $3.5 Million Face Lift," *Tribune-Review*, March 10, 1994.

11. Ibid., 9–10. According to a promotional piece issued by the McKeesport Development Corporation, the Business Growth Center would provide the entrepreneur with shared office services, reception center and "access to 15 technical and management assistance programs to strengthen and develop your company."

12. Mon Valley Initiative, *Proposal to the Heinz Endowments and the Pittsburgh Foundation*, September 12, 1988, 2.

13. Populations represented by the three CDCs in 1990 were: Brownsville Area Revitalization Corporation (Fayette County), 3,160; Braddock Housing Task Force, 4,680; East Pittsburgh Economic Development Corporation, 2,160.

14. Populations represented by the two CDCs in 1990 were: North Braddock Cares, population, 7,000; Downtown West Newton, Inc. (Westmoreland

County), 3,150. The McKeesport Development Corporation was dropped in 1993, reducing the total to seventeen.

15. Mon Valley Initiative (MVI), *Proposal to the Heinz Endowments and the Pittsburgh Foundation*, September 12, 1988, 3.

16. The MVI established a "Community Investment Fund" to channel loans and grants to the CDCs.

17. Bohdan Hodiak, "Blame for Mon Valley Group," *Pittsburgh Post-Gazette*, September 15, 1993; Eric Heyl, "Official Says Mon Valley Initiative Failing," *Tribune-Review*, September 15, 1993. Officials of McKeesport, the Steel Valley Council of Governments, and the Mon Valley Progress Council used the incident to voice criticism of the MVI as bureaucratic and ineffectual. Wes Cotter, "McKeesport Kicked Out of MVI for Renegade Tactics," *Pittsburgh Business Times*, September 13–19, 1993, 4; Cotter, "Raging Bull," ibid., September 20–26, 1993, 12.

18. Jo DeBolt to author, written commentary, August 1993.

19. Brownsville Area Revitalization Corporation, for example, publishes *The Enterprise*, and Homestead Area Revitalization Corporation, *On the Avenue*. The MVI itself publishes a quarterly newsletter under the editorial control of the board's public relations committee.

20. Allegheny Conference on Community Development, *1988 Annual Report*, 11–12; "Joint Statement: A New Partnership in the Mon Valley"; Jo DeBolt to author, written commentary, August 1993.

21. Mon Valley Initiative, *Proposal to the Heinz Endowments and the Pittsburgh Foundation*, September 1991, 11.

22. Ibid., 8.

23. University Center for Social and Urban Research, Graduate School of Public Health, Katz Graduate School of Business, University of Pittsburgh, *Greater Pittsburgh Revitalization Initiative: Evaluation of GRPI Program, Progress Report Year Three*, 1991, 26.

24. Wes Cotter, "Croft Expands Steel Valley Authority's Reach," *Pittsburgh Business Times*, June 27–July 4, 1993, 10.

25. Wes Cotter, "Early Warning Project Gets Grant from Integra Bank," *Pittsburgh Business Times*, August 17–23, 1992, 6.

26. Steel Valley Authority, *Progress Report*, 1st Quarter, 1992, 1.

27. Cotter, "Croft Expands Steel Valley Authority's Reach," 10.

28. Steel Valley Authority, "Statement to Board Members and Friends," June 2, 1992, 5.

29. "SVA initially focused entirely on a white ethnic constituency, but has since evolved a far more comprehensive approach. Its jobs-based vision now extends beyond basic manufacturing . . . and beyond its immediate white work-

ing class constituency." Bennett Harrison, "Emerging CDC Trends: Networking to Enhance Job Creation and Employment Training Initiatives," Economic Development Assistance Consortium, *Developments*, Summer/Fall 1993, 12.

30. Wes Cotter, "Agency's Strategy Draws Heavy Fire Along Mon Valley," *Pittsburgh Business Times*, October 28–November 3, 1991, 23.

31. Ibid., 1, 23. Cotter's article generated a flood of rejoinders which continued for several months: David Levdansky, state representative, 39th district: "Working with the Mon Valley Initiative, we were able to secure approximately $300,000 in loans from the Initiative to match a state DER grant in excess of $500,000. This result is that the city of Clairton . . . had established a state-of-the-art, premier recycling facility" (*Pittsburgh Business Times*, December 16–22, 1991).

Domenic J. Curinga, mayor of Clairton: "Does anybody honestly believe that the small, distressed Mon Valley communities can successfully compete for economic and community development funds against larger cities in the area that are fortunate enough to have a professional staff . . . ? Through the community organizing efforts of the MVI, Clairton now has a group of citizens who are actively rejuvenating the city's tax base, creating jobs, and stabilizing residential districts" (*Pittsburgh Business Times*, December 9–15).

William Davies, president of the Swissvale Economic Development Corporation: "The MVI staff that assists the community development corporations are hardworking, dedicated professionals that know where to go to get things done. They offer legal and technical expertise that is fundamental and necessary for the success of each local corporation" (*Pittsburgh Business Times*, December 23–29, 1991).

Howard E. Noll, president of the Monessen Community Development Corporation: "Had your staff had the time to accept my invitation to the June 6, 1991, ground-breaking ceremony for the $1.4 million incubator project in the city of Monessen, you would have been inspired with the attendance of over 100 . . . citizens who observed how grass roots citizens can improve the quality of life in their community and how, with the help of the Mon Valley Initiative, the MCDC has prepared a unique, innovative, and diversified plan for the financing of this project" (*Pittsburgh Business Times*, November 18–24, 1991).

32. Wes Cotter, "In the Mon Valley, Community Groups Duel for Turf, Clout," *Pittsburgh Business Times*, September 14–20, 1992, 31.

33. Jo DeBolt, interview, August 19, 1993, and written commentary, August 1993.

34. Ibid.

35. Letter from Jo DeBolt to author, January 20, 1993.

36. Jo DeBolt, lecture, Homestead, Pa., July 19, 1992.

37. Mon Valley Initiative, *Proposal to the Heinz Endowments and the Pittsburgh Foundation*, September 1991, 10.

38. Jo DeBolt agrees that a CDC, or the MVI, would fail if its action was identified as "politically motivated." And she refers to the by-laws which prohibit CDCs from membership in "politically-controlled organizations," thus demonstrating "our keen awareness of the need for political neutrality." What she approves of, she claims, is not that people run for office "but that the people running for office are people who had been underrepresented in the political structure—women and African Americans" (Jo DeBolt to author, written commentary, August 1993). It seems to me, however, that it makes no difference who runs for office if the political activism is identified with CDC participation or encouragement.

39. Mon Valley Initiative, *Proposal to the Heinz Endowments and the Pittsburgh Foundation*, September 12, 1988, 9.

40. Mon Valley Initiative, *5 Years of Progress: The Accomplishments of the Mon Valley Initiative*, 1993, 18.

41. Richard Florida, "Building the Future," *Executive Report*, February 1993, 16, 18–20, 32; Carnegie Mellon University, H. John Heinz III School of Public Policy and Management, *Rebuilding America: Lessons from the Industrial Heartland* (Pittsburgh, December 1992).

42. Jack Markowitz, "Sand Pit Spells Hope in Mon Valley," *Tribune-Review*, June 27, 1992. However, the city council voted against a coal-blending facility in the vicinity of the RIDC project. Tom Barnes, "Plan for Coal Blending Facility Has Friends, Foes in Duquesne," *Pittsburgh Post-Gazette*, May 3, 1993.

43. Mon Valley Initiative, *Bi-Annual Report*, January 15–July 15, 1989, 5.

44. Ibid., 6–7; Mon Valley Initiative, *1990 Year-End Report*, 16.

45. Mon Valley Initiative, *1990 Year-End Report*, 25–27.

46. Letter from Jo DeBolt to author, January 20, 1993. DeBolt maintains that this section may "overstate" her view in the sense that development and community organizing are more important and that these activities were low priority in terms of staff or board time and resources (written commentary, August 1993).

47. University Center for Social and Urban Research, Graduate School of Public Health, Katz Graduate School of Business, University of Pittsburgh, *Greater Pittsburgh Revitalization Initiative: Evaluation of GPRI Program, Progress Report Year Three*, 1991, 8.

48. Mon Valley Initiative, "MVI Funds Support Community Development," n.d. The MVI received an additional $800,000 for specific purposes: Pennsylvania Department of Community Affairs, housing; U.S. Dept. of Health and Human Services, equity grant to Monessen Business Development Center; Allegheny Foundation, housing in Braddock.

49. The MVI Board of Delegates reviews predevelopment grant requests (usually $5,000–10,000 but sometimes up to $50,000). Activity grant requests

up to $1,000 are decided by the director. If there is any question, or if the request exceeds $1,000, it is referred to the executive or finance committee. The MVI board also determines the operating budget. The Heinz Endowment did not release funds for the CIF until the Board was established, but it "never made any suggestions as to membership and were not consulted on this subject" (Jo DeBolt to author, written commentary, August 1993).

50. Mon Valley Initiative, *1990 Year End Report*, 7.

51. Draft, "Commercial District Revitalization Plan," Mon Valley Initiative, *Proposal to the Heinz Endowments and the Pittsburgh Foundation*, September 1991.

52. *Valley Vision*, Spring 1993, 1; Tom Barnes, "Mon Valley Firms Getting High-Tech Help," *Pittsburgh Post-Gazette*, March 20, 1993; Barnes, "Mon Valley Seeking Funds," *Pittsburgh Post-Gazette*, May 27, 1993. The Manufacturing Center was co-sponsored by the East Pittsburgh and Turtle Creek CDCs. LISC offered $500,000 for the Partnership for Jobs and Industry if matched locally.

Launched in March 1993, the Partnership was the first undertaking growing out of a decision by the MVI in 1992 to devise a regional plan to create and preserve jobs. LISC had advised the MVI in the development of the strategy. Also involved in the planning were Carnegie Mellon University's Center for Economic Development, the Southwestern Pennsylvania Industrial Resource Corporation and Bob Brandwein, an economic development consultant (Richard Wallace, "Statement," third annual MVI Community Development Conference, May 1, 1993; LISC, "Monongahela Valley LISC," 1993).

What the MVI envisioned, through the Partnership for Jobs and Industry, was to nudge the Mon Valley in the direction of high-performance manufacturing:

> High performance regions provide the crucial elements required for high performance manufacturing to flourish. These include: a manufacturing infrastructure of interconnected vendors and suppliers, a human infrastructure of qualified workers, engineers and researchers, and a communications and transportation infrastructure which facilitates constant sharing of information and just-in-time delivery of goods and services. New partnerships among business, labor, community and government will be required to provide these crucial inputs—to develop the broader political economy which can support the shift to high performance."

MVI, "Partnership for Jobs and Industry," 1–2.

53. Mon Valley Initiative, *Proposal to the Heinz Endowments and the Pittsburgh Foundation*, September 1991, 11. An example of this process would be the Hawthorne Avenue Program sponsored by the Swissvale Economic Development Corporation (SEDCO). Hawthorne Avenue contained a group of some twenty rowhouse units that suffered from "drug dealing, a shooting, and many lesser incidents that had many residents afraid of their own neighborhood." A SEDCO member helped organize a protest at City Council attended by the

press. The group also documented incidents and allegedly inadequate police response. Police protection improved, the housing units were offered at a sheriff's sale and were purchased by SEDCO to be turned into low-moderate income housing ("SEDCO to Begin Renovation," *Free Press*, July 22, 1993).

54. Jonathan E. Zimmer, personal interview, August 24, 1993.

55. ACTION-Housing, Inc., *1957-1992: 35 Years of Investment in Housing, Neighborhoods and People*, 7, 11. East Hills was built in four phases over 130 acres. Phase I, 187 townhouses and 91 rentals, was completed in 1964. Phase II, 326 townhouses and apartments, was completed in 1969. Phase III, 140 townhouse units, and Phase IV, a 157-unit high rise for the elderly, were completed in 1972.

56. Eastgate was privately developed on land sold by ACTION-Housing (which maintained design controls). It consisted of 120 detached sale units. No subsidies were involved. Liberty Park in East Liberty consisted of a 332-unit townhouse and apartment development along with Penn Circle Towers, 152 apartment units. Allegheny Commons East consisted of 138 apartment units in Allegheny Center, North Side. Palisades Park in Rankin encompassed 46 townhouses and Palisades Manor, a 48-unit rental apartment and commercial area. Greenway Park, located in Pittsburgh's West End, consisted of 200 cooperative townhouses and 81 apartments.

57. Brophy went on leave in May 1977 to establish the city's new housing department at the request of Mayor Caliguiri. He then became the department's director. Zimmer became acting director in May 1977, then executive director in April 1978.

58. Jonathan Zimmer, personal interview, June 3, 1993.

59. ACTION-Housing, Inc., *1957–1982: 25 Years of Housing and Neighborhood Improvements*, 17; ACTION-Housing, Inc., *Chairman's Report, 15th Annual Meeting (1973)*, 5, 6.

60. ACTION-Housing, Inc., *1957–1982*, 17.

61. ACTION-Housing, Inc. *Annual Report, 1974*, 6.

62. Barbara Gubanic, "Steps Eyed to Pump New Life into Ailing East Hills Shopping Center," *Pittsburgh Post-Gazette*, February 19, 1980.

63. Charlyne H. McWilliams, "East Hills Center Set for Change," *Pittsburgh Post-Gazette East*, August 15, 1991; "Shopping Center to be Revamped," *Pittsburgh Press*, July 25, 1991. The owners (Eastgate Associates, a New York partnership) by the summer of 1994 hoped to convert the site into a medical and social service support center. Eleanor Chute, "East Hill Site Tries to Attract Clientele," *Pittsburgh Post-Gazette*, June 15, 1994.

64. ACTION-Housing, Inc., *Chairman's Report, 15th Annual Meeting*, January 1973, 5–6.

65. Jonathan E. Zimmer, personal interview, June 3, 1993.

66. ACTION-Housing, Inc., *1957–1992*, 19. The Allegheny County Neighborhood Preservation Program affected seventeen neighborhoods and 1,354 homes. It was based on code enforcement, low-interest home improvement loans, and public investment. Participating communities included Duquesne, Homestead, Munhall, Wilkinsburg, North Braddock, Swissvale, and Bethel Park. Interest subsidies accompanied bank loans.

67. Jonathan E. Zimmer, personal interview, June 3, 1993.

68. ACTION-Housing, Inc., *Chairman's Report, 15th Annual Meeting*, 5.

69. Roger S. Ahlbrandt, "Partnerships in Meeting the Community's Housing Needs," September 1990, 22. Ahlbrandt pointed out, however, that the United Way contribution was only $250,000 toward a budget exceeding $3 million. The main part derived from contracts with government or private agencies, and from foundation grants (14).

70. Jonathan E. Zimmer, personal interview, June 3, 1993.

71. ACTION-Housing, *Annual Report, 1985*, 11.

72. ACTION-Housing, Inc. and the Advisory Committee on Housing for the Homeless, *A Comprehensive Plan to Address the Problem of Homelessness in Pittsburgh and Allegheny County*, Pittsburgh, June 25, 1985; ACTION-Housing, *Annual Report, 1989*, 8. Along with recommendations for an expanded system of short-term, emergency shelters and bridge housing, the *Comprehensive Plan* recommended: (1) Housing and services for the homeless population not able to achieve self-sufficiency because of a physical or mental disability. (2) Prevention of homelessness by programs to assist individuals faced with evictions, mortgage foreclosures, or utility shutoffs; expanding the supply of good affordable housing. (3) State and federal legislation reforming the welfare system, and extending health services, job training and economic development. Based on existing studies of the homeless problem, the report claimed that 1,800 individuals and 2,700 members of families would confront homelessness in 1985 (viii).

73. The 1982 study of personal care homes in Pittsburgh and Allegheny County led to a demonstration program of facility improvement, a model zoning ordinance for personal care homes in Pittsburgh, and a URA loan program enabling personal care providers to upgrade their facilities.

ACTION-Housing contributed to the development of six personal care facilities with over 250 beds for the frail elderly and disabled. These included the Eileen Jordan Memorial Center in North Versailles (168 beds), and the Homestead Center (62 beds). The other facilities were located in Pittsburgh's East Liberty, Northside and HIghland Park sections, as well as Bellevue. It worked with the URA and a private developer on a 137-bed personal care home on Pittsburgh's South Side. It involved the conversion of the former Saint Joseph's Nursing School and Residence. As a consultant to the Riverview Center for Jewish Seniors in Squirrel Hill, ACTION-Housing evaluated sites for a personal care facility, leading to its establishment in a section of the Center's nursing facility (fifteen beds). It also advised the Eastminster Presbyterian Church and East Liberty Family Heath Center in developing a facility for short-term care for elderly released from area hospitals.

74. ACTION-Housing, *Annual Report, 1988,* 4.

75. Ibid., 10; ACTION-Housing, *Annual Report, 1989,* 14.

76. Under contract with the Allegheny County of Development, ACTION-Housing in 1985 advised Transitional Services, Inc., on HUD funding for the rehabilitation of facilities for the mentally ill in Robinson Township and McKees Rocks (twenty individuals). In 1989, in partnership with Residential Resources, Inc., ACTION-Housing obtained funding from the Pennsylvania Department of Public Welfare and Housing Finance Agency to develop forty units of scattered-site housing for the mentally disabled.

ACTION-Housing used every opportunity to advocate community-based housing. This was the recommendation in a 1987 survey (with the Three Rivers Center for Independent Living)commissioned by the Pennsylvania Developmental Disabilities Planning Council. Also, in the late 1980s, ACTION-Housing designed "new approaches" for the community-based housing and services for the mentally ill and retarded.

77. In 1989, ACTION-Housing secured six parcels of land in Pittsburgh's Garfield and Highland Park neighborhoods, along with Swissvale and Wilkinsburg, to develop twenty-four units of scattered-site housing for the physical and mentally disabled. In 1990, ACTION-Housing and the Enterprise Corporation joined to create the Supportive Housing Management Services, Inc. It will maintain the special-needs housing facilities of ACTION-Housing and other nonprofit organizations. It is testimony to the pervasive presence of the foundations in contemporary social policy. The SHMS is supported by grants from four foundations: Alcoa, Hillman, PPG Industries, Richard King Mellon.

78. In 1989, ACTION-Housing joined Bridge to Independence in the development of Debra House II. Located in an adjoining school building, it would provide twenty units of permanent housing. Around the same time, it worked with the North Hills Affordable Housing Task Force, and Community of Benedictine Sisters, to create an eighteen-unit bridge housing facility for women and children in the vacant Street Benedict's School in Ross Township. Kathleen Neuser, "Group Works for Affordable Housing," *Franklin Park Herald,* May 2, 1990.

Sojourner House, an East End Cooperative Ministry project in Pittsburgh's East Liberty neighborhood, was designed to serve single mothers suffering from drug or alcohol problems; a bridge facility, it can accommodate fifteen mothers and children.

79. ACTION-Housing, *1986 Annual Report,* 11.

80. Jonathan E. Zimmer, personal interview, June 3, 1993.

81. Burns Heights and Cochrandale in Duquesne; Hawkins Village in Rankin; Talbot Towers in Braddock; McKees Rocks Terrace and Hays Manor in McKees Rocks. Talbot Tower was scheduled for demolition because of disrepair and poor (high rise) design.

82. Bob Hoover, "The Door to Independence," *Pittsburgh Post-Gazette,* January 17, 1991; Jonathan E. Zimmer, "Helping Vulnerable Populations to Achieve Higher Levels of Self-Sufficiency Through Community-Based Housing and Supportive Service Programs," prepared for the National Association of Housing and Redevelopment Officials, November 1988. Reprinted by National Association of Housing and Redevelopment Officials and American Public Welfare Association, September 1989.

83. ACTION-Housing, *Annual Report, 1984,* 15.

84. Ibid.

85. The weatherization and energy saving programs included:
- Rent Brake Thru Energy Conservation, funded by the Pittsburgh URA;
- Low Income Energy Assistance Program, funded by the U.S. Department of Energy and Pennsylvania Department of Community Affairs, which covered fifteen communities in northern Allegheny County;
- WeatherGrant Program, funded by Governor's Energy Council;
- Project Payback, funded by the Pittsburgh foundations, which applied to multifamily rental projects and provided inducements to landlords and tenants;
- Furnace Retrofit Program for emergency furnace repair or replacement;
- Columbia Gas Company Emergency Furnace Repair Program;
- Duquesne Light Company Weatherization Program.

In addition, ACTION-Housing had been involved in energy conservation as early as 1977 through Operation Button-Up. Administered by ACTION-Housing, and the Allegheny County Departments of Health and Redevelopment, it provided subsidies for low-income families for weatherization.

86. ACTION-Housing, *1988 Annual Report,* 14; Bill Steigerwald, "Public-Private Partnership Rescues Houses in Clairton," *Pittsburgh Post-Gazette,* April 19, 1990. The development was expected to generate $90,000 a year in taxes to Clairton and Allegheny County. As of July 1993, 87 units had been sold, and 100 rental units had been completed. At the end of the project, ACTION-Housing anticipated that 100 units would be sold, 100 rehabilitated and rented, 89 unimproved and rented at a lower rate. Ten units were lost in conversion to three-bedroom units, and the model unit would be sold. ACTION-Housing, "Plan for the Balance of Units at Century Townhomes," July 15, 1993.

Another moderate-income project was Homewood Park Estates. Initiated by Homewood-Brushton's Operation Better Block, assisted by ACTION-Housing, it will consist of eighteen single-family homes.

A grant from the Pennsylvania Department of Community Affairs enabled ACTION-Housing and the McKeesport Redevelopment Authority to launch a neighborhood preservation program in 1990. It will provide subsidized loans and technical assistance to low-income homeowners in specified neighborhoods to enable them to correct code violations.

ACTION-Housing also planned, through its AHI Development subsidiary, to build Willow Trees Apartments in the North Hills, with 234 units.

Chapter 9. Amenities and Economic Development

1. Review by David West of "The Aeneid," *Wall Street Journal*, July 25, 1991.

2. William S. Hendon and Douglas V. Shaw, "The Arts and Urban Development," in *The Future of Winter Cities*, vol. 31, ed. Gary Gappert (1987), 209–17.

3. Robert H. Mcnulty, Dorothy R. Jacobson, R. Leo Penne, *The Economics of Amenity: Community Future and Quality of Life: A Policy Guide to Urban Economic Development* (Washington, D.C.: Partners for Livable Places, 1985), emphasis in original.

4. Horton Plaza covered eleven acres of downtown San Diego near San Diego Bay. Color enhanced the visual impact and the architect, Jon Jerde, "put all the public areas outdoors." Harold R. Snedcof, *Cultural Facilities in Mixed-Use Development* (Washington, D.C., Urban Land Institute, 1985), 84–85. Witold Rybczynski, "The New Downtowns," *Atlantic* 271 (May 1993), 106.

5. An interesting example of a city which reinvigorated its downtown, not with a cultural complex, but through landscape and design, is Portland, Ore. The elements included parks, Pioneer Courthouse Square, brick sidewalks, trees and flowing water. In addition, the city prohibited ground level blank walls (even parking garages had to have stores or other activity). Philip Langdon, "How Portland Does It," *Atlantic* 270 (November 1992), 134–36, 138–39, 141–41.

6. Snedcof, *Cultural Facilities in Mixed-Use Development*, 236–55. The Morris Mechanic Theater was superseded in the mid-1970s by the nonprofit Baltimore Center for the Performing Arts. Rouse's Harborplace complex consists of two glass pavilions.

7. Ibid., 196–97. The city of Cleveland and Cuyahoga County also participated in the development of Playhouse Square.

8. Jennifer Dunning, "St. Louis Is Rebuilding Its Once-Grand Theater District," *New York Times*, August 29, 1991.

9. J. Allen Whit and Allen J. Share, "The Performing Arts as an Urban Development Strategy: Transforming the Central City," in *Deindustrialization and the Restructuring of American Industry*, ed. Michael Wallace, and Joyce Roothschild (Greenwich, Conn.: JAI Press, 1988), *Research in Politics and Society, A Research Annual* 3:162–63; J. Allen Whitt and John C. Lammers, "The Art of Growth: Ties Between Development Organizations and the Performing Arts," *Urban Affairs Quarterly* 26 (March 1991), 381–83.

Other smaller communities that have discovered "the advantages of building a performing arts center, for the economic, and social as well as the cultural benefits they[sic] bring" include Greenville, S.C.; Chattanooga, Tenn.; Helena, Ark.; Boise, Idaho. The $42 million Peace Center in Greenville included a concert hall, theater and cabaret, and riverside amphitheater. Lyn Riddle, "Building for the Performing Arts in Smaller Cities," *New York Times*, April 21, 1991.

An example of an arts- and service-driven revitalization strategy in England can be found in Birmingham. As in Pittsburgh, the steel industry disintegrated in the 1980s, and the city turned to "projects intended to attract service industries and the affluent, educated people who work in them." The City of Birmingham Symphony under Simon Rattle has become a significant force in the city's cultural revitalization. Craig R. Whitney, "Birmingham's Soot Is History. Victoria Should Visit Now," *New York Times*, December 18, 1990.

10. J. Allen Whitt, "The Arts Coalition in Strategies of urban Development," in *The Politics of Urban Development*, ed. Clarence N. Stone and Heywood T. Sanders (Lawrence: University Press of Kansas, 1987), 144–56; Paul J. DiMaggio, "The Nonprofit Instrument and the Influence of the Markertplace on Policies in the Arts," in American Assembly (Columbia University), *The Arts and Public Policy in the United States* (Englewood Cliffs, N.J.: Prentice-Hall, 1984), 23–37.

11. "The Carnegie Institute and Library became simply 'The Carnegie' in a public relations effort in the 1980s that tried to end the confusion in the public mind over the complex organizational structure of the institution" (Robert J. Gangewere, written commentary, October 1993).

12. The Wilburn era also included the establishment of the Heinz Architectural Center, and significant improvements to the Carnegie's Oakland complex: sandblasting and washing decades of dirt off the buildings, and the construction of a multilevel garage off the Scaife extension. Wilburn had formerly been Pennsylvania's secretary of education and secretary of budget and administration, president of Indiana University of Pennsylvania, and a Chase Manhattan Bank vice-president. He left the Carnegie to become president and chief executive officer of the Colonial Williamsburg Foundation. Donald Miller, "Wilburn to Leave Carnegie Institute," *Pittsburgh Post-Gazette*, April 14, 1992; Patricia Lowry, "The Carnegie Thrived Under Wilburn, a Tough Act to Follow," *Pittsburgh Press*, April 17, 1992.

13. R. Jay Gangewere, "From Zeiss to Omnimax and Digistar: The Evolution of a Science Center," *Carnegie Magazine*, September/October 1991, 20–21.

14. John G. Rangos, through the Chambers Development Charitable Foundation, gave $5 million to endow the Omnimax operating expenses. It is indeed a technological wonder and well worth experiencing on that basis.

15. For an architectural critique, see Mike May, "The Malling of the Mind: Thumbs Down to the Architecture," *In Pittsburgh*, October 2–8, 1991, 1, 6–7. It was designed by the Tasso Katselas firm—much favored by government and civic institutions in Pittsburgh.

16. This is the *U.S.S. Requin*, hauled to Pittsburgh from Tampa, Florida, where it had failed to generate much tourist traffic.

17. Donald Miller, "Science Center," *Pittsburgh Post-Gazette*, March 28, 1991; Karen Zapf, "Science Center Sparks New Vision," *Pittsburgh Business Times*, November 19, 1990, 4s; Lynne Margolis, "The Carnegie Science Center: Pittsburgh's Amusement Park for the Mind Opens," *SRO*, September 19, 1991, 7.

18. "Awaiting a Science Center," editorial, *Pittsburgh Press*, October 9, 1991.

19. Al DeSena, "A Message from the Director," *Carnegie Magazine*, September–October 1991, 22. DeSena resigned in April 1993 and was succeeded in the summer of 1994 by Seddon L. Bennington, an Australian who had been executive director of the Scitech Discovery Centre in Perth.

20. The Carnegie vacated the Buhl in the winter of 1994. Its future use remains undecided.

21. What I most looked forward to as a preteen grade school student in New York City was the occasional class trip to the Museum of Natural History (and its wondrous planetarium). There were no interactive exhibits and similar mush. It was, relatively speaking, a contemplative and therefore truly educational experience.

22. Todd DePastino, "The Selling of the Science Center," *In Pittsburgh*, March 11–17, 1993, complains that "relatively few exhibits present in an even-handed way the drawbacks and benefits of a technology; instead, most simply show the operation of technology and blandly sing its virtues." (9)

23. Mike Seate, " 'Nintendo on Steroids': Thumbs Up to the Gizmos," *In Pittsburgh*, October 2–8, 1991, 1, 7, 35.

24. Attendance in 1992 was 740,000. It dropped to 600,000 in 1993,and was 50,000 less from January to August 1994 compared to the same period in the previous year. Ellen M. Perlmutter, "A Simple Taste of Science," *Pittsburgh Post-Gazette*, August 21, 1994.

25. "Welcome for Warhol Museum," editorial, *Pittsburgh Post-Gazette*, October 9, 1989.

26. Megan Shay, "Bringing Andy Home," *In Pittsburgh*, January 24–30, 1990, 20–22.

27. Robert J. Gangewere, written commentary, October 1993.

28. Ibid. 21. The architect selected for the renovation, at the urging of the DIA Foundation, was Richard Gluckman of New York City.

29. At the outset, in 1989, Mark Francis was selected by the Carnegie to serve as both curator of contemporary art and director of the prospective Warhol Museum. But as the latter expanded in scope, the Carnegie decided it needed a full-time administrator. Armstrong faced a major funding challenge—raising the $20 million balance of the $35 million needed. Carol Vogel, "Pittsburgh Museum for Warhol Works Names a Director," *New York Times*, January 6, 1993; Donald Miller, "New Director Sizes Up an Up-Sized Warhol Museum," *Pittsburgh Post-Gazette*, January 24, 1993.

30. Carnegie Institute expansion also included the Heinz Architectural Center, opened November 1993.It was a $10 million gift of the Drue Heinz Foundation in honor of H. J. Heinz II. The entire *Carnegie Magazine* for November–December 1993 is devoted to the new center.

31. Carol Hymowitz, "This Museum Has a Liking for Artists Who Trash the Place," *Wall Street Journal*, October 17, 1991.

32. Letter from Joyce Baskin to Sandra Phillips, December 7, 1990.

33. Letter from Charles Howell to Sandra Phillips, January 11, 1991. Howell suggested that completion of the work on the primary gallery would encourage northward development of the neighborhood.

34. Barbara Luderowski, letter to Sandra McAllister Ambrozy (of the Kresge Foundation, Troy, Michigan), January 4, 1991; *The Mattress Factory Proposal to the Kresge Foundation*, January 4, 1991, 5, 12.

35. Committee on Pittsburgh Archaeology and History, "The Development of a Pittsburgh Museum of Industrial Society: A Concept Planning Document," February 1986 (based on a conference entitled "Salvaging Pittsburgh's Past: A City History Museum," November 16, 1985), 2, 1; "The Need for a City Museum," *Pittsburgh Heritage* (n.d.), 2. See also John F. Bauman, "Preserving Pittsburgh's Industrial History," *Pittsburgh Post-Gazette*, February 17, 1990.

36. Lillian Thomas, "History Marches On," *In Pittsburgh*, December 11–17, 1991, 7, 17.

37. One of the major exhibits of the new era featured life and work in Homestead. Another featured Homewood-Brushton. In pursuit of archival material, the society established new links with various ethnic communities—Polish, Jewish, Slovak, Italian. The society acquired a three-story, ten-room house built in 1852 in the working-class neighborhood of Lawrenceville; belonging to the Kins family, it would be turned into a museum depicting the life of a Polish immigrant family in 1920–1940. And the society's lecture series increasingly

focused on ethnic and working-class history. Also in keeping with the new interest in social history, the society acquired the Willow Diner, a 1930s eatery that had resided in Irwin, Westmoreland County, and will be displayed at the Regional History Center.

A significant contribution to regional ethnic and working-class history was the industrial and ethnographic survey undertaken by the Society in 1989–1991 in connection with the Steel Industry Heritage Task Force. Historical Society of Western Pennsylvania, "Society to Conduct Mon Valley Historical Survey," *Notes from the Three Rivers*, Fall 1990, 1.

A valuable addition to the Historical Society's collections was the H.J. Heinz Company's donation in December 1993 of its entire collection of 35,000 artifacts and 200,000 photographs. This was supplemented by a Heinz Company Foundation grant of $321,000 to maintain the collection and prepare exhibits.

38. Tom Barnes, "County to Aid History Center," *Pittsburgh Post-Gazette*, December 17, 1991; John A. Herbst, "Report of the Executive Director," Historical Society of Western Pennsylvania, *1992 Annual Report*, 3; John A. Herbst, "History Center Breaks New Ground," *Pittsburgh History* 77 (Summer 1994), 51. The city of Pittsburgh was to reimburse the county for half the $3.1 million upon sale of a bond issue in the spring of 1992.

39. Historical Society of Western Pennsylvania, *Making History* 2 (Winter 1993), 2; Donald Miller, "History Center Honors Heinz," *Pittsburgh Post-Gazette*, June 16, 1994. The Historical Society hopes to raise an additional $10 million to support the Center, renamed in June 1994 the Senator John Heinz Pittsburgh Regional History Center. Of the more than $22 million raised by the spring of 1994, about $11 million came from government sources; corporations and corporate foundations provided over $2 million; private foundations contributed nearly $8 million ($1.5 million from the Howard Heinz Foundation, $0.5 million from the Vira I. Heinz Foundation). Private individuals contributed about $1 million by late 1994.

40. Important to the success of the Regional History Center was recruiting author David McCullough as an advocate and fundraiser. The same was true of Frank Cahouet, chairman and CEO of Mellon Bank. William C. King, retired vice-president of Gulf Oil, played a key role in revitalizing the Historical Society after becoming president of the board of trustees in 1985.

41. Barnes, "County to Aid History Center." Frank Lucchino, county comptroller, was an influential supporter of the History Center. His law partner, Stephen Graffam, had been a trustee.

42. Historical Society of Western Pennsylvania, *1991 Annual Report*, 9; Heather S. McFeeley, "Historical Society Seeks New Homes," *Allegheny Business News*, March 27, 1991, 21; "Advance for a History Center," editorial, *Pittsburgh Post-Gazette*, November 2, 1989.

43. "Western Pa. Life to Be in Museum's Spotlight," *Greater Pittsburgh Newspaper*, October 22, 1992; "History Center Exhibit Planning Moves into

Second Busy Year," Historical Society of Western Pennsylvania, *Notes from the Three Rivers,* Fall 1990, 2; John A. Herbst, "A Tour of the Future at the Regional History Center," *Pittsburgh History* 73 (Spring 1990), 30; Eleanor Chute, "Regional History Museum Proposed for Strip District," *Pittsburgh Press,* November 28, 1989; Mike Yeomans,"Paying Homage to Pittsburgh's Past," *Pittsburgh Post-Gazette,* Sunday Magazine, August 21, 1994; Don Traub, "HSWP Preparing Major Exhibition to Tell Story of People and Development of Western Pennsylvania," Historical Society of Western Pennsylvania," *Making History,* September 1994, 4.

44. "The Pittsburgh Cultural Trust," mimeo, February 1993, 1.

45. On the earlier effort, see William J. Mallett, "The Lower Hill Renewal and Pittsburgh's Cultural District," *Pittsburgh History* 75 (Winter 1992–93), 172–90. The Heinz Endowment had offered $8 million toward a symphony hall if the city would commit itself to a broader arts center and clearance east of Crawford Street toward the Upper Hill (184).

46. Allegheny Conference on Community Development, *1984 Report,* 12; *1983 Report,* 12. The trust was brought into existence by a "consortium of Pittsburgh corporate leadership" brought together by the Allegheny Conference, the city, the county, and the Howard Heinz Endowment ("The Pittsburgh Cultural Trust," 1).

47. Pittsburgh Cultural Trust, *The First Five Years, 1984–1989,* 1.

48. Prior to the trust, Carol Brown had been deputy controller for Allegheny County, director of the Allegheny County Bureau of Cultural Programs, and director of the county's Department of Parks, Recreation, and Conservation. She joined the trust's board of trustees in 1984 and became president in 1986.

There had been a short-lived predecessor organization—the Pittsburgh/Allegheny County Cultural Alliance, established around 1980. It published in August 1982 *The State of the Arts in Pittsburgh and Allegheny County.* In March 1989, the Pittsburgh Cultural Trust released *The Economic Impact and Financial Health of the Arts in Pittsburgh,* prepared by the Pennyslvania Economy League. Both surveys, not surprisingly, found that the arts contributed greatly to the local economy.

In its capacity as arts promoter, the trust in 1990 launched the Lively Arts Getaway program involving local hotels and arts organizations. It offered weekend packages that combined hotel accommodations and performance tickets. Diana Nelson Jones, "Cultural Trust, Hotels Market City as Showplace," *Pittsburgh Post-Gazette,* March 21 1990.

49. The trust operating budget runs $10–14 million a year, and it receives a $2 million yearly subsidy. Carole Brown, personal interview, 1993.

50. The Howard Heinz Endowment was established in 1941. The Vira L. Heinz Endowment was created in 1986. Howard Heinz's son, H. J. Heinz II, served as chairman of the endowment until his death in 1987. His involvement

in the cultural initiatives was active and hands-on. Henry Beukema, personal interview, June 23, 1993.

Kyra Strassman, "The Cultural Trust's Risky Vision," *In Pittsburgh*, May 27, June 2, 1993, 8–11, argues that the Cultural Trust consumes a disproportionate portion of the local funding pie for the arts and that Pittsburgh might not be able to afford both the Cultural District and its other arts organizations: "The city's funding sources run the risk of overcommitting arts dollars to a single group which may have a flawed vision of Pittsburgh's cultural future" (9).

While the issue is arguable, the author does not provide the data or documentation to prove the point. One consideration might be that any imbalance is not entirely attributable to the Trust. It would be more accurate to say that an elite group of arts and cultural organizations gets the lion's share of funding. These would include the Carnegie Institute, Pittsburgh Symphony, Pittsburgh Opera, Pittsburgh Ballet Theatre, and, more recently, the Historical Society of Western Pennsylvania in connection with its Regional History Center. In 1987, for example, the Heinz Endowment gave $650,000 to the Pittsburgh Public Broadcasting Corporation, $525,000 to the Pittsburgh Ballet Theatre, $300,000 to the Pittsburgh Opera, and $226,800 to the Pittsburgh Symphony Society.

Another consideration is that the other organizations are funded, but in lesser amounts because their scale of operation is smaller and they are not involved in major development. Thus in that same year, the Howard Heinz Endowment provided numerous grants (starting at $3,000 for the Blatent Image Gallery) to cultural organizations. Beneficiaries included the Bach Choir of Pittsburgh, Civic Light Opera Association, Mattress Factory, Pittsburgh Center for the Arts, Pittsburgh Dance Council, Pittsburgh Filmmakers, Pittsburgh History & Landmarks Foundation, Pittsburgh New Music Ensemble, Pittsburgh Public Theater, Renaissance and Baroque Society of Pittsburgh, River City Brass Band, Three Rivers Arts Festival. And, needless to say, the Heinz Endowment was not the only source of funding for these other organizations (Howard Heinz Endowment, *Annual Report, 1987*, 13–15). Nonetheless, it is probably the case that the vitally important but less prominent arts organizations are underfunded, particularly at a time when corporate giving is reduced and foundations emphasize human services more than in the past. As Clarke Thomas remarks ("Culture's Last Grasp," *Pittsburgh Post-Gazette*, June 1, 1994):

> This community may be behind the curve in its heavy emphasis upon [the] behemoths, as against the smaller arts organizations and opportunities for arts people that increasingly are taking the spotlight in city-by-city comparisons nowadays.

One solution might be the cooperative fundraising strategy recently adopted by six smaller groups. The Contemporary Arts Stabilization Trust is a consortium consisting of the City Theater, Dance Alloy, Mattress Factory, Pittsburgh Filmmakers, Pittsburgh New Music Ensemble, and Society for Contemporary Crafts. Money raised, divided between an endowment fund and a programming fund, will be shared equally. Donald Miller, "6 Arts Groups Join Forces to Form Mutual Endowment," *Pittsburgh Post-Gazette*, September 14, 1994.

51. Marylynn Uricchio, "City's Glitter Fades Quickly at Nightfall," *Pittsburgh Post-Gazette*, August 25, 1984.

52. This was the view of Frank Brooks Robinson, head of the RIDC and member of the trust board. Marylynn Uricchio, "A Cultural District," *Pittsburgh Post-Gazette*, September 25, 1987, supplement.

53. The Allegheny Conference noted that the Howard Heinz Endowment's "generosity and foresight made possible the acquisition of the necessary properties and the employment of consultants to carry out much of the detailed planning work" (Allegheny Conference on Community Development, *1983 Report*, 12).

54. For a detailed account of the real estate dimension of the CNG/Benedum project, see Pennsylvania Economic League, *Downtown Development in Renaissance II: Cost Benefit Study*, prepared for the Urban Redevelopment Authority of Pittsburgh, April 1988, 26–29; Harry Kloman, "The Art of the Deal," *Pittsburgh*, April 1990, 39–43. Involved in the transactions was the Allegheny International Realty Development Corporation. The Public Auditorium Authority leased the land for the Benedum to that corporation which, in turn, assigned the rights to the Cultural Trust; and the Penn-Liberty Holding Company, retaining ownership of the CNG Tower land, leased it to the AIRDC for eighty-two years, payments going to the Cultural Trust. In addition, the URA gave AIRDCO a low-interest Urban Development Action Grant loan of $8.5 million for the CNG Tower (repayment over eighty-two years), but the URA transferred the note to the Cultural Trust. Allegheny International, Inc., was to be the anchor tenant for the CNG Tower, but filed for bankruptcy in winter 1988.

55. Michael Benedum, who made his fortune as an oil and gas wildcatter, and Joseph C. Trees formed the Benedum-Trees Oil Company in Wheeling; then it moved to Pittsburgh in 1907. The company acquired the Benedum-Trees Building on Fourth Avenue in 1911. Benedum established his foundation in 1944 and died in 1959 at age ninety. Susan Puskar, "Mr. Benedum," *Pittsburgh Post-Gazette*, September 25, 1987, supplement.

56. Patricia Lowry, "Treasured Tiles Escape Auction," *Pittsburgh Post-Gazette*, October 9, 1993. It should be noted that Landmarks, following the destruction of the Moose Building in 1984, elicited an agreement from the city to avoid further demolition between the Benedum and Convention Center (primarily on behalf of the blocks of historic commercial buildings) and obtained a National Register of Historic Places nomination for the section. It later become a city historic preservation district. Walter C. Kidney, *A Past Still Alive: The Pittsburgh History & Landmarks Foundation Celebrates Twenty-Five Years* (PH&LF, 1989), 20.

57. The Trust was also able to get rid of Doc Johnson's adult bookstore, housed in a three-story structure across from the Benedum. It bought the property in the spring of 1992, and the bookstore closed in March. Joyce Gannon, "Cultural Trust Buys Building," *Pittsburgh Post-Gazette*, April 17, 1992; Dan Cook, "Cultural Trust Searches for Anchor; Finds Porno Theater," *In Pittsburgh*, February 17–23, 1994, 5.

58. The trust's Art Services Division also offers financial, fundraising, and management assistance to some 200 smaller arts organizations. It maintains an arts management library in the Carnegie Library's downtown business branch. And until it closed in December 1993, it managed the TIX booth on USX Tower Plaza, which sold tickets on behalf of eighty-five arts organizations ("The Pittsburgh Cultural Trust," 6).

59. Handicrafts are sparsely represented also. There is a sales outlet in Fifth Avenue Place maintained by the Shadyside-based Pittsburgh Center for the Arts.

60. Gallery G, on Ninth Street between Penn and Liberty Avenues, had been downtown since the mid-1980s, but closed in 1993. Another gallery, 808 Penn Modern, had opened in October 1991. Following the Wood Street Galleries (October 1992) came Gallery 937 on Liberty Avenue, sponsored by the Associated Artists of Pittsburgh (January 1993), and the Stormer Gallery, Penn Avenue (February 1993). These galleries face an uncertain future in a city that does not seem capable of sustaining a flourishing visual arts gallery infrastructure. See Margie Romero, "Downtown Art," *In Pittsburgh*, June 17–23, 1993, 24–26; Patricia Lowry, "Not a Pretty Picture," *Pittsburgh Post-Gazette*, October 31, 1993.

The Trust offers shared office space for arts organizations in the Wood Street Station Building. Pittsburgh Cultural Trust, *Update*, October 1 993, 2.

61. Mary Kilroy has been a consultant to the Trust's Public Art Committee. She has directed the Philadelphia Redevelopment Authority's One Percent Arts Program (1 percent of construction costs in urban renewal areas goes to art works). Carol Brown, personal interview, October 1, 1993; Donald Miller, "Cultural Trust Names Consultant," *Pittsburgh Post-Gazette*, Weekend Magazine, August 6, 1993.

The Trust in September 1993 commissioned a mural by a New York artist, Richard Haas, a master of *trompe l'oeil*, to be painted on the Duquesne Boulevard side of the Fulton Theater, visible from the North Side. Thirty-six by fifty-six feet, it portrays a vaudeville theater interior and two Bessemer steel converters. The Trust announced in summer 1994 that it had commissioned Takamasa Kuniyasu to design a sculpture for its forthcoming parklet at Penn Avenue and Seventh Street. Tom Barnes, "Coming Attraction at Fulton: City's Third Giant Mural," *Pittsburgh Post-Gazette*, September 17, 1993; "Stacked Pottery Sculpture Commissioned for Parklet," *Tribune-Review*, July 3, 1994.

62. Bob Hoover, "The Fulton: Past, Present and Future," *Pittsburgh Post-Gazette*, May 31, 1991.

63. More than thirty organizations, presenting 150 performances, appeared at the Fulton in its first season, September 1991–August 1992.

64. The Northside Conference in 1991, to no avail, had proposed the renovation of the Garden Theater (X-rated films) and Masonic Building on North Avenue and Federal Street to accommodate the Public Theater and retail facilities. However, the nearby Federal North Project involving the improvement of a rundown commercial district progressed when the state released $3 million in July 1994 toward a Allegheny General Hospital medical education and research center at Federal North. It had been a Strategy 21 proposal. Bob Hoover, "Public Theater Weighing Move to Cultural District," *Pittsburgh Post-Gazette*, January 18, 1992; Regis M. Stefanik, "Public Theater Votes to Exit North Side," *Pittsburgh Post-Gazette*, January 21, 1992.

65. The central plaza-park would serve as a district focal point and "location for outdoor gatherings and events." The Trust plans a public competition for design of the park (23,000 square feet). The Trust also intends to include a new entrance to the Fulton Theater in the Penn and Seventh Street complex; it would open on the plaza and provide access to the parking garage. "The Pittsburgh Cultural Trust. Downtown Cultural District Development—Phase II: Seventh and Penn Land Assemblage Development," March 1992, 3.

66. Donald Miller, "A Spotlight on Theater Square," *Pittsburgh Post-Gazette*, April 11, 1993; Chris Swaney, "An Office-Theater Complex for Pittsburgh," *New York Times*, August 28 1992; Suzanne Elliott, "Trust Taps Philly's Oliver Tyrone to Develop Office/Theater Complex," *Pittsburgh Business Times*, September 21–27, 1992, 2; Pittsburgh Cultural Trust, "Request to the State Redevelopment Capital Assistance," data sheet.

67. Pittsburgh Cultural Trust, *The First Five Years*, 12.

68. Patricia Lowry and Donald Rosenberg, "A Cultural Blueprint," *Pittsburgh Press*, May 19, 1991.

69. Pittsburgh Cultural Trust, *The First Five Years*, 4. Trust plans included the creation of an entertainment center consisting of four to six nightclubs. It cited successful models in Atlanta, Orlando, Dallas, and Richmond. This was still under consideration in 1993.

The 1990 planning document also raised the possibility of a two-level riverfront park. Fort Duquesne Boulevard might then emerge "as an in-town residential area—similar to Chicago's Lake Shore Drive." Pittsburgh Cultural Trust, *A Unique Draw for Downtown: The Pittsburgh Cultural District*, 1990. This document summarized the *Strategic Implementation Study for the Cultural District*, completed in October 1990 by a group of consultants.

What is projected is a two-tier park along 2,000 feet of the Allegheny River. The lower tier, now used for parking, would connect Point State Park and the

Convention Center and be used for recreational purposes; the upper tier would become an overlook park and promenade parallel to Fort Duquesne Boulevard. The promenade tier would require extensive relocation of the westbound lanes of Fort Duquesne Boulevard South.

The Trust anticipates that the proposed park would attract private investment and "spawn a residential edge along Fort Duquesne Boulevard." To encourage residential settlement, the Trust intends to create a gap financing pool. The park-promenade, in league with the North Shore Allegheny Landing, Carnegie Science Center, Warhol Museum, and Convention Center, would "constitute a major destination for tourists." "The Pittsburgh Cultural Trust Downtown Cultural District Development—Phase II: River Promenade and Riverfront Parks," March 1992, 1.

In September 1994 the Trust announced the appointment of Michael Van Valkenburgh Associates, a Cambridge, Mass., landscape architecture firm as director of design for the park.

70. The Pennsylvania Economy League's figures for 1989–1990 activity in the Cultural District (Heinz Hall and the Benedum) are as follows. Ticket revenue: $20,043,890; performances: 427; tickets sold: 1,025,080. (Prior to the opening of the Benedum in 1987, attendance at Heinz Hall averaged 570,000 for 260 performances.)City, county, and school district tax revenues from the Cultural District in 1990 totaled $16,803,032, an increase from 1986 of $8,884,529. Pennsylvania Economy League, Western Division, *The Impact of the Cultural District on the Pittsburgh Area*, prepared for the Pittsburgh Cultural Trust, November 1990, 2; "The Pittsburgh Cultural Trust," 2.

71. Robert H. McNulty, R. Leo Penne, Dorothy R. Jacobson, *The Return of the Livable City: Learning from America's Best* (Washington, D.C.: Acropolis Books 1986), x, 50. On waterfronts as a source of community revitalization, see also Jane Holtz Kay, "Waterfront Renaissance," *World Monitor*, August 1989, 38–43; Jim Schwab, "Riverfront Gamblers," *Planning*, September 1989, 15–18.

72. The fullest account of the development of Point State Park is Robert C. Alberts, *The Shaping of the Point: Pittsburgh's Renaissance Park* (Pittsburgh: University of Pittsburgh Press 1980). The Renaissance could not have taken place without another river program—a flood control system to prevent another catastrophe like the Saint Patrick's Day flood of 1936.

73. Edward K. Muller, "Pittsburgh's Waterfront Lands: A Final Report on the Combined Meetings of the Eastern, Mid-American, and Ontario Historical Geography Associations," University of Pittsburgh, September 24, 1982. The conference was the focal point of several river-oriented events organized by Muller in collaboration with the Historical Society and other local institutions. The overall theme was "The Richness of Pittsburgh's Rivers: A Series of Exhi-

bitions, Panels, Films and Lectures." Events uncluded a river trip open to the public. Edward Muller, written commentary, September 1993.

A critique of planning flaws in Renaissance I noted that "not a single street in Pittsburgh, nor building for that matter, is effectively designed to recognize the proximity or significance of water, and few therefore receive the reflective benefits which are the rewards of water consciousness." Patrick Horsbrugh, "Contrast in Urban Design," *Landscape Architecture* 53 (April 1963), 197.

74. Ibid., 11, 15. See also Muller,"The Legacy of Industrial Rivers," *Pittsburgh History* 72 (Summer 1989), 64–75. More recently, Muller has expressed concern that city planners favor running outbound traffic on the proposed Mon Valley Expressway along the South Side down to Duquesne. The result would be "a high speed expressway on BOTH riverfronts, rather than on only one." Muller, "Maximize Riverfront Access," University of Pittsburgh Institute of Politics, *Report*, Fall 1993, 11.

75. "Facing the Rivers," editorial, *Pittsburgh Post-Gazette*, October 12, 1988; *Allegheny County 2001*, 12.

76. Allegheny County Planning Department (with Environmental Planning and Design), *Allegheny County Riverfront Policy Plan*, April 1993. The plan identified a Riverfront Zone that included the valleys and hillsides as well as the rivers. The zone encompassed sixty-nine square miles, nearly 2,700 acres of "opportunity sites for development," and 73 of the 130 Allegheny County communities with river frontage.

77. The prison's architecture is discussed by Donald Miller, "Jail Locks Up Form and Function," *Pittsburgh Post-Gazette*, September 5, 1993; Jerry Vondas, "Jailhouse Walk," *Pittsburgh Post-Gazette*, August 22, 1994.

78. The mayor and City Council in 1957 requested the Department of Parks and Recreation to prepare a riverfront plan. Representatives of the landscape architecture firm Griswold, Winters, and Swain did an inspection and described the abysmal condition of the rivers: "dumps, oil loading platforms, an abandoned crane turntable, steel beams, pilings, an abandoned pump house," not to mention "Zubik's Navy," more than two dozen barges and boats in the vicinity of the Point. They proposed some minor improvements—tree plantings, small marina at Thirth-first Street, a riverfront promenade at Fifty-first Street—and a more substantial North Shore walk and drive. The most intriguing proposal was the conversion of Herr's Island (now Washington's Landing) in the Allegheny River into a island recreation park akin to Skansen in Stockholm or the Tivoli Gardens in Copenhagen. But the fundamental premise of the report was flawed: "Most of the flat land adjacent to the rivers must continue to be occupied by the industry and commerce which support the City. However, the rivers can provide an additional opportunity for recreation without detracting from industry."

The Department of Parks and Recreation in 1959 did produce a riverfront plan which recommended hillside plantings, riverside parks, and marinas. Nothing came of this. According to a city planner at the time (William Waddell), riverfront development had low priority compared to housing and industrial development. Barbara Paull, "Rivers and Hills: A Problem of Access," *University Times*, September 17, 1970, 5–6.

79. City of Pittsburgh, Department of City Planning, *The Plan for the Pittsburgh Riverfronts*, June 1989, 34.

80. The report recommended three new parks: Nine Mile Run, Washington Boulevard, Chartiers Creek, and a Clemente Park Expansion. These would join Point Park and South Side Park.

81. The river study had moved slowly. According to Dan Sentz, Department of City Planning, it had been conceived as early as 1983, but a consultant was not hired until 1986. Margie Romero, " 'New Age' for the Rivers: Why Is It Taking Ages," *In Pittsburgh*, April 24–30, 1991, pt. 1, 4.

82. The Mayor's Working Group on Riverfront Development, *Final Report*, January 17, 1991. The group consisted of David Epperson, dean of the School of Social Work, University of Pittsburgh; state representative Tom Murphy; Jack Wagner, City Council president; Thomas Solomich, attorney; Cecile Springer, planning consultant.

83. The Citizens' League of Southwestern Pennsylvania, *Riverfront Development Study*, November 1990. The report complained that "to date, only a few elected officials, and business leaders have publicly embraced the notion that this region's rivers are a source of great beauty and recreational possibilities" (10). In addition to the reports mentioned, the URA in 1987 hired a consultant to prepare a site analysis of the North Shore from the Fort Wayne Railroad Bridge to Washington's Landing. Delivered in December 1988, it proposed various improvements: increased parking areas, better lighting, trail surfacing, piping. Robert J. Gangewere, written commentary, October 1993.

84. Jon Schmitz, "Panel Suggests Park on River's Edge," *Pittsburgh Press*, January 19, 1991.

85. One enterprise that could provide some sense of coherence or integration for disparate riverside developments and attract residents and tourists to the rivers is a water taxi service. It could link the Sandcastle Park in West Homestead and Station Square on the Monongahela to Point State Park, and then to the Strip District, Allegheny Landing, the Warhol Museum, Carnegie Science Center, Three Rivers Stadium, and Washington's Landing on the Allegheny River. Tom Barnes, "Water Taxis Seen as Wave of Future," *Pittsburgh Post-Gazette*, September 18 1991; "Taxis on the Rivers," editorial, *Pittsburgh Press*, September 19, 1991. Such a system was still not in operation by the end of 1994.

86. R. Jay Gangewere, "The Three Rivers Heritage Trail," *The Carnegie Magazine* 60 (March/April 1991), 22–30. A Heritage Trail component will be

a signage or heritage marker program. As illustrated in a draft proposal by Gangewere, when one reached the Liberty Bridge part of the trail, there would be notices explaining the impact of the automobile: "This high bridge connecting to the Liberty Tunnel is an occasion to explain the transformation of the city by the automobile era, leading to the planting of highways along both sides of the Point, parking on the Monongahela Wharf, and the elimination of waterfront access for the public." R. Jay Gangewere, "Signage Program for the Three Rivers Heritage Trail," November 21, 1991, 5.

87. Robert J. Gangewere, written commentary, October 1993. The railbanking program was created in 1983 when Congress amended the National Trails Systems Act. A railbanking request, prepared with the agreement of a railroad company, is sent to the Interstate Commerce Commission. Railbanking does not imply a free trail. The railroad may request compensation and a railroad can apply to the ICC at any time to resume rail service. ISTEA refers to the Intermodal Surface Transportation Efficiency Act of 1991, which encourages the pursuit of alternatives to the automobile for transportation.

88. Edward Muller, personal interview, September 16, 1993. Preceding the Friends of the Riverfront was a Riverfront Working Group organized in 1989 by O'Malley, John Stephen, and R. Todd Erkel. The establishment of the Friends was announced at at conference in December 1990, and incorporation took place in February 1991. John Stephen, personal interview, November 22, 1993.

89. O'Malley died in 1993, at age thirty-five. Raised in Pittsburgh, he moved to California, where he became involved in the work of the Sierra Club and helped organize the Save the Mono Lake Committee. "Martin O'Malley: 1958–1993: Chairman, Conservationist, Friend," Friends of the Riverfront, *Quarterly Newsletter*, Fall 1993, 2.

90. Margie Romero, "Trail Boss," *In Pittsburgh*, August 13–August 19, 1992, 12.

91. An example was the successful call for volunteers to participate in a Trailblazing-Cleanup on October 2, 1993, in Lawrenceville at Forty-third Street and downriver toward the Strip District. According to Dennis H. Troy, of the Lawrenceville Deveopment Corporation, residents and businessmen in the district are eager to participate in the regional trail project. As a result of a October cleanup, the LDC formed a Riverfront Watch Group to sponsor regular riverfront cleanups. Lawrenceville, he proclaimed, "once again looks to its riverfront. . . . This time, 180 years later, it is for revitalization and recreation." Dennis H. Troy, "As the City's Oldest Neighborhood,Lawrenceville Wants a Trail," Letter to the Editor, *Pittsburgh Post-Gazette*, February 26, 1994.

92. Edward Muller, personal interview, September 16, 1993. O'Malley observed that the city had made it clear that neither manpower nor money would be provided to develop the trail. "Welcome to Friends of the Riverfront," Friends

of the Riverfront, *Quarterly Newsletter*, Summer 1992, 4. In early 1994, the Friends estimated that the Heritage Trail would cost $8 million. A consultant study estimated that a completed trail would draw 750,000 users a year, provide economic benefits totaling more than $30 million, and produce $1.9 million in tax revenues. Eric Heyl, "Will Dollars Flow from City's Riverfront Trail?" *Tribune-Review*, December 11, 1993.

93. Larry Ridenour, personal interview, September 29, 1993.

94. Robert J. Gangewere, personal interview, October 18, 1993.

95. R. Todd Erkel, "Three Rivers, One Trail," *Pittsburgh Post-Gazette*, Sunday Forum, May 22, 1994.

96. "Friends of the Riverfront," promotional statements.

97. Edward Muller, written commentary, September 30, 1993.

98. "Why not," asks Tom Murphy, "a goal of continuous public access along all 35 miles of riverfront," and "developing the riverfronts within a unifying context" ("The Riverfront I Imagine," Friends of the Riverfront, *Quarterly Newsletter*, Summer 1992, 2.) The first major component of the Heritage Trail was launched in the spring of 1994. It will run on the North Side from the Seventh Street Bridge to the Sixteenth Street Bridge and eventually extend to Washington's Landing. One should note that the Three Rivers Rowing Association is based at Washington's Landing. This organization has contributed to river consciousness and recreational use.

The Murphy administration is strongly committed to the development of downtown residential housing, which is very significant for riverfront reclamation. Already mentioned in previous chapters are the plans of the South Side Local Development Company to produce, with URA assistance, up to 300 riverfront housing units between Sixteenth and Eighteenth Streets and the 100 townhouse units in progress on the downstream end of Washington's Landing. A third project, on the North Shore, would consist of two or three four-story apartments holding 200 renters. Located between the Ninth Street Bridge and Fort Wayne Railroad Bridge, it would occupy six acres acquired by the URA. The tentative developer would be the Lincoln Property Company of Dallas. Tom Barnes, "Island Townhouses Next Year," *Pittsburgh Post-Gazette*, July 15, 1994; Suzanne Elliott, "$25 Million Residential Project Planned for City's North Shore," *Pittsburgh Business Times*, May 9–15, 1994, 1, 27.

Another possibility for riverfront housing derives from the Cultural Trust's two-level riverfront park along Fort Duquesne Boulevard. The trust hopes that the project will produce residential development.

Chapter 10. Historic Preservation and Industrial Heritage in the Pittsburgh Region

1. *The Daily Graphic*, September 29, 1882 (Pittsburgh, Pa. Supplement), 636, 679; Willard Glazier, *Peculiarities of American Cities* (Philadelphia, 1885),

332–34; Waldon Fawcett, "The Center of the World of Steel," *Century* 62, n.s. 40 (June 1901), 190; Edward Hungerford, *The Personality of American Cities* (New York, 1913), 181.

2. Edward K. Muller, "Ash Pile or Steel City? H. L. Mencken Helps Mold an Image," *Pittsburgh History* 74 (Summer 1991), 54.

3. Pittsburgh Civic Commission, *Plan and Scope* (n.d.). Somewhat resentfully, the commission stated that the Survey had ignored the "civic progress" already achieved in Pittsburgh, but hoped that its findings could become the basis for the "most fundamental and comprehensive future advance ever yet made possible in America." The Civic Commission's chairman, H.D.W. English (1855–1926), was a significant influence in Pittsburgh's efforts toward civic betterment in the early twentieth century. He operated a successful life insurance business in partnership with his brother and later his nephew. English had been president of the Pittsburgh Chamber of Commerce in the years preceding his appointmentt to the Civic Commission. See "H.D.W. English, Past President of the Chamber, Dies," *Pittsburgh First* 7 (April 3, 1926), 4.

4. Pittsburgh Civic Commission, *City Planning for Pittsburgh. Outline and Procedure.* A Report by Bion J. Arnold, Chicago, John R. Freeman, Providence, Frederick Law Olmsted, Boston. Adopted by the Commission, December 1909 (June 1910). As defined by the authors, city planning in Pittsburgh "as undertaken by the Pittsburgh Civic Commission, means the city useful, convenient, economical and healthful, as well as the city beautiful" (5). Issues examined in the report included steam railroads; water transportation and flood protection; electric railroads; street systems; public lands and buildings; water systems; sewerage systems; public control over private property development; smoke abatement. It also included a special report on revising the building code.

This planning document led to city-commissioned studies of rapid transit, water supply, and sewage disposal. That on transportation, by Bion J. Arnold, was a sweeping analysis of past and present transit issues; it recommended that the present generation "rearrange the more or less haphazard combination of streets and transit facilities that have grown up within the city and to substitute therefore a comprehensive plan for both the city and its transportation." Bion J. Arnold, *Report on the Pittsburgh Transportation Problem, Submitted to Honorable William A. Magee, Mayor of the City of Pittsburgh* (Pittsburgh, December 1910), 73.

5. Pittsburgh Civic Commission, *Pittsburgh: Main Thoroughfares and the Down Town District. Improvements Necessary to Meet the City's Present and Future Needs.* A Report by Frederick Law Olmsted, Adopted by the Commission, December 1910, 21, 22.

6. Ibid., 109–11. Despite their limited possibilities for recreation, Olmsted thought that slopes of lesser gradients could be furnished with seats and terraces so that neighborhood people "can stroll and rest" and enjoy the view (111).

Olmsted's report included advocacy for both large "rural" parks and neighborhood playgrounds, recreation facilities and parks.

7. For an overview of the antecedents and aspirations of the City Beautiful, see William H. Wilson, *The City Beautiful Movement* (Baltimore 1989).

8. Charles Mulford Robinson, *The Improvement of Towns and Cities, or The Practical Basis of Civic Aesthetics* (New York, 1913 [orig. publ. 1901]), 292, 289, 210, 211. Born in Ramapo, N.Y., in 1869, Robinson grew up and lived in Rochester (B.A., University of Rochester, 1891). A journalist and writer, Robinson became the leading apostle of the City Beautiful, despite lack of technical training in architecture, planning, or engineering. Indeed, he became the first to hold the University of Illinois's Chair of Civic Design in 1913.

9. Ibid., 200.

10. Ibid., 212. Tunnard and Reed paid tribute to the City Beautiful era as a time when "Americans made amends for past errors. . . . Without it we would not have had our great libraries, museums, terminals and civic centers. . . . It was the age in which the businessman made his greatest contribution to American culture and the government followed his lead." Christopher Tunnard and Henry Hope Reed, *American Skyline: The Growth and Form of Our Cities and Towns* (New York, 1956), 136.

11. Majority Report of the Committee on Civic Improvement Appointed by the Pittsburgh Chapter, American Institute of Architects, 1904, *A Plan for the Architectural Improvement of Pittsburgh*, Sixth Annual Convention of the Architectural League of America (n.p.).

12. Montgomery Schuyler, "The Building of Pittsburgh," *Architectural Record* 30 (September 1911), 229, 243. Buildings cited by Schuyler included Carnegie Institute, Forbes Field, buildings for the University of Western Pennsylvania (University of Pittsburgh), Soldiers' Monument (Soldiers' and Sailors' Memorial), Pittsburgh Athletic Club, University Club, buildings at Carnegie Tech (Carnegie-Mellon University), the Pittsburgh and Duquesne Clubs.

13. *A Plan for the Architectural Improvement of Pittsburgh.*

14. Art Commission, *Annual Report, 1913*, 3–4, 8; Art Commission, *Annual Report, 1912*, 209; Art Commission, *Annual Report, 1915*, 8. The Art Commission reports were issued as part of the combined annual reports of the departments and offices of the city of Pittsburgh.

The Pittsburgh Civic Commission, through its Art Committee, had initiated the movement early in 1910 to create an art commission akin to those in Boston and New York. The effort was supported by such civic agencies as the Pittsburgh Art Society, the Civic Club of Allegheny County, and the Beautification Committee of the Greater Pittsburgh Association. See *An Account of the work of the Art Commission of the City of Pittsburgh. From its Creation in 1911 to January 1st, 1915.*

15. According to Baird, the City Planning Commission accomplished little in its early years outside the zoning ordinance of 1923. Disenchantment with its performance, Baird maintained, precipitated the creation of the Citizens' Committee on City Plan in 1918. George Baird, interview, 1966. Baird at this time was a senior research analyst, Department of City Planning.

16. Shade Tree Commission, *Annual Report, 1912*, 843. In *Annual Reports of the Executive Departments, City of Pittsburgh, Year ending January 31, 1913*.

17. The origins, financing, and design of Chatham Village are examined in Roy Lubove, *Twentieth-Century Pittsburgh*, vol. 1: *Government, Business, and Environmental Change* (Pittsburgh, 1995).

18. Critiques of modernism include: Brent C. Brolin, *The Failure of Modern Architecture* (New York, 1976); Peter Blake, *Form Follows Fiasco: Why Modern Architecture Hasn't Worked* (Boston, 1977); Robert Venturi, *Complexity and Contradiction in Architecture* (New York, 1966), and, with Denise Scott Brown and Steven Izenour, *Learning From Las Vegas* (Cambridge, Mass., 1972). Iconoclastic and inimitable is Tom Wolfe, *From Bauhaus to Our House* (New York, 1981). Henry Hope Reed, Jr., *The Golden City* (Garden City, N.Y., 1959) portrays the banalities of modernism in a series of pictorial contrasts in New York City: the Grand Central Terminal facade against that of the Port Authority Bus Terminal; the original wing of the Yale University Art Gallery against the new wing designed in 1953 by Louis I. Kahn; the curves and swirls of the cast iron lampposts dating from the 1890s against the characterless stainless-steel variety of today.

19. Stefan Lorant, *Pittsburgh: The Story of an American City* (Garden City, N.Y., 1964), 373.

20. Le Corbusier's design philosophy is examined in Robert Fishman, *Urban Utopias in the Twentieth Century: Ebenezer Howard, Frank Lloyd Wright, and Le Corbusier* (New York, 1977).

21. PH&LF publications that broadly survey the region's architectural heritage include: James D. Van Trump and Arthur P. Ziegler, Jr., *Landmark Architecture of Allegheny County, Pennsylvania* (PH&LF, 1967); a later survey, Walter C. Kidney, *Landmark Architecture: Pittsburgh and Allegheny County* (PH&LF, 1985); James D. Van Trump, *Life and Architecture in Pittsburgh* (PH&LF, 1983); and, in celebration of Landmark's twenty-fifth anniversary, Walter C. Kidney, *A Past Still Alive* (PH&LF, 1989). Landmarks also recently published a history of the 300-acre Allegheny Cemetery by Walter Kidney. Established in 1844, it was one of the earliest rural, romantic cemeteries in the United States. Landmarks also regularly distributes a profusely illustrated informative *Newsletter* to its members.

22. Arthur P. Ziegler, Jr., Leopold Adler II, Walter C. Kidney, *Revolving Funds for Historic Preservation: A Manual of Practice* (Pittsburgh: Ober Park Associates, 1975), 107.

23. Pittsburgh History & Landmarks Foundation, *Station Square: An Account*, March 1991) 3; PH&LF, *Fifteen Year Report: Five Year Master Plan* (1981), 44.

24. Arthur P. Ziegler, personal interview, October 12, 1993; PH&LF, *Fifteen-Year Report*, 44.

25. James Van Trump relates the P&LE saga in *Station Square: A Golden Age Retrieved*, The Stones of Pittsburgh, no. 11 (PH&LF, 1978).

26. Arthur P. Ziegler, personal interview, October 12, 1993.

27. Ibid.

28. Chuck Muer died tragically in March 1993. He was lost at sea off the Florida coast along with his wife and another couple during a violent storm. His $2 million investment was important to the success of Station Square. According to Ziegler, it was the first non-Pittsburgh investment and provided sufficient credibility to encourage investments by New York and Philadelphia banks. Also, the restaurant's immediate success led John E. Connolly to move his Clipper Fleet from the Monongahela Wharf to Station Square. Jeff Domenick, "Friends Praying for Muer," *Tribune-Review*, March 21, 1993; Johnna A. Pro, "Lost-at-Sea Muer Gave City Boost," *Pittsburgh Post-Gazette*, March 19, 1993.

29. Ziegler, Adler, and Kidney, *Revolving Funds for Historic Preservation*, 107. Many of the preservation recycling efforts in Pittsburgh received assistance from Landmarks' revolving preservation fund.

30. Landmarks had been a P&LE lessee since 1976. It purchased the original forty-one acres in 1987, and owned fifty-two acres by 1989.

31. PH&LF, *Station Square: Phase II*, 1992, 13. This publication, along with Landmarks' *Station Square: An Account*, 1991, and Van Trump's *Station Square: A Golden Age Revived*, provide factual background for the Station Square development.

32. The sale of Station Square did not involve all the grounds and buildings. The title to both grounds and buildings applied only to the Landmarks Building, Express House, East Warehouse, the parking garage, Lawrence Paint Building. John Connelly remained owner of the Sheraton Hotel, but the new owners acquired possession of the ground under the hotel; Connelly also retained ownership of the Gateway Clipper fleet and docks. The Gatehouse and Commerce Court Office Building remained under their previous ownership. The joint venture acquired the land beneath the Freight House Shops, but a development partnership, of which Landmarks owns 19 percent, retained ownership of the building.

The agreement also provides that the North Side Bidwell Training Center will contribute training services for development at Station Square and assure minority participation. This was at the request of Landmarks (PH&LD, "Release," June 15, 1994).

33. Arthur Ziegler, personal interview, September 26, 1994.

34. Besides retaining ownership of the various artifacts and part ownership of the Freight House Shops, Landmarks will continue to manage the parking facilities, landscaping, and grounds, at a fee. Another source of (contingent) income will be a small percentage of gaming fees for twenty years. Landmarks will also be responsble for restorating the exterior of the Lawrence Paint Building.

35. In May 1992 Landmarks had co-sponsored a conference, "Saving Religious Properties," the first event to create a wide awareness in Pittsburgh of the threat to historic religious properties as congregations dwindled. A $44,000 grant from the Allegheny Foundation in November 1993 led to a ten-month survey and preparation of a plan to rescue religious structures. Landmarks planned to launch a $50,000, ninety-day pilot program of grants and technical assistance for religious properties in fall 1994. "Planning to Save Religious Properties," *PH&LF News* 133 (February 1994), 1; Arthur Ziegler, personal interview, September 26, 1994.

36. Arthur Ziegler, personal interview, September 26, 1994. On the sale of Station Square, see Tom Barnes, "Station Square Being Sold," *Pittsburgh Post-Gazette*, June 16, 1994; Eric Heyl, "Station Square Sold; Buyers Pledge Growth," *Tribune-Review*, June 16, 1994; Ron DaParma, "Purchase Seen as Boon to Station Square," *Tribune-Review*, June 17, 1994; DaParma, "Landmarks Won't Miss Landlord Role," *Tribune-Review*, June 19, 1994; Tom Barnes, "Station Square Sold to Developer, Casino Firm," *Pittsburgh Post-Gazette*, September 1, 1994.

37. Within its first five years, Landmarks had already received many foundation grants, thus establishing a firm liaison with the foundation network. The Sarah Mellon Scaife Foundation, besides the $100,000 in 1966 for the Revolving Fund, provided a five-year grant for operations of $25,000 a year. The Walden Trust contributed $22,000 for operating revenue, and $10,000 came from the Edgar J. Kaufmann Charitable Trust. The Richard King Mellon Foundation gave $50,000 for restoration of the Neill Log House. The artifact program received funding from the Hunt Foundation ($1,500), and Henry Oliver Rea Charitable Trust ($2,000). The Pittsburgh Foundation provided grants for office equipment, library, and publications. Another $6,900 was given by the Alcoa Foundation for the landmark plaques installed on buildings. There were corporation as well as other foundation grants (PH&LF, *Five Year Report*, 20).

38. PH&LF, *Fifteen Year Report*, 11.

39. Arthur P. Ziegler, "Implications of Urban Social Policy: The Quest for Community Self-Determination," in *Readings in Historic Preservation: Why?*

What? How?, ed. Norman Williams, Jr., Edmund H. Kellogg, and Frank B. Gilbert (New Brunswick, N.J.: Center for Urban Policy Research, 1983), 307.

40. Arthur P. Ziegler, Jr., *Historic Preservation in Inner City Areas: A Manual of Practice*, rev. ed. (Ober Park Associates, Pittsburgh, 1974), 57–58.

41. James D. Van Trump, *1300–1335 Liverpool Street. Manchester. Old Allegheny. Pittsburgh*, The Stones of Pittsburgh, no. 2 (PH&LF, n.d.), 4–5.

42. Arthur P. Ziegler, "The Beginnings," in PH&LF, *Recollections: 25 Years*, September 1989, 3.

43. Van Trump, *1300–1335 Liverpool Street*, 20.

44. Arthur P. Ziegler, "Renewal of the Spirit and the Place," *Hud Challenge*, February 1977, 26. Ziegler added that "people suddenly sense a loss as urban space . . . vanished into bland modernity; they began to treasure the old and soon were fighting for it against our planners."

45. John DeSantis, personal interview, August 10, 1993.

46. Ziegler, "The Beginnings," 3.

47. "Manchester Once Affluent but Now Low-Income Section of Pittsburgh Will be Reborn in Unique Restoration Project," *American Preservation*, February–March 1978, 13.

48. One house, the Gustav Langenheim mansion (1315 Liverpool Street) dating from the early 1880s, was acquired by Landmarks in 1967 and saved from demolition. But Landmarks held the property longer than a decade, and sold it to Mistick Brothers, a North Side contractor. They restored it and opened it in 1980 as a section 8 subsidized rental (PH&LF, *Five Year Report*, 7; PH&LF, *Fifteen Year Report*, 12–13).

49. Ziegler, "Renewal of the Spirit," 28. ("Had they [Lowe and Cox] not been so serious and so constant, the program would have faltered long ago.")

50. Ibid., 28; "Manchester: Once Affluent," 13–14; Pittsburgh History and Landmarks Foundation, *Fifteen Year Report*, 11.

51. "Manchester: Once Affluent," 11.

52. "Practical Preservation for People in Urban Areas," *Preservation News*, Newspaper Response, Practical Preservation in Urban Areas Conference, September 10–11, 2; Nora Richter, "Pittsburgh's Innovative Renovation Record," *AIA Journal*, rpt. November 1978, 1; Julie Wortman, "Manchester—a New Constituency for Preservation," Office of Archeology and History Preservation, National Park Service, *Information Related to Responsibilities of the Secretary of the Interior*, sec. 3, Executive Order 11593 (June 1977), 1.

53. Pittsburgh Historic Review Commission, *Mexican War Streets*, December 1986. This is one of several brochures describing the city's historic districts.

54. PH&LF, *Fifteen Year Report*, 14.

55. Arthur P. Ziegler, "Renovate, Don't Relocate," *Museum News*, rpt. December 1972, 3. Apartments in the first house renovated by Landmarks after fourteen months and an outlay of $53,000 was rented to young professionals who brought "to the area a deep commitment to participate in this urban experiment." Another house was used to provide housing for moderate-income renters. Less remodeling was done, and the tenants remained in place. Landmarks used the federal sublet program in housing for low-income families. It restored "derelict" houses and rented them to the public housing authority which sublet. The five-year lease, signed before work began, enabled Landmarks to acquire mortgage funds.

56. PH&LF, *Fifteen Year Report*, 14.

57. Some residents complained that Landmarks held properties off the market for too long a time. Robin Jones, personal interview, June 1990.

58. An intriguing example of the use of preservation to build a kind of community is the restoration campaign of the North Side Calvary United Methodist Church (Allegheny and Beech) in alliance with the Allegheny Historic Preservation Society (AHPS). Built in the mid-1890s, and an official Pittsburgh landmark, the church boasts three Tiffany windows. It is involved in a $3 million restoration project, and seeks support (far beyond the congregation) based upon its architectural, not its religious significance. In April 1991 the AHPS acquired Susan Brandt to serve as preservation director in collaboration with Calvary Church. She had previously directed the restoration of the Carnegie Library in Braddock. Calvary Church seeks to stimulate interest and support for the preservation project though a newsletter, *Calvary Spirit*, pamphlets describing the church's architecture and history, and a wide variety of activities. Paralleling these is the *Newsletter* of the AHPS.

The estimated $3 million restoration will include interior renovations in the spirit of 1895.

59. Lowe joined the Murphy administration as assistant to the mayor for neighborhoods and housing. Slaughter had been vice-president of community development at Dollar Bank.

60. PH&LF, *Application Procedure for the Preservation Fund*, n.d.; Beth Pollock, "Preservation Fund Loans Benefit Communities," *Pittsburgh Business Times*, April 2–8, 1990, 25, 27. The Preservation Fund was supplemented in May 1994 by the Mellon Bank–PHLF Comprehensive Neighborhood Development Initiative. It hoped to provide up to $10 million by the end of 1995 for large-scale neighborhood revitalization. "Mellon Bank/PHLF Comprehensive Neighborhood Development," *PH&LF News* 135 (July 1994), 1; Todd Gutnick, "New Loan Program Aims at Boosting Restoration Efforts," *Tribune-Review*, May 18, 1994.

61. Walter Kidney, *Allegheny Cemetery: A Romantic Landscape in Pittsburgh* (PH&LF, 1990); Roy Lubove, "Pittsburgh's Allegheny Cemetery and the Victorian Garden of the Dead," *Pittsburgh History* 75 (Fall 1992), 148–56.

62. Kidney, *A Past Still Alive*, 124.

63. Michael Eversmeyer, personal interview, October 13, 1993.

64. Caroline Boyce, personal interview, October 12, 1993.

65. Mark Bunnell, phone interview, October 18, 1993. Bunnell became the first staff member assigned to the Historic Review Commission (and was succeeded by Caroline Boyce, 1981–1985). In 1983 Bunnell left Pittsburgh to join the Economic Development Corporation of Kansas City.

66. Whether enough staff is assigned to the HRC is another question; there have never been more than two employees, and there is currently only one.

67. The above account of the HRC is based on an interview with Joan Ivey, October 15, 1993.

68. Tom Barnes, "Landmarks: For Preservation or Profit," *Pittsburgh Post-Gazette*, November 27, 1989. Landmarks in 1985 created Landmarks Development Corporation, a for-profit subsidiary, along with three nonprofit subsidiaries: Landmarks Charitable Corporation (preservation); Landmarks Real Estate Corporation (which owned Station Square); Landmarks Financial Corporation (which managed Station Square). Although most of Station Square profits went toward development, Ziegler maintained that income would provide operating income for preservation.

69. Ziegler, *Historic Preservation in Inner City Areas.*

70. "Landmarks: Our Principles," *PH&LF News* 122 (February 1991), 12.

71. Arthur Ziegler, "Memorandum to Walter Kidney, RE: Preservation Pittsburgh Goals," October 7, 1991.

72. At the behest of the Catholic diocese, Saint Paul's Cathedral was exempted from the regulations imposed by the Oakland Historic District in 1992.

73. Mai Maki, "North Siders Debate Designation," *Pittsburgh Post-Gazette*, July 13, 1990. The Allegheny West neighborhood is described in Mike Sajna, "Return to the Gilded Age in Allegheny West," *Tribune-Review*, Sunday Focus, May 22, 1994.

74. City of Pittsburgh, Historic Review Commission, *Fourth Avenue: A City's Legacy*, brochure (n.d., n.p.).

75. Tom Barnes, "Planners Stall Bid for Historic Designation," *Pittsburgh Post-Gazette*, September 20, 1989; Ellen M. Perlmutter, "Planning Panel Rejects Downtown Historic District," *Pittsburgh Press*, September 20, 1989; Michael Eversmeyer, written commentary, November 29, 1993.

76. Joan Ivey, personal interview, October 15, 1993.

77. Michael Eversmeyer, written commentary, November 29, 1993. Eversmeyer also believes the issue was complicated by a split in the community between older, more affluent, Republican owners and newer, less affluent, Democratic ones.

78. Andrew Sheehan, "City's Historic Panel Chief May be Ousted," *Pittsburgh Post-Gazette*, March 6, 1990.

79. Eleanor Chute, "Mayor Offers Nominees for Historic Review, Other Panels," *Pittsburgh Press*, July 31, 1990; "Masloff's Candidate to Head Historic Panel Draws Fire," *Pittsburgh Post-Gazette*, August 7, 1990; Patricia Lowry, "DeSantis: Preservation to be 'Mainstream' Issue," *Pittsburgh Press*, August 12, 1990; Suzanne Elliott, "Do You Know This Man," *Pittsburgh Business Times*, February 8–14, 1993, 1, 29; Michael Eversmeyer, written commentary, November 29, 1993.

An important undertaking by the HRC since DeSantis became chairman was the preparation of a Pittsburgh Register of Historic Places. This lists all the "districts, buildings, structures, and sites in Pittsburgh that are significant and important for historical, architectural, and cultural reasons." Preservation planner Michael Eversmeyer directed the project. Currently, Pittsburgh claims thirty-two city landmarks and nine districts. These are listed in Appendix 1.

80. Landmarks had originally opposed the demolition of the Moose Building at 626 Penn Avenue. But after a study by Landmarks, the city and Heinz "interests," it concluded that demolition was "inevitable." Landmarks then advocated the creation of the Penn-Liberty Historic District (Kidney, *A Past Still Alive*, 129).

81. The following account of preservation development is based upon the author's participation in the Committee to Save the Syria Mosque, Preservation Pittsburgh, and the Coalition to Regulate Billboards.

82. In the florid and engaging prose of James Van Trump: "Stylistically, it is a curious mixture of Byzantine and Arabic elements, and its striped, two-toned brown brick walls remind one curiously of both Hagia Sophia, the great sixth-century church at Constantinople, and a large Viennese mocha torte. The confectionery note is much assisted by the frieze of Arabic script that serves as the structure's cornice—it looks rather like spidery white icing." "On the Terrace II: The Roof of the University Club in Pittsburgh," *Life and Architecture in Pittsburgh*, ed. Walter C. Kidney and Louise King Ferguson (PH&LF, 1983).

83. Arthur Ziegler had been working with Chancellor Wesley Posvar of the University of Pittsburgh on a plan to save the Syria Mosque. Pitt had been considering purchase of the building, and Posvar was surprised to suddenly discover that the Medical Center had acquired it. He still hoped to regain the building from the Medical Center and remodel it for a conference center and other uses. However, his authority was compromised as a result of newspaper revelations about his university retirement benefits. Arthur Zielger, letter to author, November 1, 1993.

84. An outstanding example of commercial historic preservation is Pittsburgh's "Firstside," directly opposite Station Square. A former Monongahela River warehouse district, it was turned into a mecca for law firms, advertising

and public relations agencies, and graphic companies. It was a product of the tax credits for historic preservation that precipitated a torrent of commercial investment until the tax "reform" bill of 1986. The federal government, as usual, proved incapable of leaving well enough alone.

A building, or building complex, which fails initially as a preservation project, can, if saved from destruction, be redeemed eventually by another commercial project or by a nonprofit organization. The Bank Center was an urban mall created in the late 1970s out of six historic buildings in Pittsburgh's Fourth Ave banking and financial center. Although it failed by 1987, it will be recycled as the Library Center, owned by Point Park College, and operated by Point Park and the Carnegie Library. Point Park will maintain an academic library for its students, and the Carnegie will maintain its Downtown Branch and Business Department. The former movie house in the Bank Center will be used for films again, as well as lectures and performances. See Robert J. Gangewere, "From Bank Vault to Book Vault," *Carnegie Magazine*, July–August 1991, 20–25; Jane-Ellen Robinet, "Point Park's Library Project Nearing $6.1 Million Goal," *Pittsburgh Business Times*, November 22–28, 5; Mark Houser, "Public-Private Library Merger Called Innovative," *Tribune-Review*, December 2, 1993.

85. After the transcendental epiphany on Liverpool Street in 1964, Ziegler and Van Trump consulted with Stanton Belfour, president of the antiquarian and somnolent Historical Society. He advised the creation of a separate organization instead of a unit within the society. They then pursued support from several acquaintances of Van Trump. Invited to dinner by Helen Clay Frick, Van Trump advised her of the Liverpool Street experience, and she requested that he and Ziegler return the next day. This produced the first grant—a check for $3,000 for a Liverpool Street analysis. At Van Trump's suggestion, they next consulted with Barbara D. Hoffstot, a trustee of the National Trust for Historic Preservation, who would serve as vice-chairman for a quarter century, and Charles C. Arnesberg, a lawyer and president of the local chapter of the Society of Architectural Historians. He would become the longtime chairman of Landmarks. William Oliver, treasurer of Jones & Laughlin, became treasurer. A group of eighty persons at a reception was informed by Theodore L. Hazlett, Jr., counsel for the URA, that many buildings would perish if they did not act.

Calvin Hamilton, director of City Planning, was supportive. He provided staff for the Liverpool Street survey, became a trustee of Landmarks, and agreed to assist in opposing plans for the demolition of the North Side's historic residential neighborhoods. PH&LF, *Fifteen Year Report*, 34; Arthur P. Ziegler, "The Beginnings," in "Recollections," 3.

86. Randy L. Udavcak, "Preservation Blues," *In Pittsburgh*, May 8–14, 1991, 10.

87. Lorraine B. Diehl, *The Late, Great Pennsylvania Station* (Lexington, Mass: Stephen Greene Press, 1985); James Dao, "Looking at Post Office," *New*

York Times, May 13, 1992; Herbert Muschamp, "In This Dream Station Future and Post Collide," *New York Times,* June 20, 1993.

88. A landmark designation would probably still not have superseded the authority of the demolition permit.

89. The range of issues that have concerned Pittsburgh in its first two years are summarized in an appendix.

90. Exasperated by the inaction of the Planning Department and mayor's office, Ferlo introduced his own legislation in March and August 1992. After it was revised by the Planning Commission and city council, it limited the size of billboards to 750 square feet in industrial zones and 378 square feet in commercial zones. Their height in commercial districts was restricted to 30 feet. Billboards could previously range as large as 1,200 square feet and 85 feet in height. New billboards were not allowed within 350 feet of tunnels, rivers, or bridges, and they were banned from the CBD. This was passed by City Council in October 1993.

Pennsylvania courts will not permit uncompensated amortization. Ferlo had attempted, unsuccessfully,to reduce the total number of billboards in Pittsburgh (about 1,400) by limiting new ones to industrial zones and requiring that for each new one an equal amount of billboard space be removed from nonconforming zones (legal when installed, but no longer so).

Witnesses testifying on behalf of Ferlo's billboard control legislation frequently condemned the prevalance of tobacco and alcohol ads, especially in poorer neighborhoods. In August 1994, Tom Armstrong, chairman of the City Planning Commission, proposed banning tobacco advertisements on billboards. The model was Baltimore, which recently had banned both tobacco and alcohol ads (excepting stadiums and industrial areas). It would be surprising if this proposal could succeed in Pittsburgh in light of state constitutional or legislative restrictions and the potency of the billboard lobby.

Neighborhoods, it would seem, must maintain eternal vigilance to prevent a billboard invasion. Manchester residents were incensed in the summer of 1994 when a monopole billboard with a 14 by 48-foot sign advertising automobile paint suddenly sprouted on a lot behind Page Street in southwest Manchester. (According to the director of City Planning, it had been approved in 1991, but the permit expired before the billboard was erected, and the more restrictive ordinance was then enacted in 1993.) The billboard is located just outside the section of Manchester designed a historic district. Mike Tysarczyk, "Billboard Upsets Manchester; Murphy Promises to Remove It," *Tribune-Review,* July 15, 1994; Kelly B. Casey, "Manchester Vows to Take Back the View," *Tribune-Review,* July 31, 1994.

And at the end of 1994 the billboard industry was permitted to invade a section of the Parkway East hitherto free of billboards (from the Pennsylvania Turnpike exit at Monroeville to Squirrel Hill). This is in the suburban Penn Hills area. The municipality had hoped to limit the size to 100 square feet, but a Common Pleas Court judge granted permission for a doubled-faced billboard (14 by 48 feet on each side). The problem was that community of Penn Hills lacked a billboad ordinance at the time the billboard company (J.B. Steven) submitted its application. See Eleanor Chute, "Parkway Stretch to Get 1st Billboard by March," *Pittsburgh Post-Gazette East*, September 22, 1994; Martin Kinnunen, "Ruling OKs Large Billboard on Parkway," *Tribune-Review*, September 26, 1994.

91. Elise Vider, "Pennsylvania Court Batters Preservation," *Historic Preservation News*, September 1991, 1–2, 27; Tom Barnes, "Ruling Rescues Historic Site Law," *Pittsburgh Post-Gazette*, November 12, 1993; Allen Freeman, "Back in the Preservation Business: Pennsylvania Supreme Court Reverses Its Far-Reaching 1991 Boyd Theater Decision of July 1991," *Historic Preservation News*, February–March 1994, 6–8. The ruling was in response to the Boyd Theater case in Philadelphia. In 1955 Philadelphia had enacted the first citywide preservation ordinance. In contrast to Pittsburgh, the Philadelphia statute permitted interior designations and lacked the extensive public hearing process.

92. Joe Napsha, "Brookville: Community in Profile," *Tribune-Review*, Sunday Focus Section, November 22, 1992; Diana Nelson Jones, "Brookville's Labor of Love," *Pittsburgh Post-Gazette*, August 21, 1994. Brookville was established in 1830. Its nineteenth-century economy was based on lumber and wood products. Currently, its largest employer is Brookville Hospital (395 employees). The Brookville Glove Manufacturing Company claims over 90 employees. In December 1992, the Pittsburgh History and Landmarks Foundation sponsored a tour to the Brookville Victorian Christmas celebration to demonstrate a successful example of economic revitalization though "careful restoration and preservation of houses, institutions, and business buildings." These included the Italianate courthouse (1869). "Holiday Tour with Landmarks," December 5, 1992.

93. Maryann G. Eidemiller, "Brownsville's Looking Pretty as a Picture," *Tribune-Review*, May 16, 1993. Examples of artist-inspired revitalization included the Torpedo Factory (Alexandria, Va.) and the German Village district of Columbia, Ohio.

94. Richard Robbins, "In This Town, Hope Springs Eternal," *Tribune-Review*, April 11, 1993. The W. A. Young complex, closed down in 1965 and acquired by the Greene County Historical Society in 1985, was inventoried and measured by a Historic American Engineering Record team in the summer of 1991. The report, consisting of drawings, photos, and oral histories, was presented at a town meeting in November. Consequently, "the people are now very interested in turning this historic foundry into a museum and using it as a focal point for revitalizing the town." Christopher Marston, "HAER Brains Find Foundry Fabulous," *Steel Heritage Chronicle* 1 (Spring 1992), 6.

95. Vandergrift Heights, developed for unskilled workers, merged with Vandergrift in 1915, and West Vandergrift was annexed in 1957.

96. See Vandergrift Borough Preservation Committee, *A Center for the Performing Arts: Reopening, Promoting, Managing, and Restoring a Historic Theater in a Historic Town*, July 1993. The committee anticipates that the restored Casino would be used for "plays, concerts, films, beauty pageants, recitals, puppet shows, lectures, ballet, acting workshops, meetings . . . and art/photo exhibits" (5). In 1991, the Casino became a member of the League of Historic American Theatres. Victorian Vandergrift Museum & Historical Society, *Casino Notes* 13 (October–December 1991), 2.

97. I attended the fourth annual Preservation Week celebration in May 1993 and encountered an impressively large and enthusiastic group of participants.

98. Richard Mandelkorn, "Lessons from Lowell," *Historic Preservation* 42 (November/December 1990), 38; Wolf Von Eckardt, "A Cultural Community Center in the Lowell Tradition," *Washington Post*, January 26, 1974; Michael Southworth, "How Park Originated," letter to *New York Times*, September 22, 1992. Southworth claims that early political support came from Rep. Brad Morse, and Senators Edward Kennedy and Edward Brooke, who sponsored bills to establish the park in the early 1970s. As for Paul Tsongas, usually identified as the prime mover, Southworth argues he had originally opposed the concept, but became helpful "after the project received wide recognition."

99. The Lowell Preservation Commission, a federal agency in the Department of the Interior, handles development in the downtown preservation district. The Lowell Historic Board controls design and preservation standards in the historic district (Mandelkorn, "Lessons from Lowell," 69).

100. Karl Zimmermann, "Cruising the Canals of a Revitalized Lowell," *New York Times*, August 4, 1991; Mandelkorn, "Lessons from Lowell," 34; Susan Diesenhouse, "A Tale of Two Cities," *New York Times*, April 1, 1990.

101. Another possible candidate for industrial park status is the group of thirteen grain elevators still standing along the Buffalo waterfront in 1990. Alan Flippen, "Buffalo's Industrial Era 'National Parks,'" *Pittsburgh Post-Gazette*, March 26, 1990.

102. Michael deCourcy Hinds, "As "'Steamtown' Grows, So Does Parks Debate," *New York Times*, November 23, 1991; Hinds, "Much Steaming Over "'Steamtown,'" *New York Times*, February 5, 1991; Kelly P. Kissel, "Battle for Steamtown," *Pittsburgh Press*, February 16, 1992; Len Barcousky, "All Aboard?" *Pittsburgh Post-Gazette*, July 3, 1994; Mike Shoup, "Steamtown: A Boon or Boondoggle?" *Philadelphia Inquirer*, August 14, 1994. Steamtown had originally been launched as a private venture. The developers failed in 1987, and the project landed in the domain of the National Park Service.

Efforts in Congress to reduce the total projected spending from $73 million to $58 million took place in 1991–1992. "Controversial Rail Park Faces Reduced Funding," *Pittsburgh Post-Gazette*, November 27, 1991; "What a Waste of Money," *Tribune-Review*, June 28, 1992; "Theme Park Funding Exposes Friction," *Tribune-Review*, June 29, 1992.

103. Bob Hoover, "RR Past Takes Turn at Altoona's Horseshoe Museum," *Pittsburgh Post-Gazette*, April 24, 1992.

104. *America's Industrial Heritage Project: Southwestern Pennsylvania*, June 1989, n.p. The nine counties were Indiana, Westmoreland, Fayette, Cambria, Somerset, Blair, Bedford, Huntingdon, Fulton. See also Allegheny Ridge Industrial Heritage Corridor Tast Force et al., *Plan for Allegheny Ridge*, April 1992; Marnaa Renn, "Packaging the Past to Preserve the Present," *Tribune-Review*, Sunday Focus, Feburary 27, 1994. A prime mover in the creation of AIHP, and executive director of the Southwestern Pennsylvania Preservation Commission, is Randy Cooley.

105. *America's Industrial Herigage Project*, n.p. The AIHP ran into problems in the summer of 1993 over complaints about bookkeeping practices that made it difficult to track federal funds or determine the scope and progress of the project. The issue seems to have evaporated by the fall of 1993, and the director of the National Park Service, Roger Kennedy, ostensibly resolved his doubts about Park Service responsibility for these heritage projects at the expense of parks and forests. Michael Blood, "Park Service Recommends AIHP Audit," *Tribune-Review*, July 29, 1993; "Park Service Alters Audit Plans at Industrial Heritage Project," *Tribune-Review*, July 30, 1993; "In Need of an Audit," *Tribune-Review*, August 2, 1993; "Auditing Our Heritage," *Pittsburgh Post-Gazette*, August 3, 1993; Richard Robbins, "Heritage Project Gets Thumbs Up," *Tribune-Review*, October, 10, 1993.

106. There is a Flood Museum in Johnstown.

107. Johnstown Area Heritage Association, *Johnstown Heritage Development Plan*, April 1991), 1–2.

108. Ibid. 3.

109. Curt Miner, "But not Out," *In Pittsburgh*, March 4–10, 1992. The ten-block Cambria City neighborhood dates back to 1853, when it was a residential community for workers at the Cambria Iron Company across the Conemaugh River. In succeeding decades, it accommodated the East European immigrants who poured into the area to work in the local iron, steel, and coal industries. A National Historic District, it "stands as a vibrant illustration of the strong cultural and religious ties that bound together an immigrant workers' community at the turn-of-the century." Johnstown Folkfest '93, *Historic Cambria City*.

110. Steel Industry Heritage Task Force, Allegheny County, Pennsylvania, *Draft Action Plan*, December 1988, 5, 7; *PH&LF News*, 115 (Fall 1990), 2. Speakers at the February 1988 conference included representatives of industrial

heritage projects around the country: Sloss Furnaces Museum, Birmingham, Ala.; Illinois & Michigan Canal, and America's Industrial Heritage Project.

111. The expanded scope of the industrial heritage project derived in part from the requirements of the state Heritage Park Program. It offered grants for planning industrial heritage corridors. Edward K. Muller, "Further Progress on Preserving Steel's Heritage," *Pittsburgh Heritage* 5 (Fall 1989), 7. The Pennsylvania State Heritage Parks Program was created in 1989–1990 and is administered by the Department of Community Affairs. Components of a heritage plan must include economic development, intergovernmental cooperation, cultural conservation, recreation, and education. In May 1994 the Oil Region Heritage Park, encompassing Crawford and Venango Counties, Titusville and Oil City, received state designation. Paul Frederick, "Oil City Planning Boom-Town Replica," *Pittsburgh Post-Gazette*, September 4, 1994.

112. Augie Carlino, "SIHC Begins Management Action Plan," *Steel Heritage Chronicle* 1 (Spring 1994), 1. The Management Action Plan is scheduled for completion by spring 1995. The state will not consider heritage designation until an action plan is submitted. The Steel Industry Heritage Task Force had earlier sponsored an additional planning document: Landmarks Design Associates, *Forging a Future for Industrial Sites:An Approach to Redesign*, September 1991. Among other things, it urged the development of riverfront amenties and public access.

113. Edward Muller, written commentary, September 30, 1993.

114. "Pork or Preservation?: Heritage Funding Should Be Based on Merit, Not Politics," editorial, *Pittsburgh Post-Gazette*, July 18, 1993.

115. Steel Industry Heritage Task Force, *Draft Action Plan*, 22.

116. Edward Muller, written commentary, September 30, 1993.

117. Doris J. Dyen, "Cultural Traditions Survey Focuses on People," *Steel Heritage Chronicle* 1 (Spring 1993), 1, 16; Gary Rotstein, "More Door-to-Door Lore," *Pittsburgh Post-Gazette*, September 29, 1993; Doris J. Dyen and Edward K. Muller, "Conserving the Heritage of Industrial Communities: The Compromising Issue of Integrity," mimeographed, 1994.

118. The Planning Council was created in September 1991.

119. Steel Industry Heritage Project, *Draft Concept Plan*, July 1992, 81.

120. A valuable account of life in the coke communities of Fayette and Westmoreland Counties is Muriel Earley Sheppard, *Cloud by Day: The Story of Coal and Coke and People* (1947; rpt. Pittsburgh: University of Pittsburgh Press, 1991).

121. Steel Industry Heritage Project, *Draft Concept Plan*, 109. The Heritage Plan also envisioned the creation of a "regional cooperative organization" to administer the program.

122. In 1990, the Pennsylvania Historical and Museum Commission awarded a contract to the Historical Society of Western Pennsylvania to undertake a nine-month survey of industrial and ethnic resources in the six-county region. This formed part of the heritage project. HSWP, *Notes from the Three Rivers,* Fall 1990, 1–2.

123. Along with the Pinkerton landing area and Carrie Furnance site, steel heritage planning for Homestead included the Bost Building on Eighth Avenue as an orientation center for visitors. Owned by the SIHC, it was the union's strike committe headquarters during the Homestead strike (also a base for the many reporters who descended on the scene).

124. John Herbst, director of the Historical Society of Western Pennsylvania, condemned the demolition of the roll shop as "a crime against the community" (Rick Teaff, "The Historic Battle of Homestead," *Pittsburgh Business Times,* July 9–15, 1990). See also Christine Vorce, "It's History Now: Homestead Roll Shop Comes Down Despite Museum Plans," *Pittsburgh Press,* June 30, 1990; "Homestead: Demolition, Disarray," editorial, *Pittsburgh Post-Gazette,* June 3, 1990; Dan Donovan, "Task Force Plans to Move 200-Ton Mill," *Pittsburgh Press,* December 27, 1990. The task force believed there was an understanding with Park Corporation to save the roll shop, but the company maintained it had always intended to demolish the structure. Mike Shanley, "Cleveland Firm Demolishes Pittsburgh's Steel Heritage," *In Pittsburgh,* March 17–23, 1994, deals with the demolition of the Big Shop.

125. The Park Corporation also objected vehemently to a land-use ordinance for the site proposed by Homestead in 1990. This Planned Economic Reuse District required setbacks from the river, view corridors, and planted buffer zones between buildings. Although the company protested the measure would interfere with development and lessen the value of the property, it was passed in December 1991. Bill Steigerwald, "Factories to Factions: Development vs. Preservation for Former Homestead Mill Site," *Pittsburgh Post-Gazette,* September 12, 1990.

126. If nothing else, a price of $1.5 million had been agreed upon for the seventy-seven acres.

127. Robert Pease, representing the Heinz Endowment, played a major role in negotiations with the Park Corporation concerning the heritage site and its cost. Margie Romero, "Sleeping Giant: When Will the Former Homestead Works Awaken?" *In Pittsburgh,* July 2–8, 1992, 9; Bohdan Hodiak, "Pending Land Sale Gives New Life to Steel Museum," *Pittsburgh Post-Gazette,* November 3, 1993; Linda Wilson Fuoco, "Steel Museum Progress is Slow," *Pittsburgh Post-Gazette,* February 13, 1994; Kelly B. Casey, "Museum Plans on Hold; Site Owner Stalls Land Sale," *Tribune-Review,* July 17, 1994).

128. Curt Miner, "Steel Heritage Task Force Documents Area's Unique Resources," *In Pittsburgh* 8 (September 25–October 1, 1991), 4.

129. Romero, "Sleeping Giant."

130. In the early months of the Task Force, Earl James asserted that "a region's heritage, especially in a period of radical and negative change, becomes the binding force maintaining its identity and, by drawing the community together, becomes the driving force for renewal." Conceived in Lowell, the heritage park concept had "come to be recognized as a powerful tool in the revitalization of the Northeast industrial belt. " Earl James, "Preserving Our History in a Park," *Pittsburgh Post-Gazette*, September 10, 1988. James was at the time director of Preservation for Landmarks and a member of the Task Force steering committee.

Randolph Harris, a community organizer for the Task Force, similarly urged that historic structures should be incorporated into the development process: "We in the Homestead, Munhall and West Homestead area are squandering valuable historic properties by following the failed development practices of the recent past that have disregarded older buildings through mass clearance of such structures. However, it is not too late if we act quickly now to adopt the successful practices of other communities that have created positive investment climates by using their history and old buildings as tools for economic development." Randolph Harris, *An Alternative Development Proposal for Site Design and Traffic Flow Incorporating Historic Buildings with New Commercial Construction*, November 1992.

Chapter 11. Conclusion

1. Besides those already mentioned, the committee included: Carol R. Brown, president of Pittsburgh Cultural Trust; Frank V. Cahouet, chairman, president, and CEO of Mellon Bank and Mellon Bank Corporation; Thomas J. Foerster, chairman of the Allegheny County Board of Commissioners; Frank R. Mascara, chairman of the Washington County Board of Commissioners; Gerald E. McGinnis, president of Respironics, Inc.; Thomas J. Murrin, dean of the A. J. Palumbo School of Business Administration, Duquesne University; Charles J. Queenan, Jr., a partner in Kirkpatrick & Lockhart; Anthony M. Sanzo, president and CEO of Allegheny General Hospital; Vincent A. Sarni, chairman of the Allegheny Conference on Community Development and former chairman and CEO, PPG Industries, Inc; Richard P. Simmons, chairman of the board of Allegheny Ludlum Corporation; Dr. Wesley W. von Schack, chairman and CEO of DQE.

2. Allegheny Conference on Community Development, *Toward a Shared Economic Vision for Pittsburgh and Southwestern Pennsylvania: A Report by the White Paper Committee for the Allegheny Conference on Community Development*, 9.

3. A useful compilation dealing with Pittsburgh region economics research is James P. DeAngelis and Sabine Deitrick, *The Regional Economic Development*

Bibliography and Data Base (TRED/Biblio): Final Report, University of Pittsburgh, Graduate School of Public and International Affairs, December 1994.

4. Between 1987 and 1992, per capita income in the Pittsburgh metropolitan area (adjusted for inflation) increased by 6.6 percent (a rate exceeded only by Houston). The area ranked twelfth among the thirty largest metropolitan statistical areas in per capita income. The unemployment rate compared favorably with the rest of the nation. But the poverty rate of 12.1 percent in 1989 was among the highest third of the thirty metropolitan areas. "A Different Focus," *Pittsburgh Post-Gazette,* September 24, 1994.

5. Max Dupuy and Mark E. Schweitzer, "Are Service-Sector Jobs Inferior?" Federal Reserve Bank of Cleveland, *Economic Commentary,* February 1, 1994,1.

6. Regional Economic Revitalization Initiative (RERI), Southwestern Pennsylvania, *The Greater Pittsburgh Region: Working Together to Compete Globally* (1994). The report was fostered by the Allegheny Conference and CMU's Center for Economic Development.

7. The area's job creation rate since December 1990 was "only slightly below the national average." Job growth favored the service sector. Although the losses in manufacturing employment slackened, the region continued to lose manufacturing jobs at a greater rate than the national average. Robert E. Gleeson, "Toward a Shared Economic Vision for Pittsburgh and Southwestern Pennsylvania: An Update on Economic Performance Since 1990," in RERI, *The Greater Pittsburgh Region,* 2:26.

8. The Enterprise Corporation of Pittsburgh, "Investing to Build Our Entrepreneurial Vitality," in ibid., 2:39. To explain the unsatisfactory rate of new company formation, the report cited (1) a deficit of 110,000 in the primage age cohort of twenty-five to thirty-five years; (2) a failure to translate university research and technology into new businesses; (3) a regional work force not oriented to small companies; (4) burdensome state and city regulations and taxes; and (5) a lack of high-risk capital.

9. *Region* is defined in different ways in the RERI report. The Greater Pittsburgh Region in one case is defined as encompassing no less than seventy counties in the three states that use the airport.

10. Proposals for promoting tourism through arts and entertainment included establishing a National Jazz Hall of Fame, a theater for long-run Broadway shows, a concentrated nightlife section akin to the Cleveland Flats of San Antonio's riverwalk, trail development, conversion of a bridge linking downtown with the North Side into a pedestrian walk lined with dining and retail facilities, support for the steel heritage project, more frequent special events like an International Day. These projects would be supplemented by an expanded convention center, more hotel space, and visitor transportation linkages.

11. The RERI proposed that the Strategy 21 partners should develop a Strategic Investment Partnership—a "consensus agenda" encompassing such

large-scale projects as industrial parks, entrepreneurial seed capital, riverfront development, conventional center improvement. also recommended was Allegheny Conference leadership in a Partnership for Regional Investment in Development and Entrepreneurship. This would be a $50 million fund inspired by precedents in Cleveland and Tulsa. In December 1994 the Murphy administration announced the creation of a $60 million revolving loan fund administered by the URA. The fund will serve various purposes, including land and property acquisition. Also announced in December 1994 was a joint venture undertaken by the Steel Valley Authority and the United Steelworkers of America union. This involved creating a nonprofit Regional Jobs corporation that would govern a for-profit subsidiary, the Industrial Valleys Investment Corporation. Favored for job creation or retention would be smaller companies that possess employee stock ownership plans or collective bargaining agreements. Fred Gustafson, "Reviving Steel Valley: Steelworkers Jobs Project," *In Pittsburgh Newsweekly*, December 14–21, 1994, 6.

12. The analysis of the five clusters defines the region as a thirteen-county area: Allegheny, Armstrong, Beaver, Bedford, Butler, Cambria, Fayette, Greene, Indiana, Lawrence, Somerset, Washington, and Westmoreland. In connection with the five key clusters, the RERI proposed a Tissue Engineering Initiative based on local university prominence in transplants and cell culture, genetics, and computer modelings; a concerted effort to become a center for maglev manufacturing, expansion of the Pittsburgh Technology Center and development of other technology parks (including a Virtual Technology Park) that would connect companies in the parks to university technology and research.

13. Infrastructure projects recommended included a Spine Line from the North Side to Oakland, extension of the East Busway, mass rail transit from downtown to the airport, completion of the Mon Valley Expressway, and improvement of airport cargo facilities.

14. The RERI also proposed connecting workers and students to the "jobs of the future." a Workplace skills Development Network was being created to connect regional training problems, and teh RERI urged that students receive work experience as part of their education.

15. RERI, *The Greater Pittsburgh Region*, 54.

16. University of Pittsburgh Center for Social and Urban Research, *Economic Benchmarks: Indices for the City of Pittsburgh and Allegheny County*, October 1994, 5.

17. RERI, *The Greater Pittsburgh Region*, 15.

18. Census estimates for the period between 1990 and July 1992 reveal that the population of the nine-county region (Allegheny, Armstrong, Beaver, Butler, Fayette, Greene, Lawrence, Washington, Westmoreland) increased by 0.5 percent (or 12,458 persons) to reach 2.62 million. (The population was 2.90 million in 1970 and 2.79 million in 1980.) Only Allegheny County experienced

a decrease; but the 2,000 loss for the county was largely attributable to Pittsburgh's drop of 2,027.

19. Dana Milbank, "Heath Care No Longer Panacea for Cities: Pittsburgh's Experience Reflects Nationwide Trend," *Wall Street Journal,* July 13, 1993; Michael DeCourcy Hinds, "Economy in Pittsburgh Braces for Health Plan," *New York Times,* October 3, 1993.

INDEX